THE
BEST JOKES
& QUOTES FROM
READER'S
DIGEST
MAGAZINE

THE BEST JOKES & QUOTES FROM READER'S DIGEST MAGAZINE

A One-of-a-Kind Collection from Reader's Digest Magazine

Reader's Digest

The Reader's Digest Association, Inc.
Pleasantville, NY/ Montreal

The Best Jokes & Quotes from Reader's Digest Magazine comprises three books previously published by Reader's Digest:

       Laughter the Best Medicine® (ISBN 978-0-89577-977-9)
       Quotable Quotes® (ISBN 978-0-89577-925-0)
       Humor in Uniform® (978-0-7621-0929-6)

PROJECT STAFF
    Laughter the Best Medicine®
        Editor: Deborah DeFord
        Art Editor: Pegi Goodman
        Research Editor: Mark LaFlaur
    Quotable Quotes®
        Editor: Deborah DeFord
        Art Editor: Judy Speicher
        Research Editor: Mark LaFlaur
    Humor in Uniform®
        Editor: Nancy Shuker
        Designer: Elizabeth Tunnicliffe

READER'S DIGEST TRADE PUBLISHING
Senior Art Director: George McKeon
Executive Editor: Dolores York
Manufacturing Manager: Elizabeth Dinda
Associate Publisher: Rosanne McManus
President and Publisher: Harold Clarke

We are committed to both the quality of our products and the service we provide to our customers. We value your comments, so please feel free to contact us.

    The Reader's Digest Association, Inc.
    Adult Trade Publishing
    Reader's Digest Road
    Pleasantville, NY 10570-7000

For more Reader's Digest products and information, visit our website:
    www.rd.com (in the United States)
    www.readersdigest.ca (in Canada)

Printed in China

1 3 5 7 9 10 8 6 4 2

CONTENTS

Laughter

THE BEST MEDICINE®

A Laugh-Out-Loud
Collection of our
Funniest Jokes,
Quotes, Stories
& Cartoons

Contents

A Note from the Editors

What's your handicap these days?" one golfer asked his companion.

"I'm a scratch golfer . . . I write down all my good scores and scratch out all my bad ones."

So relates Charles Schulz, the much-loved creator of the comic strip, *Peanuts*. Schulz is just one of the many funny folks, both professional and everyday, whose jokes appear in *Laughter, The Best Medicine*®, this year celebrating 50 years of monthly funny business in *Reader's Digest*. It is the column's vast supply of homey humor that supplied this book with an unbeatable collection.

What has made *Laughter, The Best Medicine* so popular for so long? In part, the answer lies in the department's consistent ability to pinpoint — and poke fun at — the facts and foibles of daily life. Nothing is sacred — from politics, religion, technology, doctors and lawyers, to sports, pets, children, and relationships. Add to this the quality of contributors — professional comedians, joke writers, and best of all, readers themselves — and you have a winning, winsome feature that readers look forward to month after month.

You can tell a lot about people and their times by what makes them laugh. A look through 50 years of *Laughter, The Best Medicine* offers us a glimpse of the past while tickling us in the present. Remember when knock-knock jokes were the rage? How about riddles and puns? Today's hot commodities in the humor department tend to be top ten lists and computer comedy.

While there is much more to The Digest than its jokes, its regular offerings of comic relief serve a noble and delightful purpose that has been captured in this book. Letters of thanks pour in weekly from readers who rely on *Laughter, The Best Medicine* to lift their spirits, put a twinkle in their eye or simply call up a chuckle or two after a hard day at home or the office, working or watching the kids. As you take a break from your daily business, browse through the following pages and prepare for a treat. We think you'll find that, after all is said and done, laughter really is the best medicine.

—*The Editors*

"Oh, Richard, the possibilities."

People

Courting Troubles

A man is taking a woman home from their first date, and he asks if he can come inside. "Oh, no," she says. "I never ask a guy in on the first date."

"Okay," the man replies, "how about the last date?"

—HEIDI MOSELEY

Tammy: "I'm not looking to get involved with one particular guy right now, Al."

Al: "Well, luckily for you, Tammy, I'm not exactly known for being particular."

—J. C. DUFFY, UNIVERSAL PRESS SYNDICATE

Mother to daughter: "What kind of a person is your new friend? Is he respectable?"

"Of course he is, Mum. He's thrifty, doesn't drink or smoke, has a very steady wife and three well-behaved children."

—LEA BERNER

How was your date last night, Billy?" his friend asked.

"Fabulous. We went to the concert, had a bite to eat, and then we drove around for a while until I found a nice dark spot to park. I asked her for a kiss, and she said that first I'd have to put the top down on the car. So I worked for an hour getting the top down—"

"An hour?" interrupted his pal. "I can put my top down in three minutes."

"I know," said Billy. "But you have a convertible."

—PHIL HARTMAN IN *OHIO MOTORIST*

"Who said anything about marriage? What I'm offering is an array of mutual funds, variable annuities and life insurance."

While riding a bus, I overheard one woman ask another, with great curiosity, "Well, what happened on your date with dashing Prince Lancelot?"

"Yuk!" was the disillusioned reply. "He was more like disgusting Prince Lust-a-lot—and I was the one who needed the suit of armor!"

—T. HOWIE

A college friend was going to meet a young lady he knew.
"An old flame?" I asked.
He winked and said, "More like an unlit match."

—MICHAEL HARTLAND

A bachelor, just turned 40, began feeling desperate. "I went to a singles bar," he told a friend, "walked over to this 20-year-old woman and asked, 'Where have you been all my life?' She said, 'Teething.'"

—MACK McGINNIS IN *QUOTE*

Professor to a student: "Can you think of a solution to end unemployment?"

"Yes, sir! I'd put all the men on one island and the women on another."

"And what would they be doing then?"

"Building boats!"

—SOMEN GUHA

To impress his date, the young man took her to a very chic Italian restaurant. After sipping some fine wine, he picked up the menu and ordered. "We'll have the *Giuseppe Spomdalucci,*" he said.

"Sorry, sir," said the waiter. "That's the proprietor."

—JIM STARK

I'm not saying her fiancé is cheap," whispered the office gossip. "But every time I get close to her engagement ring, I have an overwhelming desire for some Cracker Jack."

—QUOTED BY JAMES DENT IN THE CHARLESTON, W.VA., *GAZETTE*

She answered the phone to hear a repentant voice. "I'm sorry, darling," he said. "I have thought things over and you *can* have the Rolls-Royce as a wedding present, we *will* move to the Gold Coast, and your mother *can* stay with us. Now will you marry me?"

"Of course I will," she said. "And who is this speaking?"

—*THE ROTARIAN*

Striking up a conversation with the attractive woman seated beside him on a coast-to-coast flight, a would-be Romeo asked, "What kind of man attracts you?"

"I've always been drawn to Native American men," she replied. "They're in harmony with nature."

"I see," said the man, nodding.

"But, then, I really go for Jewish men who put women on a pedestal, and I can rarely resist the way Southern gentlemen always treat their ladies with respect."

"Please allow me to introduce myself," said the man. "My name is Tecumseh Goldstein, but all my friends call me Bubba."

—MATTHEW W. BOYLE

Donna: "He's so romantic. Every time he speaks to me he starts with, 'Fair lady.'"

Tina: "Romantic, my eye. He used to be a bus driver."

—STEVE JENKS

What am I supposed to do?" a young man looking to get married asked his friend. "Every woman I bring home to meet my parents, my mother doesn't like."

"Oh, that's easy," his pal replied. "All you have to do is find someone who's just like your mother."

"I did that already," he said, "and that one my father didn't like."

—MINNIE HERMAN

A bachelor asked the computer to find him the perfect mate: "I want a companion who is small and cute, loves water sports, and enjoys group activities."

Back came the answer: "Marry a penguin."

—RAINBOW

An 85-year-old widow went on a blind date with a 90-year-old man. When she returned to her daughter's house later that night, she seemed upset. "What happened, Mother?" the daughter asked.

"I had to slap his face three times!"

"You mean he got fresh?"

"No," she answered. "I thought he was dead!"

—WARREN HOLL

Altar Egos

The groom and his best man were sitting together at a table, playing poker in a small room at the back of the church. Their jackets were off, their sleeves rolled up and each man was viewing the cards he had been dealt. The door suddenly swung open, and the angry bride came barging in.

"What do you two think you're doing here? The ceremony is about to begin!" screamed the bride.

"Honey," replied the groom, "you know it's bad luck for the groom to see the bride before the wedding!"

—ROBERT HALSTEAD

At an Italian wedding ceremony, the priest asked the bride, "Do you take Franco Giuseppe Antonio to be your husband?"

Looking confused, she said, "Father, there's a mistake. I'm only marrying Frank."

—L. C.

How lovely you look, my dear!" gushed a wedding guest to the bride. And then she whispered, "Whatever happened to that dizzy blonde your groom used to date?"

"I dyed my hair," replied the bride.

—KEVIN BENNINGFIELD IN LOUISVILLE, KY., *COURIER-JOURNAL*

A Cockney asked a Roman Catholic coworker's help in choosing a bride. "I'm torn between Betty and Maria," he said. "'Ow do you Catholics make decisions?"

"I go to church," said his pal. "Then I look up and pray, and the answer comes to me."

Next day the Cockney was all excited. "I did what you told me, mate, and the answer was given to me!"

"What happened?"

"I went to your church, knelt in prayer, looked up and there it was! Written in gold, 'igh above a stained-glass window."

"What did it say?"

"It said, 'ave Maria."

—*The Jokesmith*

Overheard: "Marriage is nature's way of keeping people from fighting with strangers."

—Alan King

Attending a wedding for the first time, a little girl whispered to her mother, "Why is the bride dressed in white?"

"Because white is the color of happiness," her mother explained. "And today is the happiest day of her life."

The child thought about this for a moment. "So why is the groom wearing black?"

—Jerry H. Simpson Jr.

Why did you marry your husband?" asked the neighborhood gossip. "You don't seem to have much in common."

"It was the old story of opposites attracting each other," explained the wife. "I was pregnant and he wasn't."

—*Parts Pups*

After issuing driver's licenses for 20 years, a clerk was transferred to the marriage license bureau. Almost at once, he was in trouble. Young couples were leaving his desk red-faced and angry. His supervisor asked what was wrong.

"I can't seem to help it," muttered the dismayed clerk. "I just can't get out of the habit of asking whether they want the license for business or for pleasure."

—FRANK SCHAFF

Two neighbors were talking over the back fence. "I went to a wedding this weekend," said one, "but I don't think the marriage will last."

"Why not?" asked the other.

"Well, when the bride said 'I do,' the groom said, 'Don't use that tone of voice with me.'"

—GARY APPLE IN *SPEAKER'S IDEA FILE*

I had almost made up my mind to attend my friend's wedding when my attention was drawn to the last sentence of the wedding invitation. In bold letters it stated, "Please avoid presence."

—ROBBY ABRAHAM

A man fond of weddings was being married for a fourth time. The groom seemed very moved as he stood at the altar with his new bride, and as he stood dabbing his eyes after the ceremony, his concerned best man asked him why he was so emotional.

"Well," replied the groom, "it just occurred to me that this could be my last wedding."

—BERTE GODERSTAD

For Better or Perverse

A husband and wife drove for miles in silence after a terrible argument in which neither would budge. The husband pointed to a mule in a pasture.

"Relative of yours?" he asked.

"Yes," she replied. "By marriage."

—BOBBIE MAE COOLEY IN *THE AMERICAN LEGION MAGAZINE*

Executive overheard talking to a friend: "My wife tells me I don't display enough passion. Imagine! I have a good mind to send her a memo."

—*SPEAKER'S IDEA FILE*

Let's get one thing straight," the newlywed said to her husband. "I'm not cleaning up after you. I'm a career woman. That means I pay other people to do housework. Got it?"

"How much?"

"Eight dollars an hour. Take it or leave it."

—BILL HOLBROOK, KING FEATURES SYNDICATE

Did you hear about the dentist who married a manicurist? They fought tooth and nail.

—JOAN MCCOURT

John, an avant-garde painter, got married. Someone asked the bride a few weeks after the wedding, "How's married life, Helen?"

"It's great," she answered. "My husband paints, I cook; then we try to guess what he painted and what I cooked."

—MRS. ISTVAN PAP

Three Frenchmen were trying to define *savoir-faire*. "If I go home," said Alphonse, "and find my wife with another man, say 'Excuse me' and leave, that is savoir-faire."

"No," replied Pierre, "if I go home and find my wife with another man, and say 'Excuse me, please continue,' that is savoir-faire."

"*Au contraire*," said Jacques, "if I go home and find my wife with another man and say 'Excuse me, please continue,' and he can continue, then he has savoir-faire."

—QUOTED BY SUSIE TELTSER-SCHWARZ IN
NITE LIGHTS

Arnold complained to a coworker that he didn't know what to get his wife for her birthday. "She already has everything you could think of, and anyway, she can buy herself whatever she likes."

"Here's an idea," said the coworker. "Make up your own gift certificate that says, 'Thirty minutes of great loving, any way you want it.' I guarantee she'll be enchanted."

The next day, Arnold's coworker asked, "Well? Did you take my suggestion?"

"Yes," said Arnold.

"Did she like it?"

"Oh, yes! She jumped up, kissed me on the forehead, and ran out the door yelling, 'See you in 30 minutes!' "

—TOM MATTHEWS

Kevin: "My wife and I argue a lot. She's very touchy—the least little thing sets her off."

Christopher: "You're lucky. Mine is a self-starter."

—RON DENTINGER IN THE
DODGEVILLE, WIS., *CHRONICLE*

"Look, I know its not perfect, but, by and large, the jury system has worked very well for our marriage."

The judge was trying to change the mind of a woman filing for divorce. "You're 92," he said. "Your husband's 94. You've been married for 73 years. Why give up now?"

"Our marriage has been on the rocks for quite a while," the woman explained, "but we decided to wait until the children died."

—Quoted by Joyce Brothers

John, I can see that all your buttons are sewed on perfectly. You must be married!"

"That's right. Sewing on buttons was the first thing my wife taught me on our honeymoon."

—*Chayan*

A doctor and his wife were having a big argument at breakfast. "You aren't so good in bed either!" he shouted and stormed off to work. By midmorning, he decided he'd better make amends and phoned home. After many rings, his wife picked up the phone.

"What took you so long to answer?"

"I was in bed."

"What were you doing in bed this late?"

"Getting a second opinion."

—EDWARD B. WORBY

I was relaxing in my favorite chair on Sunday," said one office worker to another, "reading the newspaper, watching a ball game on TV and listening to another on the radio, drinking beer, eating a snack, and scratching the dog with my foot—and my wife has the nerve to accuse me of just sitting there doing nothing!"

—LOLA BRANDLI

Congratulating a friend after her son and daughter got married within a month of each other, a woman asked, "What kind of boy did your daughter marry?"

"Oh, he's wonderful," gushed the mother. "He lets her sleep late, wants her to go to the beauty parlor regularly, and insists on taking her out to dinner every night."

"That's nice," said the woman. "What about your son?"

"I'm not so happy about that," the mother sighed. "His wife sleeps late, spends all her time in the beauty parlor, and makes them eat take-out meals!"

—SABEEN

First man: I can't think what to get my wife for Christmas. If I give her something practical, I know she'll burst into tears.

Second man: In that case, buy her some handkerchiefs.

—MUSTAFA AMMI

The guys down at the bowling alley figure the delivery man has seduced every woman on our street except one," Harvey told his wife.

She thought for a moment. "I'll bet it's that snooty Mrs. Jenkins."

—G. L. GAUKROGER

Over breakfast one morning, a woman said to her husband, "I bet you don't know what day this is."

"Of course I do," he indignantly answered, going out the door on his way to the office.

At 10 AM, the doorbell rang, and when the woman opened the door, she was handed a box containing a dozen long-stemmed red roses. At 1 PM, a foil-wrapped, two-pound box of her favorite chocolates arrived. Later, a boutique delivered a designer dress.

The woman couldn't wait for her husband to come home. "First the flowers, then the candy, and then the dress!" she exclaimed. "I've never spent a more wonderful Groundhog Day in my whole life!"

—EVA C. BEAN

I was talking with an elderly relative who had just celebrated his 55th wedding anniversary. "Are there any secrets between you two?" I asked. "Do you ever hide anything from each other?"

"Well, yes," replied the old man with a sly smile. "I have ten thousand dollars in a bank that Mary doesn't know about. And she has ten thousand in a bank that I don't know about."

—JAMES A. SANAKER

A couple walking in the park noticed a young man and woman sitting on a bench, passionately kissing.

"Why don't you do that?" said the wife.

"Honey," replied her husband, "I don't even know that woman!"

—GARY R. HANDLEY

A man had just presented his wife with the fox coat she had been coaxing and cajoling him to buy her for weeks. Now he was perplexed to see her examining it with a sad look.

"What's the matter, sweetheart? Don't you like the coat?" he asked.

"I love it," she answered. "It's just that I was feeling sorry for the poor little creature who was skinned alive so that I could have the pleasure of wearing this coat."

"Why, thank you," said the husband.

—AMAL KHALIDI

I've finally found a way to get money out of my husband," a woman told her friend. "We were arguing last night, and I told him I was going home to Mother. He gave me the fare."

—CHARLES DONNE

Why Some Species Eat Their Young

A man was walking along a street when from the other side of a wall he heard someone shout, "Fifty-two!"

He stopped, and again he heard, "Fifty-two!"

Unable to overcome his curiosity, the man stood on a box that he found at the spot, peeked over, and a boy hit him with a handful of clay and shouted, "Fifty-three!"

—JULIO CESAR DA CRUZ

Wife: "Donald, when was the last time we received a letter from our son?"

Husband: "Just a second, honey, I'll go look in the checkbook."

—DIE WELTWOCHE

"Wait a minute! I smell toys."

Edgar, father of nine, reflected on how he had mellowed over the years: "When the firstborn coughed or sneezed, I called the ambulance. When the last one swallowed a dime, I just told him it was coming out of his allowance."

—JEAN SHORT

My mother always told me I wouldn't amount to anything because I procrastinate," says comedian Judy Tenuta. "I told her, 'Just wait.' "

"Mummy has no idea how to raise children," said the child to his father.

"How can you say such a thing?" replied the father.

"Well, Mummy always sends me to bed at night when I'm not sleepy, and wakes me up in the morning when I am."

—Sandor Szabo

The young wife found her husband at their baby's crib, a mixture of emotions spreading over his face. She slipped her arms around him. "A penny for your thoughts," she said, her eyes glistening.

"For the life of me," he replied, "I can't see how anybody can make a crib like this for $84.97."

—H. B. McClung

A little girl asked her mother for ten cents to give to an old lady in the park. Her mother was touched by the child's kindness and gave her the required sum.

"There you are, my dear," said the mother. "But, tell me, isn't the lady able to work any more?"

"Oh yes," came the reply. "She sells sweets."

—Harillon and Suzanne LeClercq

A couple, desperate to conceive a child, went to their priest and asked him to pray for them. "I'm going on a sabbatical to Rome," he replied, "and while I'm there, I'll light a candle for you."

When the priest returned three years later, he went to the couple's house and found the wife pregnant, busily attending to two sets of twins. Elated, the priest asked her where her husband was so that he could congratulate him.

"He's gone to Rome," came the harried reply, "to blow that candle out."

—Elizabeth Benoit

Betsy: "If you have $2, and you ask your father for $4, how much will you have?"
Billy: "Two dollars."
Betsy: "You don't know your math."
Billy: "You don't know my father."

—Lisa McNease

My Mary is so smart, she walked when she was eight months old," bragged one woman.

"You call that intelligent?" challenged her companion. "When my Cindy was that old, she let us carry her."

—Ard-Jan Dannenberg

A girl watched, fascinated, as her mother smoothed cold cream on her face. "Why do you do that?" she asked.

"To make myself beautiful," said the mother, who began removing the cream with a tissue.

"What's the matter?" asked the girl. "Giving up?"

—Nancy C. Bell

Seven-year-old John had finished his summer vacation and gone back to school. Two days later his teacher phoned his mother to tell her that John was misbehaving.

"Wait a minute," she said. "I had John here for two months and I never called you once when he misbehaved."

—F. Tracey

But, dear," said the mother to her little kid, "I didn't hear you cry when you cut your finger!"

"What's the use of crying? I thought you were outside the house."

—Hani Rushdi Ghebri Beshay

Mrs. Smith was preparing dinner when little Brad came into the kitchen. "What has mama's darling been doing all day?"

"I've been playing mailman," replied Brad.

"Mailman?" asked the mother. "How could you do that when you had no letters?"

"I had a whole bunch of letters," said Brad. "I found them in that old trunk up in the attic, all tied up with ribbon. I put one in every mailbox on the street."

—H. B. McClung

I was a very unpopular child," says comedian Rita Rudner. "I had only two friends. They were imaginary. And they would only play with each other."

The Rogue's Calorie

Horace grabbed his plate and walked up to the party buffet for the fourth time. "Aren't you embarrassed to go back for so many helpings?" asked his wife.

"Not a bit," Horace replied. "I keep telling them it's for you."

—Elinor Filice in Woman's World

Heard about the new diet? You eat whatever you want whenever you want, and as much as you want. You don't lose any weight, but it's really easy to stick to.

—George J. Tricker

Comic J. Scott Homan said he'd been trying to get in shape doing 20 sit-ups each morning. "That may not sound like a lot, but you can only hit that snooze alarm so many times."

—Atlanta Journal-Constitution

Don't tell me to reduce, Doc," said the man after his examination. "I just can't take those diets."

"No problem," said the doctor. "I'm prescribing an exercise machine."

"Really? What kind?"

"A rack. For your weight, you should be a foot and a half taller."

—GENE NEWMAN

Darn!" the man said to his pal while weighing himself in a drugstore. "I began this diet yesterday, but the scale says I'm *heavier.* Here, Norm, hold my jacket. . . . It *still* says I'm heavier. Here, hold my Twinkies."

—KEVIN FAGAN,
UNITED FEATURES SYNDICATE

How do you account for your longevity?" asked the reporter on Harvey's 110th birthday.

"You might call me a health nut," Harvey replied. "I never smoked. I never drank. I was always in bed and sound asleep by 10 o'clock. And I've always walked three miles a day, rain or shine."

"But," said the reporter, "I had an uncle who followed that exact routine and died when he was 62. How come it didn't work for him?"

"All I can say," replied Harvey, "is that he didn't keep it up long enough."

—QUOTED IN LUTHERAN DIGEST

Q: How do you get a man to do sit-ups?
A: Put the remote control between his feet.

—KATIE KENDRICK

"That weight I lost . . . I found it!"

Are the slimming exercises doing you any good?" a man asked his beer-bellied colleague. "Can you touch your toes now?"

"No, I can't touch them," the other replied, "but I'm beginning to see them."

—FRITZ HEIDI

The doctor told Uncle Fudd that if he ran five miles a day for 300 days, he would lose 75 pounds. At the end of 300 days, Uncle Fudd called the doctor to report he had lost the weight, but he had a problem.

"What's the problem?" asked the doctor.

"I'm 1,500 miles from home."

—H. B. McClung

I never eat food with additives or preservatives," boasted a health fanatic. "And I never touch anything that's been sprayed or fed chemical grain."

"Wow, that's wonderful," her friend marveled. "How do you feel?"

"Hungry," she moaned.

—S. Bader in Woman's World

Did you hear about the man who was arrested for paying his check at a cafeteria with a counterfeit 10-dollar bill?

He had been served decaffeinated coffee with a nondairy creamer and an artificial sweetener.

—Aldo Cammarota

There's a new garlic diet around. You don't lose weight, but you look thinner from a distance.

—Red Shea on The Tommy Hunter Show, TNN, Nashville

Those three hams you sold me last month were delicious," the woman told her butcher.

"If you want more, I still have 10 of the same quality."

"Give me your word they're from the same pig, and I'll take three of them."

—Almanaque Bertrand

When short hemlines came back into fashion, a woman dug an old miniskirt out of her closet. She tried it on, but couldn't figure out what to do with the other leg.

—ASHLEY COOPER IN THE CHARLESTON, S.C.,
NEWS AND COURIER

Man to clerk in video store: "I'd like to exchange this diet-and-workout tape for one on self-acceptance."

—KEVIN FAGAN,
UNITED FEATURES SYNDICATE

We're Only Human

George Burns punctuated this story with a flick of his cigar. "A woman said to me, 'Is it true that you still go out with young girls?' I said yes, it's true. She said, 'Is it true that you still smoke 15 to 20 cigars a day?' I said yes, it's true. She said, 'Is it true that you still take a few drinks every day?' I said yes, it's true.

"She said, 'What does your doctor say?' I said, 'He's dead.'"

In New York City," notes comedian Jay Leno, "they're handing out condoms to high-school students. Gee, I thought it was a big day when I got my class ring!"

At a party several young couples were discussing the difficulties of family budgets. "I really don't want a lot of money," said one yuppie. "I just wish we could afford to live the way we're living now."

—*THE LION*

My parents are the epitome of abstinence," the boy explains to his schoolmates.

"They don't smoke, they don't drink, and my sister and I are adopted children."

—*WELTWOCHE*

Two men were sitting by the swimming pool at a nudist colony when they noticed a beautiful young woman walking toward the pool. Her tan lines traced the outline of a tiny bathing suit with elaborately crisscrossed straps across the back.

"Mmm," one of the men said wistfully, "I'll bet she looks great in that suit."

—BARBARA HADLEY, QUOTED BY PATRICIA MCLAUGHLIN IN THE PHILADELPHIA *INQUIRER MAGAZINE*

A 90-year-old man checked into a posh hotel to celebrate his birthday. As a surprise, some friends sent a call girl to his room. When the man answered his door, he saw before him a beautiful young woman. "I have a present for you," she said.

"Really?" replied the bewildered gent.

"I'm here to give you super sex," she said in a whisper.

"Thanks," he said thoughtfully. "I'll take the soup."

—DORIAN GOLDSTEIN

Two friends are talking about their reading:

"I'm fascinated by medical publications. A friend of mine treated herself, using articles she read in the journals."

"You're speaking of her in the past tense. Did she die?"

"Unfortunately."

"Of what?"

"A typographical error."

—MAURICE OOGHE

The drawing is signed *Haefeli*. The desk has a sign reading "LIFESTYLE EDITOR" and a stack of trays labeled "OUT," "IN," and "VERY IN."

Q: What's the definition of a bachelor pad?

A: All the house plants are dead, but there's something growing in the refrigerator.

—MARSHALL WILLIAMS IN *THE LOS ANGELES TIMES*

A woman sat down on a park bench, glanced around and decided to stretch out her legs on the seat and relax. After a while, a beggar came up to her and said, "Hello, luv, how's about us going for a walk together?"

"How dare you," retorted the woman, "I'm not one of your cheap pickups!"

"Well then," said the tramp, "what are you doing in my bed?"

—ALZIRA INFANTE DE LA CERDA

To gain self-confidence, you must avoid using negative words such as *can't* and *not*," the counselor advised the young woman. "Do you think you could do that?"

"Well, I can't see why not."

—GREG EVANS, NORTH AMERICAN SYNDICATE

Overheard: "I'm trying to keep up with the Joneses, but every time I catch up, they just refinance!"

—DAVID A. SNELL

The best thing about getting older is that you gain sincerity," says Tommy Smothers. "Once you learn to fake that, there's nothing you can't do."

Did you hear about the self-help group for compulsive talkers? It's called On & On Anon.

—SALLY DAVIS

Bill: "Why the glum look?"
Stan: "I just don't understand today's world. My son wears an earring. My daughter has a tattoo. My wife makes twice what I do."
Bill: "So what are you going to do?"
Stan: "I'm thinking of going home to my father."

—AMERICAN SPEAKER

Heard at a bus stop:
"Hello, Lily, how are you? What have you done to your hair? It looks like a wig."
"Yes, it is a wig."
"Really, how wonderful! It looks just like real hair."

—GANESH V.

One woman was talking to another on the telephone:
"I ran into an old friend from high school the other day and she looked marvelous! She hadn't gained an ounce, and she didn't have a single wrinkle—so I ran into her again."

—SHOEBOX GREETINGS

"Dear, did something happen at the office?"

The Professions

Open Wide and Say Ha!

Three doctors were on their way to a convention when their car had a flat. They got out and examined the tire. The first doctor said, "I think it's flat."

The second doctor examined it closely and said, "It sure looks flat."

The third doctor felt the tire and said, "It feels like it's flat."

All three nodded their heads in agreement. "We'd better run some tests."

—DENISE BRIGHT

A woman and her husband interrupted their vacation to go to a dentist. "I want a tooth pulled, and I don't want Novocain because I'm in a big hurry," the woman said. "Just extract the tooth as quickly as possible, and we'll be on our way."

The dentist was quite impressed. "You're certainly a courageous woman," he said. "Which tooth is it?"

The woman turned to her husband and said, "Show him your tooth, dear."

—*Portals of Prayer*

Patient: "This hospital is no good. They treat us like dogs."
Orderly: "Mr. Jones, you know that's not true. Now, roll over."

—ANNE WOLOSYN

A physician went to heaven and met God, who granted him one question. So the physician asked, "Will health-care reform ever occur?"

"I have good news and bad news," God replied. "The answer is yes, but not in my lifetime."

—STEPHEN HUBER, MD, in *Medical World News*

A patient was anxious after a prolonged bedside discussion by hospital doctors. The head doctor even came to see him.

"There must be a lot of doubt about what is wrong with me," the patient told the doctor.

"Where did you get that idea?" the doctor replied.

"All the other doctors disagreed with you, didn't they?"

"To some extent, but don't worry," said the doctor consolingly. "In a similar case, I stood firm on my diagnosis—and the postmortem proved me right!"

—ABBAS ALI ZAHID

A woman accompanied her husband when he went for his annual checkup. While the patient was getting dressed, the doctor came out and said to the wife, "I don't like the way he looks."

"Neither do I," she said. "But he's handy around the house."

—MERRITT K. FREEMAN in *Y. B. News*

A jungle witch doctor was called to treat a man with a high fever. He made a medicine with the eye of a toad, the liver of a snake, the heart of a rat, six black beetles and half a cockroach, all mixed together with slime from the local river.

The next day he went to see his patient and found him no better. "Oh dear," said the witch doctor. "Maybe you had better try a couple of aspirins."

—CHARISMA B. RAMOS

A guy spots his doctor in the mall. He stops him and says, "Six weeks ago when I was in your office, you told me to go home, get into bed and stay there until you called. But you never called."

"I didn't?" the doctor says. "Then what are you doing out of bed?"

—RON DENTINGER in the Dodgeville, Wis., *Chronicle*

"The dentist will see you in a moment."

After giving a woman a full medical examination, the doctor explained his prescription as he wrote it out. "Take the green pill with a glass of water when you get up. Take the blue pill with a glass of water after lunch. Then just before going to bed, take the red pill with another glass of water."

"Exactly what is my problem, Doctor?" the woman asked.

"You're not drinking enough water."

—*Quote*

Doctor," the man said to his ophthalmologist, "I was looking in the mirror this morning, and I noticed that one of my eyes is different from the other!"

"Oh?" replied the doctor. "Which one?"

—JERRY H. SIMPSON JR.

A man called his doctor's office for an appointment. "I'm sorry," said the receptionist, "we can't fit you in for at least two weeks."

"But I could be dead by then!"

"No problem. If your wife lets us know, we'll cancel the appointment."

—RON DENTINGER in the Dodgeville, Wis., *Chronicle*

The woman went to a dentist to have her false teeth adjusted for the fifth time. She said they still didn't fit. "Well," said the dentist, "I'll do it again this time, but no more. There's no reason why these shouldn't fit your mouth easily."

"Who said anything about my mouth?" the woman answered. "They don't fit in the glass!"

—*The Speaker's Handbook of Humor,*
edited by Maxwell Droke

The hospital patient was worried. "Are you sure it's pneumonia, Doctor?" he asked. "I've heard of cases where a doctor treated a patient for pneumonia, and he ended up dying of something else."

"Don't worry," said the doctor. "When I treat a patient for pneumonia, he dies of pneumonia."

—WINSTON K. PENDLETON,
Funny Stories, Jokes and Anecdotes

It's the Law!

The law professor was lecturing on courtroom procedure.

"When you are fighting a case and have the facts on your side, hammer away at the facts. If you have the law on your side, hammer away with the law."

"But what if you have neither the facts nor the law on your side?"

"In that case," said the professor, "hammer away on the table."

—*The Rotarian*

What possible excuse can you give for acquitting this defendant?" the judge shouted at the jury.

"Insanity, Your Honor," replied the foreman.

"All 12 of you?"

—Martha J. Beckman in *Modern Maturity*

You admit having broken into the dress shop four times?" asked the judge.

"Yes," answered the suspect.

"And what did you steal?"

"A dress, Your Honor," replied the suspect.

"One dress?" echoed the judge. "But you admit breaking in four times!"

"Yes, Your Honor," sighed the suspect. "But three times my wife didn't like the color."

—*The Jewish Press*

And did you hear about the lawyer who didn't like what the restaurant offered? He asked for a change of menu.

—Bill Nelson in the Milwaukee *Journal*

*"It's a deal, but just to be on the safe side let's have
our lawyers look at this handshake."*

A young executive stomped into the elevator, obviously upset. "What's the matter?" asked a businessman standing there.

"Nepotism!" shouted the first man. "My boss just bypassed me and made his nephew office manager!"

"I see," the other said, handing over his business card. "If you need legal advice, please call me."

The young man glanced at the card: "O'Brien, O'Brien, O'Brien and O'Brien, Attorneys at Law."

—Norman F. Pihaly

The lawyer was cross-examining a witness. "Isn't it true," he bellowed, "that you were given $500 to throw this case?"

The witness did not answer. Instead, he just stared out the window as though he hadn't heard the question. The attorney repeated himself, again getting the same reaction—no response.

Finally, the judge spoke to the witness, "Please answer the question."

"Oh," said the startled witness, "I thought he was talking to you."

—*Sunshine* Magazine

A man visiting a graveyard saw a tombstone that read: "Here lies John Kelly, a lawyer and an honest man."

"How about that!" he exclaimed. "They've got three people buried in one grave."

—Louise Mayer in *Capper's*

Your Honor," began the defense attorney, "my client has been characterized as an incorrigible bank robber, without a single socially redeeming feature. I intend to disprove that."

"And how will you accomplish this?" the judge inquired.

"By proving beyond a shadow of a doubt," replied the lawyer, "that the note my client handed the teller was on recycled paper."

—R. C. Shebelski

Before a burglary trial, the judge explained to the defendant, "You can let me try your case, or you can choose to have a jury of your peers."

The man thought for a moment. "What are peers?" he asked.

"They're people just like you—your equals."

"Forget it," retorted the defendant. "I don't want to be tried by a bunch of thieves."

—Joey Adams

*"Your Honor, the relevance of this line of questioning
will become apparent in a moment."*

I'll need to see your license and registration," says the highway patrolman after stopping a middle-aged couple. "You were speeding."

"But, officer," says the husband, "I was way under the speed limit."

"Sir, you were doing 63 in a 55 zone."

"I was not speeding!" insists the man. "Your radar gun must be broken."

At this point, the wife leans over. "It's no use arguing with him, officer," she says apologetically. "He always gets this stubborn when he's been drinking."

—LISA MALLETTE

In darkest night, a policeman watches a staggering man trying in vain to unlock a door.

"Is this your home, after all?" the policeman asks.

"Sure, I'll prove it to you if you help me."

Inside, the man explains, "You see, this is my bedroom. And this is my wife."

"And who is the man next to her?" the policeman wants to know.

"That's me!"

—RENÉ GUYER

A junior partner in a law firm called his staff in for a meeting. "I have good news and bad news," he said, grinning. "Which do you want first?" The staff groaned, and agreed they'd better get the bad news first. "Okay," said the junior partner, "we are going to downsize. Half of you won't be here tomorrow. And the others may stay at a substantial reduction in salary."

The staff stood in horrified shock. Finally, one asked in a trembling voice, "What's the good news?"

The boss beamed. "I've been made a *full* partner!"

—*The Jokesmith*

Shrink Rap

Hello, welcome to the Psychiatric Hotline.

"If you are obsessive-compulsive, please press 1 repeatedly.

"If you are co-dependent, please ask someone to press 2.

"If you have multiple personalities, please press 3, 4, 5 and 6.

"If you are paranoid-delusional, we know who you are and what you want. Just stay on the line until we can trace the call.

"If you are schizophrenic, listen carefully and a little voice will tell you which number to press.

"If you are manic-depressive, it doesn't matter which number you press. No one will answer."

—JACQUELYN MAYERHOFER

The psychiatrist was interviewing a first-time patient. "You say you're here," he inquired, "because your family is worried about your taste in socks?"

"That's correct," muttered the patient. "I like wool socks."

"But that's perfectly normal," replied the doctor. "Many people prefer wool socks to those made from cotton or acrylic. In fact, I myself like wool socks."

"You DO?" exclaimed the man. "With oil and vinegar or just a squeeze of lemon?"

—PHYLLIS THATCHER

Psychiatrist: "Why can't you sleep at night?"
Patient: "Because I'm trying to solve all the world's problems."
Psychiatrist: "Ever get them solved?"
Patient: "Almost every time."
Psychiatrist: "Then why can't you sleep?"
Patient: "The ticker-tape parades they hold for me keep me awake."

—*Funny, Funny World*

*"Get me a psychiatrist, preferably one with
military experience."*

Psychiatrist to patient: "You have nothing to worry about—anyone who can pay my bills is certainly not a failure."

—LEA BERNER

Q: Why is psychoanalysis a lot quicker for men than for women?
A: When it's time to go back to their childhood, they're already there.

—MARTHA J. KIELEK

Don't worry," a patient told his psychiatrist. "I'll pay every cent I owe or my name isn't Alexander the Great!"

—*The Return of the Good Clean Jokes*, compiled by Bob Phillips

Is it true that Natalie's son is seeing a psychiatrist?" a woman asked her friend.

"That's what I heard," she answered.

"So what's his problem?"

"The doctor says that what he has is a terrible Oedipus complex."

"Oedipus-schmoedipus—as long as he loves his mother."

—LEO ROSTEN, *Hooray for Yiddish*

Three women started boasting about their sons. "What a birthday I had last year!" exclaimed the first. "My son, that wonderful boy, threw me a big party in a fancy restaurant. He even paid for plane tickets for my friends."

"That's very nice, but listen to this," said the second. "Last winter, my son gave me an all-expenses-paid cruise to the Greek islands. First class."

"That's nothing!" interrupted the third. "For five years now, my son has been paying a psychiatrist $150 an hour, three times a week. And the whole time he talks about nothing but me."

—*Current Comedy*

An unhappy man told his friend that he was seeing a psychiatrist about his marital problems. The shrink told him that his wife probably didn't mean the cruel things she was saying about him.

"My doctor said I have a persecution complex," the patient told his friend.

"Really? And what do you think?" the friend asked.

"That's what I expected he'd say," the man replied. "The guy hates me."

—RON DENTINGER in the Dodgeville, Wis., *Chronicle*

Jackson went to a psychiatrist. "Doc," he said, "I've got trouble. Every time I get into bed I think there's somebody under it. I get under the bed, I think there's somebody on top of it. Top, under, top, under. I'm goin' crazy!"

"Just put yourself in my hands for two years," said the shrink. "Come to me three times a week, and I'll cure you."

"How much do you charge?"

"A hundred dollars per visit."

"I'll think about it."

Jackson never went back. Six months later he met the doctor on the street. "Why didn't you ever come to see me again?" asked the psychiatrist.

"For a hundred bucks a visit? A bartender cured me for 10 dollars."

"Is that so! How?"

"He told me to cut the legs off the bed."

—LARRY WILDE, *The Ultimate Jewish Joke Book*

John, having completed a course of analysis with his psychiatrist, to friend: "I always thought I was indecisive."

Friend: "And now?"

John: "I'm not so sure."

—MRS. P. J. WOOD

Tricks of the Trades

An inexperienced real-estate salesman asked his boss if he could refund the deposit to an angry customer who had discovered that the lot he had bought was under water.

"What kind of salesman are you?" the boss scolded. "Get out there and sell him a boat."

—FELIX TESARSKI

The reading material at the barber shop consisted entirely of murder stories, mysteries, thrillers, and ghost tales.

When I asked the barber if he wanted to terrify his customers he replied, "No sir. These books make the customers' hair stand up and then it becomes easier to trim and cut."

—N. RAVI

After being laid off from five different jobs in four months, Arnold was hired by a warehouse. But one day he lost control of a forklift and drove it off the loading dock. Surveying the damage, the owner shook his head and said he'd have to withhold 10 percent of Arnold's wages to pay for the repairs. "How much will it cost?" asked Arnold.

"About $4,500," said the owner.

"What a relief!" exclaimed Arnold. "I've finally got job security!"

—DAVID E. SEES

Pete was telling a friend that he had just lost his job. "Why did the foreman fire you?" the friend asked in surprise.

"Oh," Pete said, "you know how foremen are. They stand around with their hands in their pockets watching everybody else work."

"We all know that," replied his friend. "But why did he let you go?"

"Jealousy," answered Pete. "All the other workers thought I was the foreman."

—*Sunshine* Magazine

A professor of English and the editor of the local newspaper had many friendly arguments. One Friday evening the professor was walking out of a local club with a bottle of whiskey wrapped in that day's newspaper.

"Oh!" said the editor, who was walking past. "Looks like there's something interesting in that paper."

"Aye," replied the professor. "It's the most interesting item that's been in it all week."

—ARTHUR FULLER

How's your new job at the factory?" one guy asked another.

"I'm not going back there."

"Why not?"

"For many reasons," he answered. "The sloppiness, the shoddy workmanship, the awful language—they just couldn't put up with it."

—MELL LAZARUS,
Creators Syndicate

A businessman was dining at a fancy restaurant and, so the story goes, met Lee Iacocca by the phone booth. "Mr. Iacocca," he gushed, "*the* American business hero! I've studied your career, and any success I've had comes from emulating you. Would you do me a favor? I'm with some colleagues. Please come by my table, say 'Hello, Harry,' and let me introduce you. It would mean so much to me."

Iacocca agreed. He waited for the man to sit down and then walked toward his table.

"Holy smoke!" cried one of Harry's friends. "It's Lee Iacocca, and he's heading this way!"

"Hello, Harry!" Iacocca said. "Introduce me to your friends."

Harry looked at him blankly. "Come back later, Lee," he said. "We're trying to have lunch."

—*The Jokesmith*

Approaching a passer-by, a street person asked, "Sir, would you give me a hundred dollars for a cup of coffee?"

"That's ridiculous!" the man replied.

"Just a yes or no, fella," the beggar growled. "I don't need a lecture about how to run my business."

—*Playboy*

I hear the boys are gonna strike," one worker told another.

"What for?" asked the friend.

"Shorter hours."

"Good for them. I always did think 60 minutes was too long for an hour."

—Tal D. Bonham, *The Treasury of Clean Country Jokes*

Bill attended a party where he met an old acquaintance. "Hello, Sam," he said. "How's your clothing business? I heard you lost a lot on that fall shipment of dresses."

"That's right," Sam responded.

"And you almost went bankrupt."

"That's true too."

"But I understand you made a big profit on another shipment and wound up having a pretty good season after all."

"That's correct. Then I guess you heard all about it, Bill."

"Yeah," Bill answered, "but this is the first time I'm hearing all the details."

—*Myron Cohen's Big Joke Book*

Three businessmen were having dinner at a club. When it came time to pay the check, each grabbed for it.

"It's a business expense," said one.

"I'll pay," said the second. "I'm on cost plus."

"Let me have it," argued the third. "I'm filing for bankruptcy next week."

—Joey Adams

"I've stopped going out at night. Too dangerous."

Ned took a job working alone in Canada's far frozen north. "Here's your emergency survival kit," said his boss. "It contains a box of flares, a radio, and a deck of cards."

"What are the cards for?" Ned asked.

"In case the flares don't work and the radio freezes up," replied the boss, "just take out the cards and play solitaire. In about 10 seconds someone will tap you on the shoulder and say, 'Put the red 9 on the black 10.' "

—KEVIN HILGERS in *One to One*

Football player's wife: "I hate it when my husband calls leftovers 'replays.' "

TV executive's wife: "My husband calls them 'reruns.' "

Mortician's wife: "Be grateful. My husband refers to them as 'remains.' "

—LESLIE BARANOWSKY

A very successful businessman had a meeting with his new son-in-law. "I love my daughter, and now I welcome you into the family," said the man. "To show you how much we care for you, I'm making you a 50-50 partner in my business. All you have to do is go to the factory every day and learn the operation."

The son-in-law interrupted. "I hate factories. I can't stand the noise."

"I see," replied the father-in-law. "Well, then you'll work in the office and take charge of some of the operations."

"I hate office work," said the son-in-law. "I can't stand being stuck behind a desk."

"Wait a minute," said the father-in-law. "I just made you half-owner of a money-making organization, but you don't like factories and won't work in an office. What am I going to do with you?"

"Easy," said the young man. "Buy me out."

—*Gene Perrett's Funny Business*

The Armed Farces

During our basic army training, a sergeant was telling us how a sub-machine gun sprayed bullets. He drew a circle on a blackboard and announced that it had 260 degrees.

"But, sergeant, all circles have 360 degrees," someone called out.

"Don't be stupid," the sergeant roared. "This is a small circle."

—C. A. SUTTON

A tail gunner was being court-martialed. "What did you hear in your headset?" demanded a superior officer.

"Well," replied the airman, "I heard my squadron leader holler, 'Enemy planes at 5 o'clock!'"

"What action did you take?" persisted another officer.

"Why, sir," replied the gunner, "I just sat back and waited. It was only 4:30."

—JERRY LIEBERMAN, *3,500 Good Jokes for Speakers*

During a training exercise, an army unit was late for afternoon inspection. "Where are those camouflage trucks?" the irate colonel barked.

"They're here somewhere," replied the sergeant, "but we can't find 'em."

—L. DOWNING

What's the matter with you, lad?"

"Typhoid fever, Sergeant."

"That illness either kills you or leaves you an idiot. I know because I've had it!"

—ANA MARIA SANTOS

Through the pitch-black night, the captain sees a light dead ahead on a collision course with his ship. He sends a signal: "Change your course 10 degrees east."

The light signals back: "Change yours, 10 degrees west."

Angry, the captain sends: "I'm a navy captain! Change your course, sir!"

"I'm a seaman, second class," comes the reply. "Change your course, sir."

Now the captain is furious. "I'm a battleship! I'm not changing course!"

There's one last reply. "I'm a lighthouse. Your call."

—Dan Bell

A sergeant put this problem to a recruit: "Suppose it's wartime. You're walking in the woods, and you suddenly come up against 10 of the enemy. What would you do?"

After a moment's silence the recruit's face brightened, and he replied, "Surround them, Sergeant."

—E. Meutstege

While conducting a routine inspection, the colonel arrived at the mess hall door where he met two KPs with a large soup kettle.

"Let me taste that," the colonel snapped.

One of the men fetched a big spoon and handed it respectfully to the CO, who plunged the ladle into the pot and took a large mouthful of the steaming liquid, smacking his lips critically.

Then he let out a roar that could be heard back at headquarters. "Do you call that soup?" he bellowed.

"No, sir," explained one of the KPs. "It's dishwater we were just throwing out."

—James Mutch

Top brass from the Army, Navy, and Marine Corps were arguing about who had the bravest troops. They decided to settle the dispute using an enlisted man from each branch.

The army general called a private over and ordered him to climb to the top of the base flagpole while singing "The Caissons Go Rolling Along," then let go with both hands, and salute. The private quickly complied.

Next, the admiral ordered a sailor to climb the pole, polish the brass knob at the top, sing "Anchors Aweigh," salute smartly, and jump off. The sailor did as he was told and landed on the concrete below.

Finally the marine was told to do exactly as the army and navy men had done, but in full battle gear, pack filled with bricks, loaded weapon carried high. He took one look at the marine general and said, "You're out of your mind, sir!"

The marine commander turned to the others. "Now *that's* guts!"

—RICHARD BECTON

One hazard of wartime training in England was that road signs were removed when invasion seemed imminent. A cartoon in an English newspaper during the invasion scare of 1940 pictured two German paratroopers scanning a map at a railway station. Over their heads was the one remaining sign: Gentlemen.

"I can't find this place on the map," says one to the other.

—STROME GALLOWAY in *Legion*

It happened that the platoon leader forgot the expression "Mark time." Without losing his composure, he faced his platoon and shouted, "Ten-shut! Pretend to go but don't; pretend to go but don't; pretend to go but don't . . . ."

—SYLVIA MENDES DE ABREU

"You're lucky. You never have to worry about having a bad clothes day."

During a simulated attack, the troops have to defend themselves against an imaginary enemy, as the sergeant calls it. Bawling out orders, he notices that one recruit shows little response.

"You there," the sergeant shouts, "the imaginary enemy is advancing, and you're caught in the crossfire. Action!"

The recruit takes two steps to one side.

"What are you doing, man?" yells the sergeant, purple with fury.

"I'm taking shelter behind an imaginary tree, Sergeant," answers the recruit calmly.

—MICHEL VAN KERCKHOVEN

Office Antics

One winter morning, an employee explained why he had shown up for work 45 minutes late. "It was so slippery out that for every step I took ahead, I slipped back two."

The boss eyed him suspiciously. "Oh, yeah? Then how did you ever get here?"

"I finally gave up," he said, "and started for home."

—ERIC WIGHT

Say, Bill," a man said to his pal, "how do you like your new job?"

"It's the worst job I ever had."

"How long have you been there?"

"About three months."

"Why don't you quit?"

"No way. This is the first time in 20 years that I've looked forward to going home."

—JIM YOUNG

Employee: "The stress my boss puts me under is killing me. I have migraines, my blood pressure is going through the roof, I can't sleep at night, I just found out I have an ulcer, and as long as I stay in this job, the only question is whether I'll have a stroke or a heart attack."

Friend: "So why don't you quit?"

Employee: "I have a great health plan."

—RICHARD JEROME in *The Sciences*

"Miss Bremmer, get me whatever coast I'm not on."

A lot of people complain about their dumb boss," says Joey Adams. "What they don't realize is that they'd be out of a job if their dumb boss were any smarter."

Dexter had just returned from two weeks of vacation. He asked his boss for two more weeks off to get married.

"What!" shouted the boss. "I can't give you more time now. Why didn't you get married while you were off?"

"Are you nuts?" replied Dexter. "That would have ruined my entire vacation!"

—H. B. McClung

Sign on company bulletin board: "This firm requires no physical-fitness program. Everyone gets enough exercise jumping to conclusions, flying off the handle, running down the boss, flogging dead horses, knifing friends in the back, dodging responsibility, and pushing their luck."

—*Financial Times*

The stenographer who had worked for nine years in our firm got a job elsewhere and approached the personnel officer for a certificate of experience.

"Make it out for 10 years," the steno suggested.

"But you've worked for only nine years," the personnel officer pointed out.

"But, sir," replied the steno, "what about my overtime?"

—P. R. MOHANAN

One payday, an employee received an unusually large check. She decided not to say anything about it. The following week, her check was for less than the normal amount, and she confronted her boss.

"How come," the supervisor inquired, "you didn't say anything when you were overpaid?"

Unruffled, the employee replied, "Well, I can overlook one mistake—but not two in a row!"

—*Farmers Independent*

The owner of a big electronics firm called in his personnel director. "My son will be graduating from college soon and needing a job. He's going to be your new assistant, but he's *not* to be shown any favoritism. Treat him just as you would any other son of mine."

—Quoted in *The Rotarian*

Gag-riculture

A cowboy applied for an insurance policy. "Have you ever had any accidents?" asked the agent.

"Nope," said the cowboy, "though a bronc did kick in two of my ribs last year, and a couple of years ago a rattlesnake bit my ankle."

"Wouldn't you call those accidents?" replied the puzzled agent.

"Naw," the cowboy said, "they did it on purpose."

—*Our Daily Bread*

Because of the shortage of jobs in town, a boy appeared for work on a farm. The foreman decided to give him a try and told him to milk a cow, equipping him with a stool and a bucket.

An hour later the boy returned dirty and sweaty, the bucket in one hand and the broken stool in the other.

"Extracting the milk was easy," he explained. "The worst part was getting the cow to sit on the stool!"

—Miguel José de Oliveria Neto

Willie and Ray, a couple of farmers, met at the town hardware store on Saturday. "Had some problems with my herd," lamented Willie. "My prize bull was impotent. But the vet came and gave him some special medicine, and now he seems to be doing fine."

The next week, Ray met Willie again. "My bull's had problems too," said Ray. "What was that medicine the vet prescribed?"

"I don't know," answered Willie. "But it tastes like chocolate."

—William L. Heartwell, Jr.

Van der Merwe was carrying a box when he met his friend. "Guess how many chickens I have in this box and I'll give you both of them," he said.

—*Personality*, Durban

"You want a sign that reads 'The world ends tomorrow'
. . . when do you have to have it?"

Religion

IN GOOD SPIRITS 70

COLLARED 74

YOU SHOULD DIE LAUGHING 78

In Good Spirits

When Adam came home in the small hours of the morning, Eve was jealous. "But in all of creation," Adam reasoned, "there's no one but you and me." Mollified, Eve snuggled up to him. Still, when he fell asleep, she very carefully counted his ribs.

—BILL SROKA

I used to practice meditation on an old mat. My wife was not happy about the worn-out mat.

One day I found the rug missing from its usual place.

"Where is it?" I asked her sternly.

"It has achieved nirvana," she retorted.

—ANIL BHARTI

A Christian in ancient Rome was being pursued by a lion. He ran through the city streets and into the woods, dodging back and forth among the trees. Finally it became obvious that it was hopeless—the lion was going to catch him. So he turned suddenly, faced the beast and dropped to his knees. "Lord," he prayed desperately, "make this lion a Christian."

Instantly the lion dropped to its knees and prayed, "For this meal of which I am about to partake. . . ."

—VAUNA J. ARMSTRONG

My mother always told me God hears every prayer," says comedian Mary Armstrong. "If I'd pray really hard for something and nothing happened, she would say, 'Sometimes God's answer is no.' But what if God just doesn't answer right away? You could be 42, your needs will have changed, and all of a sudden you look out at your front yard one morning and there's a Shetland pony!"

An impassioned minister was visiting a country church and began his address with a stirring reminder: "Everybody in this parish is going to die."

The evangelist was discomfited to notice a man in the front pew who was smiling broadly. "Why are you so amused?" he asked.

"I'm not in this parish," replied the man. "I'm just visiting my sister for the weekend."

—ROGER DELAHUNTY

Sol strictly observed Jewish dietary laws. But one day he went to a restaurant by himself and noticed roast pig on the menu. *Just once, I'd like to try it*, he thought, and placed his order.

The pig was brought to his table with an apple in its mouth. Just then, Sol looked up, and there was a member of his synagogue staring at him. "So I ordered a baked apple," said Sol innocently. "Who knew how they'd serve it?"

—RUTH SCHWARTZ

A Texan traveled to England on vacation. While there, he attended a religious service and was amazed at how quiet and reserved it was. Not one word was spoken out of turn. All of a sudden he heard the minister say something he really liked. "Amen!" he shouted. Everyone in the church turned and stared, and the usher came running down the aisle.

"You must not talk out loud," admonished the usher.

"But," protested the Texan, "I've got religion!"

"Well," said the usher, "you did not get it here."

—DOROTHY STARLING

Did you hear about the insomniac dyslexic agnostic? He stayed up all night wondering if there really was a dog.

—DANIEL J. KLAIMAN

A preacher was asked to give a talk at a women's health symposium. His wife asked about his topic, but he was too embarrassed to admit that he had been asked to speak about sex. Thinking quickly, he replied, "I'm talking about sailing."

"Oh, that's nice," said his wife.

The next day, at the grocery store, a young woman who had attended the lecture recognized the minister's wife. "That was certainly an excellent talk your husband gave yesterday," she said. "He really has a unique perspective on the subject." Somewhat surprised, the minister's wife replied, "Gee, funny you should think so. I mean, he's only done it twice. The first time he threw up, and the second time, his hat blew off."

—D. E. NORLING

A small town's only barber was known for his arrogant, negative attitude. When one of his customers mentioned he'd be going to Rome on vacation and hoped to meet the pope, the barber's reaction was typical. "You?" he said. "Meet the pope? Don't make me laugh! The pope sees kings and presidents. What would he want with you?"

A month later, the man returned for another haircut. "How was Rome?" asked the barber.

"Great! I saw the pope!"

"From St. Peter's Square, I suppose, with the rest of the crowd," said the barber.

"Yes, but then two guards came up, said the pope wanted to meet me, and took me right into his private apartment in the Vatican."

"Really?" the barber asked. "What did he say?"

"He said, 'Who gave you that lousy haircut?' "

—Quoted in Chelmsford, Mass.,
All Saints Church Newsletter

"My dad says Mom is a pagan because she serves
burnt offerings for dinner."

Two fellows, Murphy and Clancy, were walking past the church when Murphy said, "I haven't been to confession for a while. I believe I'll go in and get absolution." Murphy went into the confessional and acknowledged having his way with a lady.

"I know you by your voice, Murphy, and this is not the first time this has happened," said the priest. "I want to know the lady's name."

"It's not proper you should ask, and I'll not be telling you!"

"If you want absolution, you'll be telling me. Was it O'Reilly's sister?" Murphy refused to answer. "I'll ask again. Was it the widow Harrington?" Again, Murphy wouldn't reply. "One more time I'll ask: was it the Flanagan girl?"

"For the third time, I'll not be telling you!" said Murphy.

"Then you'll get no absolution from me. Out with you!"

His friend Clancy was waiting. "Well, did you get absolution?"

"No," said Murphy with a smile. "But I got three good leads!"

—WEBB CASTOR

God: "Whew! I just created a 24-hour period of alternating light and darkness on Earth."

Angel: "What are you going to do now?"

God: "Call it a day."

—DAVE COVERLY, Creators Syndicate

Collared

At a wedding reception, a priest and a rabbi met at the buffet table. "Go ahead," said the priest, "try one of these delicious ham sandwiches. Overlooking your divine rule just this once won't do you any harm."

"That I will do, dear sir," the rabbi replied, "on the day of your wedding!"

—KIM DUBOIS

The newly appointed priest was being briefed by the housekeeper on problems in the rectory that required immediate attention.

"Your roof needs repair, Father," she said. "Your water pressure is bad and your furnace is not working."

"Now, Mrs. Kelly," the priest allowed, "you've been the housekeeper here five years, and I've only been here a few days. Why not say *our* roof and *our* furnace?"

Several weeks later, when the pastor was meeting with the bishop and several other priests, Mrs. Kelly burst into the office terribly upset. "Father, Father," she blurted, "there's a mouse in our room and it's under our bed!"

—DORIS CYPHER

And did you hear about the bishop who hired a secretary who had worked for the Pentagon? She immediately changed his filing system to "Sacred" and "Top Sacred."

—IRA N. BRIGGS

The young couple invited their parson for Sunday dinner. While they were in the kitchen preparing the meal, the minister asked their son what they were having. "Goat," the little boy replied.

"Goat?" replied the startled man of the cloth. "Are you sure about that?"

"Yep," said the youngster. "I heard Pa say to Ma, 'Might as well have the old goat for dinner today as any other day.' "

—PAMELA D. MCMANUS

In a booming voice, a cantor bragged to his congregation, "Two years ago, I insured my voice with Lloyd's of London for $750,000."

The crowded room was hushed. Suddenly, an elderly woman spoke. "So," she said, "what did you do with the money?"

—JOSEPH TELUSHKIN, *Jewish Humor*

"Your sermon helped me understand my soaps better."

A young vicar about to deliver his first sermon asked the advice of a retired minister on how to capture the congregation's attention.

"Start with an opening line that's certain to grab them," the cleric told him. "For example: Some of the best years of my life were spent in the arms of a woman."

He smiled at the young vicar's shocked look before adding, "She was my mother."

The next Sunday the vicar nervously clutched the pulpit rail before the congregation and stated, "Some of the best years of my life were spent in the arms of a woman."

He was pleased at the instant reaction—then panic-stricken. "But for the life of me, I can't remember who she was!"

—GIL HARRIS

A pastor was preaching an impassioned sermon on the evils of television. "It steals away precious time that could be better spent on other things," he said, advising the congregation to do what he and his family had done. "We put our TV away in the closet."

"That's right," his wife mumbled, "and it gets awfully crowded in there."

—SHERRI DORMER

The minister was sick, and a pastor noted for his never-ending sermons agreed to fill in. When he stood up in the pulpit, he was annoyed to find only 10 worshipers present, including the choir. Afterward he complained to the sexton. "That was a very small turnout," he said. "Weren't they informed that I was coming?" "No," replied the sexton, "but word must have leaked out!"

—*Sunday Post*

The minister selected a 50-cent item at a convenience store but then discovered he didn't have any money with him.

"I could invite you to hear me preach in return," he said jokingly to the clerk, "but I'm afraid I don't have any 50-cent sermons."

"Perhaps," suggested the clerk, "I could come twice."

—GEORGE DOLAN in
Fort Worth *Star-Telegram*

While other people go to church every Sunday morning, Charles, a farmer, likes to sit in the village restaurant drinking wine.

One day the priest said to him, "Charles, I'm afraid we shall not see each other in heaven."

A worried Charles replied, "But, Father, what on earth have you done?"

—AIDA C. FUDOT

A preacher's new car broke down just after his Sunday service. Monday morning he managed to drive the vehicle to the town's one garage for repairs. "I hope you'll go easy on the cost," he told the mechanic. "After all, I'm just a poor preacher."

"I know," came the reply. "I heard you preach yesterday."

—Lutheran Digest

Unbeknown to most of the congregation, the new minister enjoyed an occasional bottle of wine. One church member, aware of this, presented the clergyman with a bottle of Bordeaux. But the gift had a string attached. The minister would have to say thank you from the pulpit.

At the conclusion of the next service, the minister made the announcements, then said, "And I want to thank my friend for giving the fine fruit, and for the spirit in which it was given."

—R. L. FINDLEY

A guru who claimed he survived on air started a cult. When some skeptics caught him munching a hamburger and french fries, the pseudo-psychic said, "You can't call this food."

—MARK PLUMMER in The Indian Post

You Should Die Laughing

Surprised to see an empty seat at the Super Bowl, a diehard fan remarked about it to a woman sitting nearby.

"It was my husband's," the woman explained, "but he died."

"I'm very sorry," said the man. "Yet I'm really surprised that another relative, or friend, didn't jump at the chance to take the seat reserved for him."

"Beats me," she said. "They all insisted on going to the funeral."

—Coffee Break

"Remember me? Bangor, Maine. Moose season, 1971."

A young couple had a fatal car accident on the way to their wedding. When they met St. Peter at the Pearly Gates, they asked if it was possible for them to marry in heaven. He said he would make some inquiries and get back to them.

A year later, St. Peter found the couple and told them they could get married. "Could we get a divorce if it doesn't work out?" they wanted to know.

"Good grief!" St. Peter exclaimed. "It took me a whole year to find a preacher up here—and now you want me to find a lawyer."

—DEE MCDONALD

An attorney died and went to heaven. As he approached the Pearly Gates, he noticed an orchestra playing and thousands of angels cheering. St. Peter himself rushed over to shake the lawyer's hand. "This is quite a reception," marveled the new arrival.

"You're very special," St. Peter explained. "We've never had anyone live to be 130 before."

The attorney was puzzled. "But I'm only 65."

St. Peter thought for a moment. "Oh," he said, "we must have added up your billing hours."

—DAVID MICUS

When her late husband's will was read, a widow learned he had left the bulk of his fortune to another woman. Enraged, she rushed to change the inscription on her spouse's tombstone.

"Sorry, lady," said the stonecutter. "I inscribed 'Rest in Peace' on your orders. I can't change it now."

"Very well," she said grimly. "Just add 'Until We Meet Again.' "

—ROBERT E. CANTELL

Two ministers died and went to heaven. St. Peter greeted them and said, "Your condos aren't ready yet. Until they're finished, you can return to earth as anything you want."

"Fine," said the first minister. "I've always wanted to be an eagle soaring over the Grand Canyon."

"And I'd like to be a real cool stud," said the second.

Poof! Their wishes were granted.

When the condos were finished St. Peter asked an assistant to bring back the two ministers. "How will I find them?" the man said.

"One is soaring over the Grand Canyon," St. Peter replied. "The other may be tough to locate. He's somewhere in Detroit—on a snow tire."

—DONNA S. TIPTON

After a preacher died and went to heaven, he noticed that a New York cabdriver had been given a higher place than he had. "I don't understand," he complained to St. Peter. "I devoted my entire life to my congregation."

"Our policy is to reward results," explained St. Peter. "Now what happened, Reverend, whenever you gave a sermon?"

The minister admitted that some in the congregation fell asleep.

"Exactly," said St. Peter. "And when people rode in this man's taxi, they not only stayed awake, they *prayed*."

—Quoted by RAYMOND A. HEIT

Two guys, Jimmy and Johnny, were standing at heaven's gate, waiting to be interviewed by St. Peter.

Jimmy: "How did you get here?"

Johnny: "Hypothermia. You?"

Jimmy: "You won't believe it. I was sure my wife was cheating on me, so I came home early one day hoping to find the guy. I accused my wife of unfaithfulness and searched the whole house without any luck. Then I felt so bad about the whole thing I had a massive heart attack."

Johnny: "Oh, man, if you had checked the walk-in freezer, we'd both be alive."

—FAIZ RAHMAN

A man asked an acquaintance how his wife was; then, suddenly remembering that she had died, he blurted out, "Still in the same cemetery?"

—MAURO BORBA COLLETES ALVES

They say when you die you see bright light at the end of a tunnel," notes comedian Ed Marques. "I think my father will see the light, then flip it off to save electricity."

—*Comic Strip Live*, Fox TV

A gold miner died and went to heaven. At the gate, St. Peter asked, "What have you done in your life?"

When the man gave his occupation, St. Peter explained that there was already a surplus of miners in heaven. "May I stay if I get rid of the others?" the fellow inquired.

St. Peter agreed. Once in, the miner wandered around until he saw a couple of familiar faces. He whispered that there was a gold strike in hell. Soon, the place was empty of miners.

But a while later, the miner asked St. Peter for permission to leave. "Even if I did start the rumor," he said, "there just might be something to it!"

—*Modern Gold Miner & Treasure Hunter*

The day after Mrs. Zelkin's funeral, the rabbi dropped in to console the widower. To his astonishment he saw the bereaved on the sofa kissing a dazzling redhead.

"Zelkin!" roared the rabbi. "Your beloved wife is not even cold in her grave, and already you're—"

Mr. Zelkin cried, "In my grief, should I know what I'm doing?"

—Leo Rosten, *Hooray for Yiddish!*

Ninety-year-old Sam bought a hairpiece, had a face lift and worked out at the gym for six months. Then he found a widow half his age to take to dinner. As they got out of his sports car, Sam was struck by lightning and died. At the Gate of Heaven, he ran up to God and asked, "Why me?"

"Oh, Sam," replied God. "I didn't recognize you!"

—Nancy Harrison

Overheard: "My greatest fear is that I will be standing behind Mother Teresa in the Final Judgment line and I'll hear God tell her, 'You know, you should have done more.' "

—*The Jokesmith*

"Sorry, bub. You're not in the database."

A Texas oilman died and went to heaven. After a few days, his bragging was getting on St. Peter's nerves. No matter what part of paradise he was shown, the oilman claimed it failed to measure up to Texas. Finally St. Peter took him to the edge of heaven so he could look straight into hell. "Have you got anything like that in Texas?" the saint demanded.

"No," the oilman replied. "But I know some ol' boys down in Houston who can put it out."

—Dana Conner

St. Peter halted a man at the entrance to heaven. "You've told too many lies to be permitted in here," he said.

"Have a heart," replied the man. "Remember, you were once a fisherman yourself."

—HAROLD HELFER in *Catholic Digest*

An angel appears at a faculty meeting and tells the dean that in return for his unselfish and exemplary behavior, the Lord will reward him with his choice of infinite wealth, wisdom, or beauty. Without hesitating, the dean selects infinite wisdom.

"Done!" says the angel, and disappears in a cloud of smoke and a bolt of lightning. Now, all heads turn toward the dean, who sits surrounded by a faint halo of light. At length, one of his colleagues whispers, "Say something."

The dean sighs and says, "I should have taken the money."

—BETSY DEVINE and JOEL E. COHEN,
Absolute Zero Gravity

Three men died and went to heaven. Upon their arrival, St. Peter asked the first if he had been faithful to his wife. The man admitted to two affairs during his marriage. St. Peter told him that he could receive only a compact car to drive in heaven.

Then St. Peter asked the second man if he had been faithful to his wife, and the man admitted to one affair. St. Peter told him he would be given a midsize car to drive.

The third man was asked about his faithfulness, and he told St. Peter he had been true to his wife until the day he died. St. Peter praised him and gave him a luxury car.

A week later the three men were driving around, and they all stopped at a red light. The men in the compact and midsize cars turned to see the man in the luxury car crying. They asked him what could possibly be the matter—after all, he was driving a luxury car.

"I just passed my wife," he told them. "She was on a skateboard."

—BOBI GORIA

"That's it? 'Keep my head down?'"

Sports

Fast Pitches

The national pastime of Tahiti is making love," says Bob Hope. "But we, silly fools, picked baseball."

After the rookie pitcher walked a third straight batter, the manager strolled to the mound. "Son," he told the southpaw, "I think you've had enough."

"But look who's coming to bat," whined the rookie. "I struck this guy out the last time he was up."

"Yeah, I know," said the manager. "But this is still the same inning."

—*Sunshine* Magazine

During a baseball game, a woman kept shouting threats at the umpire. No matter what happened on the field, she continually yelled, "Kill the umpire!" This went on for an hour. "Lady," another fan called out, "the umpire hasn't done anything wrong."

"He's my husband," she replied. "Last night he came home with lipstick on his collar. Kill the umpire!"

—*Milton Berle's Private Joke File*

Robert Orben says: "My wife claims I'm a baseball fanatic. She says all I ever read about is baseball. All I ever talk about is baseball. All I ever think about is baseball. I told her she's way off base."

Pitchers say the split-finger fastball is like sex," writes George Will. "When it's good, it's terrific, and when it's bad, it's still pretty good."

—*Men at Work*

"My man called for a fastball and your man threw a slider."

A rookie pitcher was struggling at the mound, so the catcher walked up to have a talk with him. "I've figured out your problem," he told the young southpaw. "You always lose control at the same point in every game."

"When is that?"

"Right after the national anthem."

—JEFF MACNELLY, Tribune Media Services

I have to cut down on hot dogs and beer," one bleacher bum said to another.

"Why's that?"

"Can't you see? I'm starting to get a ballpark figure."

—*The American Legion Magazine*

The morning of a New York Mets game, a fan went to see if his tickets were still on the dashboard of his car. But he discovered that the windshield was smashed.

"Someone broke in and took our tickets?" asked his wife.

"Worse than that," the man replied. "Someone left four more."

—Quoted by JAMES DENT in the Charleston, W.Va., *Gazette*

Carl and Abe are two old baseball fanatics. They agree that whoever dies first will try to come back and tell the other one if there's baseball in heaven.

One evening Abe passes away in his sleep. A few nights later Carl hears what sounds like Abe's voice. "Abe, is that you?" he asks.

"Of course it's me," Abe replies.

"I can't believe it," Carl whispers. "So tell me, is there baseball in heaven?"

"Well, I have good news and bad news," Abe says. "The good news is, yes, there's baseball in heaven. The bad news is you're pitching tomorrow night."

—DAVID DANGLER

"I don't know, 'fore' hardly seems adequate."

Chasing the
Little White Ball

Jock and Angus, two craggy Scots, were sitting before the club-house fireplace after 18 holes on a raw, blustery day. The ice slowly melted from their beards and collected in puddles under their chairs. Outside, the wind howled off the North Sea and hail rattled against the windows.

The pair sat in silence over their whiskies. Finally Jock spoke: "Next Tuesday, same time?"

"Aye," Angus replied, "weather permittin'."

—MALCOLM McNAIR in *Golf Illustrated*

Are you my caddie?" asked the golfer.

"Yes, sir," replied the boy.

"And are you any good at finding lost balls?"

"Yes, sir."

"Right, then. Find one and let's start the game."

—Stan Saacks

Three senior golfers were griping continually. "The fairways are too long," said one. "The hills are too high," said another. "The bunkers are too deep," complained the third.

Finally an 80-year-old put things into perspective. "At least," he noted, "we're on the right side of the grass."

—Harold L. Weaver

When the legendary salesman was asked his secrets of success, he gave a humble shrug. "I'm sure you all know the cardinal rules: know your product; make lots of calls; never take no for an answer. But, honestly, I owe my success to consistently missing a three-foot putt by two inches."

—Ashton Applewhite, William R. Evans III, and Andrew Frothingham,
And I Quote

You can always spot an employee who's playing golf with his boss. He's the fellow who gets a hole in one and says, "Oops!"

—Bob Monkhouse, *Just Say a Few Words*

Did you hear about the politically correct country club? They no longer refer to their golfers as having handicaps. Instead they're "stroke challenged."

—*Comedy on Call*

Husband to wife: "You're always nagging me about my golf. It's driving me mad."

Wife: "It wouldn't be a drive—just a short putt."

—HARRY LEECH

A married couple, both avid golfers, were discussing the future one night. "Honey," the wife said, "if I were to die and you were to remarry, would you two live in this house?"

"I suppose so—it's paid for."

"How about our car?" continued the woman. "Would the two of you keep that?"

"I suppose so—it's paid for."

"What about my golf clubs? Would you let her use them too?"

"Heck, no," the husband blurted out. "She's left-handed."

—DON CRIQUI on *Imus in the Morning*, WFAN, New York

A man played golf every Saturday and always got home around 2:00 in the afternoon. One Saturday, however, he rushed in at 7:30 pm and blurted to his wife, "I left the course at the normal time, but on the way home I stopped to change a flat tire for a young woman. She offered to buy me a drink, one thing led to another, and we spent the entire afternoon in a motel. I'm so sorry. I'll never do it again."

"Don't hand me that malarkey," the angry wife shouted. "You played 36 holes, didn't you?"

—GEORGE W. EDWARDS

Did you hear about Fred trying to drown himself in the water hazard on the tenth hole?" a weekend golfer asked his partner.

"No kidding!" said the other duffer. "What happened?"

"Nothing, really. He couldn't keep his head down there either."

—Quoted by ED BAER on *The Ed Baer Affair*, WHUD, Peekskill, N.Y.

Two male golfers were held up by two women players ahead, so one went forward to ask if they could play through.

He returned, looking embarrassed, and explained, "I couldn't speak to them—one is my wife, and the other is my mistress."

His partner then went forward, only to return muttering, "What an extraordinary coincidence!"

—L. D. TURNER

Marooned on a South Seas island, a man with a beard down to his knees is walking on the beach. Suddenly a beautiful woman emerges from the surf.

"Been here long?" she asks.

"Since 1981," he replies.

"How long has it been since you've had a cigarette?"

"Eleven years."

She unzips a pocket in the sleeve of her wet suit, pulls out a pack of Camels, lights one, and hands it to him. He inhales greedily. "How long since you've had a drink of whiskey?"

"Eleven years."

She unzips the other sleeve and offers him a flask. He takes a long pull and looks at her adoringly.

"How long," she asks coyly, "since you played around?"

"Eleven years," he says wistfully.

She starts to unzip the front of her wet suit. "Gosh," he says, "you got a set of golf clubs in there?"

—NED PARKER, quoted by ALEX THIEN
in the Milwaukee *Sentinel*

What's your handicap these days?" one golfer asked another.

"I'm a scratch golfer. . . . I write down all my good scores and scratch out all my bad ones."

—CHARLES SCHULZ, United Features Syndicate

"I told you this was rough hole!"

Mack the Slice, a notorious duffer, unwound on the first tee and sent a high drive far to the right. The ball sailed through an open window. Figuring that was the end of it, Mack played on.

On the eighth hole, a police officer walked up to Mack and asked, "Did you hit a ball through that window?"

"Yes, I did."

"Well, it knocked a lamp over, scaring the dog, which raced out of the house onto the highway. A driver rammed into a brick wall to avoid the dog, sending three people to the hospital. And all because you sliced the ball."

"I'm so sorry," moaned Mack. "Is there anything I can do?"

"Well," the cop replied, "try keeping your head down and close up your stance a bit."

—BILL MAJESKI in *Catholic Digest*

Golfer: "What's your handicap?"
Second golfer: "Honesty."

—*Executive Speechwriter Newsletter*

The minister was on the golf course when he heard a duffer, deep in a sand trap, let loose a stream of profanity. "I have often noticed," chided the minister, "that the best golfers are not addicted to the use of foul language."

"Of course not," screamed the man. "What do they have to swear about?"

—*Contact*

She: "How'd your doctor appointment go?"
He: "Well, there's good news and bad news. My blood pressure's high and I'm overweight. But, at the doctor's suggestion, I'm going to take up golf!"
She: "And the good news?"

—GREG EVANS, North American Syndicate

First golfer: "I have the greatest golf ball in the world. You can't lose it."

Second golfer: "How so?"

First golfer: "If you hit it into the sand, it beeps. You hit it into the water, it floats. If you want to play golf at night, it glows."

Second golfer: "Hey, sounds good. Where did you get it?"

First golfer: "Found it in the woods."

—BYRON SMIALEK in the
Washington, Pa., *Observer-Reporter*

Honey, I have a confession to make," a guy told his bride. "I'm a golf nut. You'll never see me on weekends during golf season."

"Well, dear," she murmured. "I have a confession to make too. I'm a hooker."

"No big deal," replied the groom. "Just keep your head down and your left arm straight."

—JAY TRACHMAN in *One to One*

Fish Tales and Hunting Licenses

Question: What's the difference between a hunter and a fisherman? Answer: A hunter lies in wait while a fisherman waits and lies.

—*One to One*

A fisherman accidentally left his day's catch under the seat of a bus. The next evening's newspaper carried an ad: "If the person who left a bucket of fish on the No. 47 bus would care to come to the garage, he can have the bus."

—Sri Lanka *Sunday Island*

*"Your father, may he rest in peace, was
considered quite a catch."*

Simon was an inveterate fisherman, well known for exaggerating the size of "the one that got away." But there came a day when he actually caught two enormous flounders. He immediately invited a few friends over to dine, then tried to figure out how best to serve the fish. "If I use both," he told his wife, "it will seem ostentatious."

"Why not serve a piece of each?" she suggested.

"No, if I cut them up, nobody will believe I caught two giant flounders." Simon racked his brain. Then he had an idea.

The guests were seated at the table when their host strode in with a platter, holding the biggest flounder they'd ever seen. Suddenly Simon stumbled and fell. Everyone cried out in dismay as the fish crashed to the floor, but Simon quickly brushed himself off.

"Dear," he called out to his wife, "bring in the other flounder!"

—HENRY D. SPALDING, *Jewish Laffs*

An optimist who went hunting with a pessimist wanted to show off his new dog. After the first shot, he sent his dog to fetch a duck. The dog ran across the top of the water and brought back the game. The pessimist said nothing. The dog retrieved the second and third ducks the same way—over the water. Still the pessimist did not react. Finally, the optimist could stand it no longer. "Don't you see anything unusual about my new dog?" he asked his companion.

"Yes—he can't swim."

—BOB PHILLIPS quoted by MARTHA BOLTON,
"If Mr. Clean Calls, Tell Him I'm Not In!"

Two would-be fishermen rented a boat, and one caught a large fish. "We should mark the spot," he said. The other man drew a large X in the bottom of the boat with a black marker.

"That's no good," said the first man. "Next time out we may not get the same boat."

—FLORENCE KILLAM

A hunting party was hopelessly lost. "I thought you said you were the best guide in Maine!" one of the hunters angrily said to their confused leader.

"I am," replied the guide. "But I think we're in Canada now."

—*Reminisce*

A New South Wales fisherman lost his dentures over the side of the boat in rough weather, so his prankster friend removed his own false teeth, tied them on his line and pretended he had caught the missing gnashers.

Unhooking the teeth, his grateful mate tried to put them into his mouth, then hurled them into the sea with the disgusted remark: "They're not mine—they don't fit!"

—"Column 8,"
The Sydney Morning Herald

Two Texans went up to Minnesota to go ice fishing. After setting up their tent, they started to cut a hole in the ice. As they pulled the cord on their chain saw, they heard a voice from above: "There are no fish under the ice."

When they pulled the cord again, the same voice intoned: "There are no fish under the ice."

"Is that you, God?" they asked in awe.

"No," came the reply. "I own this ice rink—and I can tell you that there are no fish under the ice."

—N. E. DUNNUCK

While hunting, Larry and Elmer got lost in the woods. Trying to reassure his friend, Larry said, "Don't worry. All we have to do is shoot into the air three times, stay where we are, and someone will find us."

They shot in the air three times, but no one came. After a while, they tried it again. Still no response. When they decided to try once more, Elmer said, "It better work this time. We're down to our last three arrows."

—ELIZABETH CLARK

The tale is told of Boudreaux, out on the bayou, fishing by dropping sticks of dynamite over the side, waiting for the "boom" and scooping the fish out with a net. After he'd done this four or five times, the game warden came out and said, "Boudreaux, you know you ain't s'posed to be fishin' that way."

Boudreaux paid him no mind. Lighting up another stick of dynamite, he handed it to the game warden and said, "You gonna talk or you gonna fish?"

—DENNIS R. EDWARDS

"I think he's had it as a bird dog."

A group of friends who went deer hunting separated into pairs for the day. That night, one hunter returned alone, staggering under an eight-point buck. "Where's Harry?" asked another hunter.

"He fainted a couple miles up the trail," Harry's partner answered.

"You left him lying there alone and carried the deer back?"

"A tough call," said the hunter. "But I figured no one is going to steal Harry."

—*The Jokesmith*

An American had been fishing for two weeks in Ireland without getting a bite. On the last day of his vacation, he caught a small salmon.

"Turlough," he said to his guide later, "that salmon cost me more than five hundred dollars."

"Well now, sir," Turlough comforted him, "aren't you lucky you didn't catch two!"

—Ian Aitken

After a long day of fishing without even a nibble, a man said disgustedly to his companion, "You know the saying, 'Give a man a fish, and he'll eat for a day; teach a man to fish, and he'll eat for a lifetime'?"

"Yes?"

"Well, whoever said it wasn't a fisherman."

—David Sahlin

Irving was boasting to a fellow fisherman about a 20-pound salmon he had caught. "Twenty pounds, huh?" remarked the other guy, with skepticism. "Were there any witnesses?"

"Of course," said Irving. "Otherwise it would have weighed 30 pounds."

—Joey Adams

The young boy protested vigorously when his mother asked him to take his little sister along fishing. "The last time she came," he objected, "I didn't catch a single fish."

"I'll talk to her," his mother said, "and I promise this time she won't make any noise."

"It wasn't the noise, Mom," the boy replied. "She ate all my bait."

—*The Rotarian*

Three men were sitting on a park bench. The one in the middle was reading a newspaper; the others were pretending to fish. They baited imaginary hooks, cast lines, and reeled in their catch.

A passing policeman stopped to watch the spectacle and asked the man in the middle if he knew the other two.

"Oh yes," he said. "They're my friends."

"In that case," warned the officer, "you'd better get them out of here!"

"Yes, sir," the man replied, and he began rowing furiously.

—ADAM T. RATTRAY

Said a fisherman after removing a tiny fish from his hook and throwing it back into the water: "Don't show up around here anymore without your parents!"

—*Der Stern*

The novice ice fisherman wasn't having any luck, but another man nearby was pulling up fish after fish through the ice. "What's your secret?" the newcomer asked.

"Mmnpximdafgltmm," mumbled the man.

"I'm sorry, I couldn't understand you," said the novice.

"Mmnpximdafgltmm!" the fisherman mumbled again.

The neophyte shook his head and began to turn away, when the other man held up his hand. Spitting twice into his coffee cup, he said, "You've got to keep the worms warm!"

—BRIAN D. HOXIE

Sitting in a rowboat, the novice fisherman asked his companion, "Got any more of those little plastic floats?"

"Why?"

"This one keeps sinking."

—ART SANSOM, Newspaper Enterprise Assn.

Three statisticians go deer hunting with bows and arrows. They spot a big buck and take aim. One shoots, and his arrow flies off 10 feet to the left. The second shoots, and his arrow goes 10 feet to the right. The third statistician jumps up and down yelling, "We got him! We got him!"

—BILL BUTZ, quoted by DIANA McLELLAN in *Washingtonian*

You Must Be Jock-ing!

Before a major college basketball game between two top-20 teams, one student nudged another and said, "Look at that player. I wonder what's the matter with him. He looks so depressed."

"You haven't heard?" asked the other. "It's because his father's always writing him for money!"

—*Ideas for Better Living*

Basketball sure is an amazing game," said one fan to another. "They pay a guy $500,000 a year to shoot the ball, and then they call it a free throw."

—JAY TRACHMAN in *One to One*

He's great on the court," a sportswriter said of a college basketball player in an interview with his coach. "But how's his scholastic work?"

"Why, he makes straight A's," replied the coach.

"Wonderful!" said the sportswriter.

"Yes," agreed the coach, "but his B's are a little crooked."

—CLARENCE PETERSEN in the Jacksonville, Fla., *Times-Union*

"He's what I call a natural."

An avid Dallas Cowboys fan took his dog to a sports bar one Sunday afternoon to watch the game. The bartender reluctantly let the dog in, and the pooch sat quietly as the game progressed. When the Cowboys got a field goal, the dog went crazy—barking, running in circles and doing back flips. "What does he do when they score a touchdown?" the amazed bartender asked.

"I don't know," replied the owner. "I've only had him two years."

—Contributed by HOWARD R. SCHROEDER

After spending all day watching football, Harry fell asleep in front of the TV and spent the night in the chair. In the morning, his wife woke him up. "Get up, dear," she said. "It's 20 to seven."

He awoke with a start. "In whose favor?"

—*Funny, Funny World*

A college football coach had recruited a top talent, but the player couldn't pass the school's entrance exam. Needing the recruit badly, the coach went to the dean and asked if the recruit could take the test orally. The dean agreed, and the following day the recruit and the coach were seated in his office. "Okay," the dean said. "What is seven times seven?"

The recruit mulled it over for a moment, then said, "I think it's 49."

Suddenly the coach leapt to his feet. "Please, Dean," he begged, "give him another chance!"

—OSCAR ZIMMERMAN

Mort Sahl sympathized with football widows. When one woman asked him how she could get her husband's attention away from the TV set, he said, "Wear something sheer."

"What if that doesn't work?" she asked.

"Then put a number on your back," Sahl replied.

—JOEY ADAMS

What position does your brother play on the football team?" Tom was asked.

"I'm not real sure," the boy replied, "but I think he's one of the drawbacks."

—Quoted in the
Milwaukee *Journal*

P.L.VEY

Anthropologists have discovered a 50-million-year-old human skull with three perfectly preserved teeth intact. They're not sure, but they think it may be the remains of the very first hockey player.

—JAY LENO

The 85-year-old woman decided to take up skydiving. After she attended instruction classes, the day came for her first jump. Strapping on a parachute, she stood awaiting her turn to leap out of the plane. But when she looked at the ground below, she lost her nerve.

Finally, she reached into her pocket, pulled out a small transmitter and radioed her instructor on the ground: "Help! I've gotten up, and I can't fall down!"

—KEN BEHRENS,
WJBC, Bloomington, Ill.

Young woman to boyfriend:

"Otto, you'd really rather watch soccer than me?"

"Yes," he says apologetically. "But I'd take you any day over the long jump, swimming, and the equestrian contest."

—ANDREA RATONYI

Bill and George were always competing against each other. After one argument over who was better at folding and packing parachutes, they went skydiving to settle the dispute. Bill jumped first, pulled the cord and began to float gently to earth. Then George jumped and pulled his cord, but nothing happened. Next he yanked on the safety cord, but that didn't work either. In a matter of seconds George, falling like a rock, flew past Bill. "So," Bill shouted, ripping off his harness, "you want to race!"

—MARIE THRUSH

A sky diver and his instructor peered down at the field 3,000 feet below. "There's nothing to worry about," the instructor said. "You jump, count to three and pull your rip cord. If that doesn't work, pull your reserve cord. There'll be a truck down there to pick you up."

The sky diver took a deep breath and plunged into the open air. After free-falling, he counted to three, then pulled his rip cord. Nothing happened. So he pulled his reserve. A few cobwebs drifted out.

"Darn," he said. "I'll bet that truck's not down there either."

—*Playboy*

Horsefeathers

The cavalryman was galloping down the road, rushing to catch up with his regiment. Suddenly his horse stumbled and pitched him to the ground. In the dirt with a broken leg, terrified of the approaching enemy, the soldier called out: "All you saints in heaven, help me get up on my horse!"

Then, with superhuman effort, he leaped onto the horse's back and fell off the other side. Once again on the ground, he called to the heavens: "All right, just half of you this time!"

—MRS. JAMES LARKIN

My wife means to lose weight. That's why she rides horseback all the time."

"And what's the result?"

"The horse lost 10 kilos last week."

—M. SPIRKOV

Overheard at the track: "Horse racing is very romantic. The horse hugs the rail, the jockey puts his arms around the horse, and you kiss your money good-bye."

—SACHIN MATADE

About to take his first horseback ride, the greenhorn was checking out the horses in the stable. The old wrangler asked whether he wanted an English saddle or a Western saddle.

"What's the difference?" asked the tenderfoot.

"The English saddle is flat, while the Western has a horn in the front."

"Better give me the English saddle," the fellow replied. "I don't expect to be riding in traffic."

—R. J. LANDSEADEL JR. in *The Rotarian*

Gasping for breath and covered with sweat, a man came into a race-track snack bar and ordered a soft drink. "What happened to you?" the waitress asked.

"I was in the paddock area," the man panted, "when I saw a $100 bill on the ground. I bent down to pick it up. While I was bent over, somebody threw a saddle on me, and a jockey jumped into the saddle. The next thing I knew, I was on the track and the jockey was whipping my flanks."

"No kidding?" said the surprised woman. "What did you do?"

"I finished third."

—Jerry H. Simpson Jr.

An elderly gentleman went to a dude ranch and asked for the rates. "Well," began the ranch director, "for people your age who can't handle horses very well, we have to charge an extra 50 dollars a day."

"Fifty dollars a day!" yelped the old-timer. "You must be putting me on!"

"No," explained the director. "That would be an additional 20 dollars."

—Ashley Cooper in Charleston, S.C., *News and Courier*

A man was walking down a country road when he heard a voice coming from behind a tree, but all he could see was a horse.

"Hello, remember me?" the voice said. "I won the Kentucky Derby two years ago."

"A talking horse!" the man exclaimed, so he rushed to a nearby field where the farmer was working and asked, "What would you take for the horse?"

"That darned horse is no good, you can have him for 20 dollars."

"Twenty dollars! I'll give you 2,000."

"Has that old haybag been giving you that baloney about winning the Kentucky Derby? Listen, I happen to know he came in last."

—*The Carpenter*

"Mom? Dad? Who are these people?."

Ententainment

Roar of the Greasepaint, Smell of the Crowd

If he starts to cry, you'll have to leave the theater," a movie-theater usher warned a young couple with an infant, "but you can ask for your money back."

Thirty minutes into the film, the husband whispered to his wife, "What do you think?"

"This film is a waste of time."

"I agree. Why not wake the baby up?"

—CARINE SCHENKEL

Sam: "I used to be a stand-up comedian before I worked here."

Joe: "I never would have guessed that."

Sam: "Ask me why I quit."

Joe: "Why did you . . ."

Sam: "Timing!"

Joe: ". . . quit?"

—MIKE SMITH

As the man and wife returned to their seats in the dark auditorium, the husband asked a fellow seated on the aisle, "Did someone step on your feet while going out at intermission?"

"Yes, you did," he replied, expecting an apology.

"Okay, honey," the man said to his wife, "this is our row."

—DUKE LARSON, quoted by Alex Thien
in the Milwaukee *Sentinel*

In Chicago there's a new Al Capone theme park. The commercial says, "Come to the park, pay your money, and nobody gets hurt."

—JOE HOBBY

When Disneyland celebrated its 40th anniversary, Disney officials buried a time capsule," reports Jay Leno. "They say it will be dug up in 50 years—or when the last person in line at Space Mountain gets to the front, whichever comes first."

A movie producer was telling his pal about giving his fiancée a string of pearls for her birthday. "Why," asked his friend, "don't you give her something practical—like a car?"

The producer answered, "Did you ever hear of a phony automobile?"

—*Another Treasury of Clean Jokes*, edited by Tal D. Bonham

You're blocking the way, sir," said the usher to a man sprawled in the aisle of a movie theater. "Please get up."

The man didn't move or reply. The usher called the manager over, who said, "I must ask you to move."

Still the prone man didn't reply. So the manager called the police. "Get up or I'll have to take you in," the officer said. "Where did you come from anyway?"

The man stirred finally and said, "The balcony."

—*Capper's*

Browsing at a video shop, a guy and a gal spot the last tape of a recent hit movie. He grabs it first. "Your VCR or mine?" he asks.

—Bill Copeland in the Sarasota, Fla., *Herald-Tribune*

Hollywood is the land of make-believe. Actors pretend they're someone else, and when the movie's finished, the producers make believe it's good.

—*Current Comedy*

"It's perfectly normal for your last film to flash before your eyes on Oscar night."

A Hollywood screenwriter coming home from work spotted a police line at the end of his street. He quickly discovered the reason: His house had burned to the ground. "What happened?" he asked a cop who was posted there.

"I'm sorry," the police officer said, "but your agent came over this afternoon and kidnapped your wife and children and then torched your house."

The screenwriter looked stunned. "My agent came to my *house*?"

—*Esquire*

Two Hollywood execs were overheard at a power breakfast. "You're *lying* to me!" shouted one, pounding the table.

"I know. You're right," said the other. "But hear me out."

—Quoted by JEFF GILES in *Newsweek*

In a darkened theater where a suspenseful mystery story was being staged, a member of the audience suddenly stood up and cried, "Where is the murderer?"

A threatening voice behind her replied, "Right in back of you, if you don't sit down!"

—PIERRE LÉAUTÉ

Movie cowboys mystify me," says Bob Hope. "How can they jump off a porch roof and onto a horse, and still sing in a normal voice?"

When I came to this country," writes comedian Yakov Smirnoff, "one of the toughest things to get used to was all the different names of rock bands like Ratt, the Grateful Dead, or Twisted Sister. Then I *saw* the people in these groups, and it began to make sense."

—*America on Six Rubles a Day*

They were watching a TV soap opera, and he became irritated by the way his wife was taking it to heart. "How can you sit there and cry about the made-up troubles of people you've never even met?" he demanded.

"The same way you can jump up and scream when some guy you've never met scores a touchdown," she replied.

—KRIS LEE in *Woman's World*

You know you're getting old when you walk into a record store and everything you like has been marked down to $1.99.

—JACK SIMMONS, *Showtime Comedy Cable*

A quiz program contestant had to identify famous slogans. After several correct responses, he was asked, "Which company originated the phrase 'Good to the last drop'?"

He thought for a moment. "Otis Elevator?"

—JACK TRACY

Mel's son rushed in the door. "Dad! Dad!" he announced. "I got a part in the school play!"

"That's terrific," Mel said proudly. "What part is it?"

"I play the part of the dad."

Mel thought this over. "Go back tomorrow," he instructed, "and tell them you want a speaking role."

—DARLEEN GIANNINI

When a plague of flying ants caused the performance at a variety theater in the Australian outback to end prematurely, the manager cabled a message to his agent: "Show stopped by flying ants!"

"Book 'em for another week," replied the agent.

—BOB BROADFIELD

A stage mother cornered the concert violinist in his dressing room and insisted he listen to a tape of her talented son playing the violin. The man agreed to listen, and the woman switched on the tape player.

What music, the violinist thought. A difficult piece, but played with such genius that it brought tears to his eyes. He listened spellbound to the entire recording.

"Madam," he whispered, "is that your son?"

"No," she replied. "That's Jascha Heifetz. But my son sounds just like him."

—*The Jokesmith*

Overheard: "I had a disturbing discussion with my wife this morning. I said that men like Sylvester Stallone and Arnold Schwarzenegger are a dime a dozen. She said, 'Here's a nickel. Get me six!' "

—*Current Comedy*

A couple of extras in the play were talking backstage at the end of the performance. "What's the matter with our leading lady?" one actress asked. "She seems really mad about something."

"Oh, she's upset because she only received nine bouquets of flowers over the footlights," the other woman answered.

"Nine!" exclaimed the first actress. "That's pretty good, isn't it?"

"Yes," her friend replied, "but she paid for 10."

—*The Safe Way*

Did you hear about the $2.7-billion write-off Sony took on its Hollywood studio? "That was quick!" says comedy writer Michael Connor. "It took the Japanese only a couple of years to master Hollywood-style bookkeeping."

—*The Los Angeles Times*

Waiter! Waiter!

Waiter," Billy roars in the restaurant. "I want a steak, but it must taste just like veal. In the soup there must be no more and no less than 16 droplets of fat, and the wine must be served at exactly 50 degrees. The crystal wineglass must sound in A-flat when I tap it."

The waiter remains stoically calm, notes down every request, and then asks: "And the toothpicks, sir? Would you like them to be Rococo, Biedermier, Jugendstil, or would you prefer something in a slightly more modern line?"

—Urbain Koopmans

When the waitress in a New York City restaurant brought him the soup du jour, the Englishman was a bit dismayed. "Good heavens," he said, "what is this?"

"Why, it's bean soup," she replied.

"I don't care what it has been," he sputtered. "What is it now?"

—Margaret Olderog

The diner was furious when his steak arrived too rare. "Waiter," he barked, "didn't you hear me say 'well done'?"

"I can't thank you enough, sir," replied the waiter. "I hardly ever get a compliment."

—A. H. Berzen

A diner called the waiter over and asked, "What's this at the bottom of my plate?"

"It's the design," replied the waiter.

"In that case," said the diner, "it's an animated drawing—it's moving!"

—*Humor Piadas e Anedotas*

"I realize we all look alike, sir, but I am Walter, a married man with two grown children, and an abiding interest in the theater, coin collecting, and small songbirds. Your waiter is Eddie. I'll send him over."

In a restaurant where the service was particularly slow, a customer was fretting because the waiter had not taken his order, although he had been waiting for a quarter of an hour. When the waiter finally appeared at his table, bearing a small dish of peanuts, he found the place empty, except for a small note from the disappointed diner: "Gone out to lunch!"

—MINA and ANDRÉ GUILLOIS

The truck driver looked askance at the soup he had just been served in a backwoods eatery. It contained dark flecks of seasoning, but two of the spots were suspicious.

"Hey," he called out to the waitress, "these particles in my soup—aren't they foreign objects?"

She scrutinized his bowl. "No, sir!" she reassured him. "Those things live around here."

—Dean Morgan

A patron in a Montreal café turned on a tap in the washroom and got scalded. "This is an outrage," he complained. "The faucet marked C gave me boiling water."

"But, Monsieur, C stands for *chaude*—French for hot. You should know that if you live in Montreal."

"Wait a minute," roared the patron. "The other tap is also marked C."

"Of course," said the manager. "It stands for cold. After all, Montreal is a bilingual city."

—*Catholic Digest*

My family and I were eating in an expensive restaurant, when I overheard the gentleman at the next table ask the waitress to pack the leftovers for their dog. It was then that his young son exclaimed loudly, "Whoopee! We're going to get a dog."

—B. S. Prabhakar

How many cups of coffee will this hold?" the man asked as he placed a large thermos on the lunch-room counter.

"Six cups," advised the waitress.

"Fine," replied the man. "Give me two cups regular, two cups black, and two with extra cream."

—George E. Bergman

The disgruntled diner summoned his waiter to the table, complaining, "My oyster stew doesn't have any oysters in it."

"Well, if that bothers you, then you better skip dessert," replied the waiter. "It's angel food cake."

—ROBERT L. RODGERS

Ours is a good restaurant," said the manager. "If you order an egg, you get the freshest egg in the world. If you order hot coffee, you get the hottest coffee in the world, and—"

"I believe you," said the customer. "I ordered a small steak."

—JIM REED, *Treasury of Ozark Country Humor*

A man walked into a crowded New York City restaurant and caught the eye of a harried waiter. "You know," he said, "it's been 10 years since I came in here."

"Don't blame me," the waiter snapped. "I'm working as fast as I can."

—NORTON MOCKRIDGE, United Features Syndicate

Inflation is creeping up," a young man said to his friend. "Yesterday I ordered a $25 steak in a restaurant and told them to put it on my American Express card—and it fit."

—DON REBER in the Reading, Pa., *Times*

Two eggs were in a pot, being boiled. One said to the other, "It's so hot in here I don't think I can stand it much longer."

The other replied, "Don't grumble. As soon as they get you out of here, they bash your head in with a spoon."

—J. JONES

"My, oh, my! What a fascinating guy you are, Vincent! But now,
if it's not too much trouble, I'd like you to take my order."

The big Texan, visiting New York for the first time, entered a fancy restaurant and ordered a steak. The waiter served it very rare. The Texan took one look at it and demanded that it be returned to the kitchen and cooked.

"It is cooked," snapped the waiter.

"Cooked—nothing!" shouted the Texan. "I've seen cows hurt worse than that get well."

—H. B. McClung

In a greasy spoon, a downhearted diner asked the waitress for meatloaf and some kind words. She brought the meatloaf but didn't say a thing. "Hey," he said, "what about my kind words?"

She replied, "Don't eat the meatloaf."

—*The Los Angeles Times*

Happy Hour

While at the pub, an Englishman, an Irishman, and a Scot each found a fly swimming around in his beer. The Englishman asked the bartender for a napkin and a teaspoon. Elegantly scooping the fly out, he placed it in the napkin and delicately folded it.

The Irishman pushed his sleeve up, immersed his hand in the beer, caught the fly, threw it on the floor, and stepped on it.

The Scot silently took his jacket off, draped it neatly over the chair, folded his shirtsleeves up, and bent over his pint. Carefully he fished the fly out by picking it up by its wings. He lifted it just above the mug, shook the fly, and in a threatening voice bellowed, "Now spit it out!"

—HANS J. GERHARDT

A college professor walked into a bar and said, "Bring me a martinus." The bartender smiled and said, "You mean martini?"

"If I want more than one," snapped the professor, "I'll order them."

—EARL WILSON

A grasshopper walks into a bar. The bartender looks at him and says, "Hey, they named a drink after you!"

"Really?" replies the grasshopper. "There's a drink named Stan?"

—FAYE SKULBERSTAD

At a party the hostess served a guest a cup of punch and told him it was spiked. Next, she served some to a minister. "I would rather commit adultery than allow liquor to pass my lips!" he shouted.

Hearing this, the first man poured his punch back and said, "I didn't know we had a choice!"

—DARRELL B. THOMPSON

Mike had stopped off at a small-town tavern and made his way to the bar when there was a commotion outside. A man at the door shouted, "Run for your lives! Big Jake's comin'!" As everyone scattered, an enormous man burst through the door, threw tables and chairs aside and strode up to the bar. "Gimme a drink!" he ordered.

Left alone at the bar, Mike quickly handed over a bottle of whiskey. The huge man downed it in one gulp, then ate the bottle. Paralyzed with fear, Mike stammered, "Can I g-get you another?"

"Nope, I gotta go," grunted the giant. "Didn't you hear? Big Jake's comin'!"

—HOWARD CHAVEZ

A fellow went to a bar and ordered a drink. He gulped it down and, to the amazement of the bartender, also ate the goblet, except for the stem. He ordered another, swallowed the drink, and again ate the goblet, leaving the stem. The bartender then called in a psychiatrist, explained the man's strange behavior, and asked whether he thought the man was eccentric. "He must be," the shrink replied. "The stem's the best part."

—P. R. ENGELE

A man walked into a second-story bar and ordered a drink. The man next to him began a conversation about wind currents in the area. The first man said he didn't understand what was so special about the wind, so the second man said, "Let me demonstrate."

With that, he went to the window, jumped out, did a little spin in midair and came back in. "See how great the currents are? You can do the same thing."

After a few more drinks and much prodding, the first man decided to test the wind currents. He went to the window, jumped out, and fell to the ground.

The bartender looked at the other man and said, "Superman, you're really mean when you're drunk."

—DARLEEN GIANNINI

Pat Muldoon, proprietor of an Irish pub, was busy pouring for his noontime trade, while trying to keep a swarm of flies away from the buffet table. When Mike Callahan, the town drunk and biggest mooch, wandered in, Pat turned a deaf ear to his plea for a nip or two on the cuff.

But when Mike offered to kill every one of the flies circling the buffet in exchange for a short one, Pat slid a shot of whiskey across the bar. As soon as he downed it, Mike rolled up his sleeves and headed for the door. "All right, Muldoon," he said. "Send 'em out one at a time."

—GORDON H. KRUEGER

A businesswoman is sitting at a bar. A man approaches her.
"Hi, honey," he says. "Want a little company?"
"Why?" asks the woman. "Do you have one to sell?"

—Quoted by CAROLYN A. STRADLEY

Late one night, after an evening of drinking, Smitty took a shortcut through the graveyard and stumbled into a newly dug grave. He could not get out, so he lay at the bottom and fell asleep. Early next morning the old caretaker heard moans and groans coming from deep in the earth. He went over to investigate, saw the shivering figure at the bottom and demanded, "What's wrong with ya, that you're makin' all that noise?"

"Oh, I'm awful cold!" came the response.

"Well, it's no wonder," said the caretaker. "You've gone and kicked all the dirt off ya!"

—DEBBIE P. WRIGHT

Overheard: "The police in this town have a very tough sobriety test. Not only do they make you blow up a balloon, but then you have to twist it into a giraffe."

—*Current Comedy*

"You guys know the rules! No discussing politics during happy hour."

A bar owner locked up his place at 2 am and went home to sleep. He had been in bed only a few minutes when the phone rang. "What time do you open up in the morning?" he heard an obviously inebriated man inquire.

The owner was so furious, he slammed down the receiver and went back to bed. A few minutes later there was another call and he heard the same voice ask the same question. "Listen," the owner shouted, "there's no sense in asking me what time I open because I wouldn't let a person in your condition in—"

"I don't want to get in," the caller interjected. "I want to get out."

—*The Carpenter*

You Betcha'

Las Vegas is loaded with all kinds of gambling devices," says Joey Adams. "Dice tables, slot machines, and wedding chapels."

A woman in Atlantic City was losing at the roulette wheel. When she was down to her last 10 dollars, she asked the fellow next to her for a good number. "Why don't you play your age?" he suggested.

The woman agreed, and then put her money on the table. The next thing the fellow with the advice knew, the woman had fainted and fallen to the floor. He rushed right over. "Did she win?" he asked.

"No," replied the attendant. "She put 10 dollars on 29 and 41 came in."

—Christine L. Castner

In Las Vegas a big-time gambler dies and a friend delivers the eulogy. "Tony isn't dead," the friend says. "He only sleeps."

A mourner in the back of the room jumps up. "I got a hundred bucks says he's dead!"

—*Solutions for Seniors*

When Salley O'Malley of County Clare won the Irish Sweepstakes, she decided to treat herself to some of the finer things in life. "I've nivver had a milk bath," she told her milkman one morning. "Wouldja be bringin' me 96 quarts o'milk tomorro'?"

"Whativver ye want, mum," answered the milkman. "Will that be pasteurized?"

"No," said she. "Up to me chest will do."

—Quoted by T. D.

Sitting by the window in her convent, Sister Eulalia opened a letter from home, and found a $10 bill inside. As she read the letter, she caught sight of a shabbily dressed stranger leaning against a lamppost below. Quickly she wrote "Don't despair, Sister Eulalia" on a piece of paper, wrapped the $10 in it and dropped it out the window.

The stranger picked it up and, with a puzzled expression and a tip of his hat, went off down the street.

The next day Sister Eulalia was told that a man was at the door, insisting on seeing her. She went down and found the stranger waiting. Without a word he handed her a roll of bills. "What's this?" she asked.

"That's the 60 bucks you have coming. Don't Despair paid five to one."

—*The Joy of Words*

Bill sat at the local bar, bragging about his athletic prowess. None of the regulars challenged him, but a visitor piped up, "I'll bet you 50 bucks that I can push something in a wheelbarrow for one block and you can't wheel it back."

Bill looked over at the skinny stranger and decided it wasn't much of a challenge. "I'll take you on," he said.

The two men and a number of regulars borrowed a wheelbarrow and took it to the corner. "Now, let's see what you're made of," taunted Bill.

"Okay," said the challenger. "Get in."

—Anne Victoria Baynas, quoted in
Old Farmer's Almanac

I'm beginning to understand exactly how the state lottery helps education," a guy told his neighbor. "Every time I buy a losing ticket, I get a little smarter."

—*One to One*

"I understand there are no slot machines in the original."

What are you so happy about?" a woman asked the 98-year-old man.

"I broke a mirror," he replied.

"But that means seven years of bad luck."

"I know," he said, beaming. "Isn't it wonderful?"

—BOB MONKHOUSE, *Just Say a Few Words*

Did you hear about the race horse that was so late coming in, they had to pay the jockey time and a half?

—TOM FITZGERALD in the San Francisco Chronicle

A confirmed horse player hadn't been to church in years even though his wife attended every week. One Sunday, however, he finally went with her.

"That wasn't so bad," he said on the way home. "The church was air-conditioned, the pews were cushioned and the singing was great. Did you notice people looking at me when I joined in with my deep baritone voice?"

"Yes, I noticed them," his wife responded. "But the next time we go to church, please try to sing 'Hallelujah, Hallelujah' and not 'Hialeah, Hialeah.' "

—Complete Speaker's Galaxy of Funny Stories, Jokes and Anecdotes, edited by
WINSTON K. PENDLETON

An excited woman called her husband at work. "I won the lottery!" she exclaimed. "Pack your clothes!"

"Great!" he replied. "Summer or winter clothes?"

"All of them—I want you out of the house by six!"

—ASHLEY COOPER in Charleston, S.C., News and Courier

With a Rub of the Lamp

Experimenting with a trick, a magician accidentally changed his wife into a sofa and his two children into armchairs. He called an ambulance and they were rushed to the hospital. Later, the worried sorcerer phoned to check their condition.

"Resting comfortably," said the doctor.

—Today

One day a man spotted a lamp by the roadside. He picked it up, rubbed it vigorously and a genie appeared.

"I'll grant you your fondest wish," the genie said.

The man thought for a moment, then said, "I want a spectacular job—a job that no man has ever succeeded at or has ever attempted to do."

"Poof!" said the genie. "You're a housewife."

—NICOLE BURKE

A despondent woman was walking along the beach when she saw a bottle on the sand. She picked it up and pulled out the cork. Whoosh! A big puff of smoke appeared.

"You have released me from my prison," the genie told her. "To show my thanks, I grant you three wishes. But take care, for with each wish, your mate will receive double of whatever you request."

"Why?" the woman asked. "That bum left me for another woman."

"That is how it is written," replied the genie.

The woman shrugged and then asked for a million dollars. There was a flash of light, and a million dollars appeared at her feet. At the same instant, in a far-off place, her wayward husband looked down to see twice that amount at his feet.

"And your second wish?"

"Genie, I want the world's most expensive diamond necklace." Another flash of light, and the woman was holding the precious treasure. And, in that distant place, her husband was looking for a gem broker to buy his latest bonanza.

"Genie, is it really true that my husband has two million dollars and more jewels than I do, and that he gets double of whatever I wish for?"

The genie said it was indeed true.

"Okay, genie, I'm ready for my last wish," the woman said. "Scare me half to death."

—TOM NEDWEK, quoted by ALEX THIEN
in the Milwaukee *Sentinel*

Overheard: "For some reason I didn't like that Disney movie. Aladdin rubbed me the wrong way."

—GARY APPLE in *Speaker's Idea File*

A man was trying to obtain a flat in Bombay. After many days of fruitless search he was returning to his slum home when he stopped to buy a tender coconut. But when he cut open the top of the coconut, smoke issued out and to the poor man's astonishment a huge genie materialized.

"Command and I will obey!" thundered the genie.

With awakening hope the man stuttered out, "I want a flat in Bombay."

"If I could get a flat for myself in Bombay," retorted the genie, "do you think I would have stayed inside a coconut?"

—RAJIV NAIR

Then there was the fellow who always had bad luck. Once he found a magic lamp, rubbed it, and a genie appeared and gave him the Midas touch. For the rest of his life, everything he touched turned into a muffler.

—*Orben's Comedy Fillers*

Arthur rubbed the old lamp he'd purchased at a flea market, and sure enough, a genie appeared. "Thanks for setting me free," said the grateful spirit.

"Aren't you going to grant me a wish?" asked Arthur.

"Are you kidding?" answered the genie. "If I could grant wishes, would I have been in that lousy lamp all this time?"

—STEVE KEUCHEL

"I thought you had the camera."

Travel

Up in the Air

It doesn't make sense," says comedian Elayne Boosler. "You're flying at 500 m.p.h., 30,000 feet in the air, and the pilot tells you to feel free to roam around the plane. But when you're on the ground taxiing to the gate at one m.p.h., he tells you to remain seated for your own safety."

Why is there mistletoe hanging over the baggage counter?" asked the airline passenger, amid the holiday rush.

The clerk replied, "It's so you can kiss your luggage good-bye."

—SEYMOUR ROSENBERG in the Spartanburg,
S.C., *Herald-Journal*

A student-pilot was making his first helicopter flight. After the take-off, the instructor explained the instruments and, pointing to the rotor blades, said, "That's the air conditioning."

The pupil looked at him in astonishment, and the instructor said, "You don't believe me, do you? Just wait until we reach 3,000 feet and I shut it off. Then you'll see what a hot spot this can be!"

—P. VAN WINKEL

An elderly woman was nervous about making her first flight in an airplane, so before takeoff she went to speak to the captain about her fears.

"You will bring me down safely, won't you?" she anxiously inquired.

"Don't worry, madam," was his friendly reply. "I haven't left anyone up there yet."

—COLLEEN BURGER

"I happen to be a frequent flyer, and this just doesn't feel right to me."

A jet ran into some turbulent weather. To keep the passengers calm, the flight attendants brought out the beverage carts.

"I'd like a soda," said a passenger in the first row. Moving along, the attendant asked the man behind her if he would like something.

"Yes, I would," he replied. "Give me whatever the pilot is drinking!"

—MARY J. MILLER

A small plane with an instructor and student on board hit the runway and bounced repeatedly until it came to a stop. The instructor turned to the student and said, "That was a very bad landing you just made."

"Me?" replied the student. "I thought you were landing."

—The Cockle Bur

The 747 was halfway across the Atlantic when the captain got on the loudspeaker: "Attention, passengers. We have lost one of our engines, but we can certainly reach London with the three we have left. Unfortunately, we will arrive an hour late as a result."

An hour later the captain made another announcement: "Sorry, but we lost another engine. Still, we can travel on two. I'm afraid we will now arrive two hours late."

Shortly thereafter, the passengers heard the captain's voice again: "Guess what, folks. We just lost our third engine, but please be assured we can fly with only one. We will now arrive in London three hours late."

At this point, one passenger became furious. "For Pete's sake," he shouted. "If we lose another engine, we'll be up here all night!"

—NATHANIEL SCOTT MILLER

At an airline ticket counter, a small boy, with his mother, told the agent he was two years old. The man looked at him suspiciously and asked, "Do you know what happens to little boys who lie?"

"Yes. They get to fly at half-price."

—MARLENE FREEDMAN in *Chevron USA*

Pilot to airline passengers: "Ladies and gentlemen, I have some good news and some bad news. The bad news is that we have a hijacker on board. The good news is, he wants to go to the French Riviera."

—Parts Pups

Q: What's a sure sign you're flying the wrong airline?

A: The pilot has a heart attack, and the air-traffic controller talks a flight attendant through takeoff.

—PETER S. LANGSTON

The Concorde is great," says Howie Mandel. "Traveling at twice the speed of sound is fun—except you can't hear the movie till two hours after you land."

Two pilots were discussing the merits of a twin-engine, propeller-driven aircraft undergoing service trials. "How does it handle?" asked the pilot who hadn't yet flown the new plane.

"Oh, it's not bad," was the reply.

"How is it in asymmetric flight? One engine out?"

After thinking for a moment, the other pilot replied, "Ah, that's where it becomes tricky. If one engine quits, the other engine immediately takes you to the scene of the crash."

—JIM McCORKLE

Wheeling

Lost on back roads in Vermont, a tourist collided with a local man at an intersection. He and the local got out to examine their bent fenders.

"Well, don't look like much," observed the local. "Whyn't we just take a little pull to steady our nerves." He grabbed a jug from his battered pickup, removed the stopper and handed it to the tourist.

After taking a good slug, the tourist handed the jug back to the local, who banged in the stopper and set the jug back in his truck.

"Aren't you going to have some?" asked the tourist.

The local shook his head. "Not till after the trooper comes."

—JAMES SHANNON

Anytime you see a young man open a car door for his girlfriend, either the car is new or the girlfriend is.

—Robert E. Limbaugh II in *Boys' Life*

A juggler, driving to his next performance, is stopped by the police. "What are those machetes doing in your car?" asks the cop.

"I juggle them in my act."

"Oh, yeah?" says the doubtful cop. "Let's see you do it." The juggler gets out and starts tossing and catching the knives. Another man driving by slows down to watch.

"Wow," says the passer-by. "I'm glad I quit drinking. Look at the test they're giving now!"

—Natalie Kaplowitz

A young man was trying to park his car between two others. He put it in reverse, and bang—right into the car behind him. He then went forward and bang—right into the car in front.

A young woman watching the maneuver couldn't contain herself. "Do you always park by ear?" she asked.

—Venderci Martins Valente

A traffic cop pulled over a speeding motorist and asked, "Do you have any ID?"

The motorist replied, "About what?"

—Martha B. Roberts

After he finished his route, a bus driver had to explain to the supervisor why he was 10 minutes late: "I was stuck behind a big truck."

"But yesterday you were 10 minutes early," reminded the boss.

"Yeah," the bus driver replied. "But yesterday I was stuck behind a Porsche."

—Tim Harvey

Late for a return flight from Dublin, an American tourist in Ireland jumped into a cab. "Quick," he said, "get me to the airport as fast as you can!" The cabbie nodded and floored the gas pedal. Soon they were barreling along at more than 70 miles an hour.

Just ahead a stoplight was bright red. The cab shot through the intersection without slowing down in the slightest. "Are you blind?" shouted the tourist. "That was a red light!"

The cabbie was unfazed. "I don't believe in red lights, sir, nor do any of my five cab-driving brothers." After two more hair-raising hurtles through red lights, the tourist was relieved to see a green light. But right before the intersection, the cabbie slammed on the brakes. "Are you insane?" yelled the passenger. "That was a green light!"

"True, sir," replied the cabbie. "But you never know when one of my brothers may be coming through."

—E. H.

The truck driver stopped at a roadside diner. His waitress brought him a hamburger, a cup of coffee, and a piece of pie.

As the trucker was about to start eating, three men in leather jackets pulled up on motorcycles and came inside. One grabbed the man's hamburger, the second one drank his coffee and the other one took his pie. The truck driver didn't say a word. He got up, put on his jacket, paid the cashier and left.

One of the bikers said to the cashier, "Not much of a man, is he?"

"He's not much of a driver either," she replied. "He just ran his truck over three motorcycles."

—MICHAEL IAPOCE in *A Funny Thing Happened on the Way to the Boardroom*

Driving tip: If you rear-end a car on the freeway, your first move should be to hang up the phone.

—TOM ADAMS in *Comic Highlights*

"Fill'er up, sir?"

The driving instructor was giving lessons to an extremely nervous student who panicked whenever another car approached on a particular two-lane road. One day, however, they got to the same stretch of road, and she remained completely calm.

"This time you're doing fine!" exclaimed the instructor.

"Yes," the novice driver agreed. "Now when I see another car coming, I shut my eyes."

—M. HERBRINK

Driving back from car-repair class, John said to his buddy, Joe, "I'm going to turn now. Could you stick your head out the window to see if the blinker's working?"

"Sure," Joe replied as he peeked outside. "It is, no it isn't, yes it is, no it isn't, yes it is . . . ."

—PAULO CESAR MENEGUSSO

The young woman sat in her stalled car, waiting for help. Finally two men walked up to her.

"I'm out of gas," she purred. "Could you push me to a service station?"

They readily put their muscles to the car and rolled it several blocks. After a while, one looked up, exhausted, to see that they had just passed a filling station.

"How come you didn't turn in?" he yelled.

"I never go there," the woman shouted back. "They don't have full service."

—*Super Automotive Service*

What an automated society we live in. Have you ever noticed that when a traffic signal turns green, it automatically activates the horn of the car behind you?

—ROBERT ORBEN in *The American Legion Magazine*

Driving down a winding country road, a man came upon a youth running hard, three huge dogs snarling at his heels. The man screeched his car to a halt and threw open the door. "Get in, get in!" he shouted.

"Thanks," gasped the youth. "You're terrific. Most people won't offer a ride when they see I have three dogs!"

—P. A. ISAACSON

Wife: "There's trouble with the car. It has water in the carburetor."

Husband: "Water in the carburetor? That's ridiculous."

Wife: "I tell you the car has water in the carburetor."

Husband: "You don't even know what a carburetor is. Where's the car?"

Wife: "In the swimming pool."

—Executive Speechwriter Newsletter

The villager on his first trip to the city was waiting at a bus stop one morning. After some hesitation he asked a woman, "Which bus should I take for Mahim?"

"Bus Number 177," the woman replied, and caught the next bus.

The same evening, the woman got off a bus at the same stop and found the villager still waiting. "Didn't you get the bus to Mahim?" she exclaimed.

"Not yet," he said wearily. "So far 168 buses have come and gone—eight more before mine arrives."

—C. P. MURGUDKAR

Did you hear about the director of the Department of Motor Vehicles who resigned on Tuesday?

He tried to resign on Monday, but found he'd been standing in the wrong line.

—DAVE MARGOLIS in *The Los Angeles Times*

You know it's time to get a new car when—

The traffic reporter on the radio begins to refer to you by name.

You make a *left* turn and your date falls out.

You lose the "stoplight challenge" to a 16-year-old on a moped.

—JAY TRACHMAN IN ONE TO ONE

"North face of Everest: howling winds, sub-zero cold, insufficient oxygen, menswear."

Explorations

One stupid guy reads an ad about a vacation cruise that costs only $100. After he signs up and pays, the travel agent hits him with a bat, knocks him unconscious, and throws him out the back door into the river. Soon another guy comes in, pays his fee, and gets the same treatment.

Fifteen minutes later, as the two are floating down the river together, the first man says, "I wonder if they're serving any food on this cruise."

"I don't know," the second guy replies. "They didn't last year."

—MEL SMITH in *The Los Angeles Times*

An Irish lad named Sean was doing so well with his furniture business that he decided to take a trip to France. When he returned to Ireland, his friend Brendan asked him, "Why did you go to France and you not speaking a word of the language? How could you make yourself understood?"

"Let me tell you," said Sean. "I met this lass in the park. I drew a picture of plates and food, and so we went out to eat. After drawing a picture of people dancing, we went to a nightclub. At midnight, could you imagine, she took my pen and drew a picture of a bed."

"Faith 'n' begorra!" exclaimed Brendan. "How did she know you were in the furniture business?"

—Thomas R. McGuinness

Just before heading to Florida for spring break, a college student bought a skimpy bikini. She modeled it for her mother. "How do you like it?"

The parent stared in silence for a few moments, and then replied, "If I had worn a bathing suit like that when I was your age, you'd be four years older than you are right now."

—Quoted by James Dent in Charleston, W. Va., *Gazette*

Two explorers, camped in the heart of the African jungle, were discussing their expedition. "I came here," said one, "because the urge to travel was in my blood. City life bored me, and the smell of exhaust fumes on the highways made me sick. I wanted to see the sun rise over new horizons and hear the flutter of birds that never had been seen by man. I wanted to leave my footprints on sand unmarked before I came. In short, I wanted to see nature in the raw. What about you?"

"I came," the second man replied, "because my son was taking saxophone lessons."

—Al Batt in *Capper's*

Heading into the jungle on his first safari, the American visitor was confident he could handle any emergency. He sidled up to the experienced native guide and said smugly, "I know that carrying a torch will keep lions away."

"True," the guide replied. "But it depends on how fast you carry the torch."

—E. H.

From a passenger ship one can see a bearded man on a small island who is shouting and desperately waving his hands.

"Who is it?" a passenger asks the captain.

"I've no idea. Every year when we pass, he goes mad."

—*Chayan*

One day, an explorer was captured by native warriors and taken to their chieftain, a gigantic man with teeth filed to dagger-like points. Desperately, the explorer tried to think of a way to save himself. He pulled out his cigarette lighter, held it in front of the chief's face and lit it, exclaiming, "Look! *Magic!*"

The chief's eyes were huge in astonishment. "It certainly must be magic," he said. "I have never seen a lighter light on the first try!"

—*Nuggets*

One hot, dry day in the West, a traveler arrived at a small highway café. Wiping the sweat from his brow, he turned to a deeply tanned old-timer sitting at the counter and asked, "When was the last time it rained here?"

The old man looked at him. "Son, you remember in the Bible when it says it rained for 40 days and 40 nights?"

"Well, yes, I sure do."

The old man continued, "We got an inch."

—DOUGLAS IRVING in *Arizona Highways*

On our railway, children age 10 and under travel at half-price. As the conductor began checking tickets, a woman sitting next to me told her daughter, "Now remember, you are only 10." The girl nodded her head.

The conductor approached and asked the girl, "How old are you?"

"Ten, sir."

"And when will you be 11?"

"When I get off this train!"

—THEODORUS HARI WAHUANTO

Two passengers on a ship are talking. "Can you swim?" asks one. "No," says the other, "but I can shout for help in nine languages."

—MRS. ATTILANE NAGY

The sociologist on an African jungle expedition held up her camera to take pictures of the native children at play. Suddenly the youngsters began to yell in protest.

Turning red, the sociologist apologized to the chief for her insensitivity and told him she had forgotten that certain tribes believed a person lost his soul if his picture was taken. She explained to him, in long-winded detail, the operation of a camera. Several times the chief tried to get a word in, but to no avail.

Certain she had put all the chief's fears to rest, the sociologist then allowed him to speak. Smiling, he said, "The children were trying to tell you that you forgot to take off the lens cap!"

—SHARON SPENCE

"It's faster if you use the stairs inside."

"No, no, not a pride. It's a bunch of tourists."

Tourism Department

What's this daily charge for 'fruit'?" the hotel patron asked the manager. "We didn't eat any."

"But the fruit was placed in your room every day. It isn't our fault you didn't take advantage of it."

"I see," said the man as he subtracted $150 from the bill.

"What are you doing?" sputtered the manager.

"I'm subtracting 50 dollars a day for your kissing my wife."

"*What*? I didn't kiss your wife."

"Ah," replied the man, "but she was there."

—JAMES DENT in the Charleston, W. Va., *Gazette*

Travel agent: "I can get you three days and two nights in Rome for a hundred bucks."

Customer: "How come so cheap?"

Travel agent: "The days are July 11, 12 and 13. The nights are July 21 and 22."

—BRANT PARKER & JOHNNY HART, North America Syndicate

Asia was by far my favorite destination," the woman bragged at the party, though she had never been out of the United States. "Enigmatic and magical, beautiful beyond belief. And China, of course, is the pearl of the Asian oyster."

"What about the pagodas?" a man beside her asked. "Did you see them?"

"Did I *see* them? My dear, I had *dinner* with them."

—LORD-NELSON QUIST in *Playboy*

In a panic, a traveler called down to the hotel's front desk soon after checking in. "Help!" he yelled. "I'm trapped inside my room!"

"What do you mean, trapped?"

"Well, I see three doors," the man explained. "The first opens to a closet, and the second to a bathroom. And the third door has a 'Do Not Disturb' sign hanging on it."

—PETER S. GREENBERG, Los Angeles Times Syndicate

When the fellow called a motel and asked how much they charged for a room, the clerk told him that the rates depended on room size and number of people. "Do you take children?" the man asked.

"No, sir," replied the clerk. "Only cash and credit cards."

—*Successful Meetings Magazine*

"What do you say, honey? This looks like our kind of place."

An English traveler, asked by Australian immigration if he had a criminal record, expressed some surprise that such a qualification was still required.

—New Zealand *Herald*

A vacationer telephoned a seaside hotel to ask where it was. "It's only a stone's throw from the beach," he was told. "How will I recognize it?" asked the man. Back came the reply, "It's the one with all the broken windows."

—BOB STERLING

A pair of honeymooners checked into the Watergate Hotel in Washington, D.C. That night, as the husband was about to turn off the light, his bride asked, "Do you think this room is bugged?"

"That was a long time ago, sweetheart," he reassured her.

"But what if there's a microphone somewhere? I'd be so embarrassed."

So the groom searched under tables and behind pictures. Then he turned back the rug. Sure enough, there was a funny-looking gizmo in the floor. He took out the screws, got rid of the hardware, and climbed into bed.

The next morning the newlyweds were awakened by a hotel clerk who wanted to know if they had slept well.

"We did," replied the groom. "Why do you ask?"

"It's rather unusual," the clerk answered. "Last night the couple in the room below yours had a chandelier fall on them."

—HENNY YOUNGMAN, quoted by ALEX THIEN in the Milwaukee *Sentinel*

A New York retail clerk was suffering from aching feet. "It's all those years of standing," his doctor declared. "You need a vacation. Go to Miami, soak your feet in the ocean and you'll feel better."

When the man got to Florida, he went into a hardware store, bought two large buckets and headed for the beach. "How much for two buckets of that sea water?" he asked the lifeguard.

"A dollar a bucket," the fellow replied with a straight face.

The clerk paid him, filled his buckets, went to his hotel room and soaked his feet. They felt so much better he decided to repeat the treatment that afternoon. Again he handed the lifeguard two dollars. The young man took the money and said, "Help yourself."

The clerk started for the water, then stopped in amazement. The tide was out. "Wow," he said, turning to the lifeguard. "Some business you got here!"

—CARL D. KIRBY

A tourist was visiting New Mexico and was amazed at the dinosaur bones lying about.

"How old are these bones?" the tourist asked an elderly Native American, who served as a guide.

"Exactly one hundred million and three years old."

"How can you be so sure?" inquired the tourist.

"Well," replied the guide, "a geologist came by here and told me these bones were one hundred million years old, and that was exactly three years ago."

—ALLAN E. OSTAR

To celebrate their silver anniversary, a couple went to Niagara Falls and asked a motel clerk for a room. "We only have the honeymoon suite available," she told them.

"My wife and I've been married 25 years," the man said. "We don't need the honeymoon suite."

"Look, buddy," replied the clerk. "I might rent you Yankee Stadium, but you don't have to play baseball in it!"

—*Parts Pups*

An American couple visiting in a German village stepped into a small shop to look for souvenirs. The woman sneezed.

"*Gesundheit!*" said the clerk.

"Charles," said the American woman to her husband, "we're in luck. There's somebody here who speaks English."

—*Ohio Motorist*

At a swanky hotel, a guy walks up to the front desk and asks the clerk, "Do I register with you?"

"Not by any stretch of the imagination," snaps the woman.

—ASHLEY COOPER in the Charleston, S.C., *Post and Courier*

"His majesty the Kingpin!"

Public Domain

International Boundaries

Two highway workers are at a construction site when a car with diplomatic plates pulls up. *"Parlez-vous français?"* the driver asks. The two just stare.

"Hablan ustedes español?" the driver tries. They stare some more.

"Sprechen Sie Deutsch?" They continue to stare.

"Parlate italiano?" Nothing. Finally the man drives off in disgust.

One worker turns to the other and says, "Maybe we should learn a foreign language."

"What for?" the other replies. "That guy knew four of them, and a fat lot of good it did him."

—MAXIME COSMA, *The Best Jokes of Romania*

A minister was urged by his congregation to explain the difference between heaven and hell. "They're not as different as you might think," he said. "In heaven, the British are the policemen, the Germans are the mechanics, the Swiss run the trains, the French do the cooking, and the Italians are the lovers. In hell, only minor changes take place. The Germans are the policemen, the French are the mechanics, the Italians run the trains, the British do the cooking, and the Swiss are making love."

—JOHN MOLYNEUX in *The Bulletin*

Was Grandpa mad when they went through his luggage at the border?"

"Not in the least. They found his glasses that he'd lost two weeks earlier."

—MIKLOS MADARASZ

*"In the interests of restoring calm to world trouble spots,
UN peacekeepers invade Buckingham Palace."*

A near-sighted diplomat attended a ball at a South American embassy. When the orchestra struck up a tune, he felt he should start the dancing. Accordingly he walked over to a figure clad in red and said, "Beautiful lady in scarlet, would you do me the honor of waltzing with me?"

"Certainly not!" came the reply. "In the first place, this is not a waltz, but a tango. And in the second place, I am not a beautiful lady in scarlet. I'm the papal nuncio."

—ROBERT L. CLARKE, quoted by WILLIAM SAFIRE and
LEONARD SAFIR in *Leadership*

Overheard: "The tragedy of Canada is that they had the opportunity to have French cuisine, British culture, and American technology, and instead they ended up with British cuisine, American culture, and French technology."

—Will Shetterly

An Englishman awaiting the train to Paris at the station restaurant in Calais beckoned to the waiter and asked him in French laden with a heavy British accent, "Do you know the man smoking a pipe and reading a newspaper over by the heater?"

"No, sir. So many of our patrons are just passing through."

"Well, please call the manager for me then."

When the manager arrived, the Englishman repeated his question. The manager scrutinized the man by the heater.

"I'm sorry, sir, but I've never seen him before."

With that, the Englishman rose and walked over to the man. "Please accept my apologies, sir, for speaking to you without having been properly introduced," he said, "but your coat is on fire!"

—François Chauvière

There is a story that Soviet General Secretary Mikhail Gorbachev was late for a meeting and told his chauffeur to step on it. The chauffeur refused on the ground that it would be breaking the speeding laws. So Gorbachev ordered him into the back seat and got behind the wheel.

After a few miles, the car was stopped by a police patrol. The senior officer sent his subordinate to arrest the offender.

A moment later, the officer returned saying that the person was much too important to prosecute.

"Who is it?" demanded the police chief.

"I'm not sure, sir," replied the officer, "but Comrade Gorbachev is his chauffeur."

—"Observer" in *Financial Times*

A secret agent was sent to Ireland to pick up some sensitive information from an agent named Murphy. His instructions were to walk around town using a code phrase until he met his fellow agent.

He found himself on a desolate country road and finally ran into a farmer. "Hello," the agent said, "I'm looking for a man named Murphy."

"Well, you're in luck," said the farmer. "As it happens, there's a village right over the hill where the butcher is named Murphy, the baker is named Murphy, and three widows are named Murphy. Matter of fact, my name is Murphy."

Aha, the agent thought, here's my man. So he whispered the secret code: "The sun is shining…the grass is growing…the cows are ready for milking."

"Oh," said the farmer, "you're looking for Murphy the spy—he's in the village over in the other direction."

—RAYMOND W. SMITH in
Vital Speeches of the Day

On a visit to the United States, Gorbachev met a Russian who had immigrated to this country. "What do you do for a living here?" the Soviet leader asked him.

"My brother, my sister, and I work in a big factory."

"How do these capitalist bosses treat you?"

"Just fine," answered the man. "In fact, if you are walking home from work, the boss picks you up in his big car and drives you to your door. Another time, he treats you to a dinner in an expensive restaurant. Sometimes he takes you home for the weekend and buys you presents."

Gorbachev was stunned. "How often does this happen?"

"Well, to me, actually never. But to my sister, several times."

—Quoted by JAMES DENT in the
Charleston, W.Va., *Gazette*

Government at Its Biggest

A young man visited his local welfare office and was asked to give his surname—all other details would be on computer. The assistant typed in his name, then read from the screen: "You are James Herbert Roberts of Oldfield Lane, London, age 22; single; unemployed for one year; now working as a plumber for Jones & Co. It's all here, every last detail. Now, what is your query?"

"Well," said the man, "it's about the widow's pension you keep sending me."

—BILL NAYLOR

The president receives the news that his government is divided between optimists and pessimists. "Who are the optimists?" the president asks.

"They are those who believe that we will be eating grass by the end of the year," says the adviser.

"And the pessimists?"

"They are those who think that there won't be enough grass for everybody."

—*Veja*

Question: Why wasn't Rome built in a day?
Answer: Because it was a government job.

—GLENN E. SPRADLIN in the Louisville *Courier-Journal*

Why does the capital have so many one-way streets? So that all the civil servants coming in late won't collide with those going home early.

—ARNIE BENJAMIN, *The Daily News*

Man to friend: "I figured out why the Postal Service raised the postage rates. The extra four cents is for storage."

—ANGIE PAPADAKIS

You don't see me at Vegas or the track throwing my money around anymore," says Bob Hope. "I've got a government to support."

A veteran congressman was asked what he had learned in the rough-and-tumble of the political arena. "Well," he said, "I found it wasn't so much whether you won or lost, but how you placed the blame."

—*American Agriculturalist Magazine*

At a Washington cocktail party, two strangers struck up a conversation. After a few minutes of small talk, one said, "Have you heard the latest White House joke?"

The second fellow held up his hand. "Wait, before you begin, I should tell you that I work in the White House."

"Oh, don't worry," the first man replied. "I'll tell it very slowly."

—T. J. MCINERNEY in *Globe*

Overheard at the Food and Drug Administration: "If laughter is the best medicine, shouldn't we be *regulating* it?"

—BALOO in *The Wall Street Journal*

Highway sign: "SPEED LIMIT 65 for most cars and some trucks under 8,000 pounds—only if they're empty, unless you weigh over 300 pounds—then divide by six. For additional information call the IRS, which helped write this."

—MIKE PETERS, Tribune Media Services

"Ladies and gentlemen, I believe I can announce that at long last we've isolated the gene that determines political affiliation."

Four friends met at a restaurant for lunch. For quite a while, no one said a word. Finally the first man mumbled, "Oh, boy!" To which the next one said, "It's awful." The third then muttered, "What are ya gonna do?"

"Listen," exclaimed the last friend, "if you guys don't stop talking politics, I'm leaving!"

—*The Big Book of Jewish Humor,* edited by
WILLIAM NOVAK and MOSHE WALDOKS

It's a Crime

Did you hear about the desperado who tried to hijack a bus full of Japanese tourists? Fortunately, police had 5,000 photographs of the suspect.

—BARRY CRYER on *American Radio Theater*

Can you describe your assailant?" asked the officer as he helped the bruised and battered man get up.

"Sure," the man replied. "That's what I was doing when he hit me."

—ALAN THOMAS in *Quote*

A man was applying for a job as a prison guard. The warden said, "Now these are real tough guys in here. Do you think you can handle it?"

"No problem," the applicant replied. "If they don't behave, out they go!"

—JOEY ADAMS

When a Colorado mine operator found that his office safe had jammed, he called the nearby state prison and asked whether any of the inmates might know how to open it. Soon, a convict and a prison guard showed up at the office. The inmate spun the dials, listened intently and calmly opened the safe door.

"I'm much obliged," said the mine operator. "How much do you figure I owe you?"

"Well," said the prisoner, "the last time I opened a safe I got $25,000."

—W. T. LITTLE

Two prisoners were making their escape over the jailhouse roof when one of them dislodged a tile. "Who's there?" shouted a guard.

The first prisoner replied with a convincing imitation of a cat's meow. Reassured, the guard went back to his rounds.

But then the second prisoner dislodged another tile. The guard repeated, "Who's there?"

"The other cat," answered the prisoner.

—LAURENT GREBERT

Sent to prison as a first offender, a student of English was told by a longtime inmate that if he made amorous advances to the warden's wife, she'd get him released quickly.

"But I can't do that," he protested. "It's wrong to end a sentence with a proposition."

—*Financial Times*

Comedy writer Paul Ryan tells of the cable TV repairman who was charged with faking his own kidnapping. Police became suspicious when they had to wait at home with the ransom from 9 am to 5 pm.

—*The Los Angeles Times*

Outside city hall, a boy selling newspapers bellowed, "Extra! Extra! Read all about it! Two men swindled!" A man walked up to the boy, bought a paper, and sat down to read it. "Hey, kid," he protested a few moments later, "there's nothing in here about two men being cheated."

"Extra! Extra!" shouted the boy. "Three men swindled!"

—MIKE LESSITER in *Country Chuckles,*
Cracks & Knee-Slappers

"Mr. Cosgrove has stepped away from his desk.
May I take a message?"

Three friends who always argued about who was the smartest are sitting on death row. The first one's number comes up, but when he sits down in the electric chair, nothing happens. The warden commutes his sentence on the spot and releases him.

Same thing happens with the second friend and he's let go. Then the third guy steps up to the platform and sits down.

The switch is pulled and again there's no charge. But before the warden can say anything, the prisoner starts pointing excitedly. "You know," he says, "if you'd just cross that black wire with the yellow one. . . ."

—Quoted on *The Gary McKee Hometown Radio Show*,
WSB-AM, Atlanta

People say New Yorkers can't get along. Not true. I saw two New Yorkers, complete strangers, sharing a cab. One guy took the tires and the radio; the other guy took the engine.

—*Late Show with David Letterman*

The inmate was aware that all prison mail passes through censors. When he got a letter from his wife asking about the family garden— "Honey, when do I plant potatoes?"—he wrote back, "Do not, under any circumstances, dig up our old garden spot. That's where I buried all my guns."

Within days his wife wrote back, "Six investigators came to the house. They dug up every square inch of the back yard."

By return mail she got his answer: "Now is the time to plant potatoes."

—REV. ROBERT MOORE Jr., quoted by CHARLES ALLBRIGHT
in the *Arkansas Democrat Gazette*

Higher Education

During a college examination, the professor found a student peeking at a classmate's answers.

"How can you cheat so blatantly?" the professor shouted. "You have already stolen more than one look at your classmate's paper!"

"Don't blame me, sir," replied the student. "If his handwriting weren't so bad, I could have got it all at one glance."

—SHIH YU HSIEH

Q: What's the difference between ignorance and apathy?
A: I don't know and I don't care.

—*Daily Telegraph*

A young man hired by a supermarket reported for his first day of work. The manager greeted him with a warm handshake and a smile, gave him a broom and said, "Your first job will be to sweep out the store."

"But I'm a college graduate," the young man replied indignantly.

"Oh, I'm sorry. I didn't know that," said the manager. "Here, give me the broom—I'll show you how."

—Richard L. Weaver II in *Vital Speeches of the Day*

During a lecture for medical students, the professor listed as the two best qualities of a doctor the ability to conquer revulsion and the need for keen powers of observation. He illustrated this by stirring a messy substance with his finger and then licking his finger clean. Then he called a student to the front and made him do the same.

Afterward the professor remarked, "You conquered your revulsion, but your powers of observation are not very good. I stirred with my forefinger, but I licked my middle finger."

—S.K.D.

Our son came home from college for the weekend and I asked him, "How are things going?"

He said, "Good."

I said, "And the dormitory?"

He said, "Good."

I said, "They've always had a strong football team. How do you think they'll do this year?"

He said, "Good."

I said, "Have you decided on your major yet?"

He said, "Yes."

I said, "What is it?"

He said, "Communications."

—*Orben's Current Comedy*

"Is this any way to treat a dissident?"

"Our economics professor talks to himself. Does yours?"
"Yes, but he doesn't realize it. He thinks we're listening!"

—CHARISMA B. RAMOS

During class, the chemistry professor was demonstrating the properties of various acids. "Now I'm dropping this silver coin into this glass of acid. Will it dissolve?"

"No, sir," a student called out.

"No?" queried the professor. "Perhaps you can explain why the silver coin won't dissolve."

"Because if it would, you wouldn't have dropped it in."

—HERBERT V. PROCHNOW, *Speaker's and Toastmaster's Handbook*

I'd like to donate a million dollars, tax-free, to this institution," a Texan announced to the president of a small college. "But there's a condition. I would like an honorary degree for my horse."

"Horse?" stammered the president.

"Yes, for my mare, Betsy. She's carried me faithfully for many years, and I think she deserves a doctorate in transportation."

"But we can't give a degree to a horse!"

"Sorry, then you don't get the million dollars."

The board of trustees was hastily convened and each member in turn condemned the idea as a disgrace. Finally the oldest trustee spoke. "Let's take the money," he said. "It's about time we gave a degree to a *whole* horse!"

—Isaac Asimov, *Asimov Laughs Again*

An engineer, a mathematician, and a physicist were standing around the university flagpole when an English professor wandered by. "What are you doing?" he asked.

"We need to know the height of the flagpole," answered one, "and we're discussing the formulas we might use to calculate it."

"Watch!" said the English professor. He pulled the pole from its fitting, laid it on the grass, borrowed a tape measure and said, "Exactly 24 feet." Then he replaced the pole and walked away.

"English professor!" sneered the mathematician. "We ask him for the height, and he gives us the length."

—*The Jokesmith*

"We super-rich are few in number. People should value us instead of always picking on us!"

Money Matters

The Rich and the Foolish

A tightwad was convinced by a friend to buy a couple of tickets in the state lottery. But after he won the big prize, he didn't seem happy. "What's wrong?" the friend asked. "You just became a millionaire!"

"I know," he groaned. "But I can't imagine why I bought that second ticket!"

—OHIO MOTORIST

A stockbroker had made millions of dollars for an Arabian oil sheik. The sheik was so pleased he offered her rubies, gold, and a silver-plated Rolls-Royce. She declined the gifts, telling him she had merely done her job. But the sheik insisted.

"Well," the woman said, "I've recently taken up golf. A set of golf clubs would be a fine gift."

Weeks went by. One morning the stockbroker received a letter from him.

"So far I have bought you three golf clubs," it said, "but I hope you will not be disappointed because only two of them have swimming pools."

—ALEX THIEN IN THE MILWAUKEE SENTINEL

Selling at an auction was halted when the auctioneer announced, "Someone in the room has just lost his wallet containing $1,000. He is offering a reward of $250 for its immediate return." After a moment of silence, there was a call from the back of the room, "$255."

—ROTARY DOWN UNDER

An MG Midget pulled alongside a Rolls-Royce at a traffic light. "Do you have a car phone?" its driver asked the guy in the Rolls. "Of course I do," replied the haughty deluxe-car driver.

"Well, do you have a fax machine?"

The driver in the Rolls sighed. "I have that too."

"Then do you have a double bed in the back?" the Midget driver wanted to know.

Ashen-faced, the Rolls driver sped off. That afternoon, he had a mechanic install a double bed in his auto.

A week later, the Rolls driver passes the same MG Midget, which is parked on the side of the road—back windows fogged up and steam pouring out. The arrogant driver pulls over, gets out of the Rolls and bangs on the Midget's back window until the driver sticks his head out. "I want you to know that I had a double bed installed," brags the Rolls driver.

The Midget driver is unimpressed. "You got me out of the shower to tell me that?"

—Quoted by DAVID GREASON, New York Times News Service

A 70-year-old millionaire had just married a beautiful 20-yearold.

"You crafty old codger," said his friend. "How did you get such a lovely young wife?"

"Easy," the millionaire replied. "I told her I was 95."

—FIONA GOLDING

The miserly millionaire called a family conference. "I'm placing a box of money in the attic," he said. "When I die, I intend to grab it on my way up to heaven. See to it that no one touches it until it's my time to go."

The family respected his wishes. After his death the millionaire's wife looked in the attic. The box was still there. "The fool!" she said. "I told him he should have put it in the basement."

—GENE JENNINGS

A yuppie was driving his new BMW convertible. He had the top-down, his right hand on the wheel, and his left arm hanging over the door. With the tape deck going full blast, he didn't notice the rust bucket that pulled around to pass until it sideswiped him. The yuppie pulled to a stop.

"My car!" he cried. "My beautiful car!"

When a policeman came by, the yuppie told him about the accident. His car was a wreck, and it didn't even have 50 miles on it.

"You've got more to worry about than your car," the officer replied. "You need an ambulance. Your arm is badly injured."

The yuppie looked at his arm and cried, "My Rolex watch—my beautiful Rolex!"

—ALEX THIEN IN THE MILWAUKEE SENTINEL

When the preacher's car broke down on a country road, he walked to a nearby roadhouse to use the phone. After calling for a tow truck, he spotted his old friend, Frank, drunk and shabbily dressed at the bar. "What happened to you, Frank?" asked the good reverend. "You used to be rich."

Frank told a sad tale of bad investments that had led to his downfall. "Go home," the preacher said. "Open your Bible at random, stick your finger on the page and there will be God's answer."

Some time later, the preacher bumped into Frank, who was wearing Gucci shoes, sporting a Rolex watch, and had just stepped out of a Mercedes. "Frank," said the preacher, "I am glad to see things really turned around for you."

"Yes, preacher, and I owe it all to you," said Frank. "I opened my Bible, put my finger down on the page and there was the answer—Chapter 11."

—PATRICK DIXON

*"I don't think you're trying very hard to look at things
from a royal perspective."*

And then there's the shop-a-holic whose friend complimented her
on her new car. "Oh, thanks," the woman replied. "I'm getting about
20 malls per gallon!"

—NUGGETS

Only the billionaire and his friend remained after all the guests at his weekend ranch party scurried off for the afternoon's entertainment. The host answered the phone and slammed down the receiver in disgust. "I have to go to Dallas, and I've no way to get there!"

"Sure you do," his friend reassured him. "Isn't that a Cadillac convertible with the keys in it?"

"Yes, but that's my wife's car."

"So why can't you use it?"

"Are you kidding? The windshield's ground to her prescription."

—DAVID COX

Having purchased a new car, my friend was chary of hiring a new chauffeur because he had been warned that most chauffeurs exchanged new car parts for old and made some money on the sly. However, since my friend did not know how to drive, he had to engage a chauffeur, but he questioned every movement of the driver.

Once when we were riding together, the car slowed, then picked up speed.

"What happened?" my friend asked the driver.

"I just changed the gear, sir," the driver replied.

Turning to me, my friend whispered, "I have to fire this fellow. He not only changed the gear but has the audacity to admit it!"

—M. L. BHAGAT

A guy walks up to the owner of a store and says, "You probably don't remember me, but about five years ago I was broke. I came in here and asked you for $10, and you gave it to me."

The store owner smiles and replies, "Yes, I remember."

The guy says, "Are you still game?"

—RON DENTINGER IN THE DODGEVILLE, WIS., CHRONICLE

A farmer who was notoriously miserly called a doctor to attend his sick wife.

"They say you're a skinflint," said the doctor. "Can I be sure of my fee?"

"Whether you kill my wife or cure her, you'll get your money without having to sue," said the farmer.

But the woman died, despite all the doctor's efforts to save her. He duly asked for his payment.

"Did you cure my wife?" asked the man.

"No," admitted the doctor.

"Did you kill her?"

"Certainly not!" the doctor said indignantly.

"Well, then, I owe you nothing."

—MICHELE VACQUIER

Mrs. Flinders decided to have her portrait painted. She told the artist, "Paint me with diamond earrings, a diamond necklace, emerald bracelets, and a ruby pendant."

"But you're not wearing any of those things."

"I know," said Mrs. Flinders. "It's in case I should die before my husband. I'm sure he'd remarry right away, and I want her to go nuts looking for the jewelry."

—MAE MORRISON

Take a pencil and paper," the teacher said, "and write an essay with the title 'If I Were a Millionaire.' "

Everyone but Philip, who leaned back with arms folded, began to write furiously.

"What's the matter," the teacher asked. "Why don't you begin?"

"I'm waiting for my secretary," he replied.

—BERNADETTE NAGY

"I like to think of myself as an artist, and money is the medium in which I work best."

High Finance

Houston stockbroker to client: "If you put one hundred thousand dollars in a certificate of deposit at the bank, you get either a toaster or an offshore drilling rig. But hurry. The toasters are going fast."

—BILL SHEPHERD, QUOTED BY PAUL HARASIM
IN THE HOUSTON POST

Chicken Little on Wall Street: "The sky is making a technical correction!"

—CURRENT COMEDY

A pair of economists went to a restaurant for lunch. "Never mind the food," one said to the waitress. "Just bring us the bill so we can argue about it."

—CAROL SIMPSON IN FUNNY TIMES

I'm thinking of leaving my husband," complained the economist's wife. "All he ever does is stand at the end of the bed and tell me how good things are going to be."

—JAY TRACHMAN IN ONE TO ONE

The sales manager was complaining to a colleague about one of his salesmen. "George is so forgetful that it's a wonder he can sell anything. I asked him to pick up some sandwiches on his way back from lunch, but I'm not sure he'll even remember to come back."

Just then, the door flew open and in came George. "You'll never guess what happened!" he shouted. "At lunch, I met Fred Brown, the president of a Fortune 500 company. He hadn't bought anything from us in 10 years. Well, we got to talking, and he gave me an order worth 15 million dollars!"

"See?" said the sales manager. "I told you he'd forget the sandwiches."

—EXECUTIVE SPEECHWRITER NEWSLETTER

The economy is weird," remarked one worker to another. "My bank failed before the toaster did."

—COFFEE BREAK

"A monster called the commodities market tried to eat me today."

A bank in New York City is now making it possible to buy and sell stock using their ATM machines. This is great—it gives muggers a chance to diversify their portfolios.

—Late Show with David Letterman

A man was forever writing to his bank asking for his overdraft limit to be increased. The bank had always obliged, but when things eventually started to get critical, he received a letter from the manager that began: "Dear Sir. We are concerned about three overdrawn accounts at this bank, your own, Mexico's and Brazil's—in that order."

—VINCENT MURPHY

Question: What do you need to make a small fortune on Wall Street?

Answer: A large fortune.

—Country

Overheard: "Things are still bad in the banking industry. The other day, a friend of mine went to the bank and asked the teller to check her balance. The guy leaned over and pushed her!"

—TOM BLAIR in the San Diego Union-Tribune

A woman visited the bank to close her account because she was convinced the institution was going under.

Asked by a startled manager why she thought so, she produced one of her checks, endorsed by the bank, "Insufficient funds."

—Financial Mail

Loan Officer: "Based on your credit history, it seems the only kind of loan you qualify for is an auto loan."

Customer: "You mean money to buy a car?"

Loan Officer: "I mean money you lend yourself."

—J. C. DUFFY, Universal Press Syndicate

At a testimonial dinner in his honor, a wealthy businessman gave an emotional speech. "When I came to this city 50 years ago," he said, "I had no car, my only suit was on my back, the soles of my shoes were thin, and I carried all my possessions in a paper bag."

After dinner, a young man nervously approached. "Sir, I really admire your accomplishments. Tell me, after all these years, do you still remember what you carried in that brown paper bag?"

"Sure, son," he said. "I had $300,000 in cash and $500,000 in negotiable securities."

—The Lion

T. Boone Pickens told this joke to a group of bankers:

A banker calls in an oilman to review his loans. "We loaned you a million to revive your old wells, and they went dry," says the banker.

"Coulda been worse," the oilman replies.

"Then we loaned you a million to drill new wells, and they were dry."

"Coulda been worse."

"Then we loaned you another million for new drilling equipment, and it broke down."

"Coulda been worse."

"I'm getting tired of hearing that!" snaps the banker. "How could it have been worse?"

"Coulda been my money," says the oilman.

An accountant answered an advertisement for a top job with a large firm. At the end of the interview, the chairman said, "One last question—what is three times seven?"

The accountant thought for a moment and replied, "Twenty-two."

Outside he checked himself on his calculator and concluded he had lost the job. But two weeks later he was offered the post. He asked the chairman why he had been appointed when he had given the wrong answer.

"You were the closest," the chairman replied.

—S. NETTLE

I think my wages are frozen," one worker said to another. "When I opened my pay envelope, a little light went on."

—ROGER DEVLIN IN THE TULSA TRIBUNE

Answer: Rugs, fish batter, and savings and loan executives.
Question: List three things that should be beaten every Friday.

—JOHNNY CARSON ON THE TONIGHT SHOW

Edith and Norbert had a knock-down, drag-out battle over his inability to earn a better living. She told him he wasn't forceful enough in asking the boss for a raise.

"Tell him," she yelled, "that you have seven children. You also have a sick mother, you have to sit up many nights, and you have to clean the house because you can't afford a maid."

Several days later, Norbert came home from work, stood before his wife and calmly announced that the boss had fired him. "Why?" asked Edith.

"He says I have too many outside activities."

—THE LARRY WILDE TREASURY OF LAUGHTER

Dialogue between a sharp-tongued boss and a dissatisfied employee seeking a raise: "I know perfectly well you aren't beingpaid what you're worth!"

"So . . ." asked the employee, his hope returning.

"But I can't allow you to starve to death, can I?"

—MADAME B. LEGÉ

Buyers Beware

Said a skeptical customer to a used-car dealer: "And how is your customer service?"

"Oh, that's first class. Anybody who buys a car from us gets a free copy of the latest railroad train schedules!"

—DER STERN

Sign in store window: "Any faulty merchandise will be cheerfully replaced with merchandise of equal quality."

—MARTHA JANE B. CATLETT

In Jaipur, India, a man broke his own world record for tiny writing. He squeezed 1,314 characters onto a single grain of rice. When he finished, he went back to his old job of printing rental-car contracts.

—JOHNNY CARSON ON THE TONIGHT SHOW

Husband, holding mail-order catalog, to wife: "It says on the cover that if we don't buy $10 worth of merchandise, they'll send our name to every catalog in the country!"

—SCHOCHET IN THE WALL STREET JOURNAL

When he found a six-year-old shoe-repair ticket in the pocket of an old suit, Brown called the shop to see if the shoes were still around.
"Were they black wingtips needing half soles?" asked a clerk.
"Yes," said Brown.
"We'll have them ready in a week."

—QUOTED IN LUTHERAN DIGEST

An optometrist was instructing a new employee on how to charge a customer. "As you are fitting his glasses, if he asks how much they cost, say '$75.' If his eyes don't flutter, say 'For the frames. The lenses will be $50.' If his eyes still don't flutter, you add 'Each.'"

—MAMIE BROWN

A gentleman entered a busy florist shop that displayed a large sign that read "Say It with Flowers."
"Wrap up one rose," he told the florist.
"Only one?" the florist asked.
"Just one," the customer replied. "I'm a man of few words."

—DOMENICA DEL CORRIERE

"You call that the trappings of wealth?"

Overheard: "I think our bank is in trouble. I was about to complete a withdrawal at the ATM and the machine asked me if I wanted to go double or nothing."

—THE ROTARIAN

These yuppies are really getting to me," a man complained to his friend. "Have you seen the new funeral home in New York? It's called 'Death 'n' Things.' "

—JIM KERR, WWPR, NEW YORK

I think it's wrong," says comedian Steven Wright, "that only one company makes the game Monopoly."

I went to a bookstore today," says comic Brian Kiley, "and I asked the manager where the self-help section was. She said, 'If I told you, that would defeat the whole purpose.'"

I can't believe what's happened to gas prices! The other day I handed the kid at the pump a $20 bill, and he used it to wipe the dipstick!

—QUOTED BY PETE SUMMERS, WLAD, DANBURY, CONN.

As the cashier totaled the man's purchases, she asked, "Do you wish to charge?"

Looking at the amount, he answered, "No. I think I'll surrender."

—GEORGE E. BERGMAN

If It Isn't Death, It's Taxes

Once, a man with an alligator walked into a pub and asked the bartender, "Do you serve IRS agents here?"

"Sure do," the barkeep replied.

"Good, give me a beer," said the man. "And my gator'll have an IRS agent."

—FARMER'S DIGEST

Discussing the environment with his friend, one man asked,

"Which of our natural resources do you think will become exhausted first?"

"The taxpayer," answered the other.

—WINSTON K. PENDLETON, COMPLETE SPEAKER'S GALAXY OF
FUNNY STORIES, JOKES AND ANECDOTES

Two IRS agents were traveling through a rural area when their car broke down. They walked to a nearby mansion and knocked on the door. A beautiful widow answered and said they were welcome to spend the night while her hired hands worked on the car.

Months later one of the agents received a package of legal documents.

After surveying the contents, he quickly called the other agent.

"When we were up in the country," the first agent asked, "did you slip away in the night and go to that widow's bedroom?"

"Yes," the second agent admitted.

"Did you use my name?"

"Why, yes, but how'd you find out?"

"She died and left me her estate."

—GAYLEN K. BUNKER

A grieving widow was discussing her late husband with a friend. "My Albert was such a good man, and I miss him so. He provided well for me with that fifty-thousand-dollar insurance policy—but I would give a thousand of it just to have him back."

—FARMER'S DIGEST

Mrs. Willencot was very frugal. When her husband died, she asked the newspaper how much it would cost for a death notice.

"Two dollars for five words."

"Can I pay for just two words?" she asked. "Willencot dead."

"No, two dollars is the minimum. You still have three words."

Mrs. Willencot thought a moment. "Cadillac for sale."

—PATRICIA SCHULTZ

My tax man is so considerate and compassionate," says Joey Adams. "He's the only accountant I know with a recovery room."

"Look, I know it's not fair, but taking everyone at the flat age of 37 greatly simplifies the system."

On her eightieth birthday, a woman from Brooklyn decides to prepare her last will and testament. She goes to her rabbi to make two final requests. First, she insists on cremation.

"What is your second request?" the rabbi asks.

"I want my ashes scattered over Bloomingdale's."

"Why Bloomingdale's?"

"Then I'll be sure that my daughters visit me twice a week."

—THE BIG BOOK OF JEWISH HUMOR, EDITED BY
WILLIAM NOVAK AND MOSHE WALDOKS

The couple had reached an age where the wife thought it was time to start considering wills and funeral arrangements rather than be caught unprepared. Her husband, however, wasn't too interested in the topic. "Would you rather be buried or cremated?" she asked him.

There was a pause, then he replied from behind his paper, "Surprise me."

—JIM GIBSON IN THE VICTORIA, B.C., TIMES-COLONIST

A guy walked into the tax collector's office with a huge bandage on his nose. "Had an accident?" asked the tax agent.

"No," answered the man. "I've been paying through it for so long, it gave way under the strain."

—RALPH GOLDSMITH IN THE BOSCOBEL, WIS., DIAL

Fire swept the plains and burned down the farmer's barn. While he surveyed the wreckage, his wife called their insurance company and asked them to send a check for $50,000, the amount of insurance on the barn.

"We don't give you the money," a company official explained. "We replace the barn and all the equipment in it."

"In that case," replied the wife, "cancel the policy I have on my husband."

—NAOMI WILKINS IN WOMAN'S WORLD

President Clinton says he looks forward to the day a citizen can call the IRS and get the right answer to a question," says Jay Leno. "I look forward to the day I can call the IRS and get a voice that says, 'Sorry, that number has been disconnected.'"

*"I suppose it's inevitable that we occasionally lose
someone to a better mousetrap!"*

Technology

Gadgets and Gizmos

Frank was setting up a sundial in his yard when a neighbor asked, "What's that for?"

Frank stopped to explain, "The sun hits that small triangular spike and casts a shadow on the face of the sundial. Then, as the sun moves across the sky, the shadow also moves across the calibrated dial, enabling a person to determine the correct time."

The neighbor shook his head. "What will they think of next?"

—RON DENTINGER in the
Dodgeville, Wis., *Chronicle*

Son to his father as they watch television: "Dad, tell me again how when you were a kid you had to walk all the way across the room to change the channel."

—BUCELLA in *VFW*

Overheard: "I hate talking cars. A voice out of nowhere says things like, 'Your door is ajar.' Why don't they say something really useful, like 'There's a state trooper hiding behind that bush.'"

—*Current Comedy*

And then there's the fellow who's sorry he ever installed a car telephone. He finds it such a nuisance having to run to the garage every time it rings.

—*The Rotarian*

One hypochondriac to another: "My doctor is on the cutting edge of technology. He told me to take two aspirin and fax him in the morning."

—*Current Comedy*

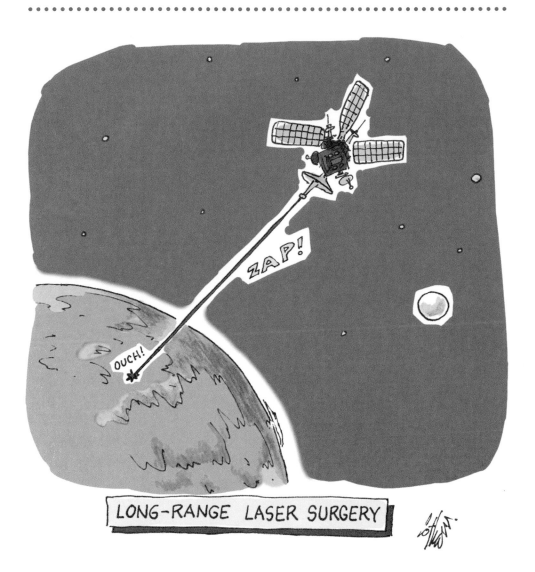

LONG-RANGE LASER SURGERY

Dragnet's Sgt. Joe Friday decided to upgrade the office communication system, so he went to an electronics store to see what was available. A saleswoman showed Friday the latest in cellular phones, intercoms, facsimile machines, and two-way radios. "Are you interested in purchasing a new telephone system?" she asked.

"No," replied Friday. "Just the fax, ma'am."

—TIM MOORE

Clem decided it was time to purchase a new saw to help clear his heavily timbered property. A salesman showed him the latest model chain saw and assured him that he could easily cut three or four cords of wood per day with it.

But the first day Clem barely cut one cord of wood. The second morning he arose an hour earlier and managed to cut a little over one cord. The third day he got up even earlier but only managed to achieve a total of 1 1/2 cords of wood.

Clem returned the saw to the store the next day and explained the situation. "Well," said the salesman, "let's see what's the matter." He then pulled the cable and the chain saw sprang into action.

Leaping back, Clem exclaimed, "What the heck is that noise?"

—GREGORY POTTER

Overheard: "Even my mother is getting caught up in our high-tech environment. Just the other day she was complaining, 'You don't write, you don't call, you don't fax.' "

—*Current Comedy for Speakers*

Did you hear about the high-tech ventriloquist?
He can throw his voice mail.

—GARY APPLE in *Speaker's Idea File*

And what would you like for Christmas this year?" a department store Santa asked the cute kid sitting on his lap.

The little girl was indignant. "Didn't you get the fax I sent you?"

—Quoted by ELSTON BROOKS in the Fort Worth *Star-Telegram*

There's a new telephone service that lets you test your IQ over the phone," says Jay Leno. "It costs $3.95 a minute. If you make the call at all, you're a moron. If you're on the line for three minutes, you're a complete idiot."

Overheard: "Yesterday I got my tie stuck in the fax machine. Next thing I knew, I was in Los Angeles."

—STEVE HAUPT

When I was a youngster," complained the frustrated father, "I was disciplined by being sent to my room without supper. But my son has his own color TV, phone, computer, and CD player."

"So what do you do?" asked his friend.

"I send him to my room!"

—*Capper's*

They say by the year 2000, video cameras will be the size of postage stamps and will cost 50 dollars. Of course by then postage stamps will cost 60 dollars . . . .

—WAYNE COTTER, *Comic Strip Live*, FOX TV

Satan agreed to be interviewed on the Larry King show. Asked what he thought were his greatest accomplishments, the devil thought for a minute.

"I always look back with a smile on the sinking of the *Titanic*," he mused. "But there are so many fond memories of wars, disasters, and cities laid waste, it's hard to pick out a favorite."

"Come on," pressed King. "There must be one foul deed you consider your crowning achievement."

"Well, yes," admitted Satan. "I invented Call Waiting."

—ARGUS HAMILTON in Oklahoma City *Daily Oklahoman*

My sister gave birth in a state-of-the-art delivery room," said one man to another. "It was so high-tech that the baby came out cordless."

—*Current Comedy*

Department store automatic answering machine:

"If you are calling to order or send money, press 5.

"If you are calling to register a complaint, press 6 4 5 9 8 3 4 8 2 2 9 5 5 3 9 2.

"Have a good day."

—HAL THUROW

Patron: "What time do you have?"

Bartender: "I don't have a watch anymore. I bought one that was waterproof, dustproof, and shockproof."

Patron: "Well, where is it?"

Bartender: "It caught fire."

—YOUNG and DRAKE, King Features Syndicate

Phone-answering machines for the rich and famous:
•Sylvester Stallone—"Yo. You. Message. Now."
•Sally Field—"If you like me—if you really *like* me—leave your name and number after the beep."
•Clint Eastwood—"Go ahead, leave a message. Make my day."
•Shirley MacLaine—"I already know who you are and what you're calling about. Simply leave a brief description of your present incarnation."

—Maureen Larkin in *Ladies' Home Journal*

Did you hear about the robot that was so ugly it had a face only a motor could love?

—Shelby Friedman

Two executives in expensive suits stopped off at a small country bar. As the bartender served them, he heard a muffled *beep beep* sound and watched as one of the men calmly removed a pen from his inside coat pocket and began carrying on a conversation. When he was done talking, the exec noticed the bartender and other customers giving him puzzled looks. "I was just answering a call on my state-of-the-art cellular pen," he explained.

A short while later another odd tone was heard. This time the second executive picked up his fancy hat, fiddled with the lining and started talking into it. After a few minutes he put the hat back on the bar. "That was just a call on my state-of-the-art cellular hat," he said matter-of-factly.

A few stools down one of the locals suddenly let out a loud burp. "Quick!" he exclaimed. "Anybody got a piece of paper? I have a fax comin' in!"

—*John Boy & Billy,* Radio Network

While Milgrom waited at the airport to board his plane, he noticed a computer scale that would give your weight and a fortune. He dropped a quarter in the slot, and the computer screen displayed: "You weigh 195 pounds, you're married, and you're on your way to San Diego." Milgrom stood there dumbfounded.

Another man put in a quarter and the computer read: "You weigh 184 pounds, you're divorced, and you're on your way to Chicago."

Milgrom said to the man, "Are you divorced and on your way to Chicago?"

"Yes," came the reply.

Milgrom was amazed. Then he rushed to the men's room, changed his clothes and put on dark glasses. He went to the machine again. The computer read: "You still weigh 195 pounds, you're still married, and you just missed your plane to San Diego!"

—STEVE WOZNIAK and LARRY WILDE,
The Official Computer Freaks Joke Book

Bright Ideas

Q: How many car salesmen does it take to change a light bulb?
A: I'm just going to work this out on my calculator, and I think you're going to be pleasantly surprised.

—ROBERT WILBURN, quoted by
MARY ANN MADDEN in *New York*

How many politicians does it take to change a light bulb?
A. Five—one to change it and four to deny it.

—TINA FRENCH

Q: How many bullies does it take to change a light bulb?
A: Four. Do you have a problem with that?

—DENNIS LEEKE

Q: "How many bureaucrats does it take to change a light bulb?"

A: "Two. One to assure us that everything possible is being done while the other screws the bulb into a water faucet."

—Voice for Health

Q: How many unemployed actors does it take to change a light bulb?

A: 100. One to change it, and 99 to stand around and say, "Hey, I could've done that!"

—One to One

Q: How many economists does it take to change a light bulb?

A: How many did it take this time last year?

—The Jokesmith

Q: How many real-estate agents does it take to change a light bulb?

A: Ten. But we'll accept eight.

—BILL HOMISAK, quoted by
MARY ANN MADDEN in New York

Q: How many liberated women does it take to change a light bulb?

A: Five! One to turn it, and four to form a support group.

—JAY TRACHMAN in One to One

Q: How many surrealist painters does it take to change a light bulb?

A: A fish.

—HORACE DAVIES, quoted by
MARY ANN MADDEN in New York

"I'll make a deal with you. I'll tell you the secret of life if you'll tell me how to program my VCR."

Q: How many feminists does it take to change a light bulb?
A: That's not funny.

—CHRISTINA HOFF SOMMERS,
Who Stole Feminism?

Thomas Edison spent years trying to invent the electric light, testing and retesting. Finally, late one night, he got the bulb to glow. He ran out of his laboratory, through the house, up the stairs to his bedroom. "Honey," Edison called to his wife, "I've done it!"

She rolled over and said, "Will you turn off that light and come to bed!"

—RON DENTINGER in
Work Sheet

Q: How many country-western singers does it take to change a light bulb?

A: Five. One to put in the new bulb, and four to sing about how much they long for the old one.

—LESLIE R. TANNER

:) \&/HA HA!

Delbert and Fletch, two industrial robots, escaped from the engineering lab one Saturday night. They decided to separate, pick up some dates and meet later.

A few hours passed and Delbert arrived at the meeting place. He found Fletch standing in front of a mailbox and a fire alarm. "Who are your two friends?" asked Delbert.

"Forget them," sighed Fletch. "The short, fat one with the big mouth just stands there, and if you touch the redhead she screams her lungs out."

—ED MCMANUS, quoted by STEVE WOZNIAK and LARRY WILDE in *The Official Computer Freaks Joke Book*

Mrs. B: "Why are you laughing?"
Mrs. D: "A salesman tried to sell my husband a lap-top computer."
Mrs. B: "What's so funny about that?"
Mrs. D: "My husband hasn't had a lap in 20 years!"

—YOUNG and DRAKE, King Features Syndicate

Did you hear about the new computer Apple has developed, small enough to be carried in a fanny pack? It will be called the Macintush.

—TOM CLOUD, quoted by ABIGAIL VAN BUREN, Universal Press Syndicate

A computer salesman dies and meets St. Peter at the Pearly Gates. St. Peter tells the salesman that he can choose between heaven and hell. First he shows the man heaven, where people in white robes play harps and float around. "Dull," says the salesman.

Next, St. Peter shows him hell: toga parties, good food and wine, and people looking as though they're having a fine time. "I'll take hell," he says.

He enters the gates of hell and is immediately set upon by a dozen demons, who poke him with pitchforks. "Hey," the salesman demands as Satan walks past, "what happened to the party I saw going on?"

"Ah," Satan replies. "You must have seen our demo."

—Digital Review

Chip Ahoy
I bought the latest computer;
It came completely loaded.
It was guaranteed for 90 days,
But in 30 was outmoded.

—BILL IHLENFELDT in *The Wall Street Journal*

That computer you sold me is no good," complained the customer. "It keeps flashing insulting messages, like 'Look it up yourself, stupid.' "

"Oh," replied the store clerk, "you must have one of our new 'User Surly' models."

—JOHNNY HART, Creators Syndicate

The computer programmer, it seems, had allowed for every contingency. One day the operator became frustrated with her work and punched in a highly unladylike message. On the console a response immediately flashed up: "Tut, tut, improper expression."

—JANE ROUX

Q: Why is a modem better than a woman?

A: A modem doesn't complain if you sit and play at the computer all night. A modem doesn't mind if you talk to other modems. A modem will sit patiently and wait by the phone. A modem comes with an instruction manual.

—JAY TRACHMAN in *One to One*

The exec was making a presentation to the company board. "Computers have allowed us to cut costs," he explained. "We expect even more dramatic improvements as computers become increasingly self-sufficient." He unveiled a large chart showing a man, a dog, and a computer. "Here is our organization plan of the future."

"What kind of plan is that?" demanded a board member.

"It's simple," replied the exec. "The man's job is to feed the dog. The dog's job is to bite the man if he touches the computer."

—LOUIS A. MAMAKOS

Space Invaders

Upon their return from an excursion to our planet, two Martians presented their chief with a television set. "We couldn't manage to capture any Earthlings," they explained, "but we did get our hands on one of their gods."

—MINA and ANDRÉ GUILLOIS

A pair of Martians landed on a country road on Earth in the middle of the night. "Where are we?" one asked.

"I think we're in a cemetery," his companion answered. "Look at the gravestone over there—that man lived to be 108."

"What was his name?"

"Miles to Omaha."

"Take me to your remote control."

A service station attendant watching a Martian put gas into its spacecraft noticed that "UFO" was printed on the spaceship's side. "Does that stand for 'Unidentified Flying Object'?" he asked the Martian.

"No," the creature replied. " 'Unleaded Fuel Only.' "

—Delfort D. Minor

The White House is proposing we collaborate with Russia to build a new space station," says Jay Leno. "Know what that means? We're going to wind up with a space station that has a $30-million-dollar toilet—and no toilet paper."

The week before a space launch, an astronaut tries to relax at an out-of-the-way pub. But the bartender recognizes him and says, "You fellows at NASA think you're something, going to the moon. But we've got a couple of guys here who've been building their own spaceship out back."

Reluctantly, the astronaut goes outside to look—the spaceship is a mess of beer bottles, cans and junk. "We're planning to go to the sun," boasts one guy.

"This thing will be incinerated before you can get close to the sun," the astronaut warns.

"We got that all figured out—we're going at night!"

—Herman Gollob in *Texas Monthly*

It's the year 2210, and the planets have long been colonized. Interplanetary flight is as everyday as transcontinental flight, and on one of these interplanetary liners a Martian colonist strikes up a conversation with the passenger next to him. "Where are you from?" he asks.

"Earth," is the reply.

"Oh, really? By any chance do you know . . .?"

—Mark S. Zuelke

"See you, Roger. I'm returning to the private sector."

Talking Animals

PET PEEVES 204

WILD THINGS 212

Pet Peeves

Is our parrot a daddy or a mommy?" asked the young boy of his mother on a crowded bus.

"She is a mommy parrot," the mother replied.

"How do we know?" the boy asked.

A hush fell over the passengers as they listened for how the mother would cope with this one. But she was ready for the challenge and replied, "She has lipstick on, hasn't she?"

—R. Sarangapani

The neighbor's young son came knocking at the housewife's door every day to ask if he could take her dog for a walk. Her husband, who was a carpenter, almost always took the animal with him to his jobs, so she told the child, "I'm sorry, but the dog is at work with my husband." Because the boy kept coming over every day with the same request, she always gave him the same response.

The youngster met the woman on the street one day, stopped and eyed her suspiciously. "Say," he asked, "what does your dog do for a living?"

—Mette R. Nyhus

John, teaching his parrot to talk: "Repeat after me, 'I can walk.'"
Parrot: "I can walk."
John: "I can talk."
Parrot: "I can talk."
John: "I can fly."
Parrot: "That's a lie."

—Fateh Zung Singh

Overheard: "My neighbor's dog is taking the advanced course at obedience school. He knows how to fetch, heel and beg—now he's learning to fax."

—Jay Trachman in *One to One*

When the farmer arrived at the obedience school to pick up his newly trained bird dog, he asked the instructor for a demonstration. The two men and the dog went to a nearby field, where the dog immediately pointed to a clump of brush, then rolled over twice.

"There are two birds in there," the instructor said, and sure enough, two birds were flushed. A minute later, the dog pointed to another bunch of bushes, and then rolled over five times.

"There are five birds in there," the instructor noted, and indeed five birds were driven from the brush. Then the dog pointed to a third clump. He began to whine and run in circles until he found a stick, which he shook mightily and dropped at the men's feet.

"And in that clump of brush there," the proud instructor concluded, "there are more birds than you can shake a stick at!"

—*Country*

Sign seen in a veterinarian's office: The doctor is in. Sit. Stay.

—Gale Shipley

An agent arranged an audition with a TV producer for his client, a talking dog that told jokes and sang songs. The amazed producer was about to sign a contract when suddenly a much larger dog burst into the room, grabbed the talking pooch by the neck and bounded back out.

"What happened?" demanded the producer.

"That's his mother," said the agent. "She wants him to be a doctor."

—*Cheer*

Overheard at the veterinarian's: "I had my cat neutered. He's still out all night with the other cats, but now it's in the role of consultant."

—*Current Comedy*

Walking down the street, a dog saw a sign in an office window. "Help wanted. Must type 70 words a minute. Must be computer literate. Must be bilingual. An equal-opportunity employer."

The dog applied for the position, but he was quickly rebuffed. "I can't hire a dog for this job," the office manager said. But when the dog pointed to the line that read "An equal-opportunity employer," the office manager sighed and asked, "Can you type?" Silently, the dog walked over to a typewriter and flawlessly banged out a letter. "Can you operate a computer?" the manager inquired. The dog then sat down at a terminal, wrote a program and ran it perfectly.

"Look, I still can't hire a dog for this position," said the exasperated office manager. "You have fine skills, but I need someone who's bilingual. It says so right in the ad."

The dog looked up at the manager and said, "Meow."

—DONALD WEINSTEIN, quoted by LAWRENCE VAN GELDER
in *The New York Times*

A dog goes into the unemployment office and asks for help finding a job. "With your rare talent," says the clerk, "I'm sure we can get you something at the circus."

"The circus?" echoes the dog. "What would a circus want with a plumber?"

—JAY TRACHMAN in *One to One*

Did you hear about the cat that gave birth in a Singapore street? It got fined for littering.

—DAWN FUNG

"Have you noticed how Ed has changed since he started going to law school?"

Please keep your dog beside you, sir," a woman said crossly to the man sitting opposite her on the bus. "I can feel a flea in my shoe."

"Bello, come here," replied the man. "That woman has fleas."

—J. G.

Mrs. Klapisch brought her cat to the veterinarian. The doctor had her hold the animal on the examining table as he touched and gently squeezed it. He then walked slowly around the table, all the while looking back and forth, back and forth. When he was done, he gave out some medication and presented Mrs. Klapisch with the bill.

"What?" she cried. "One hundred fifty dollars for two pills?"

"Not just for pills," said the vet. "I gave her a cat scan too."

—David W. Fleeton

Henry's new job had him spending a lot of time on the road, and out of concern for his wife's safety he visited a pet shop to look at watchdogs.

"I have just the dog for you," said the salesman, showing him a miniature Pekingese.

"Come on," Henry protested, "that little thing couldn't hurt a flea."

"Ah, but he knows karate," the salesman replied. "Here, let me show you." He pointed to a cardboard box and ordered, "Karate the box!" Immediately the dog shredded it. The salesman then pointed to an old wooden chair and instructed, "Karate the chair!" The dog reduced the chair to matchsticks. Astounded, Henry bought the dog.

When he got home, Henry announced that he had purchased a watchdog, but his wife took one look at the Pekingese and was unimpressed. "That scrawny thing couldn't fight his way out of a paper bag!" she said.

"But this Pekingese is special," Henry insisted. "He's a karate expert."

"Now I've heard everything," Helen replied. "Karate my foot!"

—JIM ELLSWORTH

Several racehorses are in a stable. One of them starts boasting about his track record.

"Of my last 15 races," he says, "I've won eight."

Another horse breaks in, "Well, I've won 19 of my last 27!"

"That's good, but I've taken 28 of 36," says another, flicking his tail.

At this point a greyhound who's been sitting nearby pipes up. "I don't mean to boast," he says, "but of my last 90 races, I've won 88."

The horses are clearly amazed. "Wow," says one after a prolonged silence, "a talking dog!"

—PETER S. LANGSTON

I'm really worried about my dog," Ralph said to the veterinarian. "I dropped some coins on the floor and before I could pick them up, he ate them." The vet advised Ralph to leave his dog at the vet's office overnight.

The next morning, Ralph called to see how his pet was doing. The vet replied, "No change yet."

—MIKE WALT, SR.

The pet-shop customer couldn't believe his good fortune. The parrot he had just bought could recite Shakespeare's sonnets, imitate opera stars and intone Homer's epic poems in Greek. And he cost only $600.

Once the man got the bird home, however, not another word passed his beak. After three weeks the disconsolate customer returned to the shop and asked for his money back. "When we had this bird," said the proprietor, "he could recite poetry and sing like an angel. Now you want me to take him back when he's no longer himself? Well, all right. Out of the goodness of my heart I'll give you $100."

Reluctantly the man accepted his loss. Just as the door shut behind him he heard the parrot say to the shop owner, "Don't forget—my share is $250."

—C. A. HENDERSON

A man answered his doorbell, and a friend walked in, followed by a very large dog. As they began talking, the dog knocked over a lamp, jumped on the sofa with his muddy paws and began chewing a pillow. The outraged householder, unable to contain himself any longer, burst out, "Can't you control your dog better?"

"*My* dog!" exclaimed the friend. "I thought it was *your* dog."

—*The Great Clean Jokes Calendar*

"I'm sick and tired of begging."

A man trained his dog to go around the corner to Bud's Lounge every day with two dollar bills under his collar to get a pack of cigarettes. Once the man only had a five, so he put it under the collar and sent the dog on his way.

An hour passed and the pooch still hadn't returned. So the man went to Bud's and found his dog sitting on a bar stool, drinking a beer. He said, "You've never done this before."

Replied the dog, "I never had the money before."

—GARRISON KEILLOR, *We Are Still Married*

• •

A guy walks into a bar and orders a beer. "Listen," he says to the bartender. "If I show you the most amazing thing you've ever seen, is my beer on the house?"

"We'll see," says the bartender. So the guy pulls a hamster and a tiny piano out of a bag, puts them on the bar, and the hamster begins to play. "Impressive," says the bartender, "but I'll need to see more."

"Hold on," says the man. He then pulls out a bullfrog, and it sings "Old Man River." A patron jumps up from his table and shouts, "That's absolutely incredible! I'll give you $100 right now for the frog."

"Sold," says the guy. The other patron takes the bullfrog and leaves.

"It's none of my business," says the bartender, "but you just gave away a fortune."

"Not really," says the guy. "The hamster is also a ventriloquist."

—ANDY BALE, WHUD, Peekskill, N.Y.

A man went to the movies and was surprised to find a woman with a big collie sitting in front of him. Even more amazing was the fact that the dog always laughed in the right places through the comedy.

"Excuse me," the man said to the woman, "but I think it's astounding that your dog enjoys the movie so much."

"I'm surprised myself," she replied. "He hated the book."

—GRAHAM FOSTER in Tomahawk, Wis., *Leader,*
quoted by DEBBIE CHRISTIAN in the Milwaukee *Journal*

Kerry the tomcat was scampering all over the neighborhood—down alleys, up fire escapes, into cellars. A disturbed neighbor knocked on the owner's door and said, "Your cat is rushing about like mad."

"I know," the man conceded. "Kerry's just been neutered, and he's running around canceling engagements."

—LARRY WILDE, *Library of Laughter*

Wild Things

A forest ranger, trekking through a remote campground area, caught a whiff of something burning in the distance. Farther along the trail he found an old hermit making his evening meal.

"What are you cooking?" the ranger asked.

"Peregrine falcon," answered the hermit.

"*Peregrine falcon!*" the conservationist said, shocked. "You can't cook that! It's on the endangered species list."

"How was I to know?" the hermit questioned. "I haven't had contact with the outside world in ages."

The ranger told the recluse he wouldn't report him this time, but he wasn't to cook peregrine falcon ever again. "By the way," he asked, "what does it taste like?"

"Well," replied the hermit, "I'd say it's somewhere between a dodo bird and a whooping crane."

—RICHARD SCHULDt, quoted by Alex Thien
in the Milwaukee *Sentinel*

A father took his children to the zoo. All were looking forward to seeing the monkeys. Unfortunately, it was mating time and, the attendant explained, the monkeys had gone inside their little sanctuary for some togetherness. "Would they come out for some peanuts?" asked the father.

"Would you?" responded the attendant.

—CHARLEY MANOS in *The Detroit News*

When a snail crossed the road, he was run over by a turtle. Regaining consciousness in the emergency room, he was asked what caused the accident.

"I really can't remember," the snail replied. "You see, it all happened so fast."

—CHARLES MCMANIS

"I don't know why I even made this trip—I'm not even sexually active."

The photographer had been trying for hours to get some action shots of a bear that preferred to sleep in its cage. "What kind of bear is that?" he finally asked the zoo keeper.

"Himalayan," was the reply.

"I know that," snarled the photographer. "What I want to know is when him a getting up."

—RICHARD A. UECKER

The zoo built a special eight-foot-high enclosure for its newly acquired kangaroo, but the next morning the animal was found hopping around outside. The height of the fence was increased to 15 feet, but the kangaroo got out again. Exasperated, the zoo director had the height increased to 30 feet, but the kangaroo still escaped. A giraffe asked the kangaroo, "How high do you think they'll build the fence?"

"I don't know," said the kangaroo. "Maybe a thousand feet if they keep leaving the gate unlocked."

—Jerry H. Simpson, Jr.

A woman lion tamer had the big cats under such control they took a lump of sugar from her lips on command. "Anyone can do that!" a skeptic yelled.

The ringmaster came over and asked, "Would you like to try it?"

"Sure," replied the man, "but first get those crazy lions out of there!"

—*Healthwise*

A rooster was strutting around the henhouse one Easter morning and came across a nest of eggs dyed every color of the rainbow. The rooster took one look at the colorful display, ran outside and beat the heck out of the resident peacock.

—Seymour Rosenberg in the
Spartanburg, S.C., *Herald-Journal*

As spring migration approached, two elderly vultures doubted they could make the trip north, so they decided to go by airplane.

When they checked their baggage, the attendant noticed that they were carrying two dead armadillos. "Do you wish to check the armadillos through as luggage?" she asked.

"No, thanks," replied the vultures. "They're carrion."

—Fred Brice

The old big-game hunter is recounting his adventures to his grandson:

"I remember, I once had to brave eight ferocious lions with no gun, nothing but a knife to defend me. My life was at stake. . . ."

"Granddad, the last time you told this story, there were only three lions!"

"Yes, but then you were too young to hear the terrible truth."

—ADAM WOLFART

Did you hear about the scientist who crossed a carrier pigeon with a woodpecker?

He got a bird that not only delivers messages to their destination but knocks on the door when it gets there.

—JOHN R. FOX

An antelope and a lion entered a diner and took a booth near the window. When the waiter approached, the antelope said, "I'll have a bowl of hay and a side order of radishes."

"And what will your friend have?"

"Nothing," replied the antelope.

The waiter persisted. "Isn't he hungry?"

"Hey, if he were hungry," said the antelope, "would I be sitting here?"

—*Current Comedy*

An expert on whales was telling friends about some of the unusual findings he had made. "For instance," he said, "some whales can communicate at a distance of 300 miles."

"What on earth would one whale say to another 300 miles away?" asked an astounded member of the group.

"I'm not absolutely sure," answered the expert, "but it sounds something like 'Can you still hear me?' "

—STEVE KEUCHEL

"Forgive me? It must have been the beast in me talking."

We have a skunk in the basement," shrieked the caller to the police dispatcher. "How can we get it out?"

"Take some bread crumbs," said the dispatcher, "and put down a trail from the basement out to the backyard. Then leave the cellar door open."

Sometime later the resident called back. "Did you get rid of it?" asked the dispatcher.

"No," replied the caller. "Now I have two skunks in there!"

—*Ohio Motorist*

And then there was the male spotted owl who told his wife, "What do you mean you have a headache? We're an endangered species!"

—JOHN BUNZEL, quoted by HERB CAEN
in the San Francisco *Chronicle*

While drinking at the lake, a young bear admires its reflection and growls, "I am the king of beasts!"

Along comes a lion and roars, "What was that I just heard?"

"Oh, dear," says the bear, "you say strange things when you've had too much to drink."

—LEA BERNER

Dad," a polar bear cub asked his father, "am I 100 percent polar bear?"

"Of course you are," answered the elder bear. "My parents are 100 percent polar bear, which makes me 100 percent polar bear. Your mother's parents are all polar bear, so she's 100 percent polar bear. Yep, that makes you 100 percent polar bear too. Why do you want to know?"

Replied the cub, " 'Cause I'm freezing!"

—"T & T," KCYY, San Antonio

A male crab met a female crab and asked her to marry him. She noticed that he was walking straight instead of sideways. *Wow*, she thought, *this crab is really special. I can't let him get away.* So they got married immediately.

The next day she noticed her new husband walking sideways like all the other crabs, and got upset. "What happened?" she asked. "You used to walk straight before we were married."

"Oh, honey," he replied, "I can't drink that much every day."

—GITY KAZEMIAN

"QUOTABLE Quotes®

Wit & Wisdom
for Every Occasion

Contents

A Note from the Editors

"The only thing sure about luck is that it will change."

That quote from Bret Harte is as appealing today as when it ran in the very first appearance of Quotable Quotes® — in the May 1933 issue of Reader's Digest. Since then, thousands of quotes have graced the feature, delighting and inspiring generations of readers.

In a publication that prides itself on the art of condensation, the quotations in this popular collection represent the finest tradition of brevity: they package profound ideas in just a few words. In compiling this column, we search out quotes that are serious and those that are amusing. We look for provocative comments, well expressed, on universal themes. Ideal candidates can be contemporary or classic, timeless or topical, whimsical or earnest.

We cull quotes from a wide variety of sources — books, newspapers, magazines, television, radio, movies, the Internet, anywhere we come across a likely thought pithily expressed. And these gems have a life span that endures long after and far beyond their appearance in The Digest. They can be found on refrigerator doors, sprinkled into commencement speeches, enlivening sales pitches, wherever someone thinks they can do the most good. Humorists and social commentators have thrived on them. And more than a few have wound their way into a poignant eulogy.

By their very nature, Quotable Quotes beg to be repeated, whether you share them during trying times or use them to drive home a point. What you derive from Quotable Quotes is of course personal, yet these brief words can also serve as a bridge to connect people or ideas.

In Quotable Quotes you'll find the wit and wisdom of men and women from all walks of life and from all ages — from Benjamin Franklin to Colin Powell, Abraham Lincoln to Mother Teresa of Calcutta, Margaret Mead to Garrison Keillor. Read what they have to say. And enjoy it!

WITHIN OURSELVES

"

It is only with the heart that one can see rightly; what is essential is invisible to the eye.

—ANTOINE DE SAINT-EXUPERY,
  THE LITTLE PRINCE

"

THE ADVANTAGE OF SOLITUDE . . .

1 Be able to be alone. Lose not the advantage of solitude.

—SIR THOMAS BROWNE

2 When we cannot bear to be alone, it means we do not properly value the only companion we will have from birth to death—ourselves.

—EDA LESHAN
in *Newsday* (Long Island, New York)

3 We visit others as a matter of social obligation. How long has it been since we have visited with ourselves?

—MORRIS ADLER

4 We cannot confront solitude without moral resources.

—HONORÉ DE BALZAC
Madame de la Chanterie

5 The result of joining two solitudes will always be a greater solitude.

—PEDRO LUIS
Flores de Otuno

6 Solitude is a good place to visit but a poor place to stay.

—JOSH BILLINGS

7 The same fence that shuts others out shuts you in.

—BILL COPELAND

8 There's one thing worse than being alone: wishing you were.

—BOB STEELE

9 Loneliness and the feeling of being uncared for and unwanted are the greatest poverty.

—MOTHER TERESA OF CALCUTTA

10 Of all things that can happen to us, triumph is the most difficult to endure when we are alone. Deprived of witnesses, it shrinks at once.

—GABRIELLE ROY
La Detresse et L'enchantement

11 Our language has wisely sensed the two sides of being alone. It has created the word "loneliness" to express the pain of being alone. And it has created the word "solitude" to express the glory of being alone.

—PAUL TILLICH
The Eternal Now

12 The man who goes alone can start today; but he who travels with another must wait until the other is ready.

—HENRY DAVID THOREAU

13 What a lovely surprise to finally discover how unlonely being alone can be.

—ELLEN BURSTYN

1 Man loves company—even if it is only that of a small burning candle.

—GEORG CHRISTOPH LICHTENBERG

THE RIGHT MEASURE OF HIMSELF . . .

2 Fortunate, indeed, is the man who takes exactly the right measure of himself and holds a just balance between what he can acquire and what he can use.

—PETER LATHAM

3 Integrity is not a conditional word. It doesn't blow in the wind or change with the weather. It is your inner image of yourself, and if you look in there and see a man who won't cheat, then you know he never will.

—JOHN D. MACDONALD
The Turquoise Lament

4 Integrity has no need of rules.

—ALBERT CAMUS

5 We get so much in the habit of wearing a disguise before others that we eventually appear disguised before ourselves.

—JIM BISHOP

6 We don't know who we are until we see what we can do.

—MARTHA GRIMES
Writer's Handbook

7 What we must decide is how we are valuable rather than how valuable we are.

—EDGAR Z. FRIEDENBERG

8 Our credulity is greatest concerning the things we know least about. And since we know least about ourselves, we are ready to believe all that is said about us. Hence the mysterious power of both flattery and calumny.

—ERIC HOFFER
The Passionate State of Mind

9 No one beneath you can offend you. No one your equal would.

—JAN L. WELLS

10 The superior man is distressed by the limitations of his ability; he is not distressed by the fact that men do not recognize the ability he has.

—CONFUCIUS

11 No man, for any considerable time, can wear one face to himself and another to the multitude without finally getting bewildered as to which may be the true.

—NATHANIEL HAWTHORNE

12 Maybe taking ourselves for somebody else means that we cannot bear to see ourselves as we are.

—ALBERT BRIE
Le Devoir

1 Until you make peace with who you are, you'll never be content with what you have.

—Doris Mortman
Circles

2 If we have our own "why" of life, we can bear almost any "how."

—Friedrich Nietzsche

3 Man shies away from nothing as from a rendezvous with himself— which makes the entertainment industry what it is.

—Fritz Muliar

4 To have doubted one's own first principles is the mark of a civilized man.

—Oliver Wendell Holmes Jr.

5 When one is out of touch with oneself, one cannot touch others.

—Anne Morrow Lindbergh
Gift From the Sea

6 Everything that irritates us about others can lead us to an understanding of ourselves.

—Carl G. Jung
Memories, Dreams, Reflections

7 Fair play is primarily not blaming others for anything that is wrong with us.

—Eric Hoffer
Working and Thinking on the Waterfront

8 Our opinion of people depends less upon what we see in them than upon what they make us see in ourselves.

—Sarah Grand

9 One can only face in others what one can face in oneself.

—James Baldwin

10 I have had more trouble with myself than with any other man I have ever met!

—Dwight L. Moody

11 Being yourself is not remaining what you were, or being satisfied with what you are. It is the point of departure.

—Sydney J. Harris

12 People often say that this or that person has not yet found himself. But the self is not something that one finds. It is something one creates.

—Thomas Szasz
The Second Sin

13 You have to start knowing yourself so well that you begin to know other people. A piece of us is in every person we can ever meet.

—John D. MacDonald
introduction to *Night Shift*
by Stephen King

1 The best vision is insight.

—MALCOLM S. FORBES
in *Forbes* magazine

2 Men go abroad to wonder at the heights of mountains, at the huge waves of the sea, at the long courses of the rivers, at the vast compass of the ocean, at the circular motions of the stars; and they pass by themselves without wondering.

—ST. AUGUSTINE

3 If a man happens to find himself, he has a mansion which he can inhabit with dignity all the days of his life.

—JAMES A. MICHENER

4 No sooner do we think we have assembled a comfortable life than we find a piece of ourselves that has no place to fit in.

—GAIL SHEEHY

5 Not until we are lost do we begin to understand ourselves.

—HENRY DAVID THOREAU

6 You may find the worst enemy or best friend in yourself.

—ENGLISH PROVERB

7 Know yourself. Don't accept your dog's admiration as conclusive evidence that you are wonderful.

—ANN LANDERS

Be yourself. No one can ever tell you you're doing it wrong. 8

—JAMES LEO HERLIHY

Often we change jobs, friends and spouses instead of ourselves. 9

—AKBARALI H. JETHA
Reflections

Everybody thinks of changing humanity and nobody thinks of changing himself. 10

—LEO TOLSTOY

Everyone complains of his memory, and nobody complains of his judgment. 11

—FRANÇOIS DE LA ROCHEFOUCAULD

SO SOOTHING TO OUR SELF-ESTEEM . . .

Nothing is so soothing to our self-esteem as to find our bad traits in our forebears. It seems to absolve us. 12

—VAN WYCK BROOKS
From a Writer's Notebook

I don't want everyone to like me; I should think less of myself if some people did. 13

—HENRY JAMES

When we are confident, all we need is a little support. 14

—ANDRÉ LAURENDEAU
Une Vie D'Enfer

1 We may not return the affection of those who like us, but we always respect their good judgment.

—LIBBIE FUDIM

2 A man can stand a lot as long as he can stand himself.

—AXEL MUNTHE

3 Misfortunes one can endure—they come from outside; they are accidents. But to suffer for one's own faults—ah, there is the sting of life.

—OSCAR WILDE

4 We are all worms, but I do believe I am a glowworm.

—WINSTON CHURCHILL

5 The most difficult secret for a man to keep is the opinion he has of himself.

—MARCEL PAGNOL

6 Appearances give us more pleasure than reality, especially when they help to satisfy our egos.

—ÉMILE CHEVALIER

7 The ingenuities we practice in order to appear admirable to ourselves would suffice to invent the telephone twice over on a rainy summer morning.

—BRENDAN GILL

8 We have to learn to be our own best friends because we fall too easily into the trap of being our worst enemies.

—RODERICK THORP
Rainbow Drive

9 A human being's first responsibility is to shake hands with himself.

—HENRY WINKLER

10 If you want your children to improve, let them overhear the nice things you say about them to others.

—HAIM GINOTT

11 We appreciate frankness from those who like us. Frankness from others is called insolence.

—ANDRÉ MAUROIS

12 We probably wouldn't worry about what people think of us if we could know how seldom they do.

—OLIN MILLER

13 We judge ourselves by what we feel capable of doing, while others judge us by what we have already done.

—HENRY WADSWORTH LONGFELLOW

14 Argue for your limitations and, sure enough, they're yours.

—RICHARD BACH
Illusions

15 Morale is self-esteem in action.

—AVERY WEISMAN, MD

1 Lack of something to feel important about is almost the greatest tragedy a man may have.

—ARTHUR E. MORGAN

2 Once in a century a man may be ruined or made insufferable by praise. But surely once in a minute something generous dies for want of it.

—JOHN MASEFIELD

3 In the depth of winter I finally learned that there was in me an invincible summer.

—ALBERT CAMUS
Lyrical and Critical Essays

4 Self-respect is the fruit of discipline; the sense of dignity grows with the ability to say no to oneself.

—ABRAHAM JOSHUA HESCHEL

5 The better we feel about ourselves, the fewer times we have to knock somebody else down to feel tall.

—ODETTA

6 A man can't ride your back unless it's bent.

—REV. MARTIN LUTHER KING JR.

7 Never feel self-pity, the most destructive emotion there is. How awful to be caught up in the terrible squirrel cage of self.

—MILLICENT FENWICK

8 Self-pity in its early stages is as snug as a feather mattress. Only when it hardens does it become uncomfortable.

—MAYA ANGELOU
Gather Together in My Name

9 Trust yourself. You know more than you think you do.

—BENJAMIN SPOCK, MD
Baby and Child Care

IMAGINATION IS A GOOD HORSE TO CARRY YOU . . .

10 Imagination is a good horse to carry you over the ground—not a flying carpet to set you free from probability.

—ROBERTSON DAVIES
The Manticore

11 Imagination is the true magic carpet.

—NORMAN VINCENT PEALE

12 The man who has no imagination has no wings.

—MUHAMMAD ALI

1 Imagination offers people consolation for what they cannot be, and humor for what they actually are.
—ALBERT CAMUS

2 There are lots of people who mistake their imagination for their memory.
—JOSH BILLINGS

3 You can't depend on your judgment when your imagination is out of focus.
—MARK TWAIN

4 He who has imagination without learning has wings but no feet.
—JOSEPH JOUBERT

5 Imagination will often carry us to worlds that never were. But without it, we go nowhere.
—CARL SAGAN
Cosmos

6 Imagination is the highest kite that one can fly.
—LAUREN BACALL
Lauren Bacall, By Myself

7 Imagination is as good as many voyages—and much cheaper.
—GEORGE WILLIAM CURTIS

8 I believe in the imagination. What I cannot see is infinitely more important than what I can see.
—DUANE MICHALS
Real Dreams

9 The opportunities of man are limited only by his imagination. But so few have imagination that there are ten thousand fiddlers to one composer.
—CHARLES F. KETTERING

10 Imagination is more important than knowledge.
—ALBERT EINSTEIN

11 He turns not back who is bound to a star.
—LEONARDO DA VINCI

12 Perhaps imagination is only intelligence having fun.
—GEORGE SCIALABBA
in *Harvard* magazine

13 I doubt that the imagination can be suppressed. If you truly eradicated it in a child, he would grow up to be an eggplant.
—URSULA K. LE GUIN
The Language of the Night

14 One of the virtues of being very young is that you don't let the facts get in the way of your imagination.
—SAM LEVENSON

15 If one is lucky, a solitary fantasy can totally transform one million realities.
—MAYA ANGELOU

THE BEST REASON FOR HAVING DREAMS . . .

1 The best reason for having dreams is that in dreams no reasons are necessary.

—Ashleigh Brilliant

2 There are no rules of architecture for a castle in the clouds.

—G. K. Chesterton

3 Hold fast to dreams/For if dreams die,
Life is a broken-winged bird/That cannot fly.

—Langston Hughes
The Dream Keeper and Other Poems

4 No bird soars too high if he soars with his own wings.

—William Blake

5 The best way to make your dreams come true is to wake up.

—J. M. Power

6 Nothing happens unless first a dream.

—Carl Sandburg
Slabs of the Sunburnt West

7 A rock pile ceases to be a rock pile the moment a single man contemplates it, bearing within him the image of a cathedral.

—Antoine de Saint-Exupéry
Flight to Arras

8 To fulfill a dream, to be allowed to sweat over lonely labor, to be given a chance to create, is the meat and potatoes of life. The money is the gravy.

—Bette Davis
The Lonely Life

9 The years forever fashion new dreams when old ones go. God pity a one-dream man!

—Robert Goddard

10 A man must have his dreams— memory dreams of the past and eager dreams of the future. I never want to stop reaching for new goals.

—Maurice Chevalier

11 Dreams and dedication are a powerful combination.

—William Longgood
Voices from the Earth

12 I like the dreams of the future better than the history of the past.

—Thomas Jefferson

13 We all live under the same sky, but we don't have the same horizon.

—Konrad Adenauer

1 The moment after Christmas every child thinks of his birthday.

—STEPHEN UYS

2 Everything starts as somebody's daydream.

—LARRY NIVEN
Niven's Laws

3 Rose-colored glasses are never made in bifocals. Nobody wants to read the small print in dreams.

—ANN LANDERS

4 How many of our daydreams would darken into nightmares, were there a danger of their coming true!

—LOGAN PEARSALL SMITH
Afterthoughts

5 Dreaming permits each and every one of us to be safely insane every night of the week.

—DR. CHARLES FISHER

ESTABLISHING GOALS IS ALL RIGHT . . .

6 Establishing goals is all right if you don't let them deprive you of interesting detours.

—DOUG LARSON

7 Discipline is remembering what you want.

—DAVID CAMPBELL

8 Goals are dreams with deadlines.

—DIANA SCHARF HUNT

9 The trouble with not having a goal is that you can spend your life running up and down the field and never scoring.

—BILL COPELAND

10 In the long run men hit only what they aim at.

—HENRY DAVID THOREAU

11 Don't bunt. Aim out of the ballpark.

—DAVID OGILVY

12 Aim at Heaven and you will get Earth thrown in. Aim at Earth and you get neither.

—C. S. LEWIS

13 Keep high aspirations, moderate expectations and small needs.

—H. STEIN

14 Goals determine what you're going to be.

—JULIUS ERVING

15 The trouble with our age is that it is all signposts and no destination.

—*The War Cry*

16 To live only for some future goal is shallow. It's the sides of the mountain that sustain life, not the top.

—ROBERT M. PIRSIG
Zen and the Art of Motorcycle Maintenance

1 When you aim for perfection, you discover it's a moving target.

—GEORGE FISHER

2 Intelligence without ambition is a bird without wings.

—C. ARCHIE DANIELSON

3 Whoever wants to reach a distant goal must take many small steps.

—HELMUT SCHMIDT

4 I've always wanted to be somebody, but I see now I should have been more specific.

—LILY TOMLIN

5 There is nothing worse than being a doer with nothing to do.

—ELIZABETH LAYTON

THE MOST IMPORTANT THINGS IN LIFE . . .

6 The most important things in life aren't things.

—Quoted in bulletin of The First Christian Church of Fairfield, Illinois

7 Origins are of the greatest importance. We are almost reconciled to having a cold when we remember where we caught it.

—MARIE VON EBNER-ESCHENBACH

8 To see what is in front of one's nose requires a constant struggle.

—GEORGE ORWELL

9 If people concentrated on the really important things in life, there'd be a shortage of fishing poles.

—DOUG LARSON

10 If you can play golf and bridge as though they were games, you're just about as well adjusted as you are ever going to be.

—Manitoba Co-Operator

11 The only person you should ever compete with is yourself. You can't hope for a fairer match.

—TODD RUTHMAN

12 The great thing in this world is not so much where we stand as in what direction we are moving.

—OLIVER WENDELL HOLMES SR.

13 To have more, desire less.

—Table Talk

14 When we have provided against cold, hunger and thirst, all the rest is but vanity and excess.

—SENECA

15 A glimpse is not a vision. But to a man on a mountain road by night, a glimpse of the next three feet of road may matter more than a vision of the horizon.

—C. S. LEWIS

16 The last thing one knows is what to put first.

—BLAISE PASCAL

1 We need to learn to set our course by the stars, not by the lights of every passing ship.
—GEN. OMAR N. BRADLEY

2 What was most significant about the lunar voyage was not that men set foot on the moon but that they set eye on the earth.
—NORMAN COUSINS

3 The hardest thing to learn in life is which bridge to cross and which to burn.
—LAURENCE J. PETER

4 Take your work seriously but yourself lightly.
—C. W. METCALF

5 If you treat every situation as a life-and-death matter, you'll die a lot of times.
—DEAN SMITH

6 Do not take life too seriously. You will never get out of it alive.
—ELBERT HUBBARD

7 It's a funny thing about life; if you refuse to accept anything but the best, you very often get it.
—W. SOMERSET MAUGHAM

8 It is not the man who has too little who is poor, but the one who craves more.
—SENECA

Think big thoughts but relish small pleasures. 9
—H. JACKSON BROWN JR.
Life's Little Instruction Book

To be upset over what you don't have is to waste what you do have. 10
—KEN S. KEYES JR.
Handbook to Higher Consciousness

The pursuit of perfection often impedes improvement. 11
—GEORGE WILL
in *Newsweek*

One cannot collect all the beautiful shells on the beach. One can collect only a few, and they are more beautiful if they are few. 12
—ANNE MORROW LINDBERGH
Gift from the Sea

Look at everything as though you were seeing it either for the first or last time. Then your time on earth will be filled with glory. 13
—BETTY SMITH
A Tree Grows in Brooklyn

Climb up on some hill at sunrise. Everybody needs perspective once in a while, and you'll find it there. 14
—ROBB SAGENDORPH

The man who can't dance thinks the band is no good. 15
—POLISH PROVERB

1 Nothing is so good as it seems
beforehand.

—GEORGE ELIOT
Silas Marner

2 In order to maintain a well-bal-
anced perspective, the person
who has a dog to worship him
should also have a cat to ignore
him.

—*Peterborough Examiner*

CONSCIENCE IS THAT STILL, SMALL VOICE . . .

3 Conscience is that still, small voice
that is sometimes too loud for
comfort.

—BERT MURRAY
in *The Wall Street Journal*

4 Conscience is a small inner voice
that doesn't speak your language.

—*Merit Crossword Puzzles Plus*

5 The ultimate test of man's conscience may be his willingness to
sacrifice something today for
future generations whose words
of thanks will not be heard.

—GAYLORD NELSON
in *The New York Times*

6 Conscience is God's presence in
man.

—EMANUEL SWEDENBORG

7 Reason deceives us; conscience,
never.

—JEAN JACQUES ROUSSEAU

8 Conscience is a mother-in-law
whose visit never ends.

—H. L. MENCKEN

9 A conscience, like a buzzing bee,
can make a fellow uneasy without
ever stinging him.

—*American Farm & Home Almanac*

10 The one thing that doesn't abide
by majority rule is a person's
conscience.

—HARPER LEE
To Kill a Mockingbird

11 The truth of the matter is that you
always know the right thing to do.
The hard part is doing it.

—GEN. H. NORMAN SCHWARZKOPF

12 To know what is right and not to
do it is the worst cowardice.

—CONFUCIUS

13 Self-discipline is when your conscience tells you to do something
and you don't talk back.

—W. K. HOPE

1 In matters of conscience, the law of majority has no place.
—MOHANDAS K. GANDHI

2 People who wrestle with their consciences usually go for two falls out of three.
—Los Angeles Times Syndicate

3 There is no pillow so soft as a clear conscience.
—FRENCH PROVERB

4 A long habit of not thinking a thing wrong gives it a superficial appearance of being right.
—THOMAS PAINE

5 A lot of people mistake a short memory for a clear conscience.
—DOUG LARSON

6 Many people feel "guilty" about things they shouldn't feel guilty about, in order to shut out feelings of guilt about things they should feel guilty about.
—SYDNEY J. HARRIS

7 A good conscience is a continual Christmas.
—BENJAMIN FRANKLIN

8 A man cannot be comfortable without his own approval.
—MARK TWAIN

WISDOM IS THE REWARD . . .

Wisdom is the reward you get for 9 a lifetime of listening when you'd have preferred to talk.
—DOUG LARSON

No man was ever wise by chance. 10
—SENECA

It requires wisdom to understand 11 wisdom; the music is nothing if the audience is deaf.
—WALTER LIPPMANN
A Preface to Morals

What we do not understand we 12 do not possess.
—JOHANN WOLFGANG VON GOETHE

One of the functions of intelli- 13 gence is to take account of the dangers that come from trusting solely to the intelligence.
—LEWIS MUMFORD

What the heart knows today, the 14 head will understand tomorrow.
—JAMES STEPHENS

Science at best is not wisdom; it is 15 knowledge. Wisdom is knowledge tempered with judgment.
—LORD RITCHIE-CALDER

Never mistake knowledge for wis- 16 dom. One helps you make a living; the other helps you make a life.
—SANDRA CAREY

1 "Next time I will . . ." "From now on I will . . ." What makes me think I am wiser today than I will be tomorrow?

—HUGH PRATHER

2 There is a great difference between knowing a thing and understanding it.

—CHARLES KETTERING WITH T. A. BOYD
Prophet of Progress

3 The day the child realizes that all adults are imperfect he becomes an adolescent; the day he forgives them, he becomes an adult; the day he forgives himself he becomes wise.

—ALDEN NOWLAN
Between Tears and Laughter

4 Everyone is a damn fool for at least five minutes every day. Wisdom consists in not exceeding the limit.

—ELBERT HUBBARD

5 Wisdom too often never comes, and so one ought not to reject it merely because it comes late.

—FELIX FRANKFURTER

6 The wise person questions himself, the fool others.

—HENRI ARNOLD

7 The most manifest sign of wisdom is continued cheerfulness.

—MONTAIGNE

8 The art of living consists in knowing which impulses to obey and which must be made to obey.

—SYDNEY J. HARRIS

9 Wisdom consists of the anticipation of consequences.

—NORMAN COUSINS
in *Saturday Review*

10 Wisdom is the quality that keeps you from getting into situations where you need it.

—DOUG LARSON

11 It is only with the heart that one can see rightly; what is essential is invisible to the eye.

—ANTOINE DE SAINT-EXUPÉRY
The Little Prince

12 The more a man knows, the more he forgives.

—CATHERINE THE GREAT

13 Keep me away from the wisdom which does not cry, the philosophy which does not laugh and the greatness which does not bow before children.

—KAHLIL GIBRAN

14 The best-educated human being is the one who understands most about the life in which he is placed.

—HELEN KELLER

1 It is easier to be wise for others than for ourselves.

—ALEKSANDR I. SOLZHENITSYN
The First Circle

2 People far prefer happiness to wisdom, but that is like wanting to be immortal without getting older.

—SYDNEY J. HARRIS

3 Learning sleeps and snores in libraries, but wisdom is everywhere, wide awake, on tiptoe.

—JOSH BILLINGS

4 Nothing in life is to be feared. It is only to be understood.

—MARIE CURIE

5 Discretion is knowing how to hide that which we cannot remedy.

—SPANISH PROVERB

THE FIRST SIGN OF MATURITY . . .

6 The first sign of maturity is the discovery that the volume knob also turns to the left.

—"SMILE" ZINGERS
in Chicago *Tribune*

7 Life begins as a quest of the child for the man and ends as a journey by the man to rediscover the child.

—LAURENS VAN DER POST
The Lost World of the Kalahari

8 A child becomes an adult when he realizes he has a right not only to be right but also to be wrong.

—THOMAS SZASZ
The Second Sin

9 Maturity is the ability to do a job whether or not you are supervised, to carry money without spending it and to bear an injustice without wanting to get even.

—ANN LANDERS

10 You are not mature until you expect the unexpected.

—Chicago *Tribune*

11 The young man knows the rules, but the old man knows the exceptions.

—OLIVER WENDELL HOLMES SR.

12 You're never too old to grow up.

—SHIRLEY CONRAN
Savages

13 You grow up the day you have your first real laugh—at yourself.

—ETHEL BARRYMORE

14 Age is a high price to pay for maturity.

—TOM STOPPARD

15 To exist is to change, to change is to mature, to mature is to go on creating oneself endlessly.

—HENRI BERGSON

1 Maturity begins when we're content to feel we're right about something without feeling the necessity to prove someone else wrong.

—SYDNEY J. HARRIS

2 Maturity is reached the day we don't need to be lied to about anything.

—FRANK YERBY

3 Maturity means reacquiring the seriousness one had as a child at play.

—FRIEDRICH NIETZSCHE

4 Youth is when you blame all your troubles on your parents; maturity is when you learn that everything is the fault of the younger generation.

—HAROLD COFFIN

As we grow old . . .

5 As we grow old, the beauty steals inward.

—RALPH WALDO EMERSON

6 How old would you be if you didn't know how old you was?

—SATCHEL PAIGE

7 Whatever a man's age may be, he can reduce it several years by putting a bright-colored flower in his buttonhole.

—MARK TWAIN

8 When it comes to staying young, a mind-lift beats a face-lift any day.

—MARTY BUCELLA
in *Woman* magazine

9 It's easier to have the vigor of youth when you're old than the wisdom of age when you're young.

—RICHARD J. NEEDHAM
*A Friend in Needham, or,
A Writer's Notebook*

10 Adults are obsolete children.

—DR. SEUSS

11 We all wear masks, and the time comes when we cannot remove them without removing some of our own skin.

—ANDRÉ BERTHIAUME
Contretemps

12 After a certain number of years, our faces become our biographies.

—CYNTHIA OZICK
The Paris Review

13 The mask, given time, comes to be the face itself.

—MARGUERITE YOURCENAR
Memoirs of Hadrian

14 The secret of staying young is to live honestly, eat slowly and just not think about your age.

—LUCILLE BALL

1 If youth only knew; if age only could.

—HENRI ESTIENNE

2 When the problem is not so much resisting temptation as finding it, you may just be getting older.

—*Los Angeles Times*

3 The person who says youth is a state of mind invariably has more state of mind than youth.

—*American Farm and Home Almanac*

4 If you carry your childhood with you, you never become older.

—ABRAHAM SUTZKEVER

5 Most people say that as you get old, you have to give up things. I think you get old because you give up things.

—SEN. THEODORE FRANCIS GREEN

6 You don't stop laughing because you grow old; you grow old because you stop laughing.

—MICHAEL PRITCHARD

7 We are only young once. That is all society can stand.

—BOB BOWEN

8 I've always believed in the adage that the secret of eternal youth is arrested development.

—ALICE ROOSEVELT LONGWORTH

9 The joy that is felt at the sight of new-fallen snow is inversely proportional to the age of the beholder.

—PAUL SWEENEY

10 Age does not protect you from love. But love, to some extent, protects you from age.

—JEANNE MOREAU

11 Age appears best in four things: old wood to burn, old wine to drink, old friends to trust and old authors to read.

—FRANCIS BACON

12 Growing up is usually so painful that people make comedies out of it to soften the memory.

—JOHN GREENWALD

13 Old age lives minutes slowly, hours quickly; childhood chews hours and swallows minutes.

—MALCOLM DE CHAZAL

14 When I no longer thrill to the first snow of the season, I'll know I'm growing old.

—LADY BIRD JOHNSON

15 Just remember, when you're over the hill, you begin to pick up speed.

—CHARLES SCHULZ

1 People are living longer than ever before, a phenomenon undoubtedly made necessary by the 30-year mortgage.

—DOUG LARSON

2 There is always some specific moment when we become aware that our youth is gone; but, years after, we know it was much later.

—MIGNON MCLAUGHLIN

3 It takes about ten years to get used to how old you are.

—Quoted by RAYMOND A. MICHEL
in *The Leaf*

4 Middle age is the time when a man is always thinking that in a week or two he will feel just as good as ever.

—DON MARQUIS

5 Middle age is the awkward period when Father Time starts catching up with Mother Nature.

—HAROLD COFFIN

6 Middle age is when you begin to wonder who put the quicksand into the hourglass of time.

—*The Orben Comedy Letter*

7 Midlife crisis is that moment when you realize your children and your clothes are about the same age.

—BILL TAMMEUS
in Kansas City *Star*

8 Youth is when you're allowed to stay up late on New Year's Eve. Middle age is when you're forced to.

—BILL VAUGHN

9 What most persons consider as virtue, after the age of 40 is simply a loss of energy.

—VOLTAIRE

10 I don't know what the big deal is about old age. Old people who shine from inside look 10 to 20 years younger.

—DOLLY PARTON
in *Ladies' Home Journal*

11 I have no romantic feelings about age. Either you are interesting at any age or you are not. There is nothing particularly interesting about being old—or being young, for that matter.

—KATHARINE HEPBURN

12 Old age is having too much room in the house and not enough in the medicine cabinet.

—Orben's Current Comedy

13 When grace is joined with wrinkles, it is adorable. There is an unspeakable dawn in happy old age.

—VICTOR HUGO

14 A young boy is a theory; an old man is a fact.

—ED HOWE

1 Never lose sight of the fact that old age needs so little but needs that little so much.
—Margaret Willour

2 The older I grow the more I distrust the familiar doctrine that age brings wisdom.
—H. L. Mencken
Prejudices

3 Wisdom doesn't necessarily come with age. Sometimes age just shows up all by itself.
—Tom Wilson

4 You can judge your age by the amount of pain you feel when you come in contact with a new idea.
—John Nuveen

5 Sometimes the child in one behaves a certain way and the rest of oneself follows behind, slowly shaking its head.
—James E. Shapiro
Meditations From the Breakdown Lane

6 The best thing about being young is, if you had to do it all over again, you would still have time.
—Sandra Clarke

7 If life were just, we would be born old and achieve youth about the time we'd saved enough to enjoy it.
—Jim Fiebig

8 Everybody has been young before, but not everybody has been old before.
—African proverb

9 You will stay young as long as you learn, form new habits and don't mind being contradicted.
—Marie von Ebner-Eschenbach

10 You are young at any age if you are planning for tomorrow.
—*The Sword of the Lord*

11 A grownup is a child with layers on.
—Woody Harrelson

12 When people tell you how young you look, they are also telling you how old you are.
—Cary Grant

13 To age with dignity and with courage cuts close to what it is to be a man.
—Roger Kahn

14 I speak truth, not so much as I would, but as much as I dare; and I dare a little the more, as I grow older.
—Montaigne

15 The older you get, the more important it is not to act your age.
—Ashleigh Brilliant

1 The trick is growing up without growing old.

—CASEY STENGEL

2 Growing older is not upsetting; being perceived as old is.

—KENNY ROGERS

3 The trouble with class reunions is that old flames have become even older.

—DOUG LARSON

4 A person is always startled when he hears himself seriously called an old man for the first time.

—OLIVER WENDELL HOLMES SR.

5 After thirty, a body has a mind of its own.

—BETTE MIDLER

6 We grow neither better nor worse as we grow old, but more like ourselves.

—MAY LAMBERTON BECKER

7 The best thing about growing older is that it takes such a long time.

—WALTERS KEMP

8 One advantage in growing older is that you can stand for more and fall for less.

—MONTA CRANE

9 The best birthdays of all are those that haven't arrived yet.

—ROBERT ORBEN

10 The older I grow, the more I listen to people who don't talk much.

—GERMAIN G. GLIDDEN

11 We've put more effort into helping folks reach old age than into helping them enjoy it.

—FRANK A. CLARK

MEMORY IS THE DIARY . . .

12 Memory is the diary we all carry about with us.

—OSCAR WILDE

13 Count reminiscences like money.

—CARL SANDBURG

14 It's surprising how much of memory is built around things unnoticed at the time.

—BARBARA KINGSOLVER
Animal Dreams

15 We do not remember days; we remember moments.

—CESARE PAVESE
The Burning Brand

16 The moment may be temporary, but the memory is forever.

—BUD MEYER

1 Don't brood on what's past, but never forget it either.

—THOMAS H. RADDALL

2 Recall it as often as you wish, a happy memory never wears out.

LIBBIE FUDIM

3 Each of us is the accumulation of our memories.

—ALAN LOY MCGINNIS
The Romance Factor

4 One form of loneliness is to have a memory and no one to share it with.

—PHYLLIS ROSE
in *Hers: Through Women's Eyes*

5 Memories are the key not to the past, but to the future.

—CORRIE TEN BOOM WITH
JOHN AND ELIZABETH SHERRILL
The Hiding Place

6 May you look back on the past with as much pleasure as you look forward to the future.

—Quoted by PAUL DICKSON in *Toasts*

7 Keep some souvenirs of your past, or how will you ever prove it wasn't all a dream?

—ASHLEIGH BRILLIANT

8 To live without a memory is to live alone.

—GILLES MARCOTTE

There is no fence or hedge round 9 time that has gone. You can go back and have what you like if you remember it well enough.

—RICHARD LLEWELLYN
How Green Was My Valley

Everybody needs his memories. 10 They keep the wolf of insignificance from the door.

—SAUL BELLOW

Each day of our lives we make 11 deposits in the memory banks of our children.

—CHARLES R. SWINDOLL
The Strong Family

You never know when you're 12 making a memory.

—RICKIE LEE JONES
"Young Blood"

Our memories are card indexes— 13 consulted, and then put back in disorder, by authorities whom we do not control.

—CYRIL CONNOLLY

What is memory? Not a storehouse, 14 not a trunk in the attic, but an instrument that constantly refines the past into a narrative, accessible and acceptable to oneself.

—STANLEY KAUFFMANN
The New Republic

1 Memory is a child walking along a seashore. You never can tell what small pebble it will pick up and store away among its treasured things.

—PIERCE HARRIS
Atlanta Journal

2 I'm always fascinated by the way memory diffuses fact.

—DIANE SAWYER
in *TV Guide*

3 When I was younger, I could remember anything, whether it had happened or not.

—MARK TWAIN

4 You can close your eyes to reality but not to memories.

—STANISLAW J. LEC
Unkempt Thoughts

5 There are times when forgetting can be just as important as remembering—and even more difficult.

—HARRY AND JOAN MIER
Happiness Begins Before Breakfast

6 Remembering is a dream that comes in waves.

—HELGA SANDBUR
". . . Where Love Begins"

7 Memory is a complicated thing, a relative to truth, but not its twin.

—BARBARA KINGSOLVER
Animal Dreams

8 Recollection is the only paradise from which we cannot be turned out.

—JEAN PAUL RICHTER

9 The true tomb of the dead is the heart of the living.

—JEAN COCTEAU

10 There is something terrible yet soothing about returning to a place where you once lived. You are one of your own memories.

—MARY MORRIS
Crossroads

11 Some folks never exaggerate— they just remember big.

—AUDREY SNEAD

12 The older a man gets, the farther he had to walk to school as a boy.

—*Commercial Appeal*
(Danville, Virginia)

13 God gave us our memories so that we might have roses in December.

—JAMES M. BARRIE

14 No memory is ever alone; it's at the end of a trail of memories, a dozen trails that each have their own associations.

—LOUIS L'AMOUR
Ride the River

IF YOU'RE YEARNING FOR THE GOOD OLD DAYS . . .

1 If you're yearning for the good old days, just turn off the air conditioning.

> —GRIFF NIBLACK
> in Indianapolis *News*

2 We have all got our "good old days" tucked away inside our hearts, and we return to them in dreams like cats to favorite armchairs.

> —BRIAN CARTER
> *Where The Dream Begins*

3 Things ain't what they used to be and probably never was.

> —WILL ROGERS

4 Nostalgia is a file that removes the rough edges from the good old days.

> —DOUG LARSON

5 In the old days, when things got rough, what you did was without.

> —BILL COPELAND

6 Nostalgia is like a grammar lesson: you find the present tense and the past perfect.

> —*The United Church Observer*

7 The essence of nostalgia is an awareness that what has been will never be again.

> —MILTON S. EISENHOWER
> *The Wine Is Bitter*

8 There has never been an age that did not applaud the past and lament the present.

> —LILLIAN EICHLER WATSON
> *Light from Many Lamps*

9 Nothing seems to go as far as it did. Even nostalgia doesn't reach back as far as it used to.

> —*Changing Times*

10 You can clutch the past so tightly to your chest that it leaves your arms too full to embrace the present.

> —JAN GLIDEWELL
> in St. Petersburg *Times*

11 A trip to nostalgia now and then is good for the spirit, as long as you don't set up housekeeping.

> —DAN BARTOLOVIC
> KPUG-KNWR, Bellingham, Wasington.

12 The past should be a springboard, not a hammock.

> —IVERN BALL

13 The older you get, the greater you were.

> —LEE GROSSCUP

PEOPLE TOGETHER

It's the things in common that make relationships enjoyable, but it's the little differences that make them interesting.

—TODD RUTHMAN

HOME IS A PLACE . . .

1 Home is a place you grow up wanting to leave, and grow old wanting to get back to.

—JOHN ED PEARCE
in Louisville *Courier-Journal Magazine*

2 The fireside is the tulip bed of a winter day.

—PERSIAN PROVERB

3 The home is not the one tame place in the world of adventure. It is the one wild place in the world of rules and set tasks.

—G. K. CHESTERTON

4 One of the oldest human needs is having someone to wonder where you are when you don't come home at night.

—MARGARET MEAD

5 The strength of a nation derives from the integrity of the home.

—CONFUCIUS

6 Where we love is home—home that our feet may leave, but not our hearts.

—OLIVER WENDELL HOLMES SR.

7 Where is home? Home is where the heart can laugh without shyness. Home is where the heart's tears can dry at their own pace.

—VERNON G. BAKER
in *Courant* (Hartford, Connecticut)

My home is here. I feel just as 8 at home overseas, but I think my roots are here and my language is here and my rage is here and my hope is here. You know where your home is because you've been there long enough. You know all the peculiarities of the people around you, because you are one of them. And naturally, memories are the most important. Your home is where your favorite memories are.

—PIETER-DIRK UYS

A child on a farm sees a plane fly 9 overhead and dreams of a faraway place. A traveler on the plane sees the farmhouse . . . and dreams of home.

—CARL BURNS
The Drug Shop

When you finally go back to your 10 old hometown, you find it wasn't the old home you missed but your childhood.

—SAM EWING
in *National Enquirer*

The reality of any place is what its 11 people remember of it.

—CHARLES KURALT
North Carolina Is My Home

A small town is a place where 12 there is little to see or do, but what you hear makes up for it.

—IVERN BALL

1 A small town is a place where everyone knows whose check is good and whose husband is not.

—SID ASCHER

2 A place is yours when you know where all the roads go.

—Quoted by STEPHEN KING in *Down East*

3 There's nothing people like better than being asked an easy question. For some reason, we're flattered when a stranger asks us where Maple Street is in our hometown and we can tell him.

—ANDREW A. ROONEY
And More by Andy Rooney

4 A man travels the world over in search of what he needs and returns home to find it.

—GEORGE MOORE

5 Visitors should behave in such a way that the host and hostess feel at home.

—J. S. FARYNSKI

A TRUE FRIEND . . .

6 A true friend is one who overlooks your failures and tolerates your successes.

—DOUG LARSON

7 One does not make friends. One recognizes them.

—GARTH HENRICHS

8 In prosperity, our friends know us; in adversity, we know our friends.

—JOHN CHURTON COLLINS

9 Strangers are friends that you have yet to meet.

—ROBERTA LIEBERMAN

10 Lots of people want to ride with you in the limo, but what you want is someone who will take the bus with you when the limo breaks down.

—OPRAH WINFREY

11 I value the friend who for me finds time on his calendar, but I cherish the friend who for me does not consult his calendar.

—ROBERT BRAULT

12 It may be true that a touch of indifference is the safest foundation on which to build a lasting and delicate friendship.

—W. ROBERTSON NICOLL
People and Books

13 Getting people to like you is only the other side of liking them.

—NORMAN VINCENT PEALE

14 It's the things in common that make relationships enjoyable, but it's the little differences that make them interesting.

—TODD RUTHMAN

1 The only way to have a friend is to be one.
—RALPH WALDO EMERSON

2 Be slow in choosing a friend, slower in changing.
—BENJAMIN FRANKLIN

3 Don't make friends who are comfortable to be with. Make friends who will force you to lever yourself up.
—THOMAS J. WATSON SR.

4 The bird a nest, the spider a web, man friendship.
—WILLIAM BLAKE

5 True friendship is a plant of slow growth.
—GEORGE WASHINGTON

6 It takes a long time to grow an old friend.
—JOHN LEONARD
in *Friends and Friends of Friends* by Bernard Pierre Wolff

7 The most called-upon prerequisite of a friend is an accessible ear.
—MAYA ANGELOU
The Heart of a Woman

8 Men kick friendship around like a football, but it doesn't seem to crack. Women treat it like glass and it goes to pieces.
—ANNE MORROW LINDBERGH

9 Could we see when and where we are to meet again, we would be more tender when we bid our friends good-by.
—MARIE LOUISE DE LA RAMÉE

10 Friends are relatives you make for yourself.
—EUSTACHE DESCHAMPS

11 The golden rule of friendship is to listen to others as you would have them listen to you.
—DAVID AUGSBURGER

12 You can make more friends in a month by being interested in them than in ten years by trying to get them interested in you.
—CHARLES L. ALLEN
Roads to Radiant Living

13 We need old friends to help us grow old and new friends to help us stay young.
—LETTY COTTIN POGREBIN
Among Friends

14 If you want an accounting of your worth, count your friends.
—MERRY BROWNE
in *National Enquirer*

15 My friends are my estate. Forgive me then the avarice to hoard them!
—EMILY DICKINSON

1 Friendship is a single soul dwelling in two bodies.
—ARISTOTLE

2 In my friend, I find a second self.
—ISABEL NORTON

3 No man is the whole of himself; his friends are the rest of him.
—HARRY EMERSON FOSDICK

4 Friendships multiply joys and divide griefs.
—H. G. BOHN

5 A friend is someone you can do nothing with, and enjoy it.
—The Optimist Magazine

6 We cherish our friends not for their ability to amuse us, but for our ability to amuse them.
—EVELYN WAUGH

7 A loyal friend laughs at your jokes when they're not so good, and sympathizes with your problems when they're not so bad.
—ARNOLD H. GLASOW
in The Wall Street Journal

8 How rare and wonderful is that flash of a moment when we realize we have discovered a friend.
—WILLIAM ROTSLER

9 To a friend's house, the road is never long.
—ANONYMOUS

10 A friend hears the song in my heart and sings it to me when my memory fails.
—Pioneer Girls Leaders' Handbook

11 True friendship is like phosphorescence—it glows best when the world around you goes dark.
—DENISE MARTIN

12 The proper office of a friend is to side with you when you are in the wrong. Nearly anybody will side with you when you are right.
—MARK TWAIN

13 A true friend never gets in your way unless you happen to be going down.
—ARNOLD H. GLASOW

14 It is important for our friends to believe that we are unreservedly frank with them, and important to friendship that we are not.
—MIGNON MCLAUGHLIN
The Neurotic's Notebook

15 The surest way to lose a friend is to tell him something for his own good.
—SID ASCHER

16 If it's painful for you to criticize your friends, you're safe in doing it; if you take the slightest pleasure in it, that's the time to hold your tongue.
—ALICE DUER MILLER

1 Only your real friends will tell you when your face is dirty.

—SICILIAN PROVERB

2 A friend is a lot of things, but a critic he isn't.

—BERN WILLIAMS

3 A friend is someone who can see through you and still enjoys the show.

—*Farmers Almanac*

4 Friends are those rare people who ask how we are and then wait to hear the answer.

—ED CUNNINGHAM

5 The most beautiful discovery true friends make is that they can grow separately without growing apart.

—ELISABETH FOLEY

6 Some of the most rewarding and beautiful moments of a friendship happen in the unforeseen open spaces between planned activities. It is important that you allow these spaces to exist.

—CHRISTINE LEEFELDT AND ERNEST CALLENBACH
The Art of Friendship

7 We love those who know the worst of us and don't turn their faces away.

—WALKER PERCY
Love in the Ruins

8 No man can be called friendless when he has God and the companionship of good books.

—ELIZABETH BARRETT BROWNING

9 An enemy who tells the truth contributes infinitely more to our improvement than a friend who deludes us.

—LOUIS-N. FORTIN
Pensées, Proverbes, Maximes

10 It pays to know the enemy—not least because at some time you may have the opportunity to turn him into a friend.

—MARGARET THATCHER
Downing Street Years

11 Pay attention to your enemies, for they are the first to discover your mistakes.

—ANTISTHENES

12 A friend is someone who makes me feel totally acceptable.

—ENE RIISNA

13 The best mirror is a friend's eye.

—GAELIC PROVERB

THE BEST HELPING HAND . . .

14 Sometimes the best helping hand you can get is a good, firm push.

—JOANN THOMAS

1 What do we live for if it is not to make life less difficult for each other?

—George Eliot

2 Whoever is spared personal pain must feel himself called to help in diminishing the pain of others.

—Albert Schweitzer
Memoirs of Childhood and Youth

3 Be not forgetful to entertain strangers: for thereby some have entertained angels unawares.

—Hebrews 13:2

4 No one is useless in this world who lightens the burden of it for anyone else.

—Charles Dickens

5 Great opportunities to help others seldom come, but small ones surround us every day.

—Sally Koch
in *Wisconsin*

6 I have always held firmly to the thought that each one of us can do a little to bring some portion of misery to an end.

—Albert Schweitzer

7 We ourselves feel that what we are doing is just a drop in the ocean. But the ocean would be less because of that missing drop.

—Mother Teresa of Calcutta

8 It is well to give when asked, but it is better to give unasked, through understanding.

—Kahlil Gibran
The Prophet

9 He who helps early helps twice.

—Tadeusz Mazowiecki

10 Expect people to be better than they are; it helps them to become better. But don't be disappointed when they are not; it helps them to keep trying.

—Merry Browne
in *National Enquirer*

11 You may give gifts without caring—but you can't care without giving.

—Frank A. Clark

12 Never hesitate to hold out your hand; never hesitate to accept the outstretched hand of another.

—Pope John XXIII

13 It is one of the beautiful compensations of this life that no one can sincerely try to help another without helping himself.

—Charles Dudley Warner

14 We love those people who give with humility, or who accept with ease.

—Freya Stark
Perseus in the Wind

1 Basically, the only thing we need is a hand that rests on our own, that wishes it well, that sometimes guides us.

—HECTOR BIANCIOTTI
Sans La Misericorde du Christ

2 Extending your hand is extending yourself.

—ROD MCKUEN
Book of Days

3 The miracle is this—the more we share, the more we have.

—LEONARD NIMOY

4 To ease another's heartache is to forget one's own.

—ABRAHAM LINCOLN

5 The more sympathy you give, the less you need.

—MALCOLM S. FORBES
in *Forbes* magazine

6 He is not an honest man who has burned his tongue and does not tell the company that the soup is hot.

—YUGOSLAV PROVERB

7 Honesty is stronger medicine than sympathy, which may console but often conceals.

—GRETEL EHRLICH

8 Correction does much, but encouragement does more.

—JOHANN WOLFGANG VON GOETHE

9 Money-giving is a good criterion of a person's mental health. Generous people are rarely mentally ill people.

—DR. KARL MENNINGER

10 The impersonal hand of government can never replace the helping hand of a neighbor.

—HUBERT H. HUMPHREY

11 You can't get rid of poverty by giving people money.

—P. J. O'ROURKE
A Parliament of Whores

12 We'd all like a reputation for generosity, and we'd all like to buy it cheap.

—MIGNON MCLAUGHLIN

13 The greatest pleasure I know is to do a good action by stealth and have it found out by accident.

—CHARLES LAMB

14 Real charity doesn't care if it's tax-deductible or not.

—DAN BENNETT

15 Criticism, like rain, should be gentle enough to nourish a man's growth without destroying his roots.

—FRANK A. CLARK

16 Nobody wants constructive criticism. It's all we can do to put up with constructive praise.

—MIGNON MCLAUGHLIN

1 The greatest good you can do for another is not just to share your riches but to reveal to him his own.

—BENJAMIN DISRAELI

2 The pleasure we derive from doing favors is partly in the feeling it gives us that we are not altogether worthless.

—ERIC HOFFER

3 Deceiving someone for his own good is a responsibility that should be shouldered only by the gods.

—HENRY S. HASKINS

4 Life's unfairness is not irrevocable; we can help balance the scales for others, if not always for ourselves.

—HUBERT H. HUMPHREY

5 We ought to be careful not to do for a fellow what we only intended to help him do.

—FRANK A. CLARK

6 The more help a person has in his garden, the less it belongs to him.

—WILLIAM H. DAVIS

7 The difference between a helping hand and an outstretched palm is a twist of the wrist.

—LAURENCE LEAMER
King of the Night

Few things help an individual more than to place responsibility upon him and to let him know that you trust him. 8

—BOOKER T. WASHINGTON

Do not free a camel of the burden of his hump; you may be freeing him from being a camel. 9

—G. K. CHESTERTON

No matter what accomplishments you achieve, somebody helps you. 10

—ALTHEA GIBSON

Do not commit the error, common among the young, of assuming that if you cannot save the whole of mankind you have failed. 11

—JAN DE HARTOG
The Lamb's War

If you can't feed a hundred people, then feed just one. 12

—MOTHER TERESA OF CALCUTTA

From what we get, we can make a living; what we give, however, makes a life. 13

—ARTHUR ASHE
Days of Grace

No person was ever honored for what he received. Honor has been the reward for what he gave. 14

—CALVIN COOLIDGE

1 The dead take to the grave, clutched in their hands, only what they have given away.

—DeWitt Wallace

2 The only things we ever keep are what we give away.

—Louis Ginsberg
The Everlasting Minute and Other Lyrics

3 The fragrance always stays in the hand that gives the rose.

—Hada Bejar

Love doesn't just sit there . . .

4 Love doesn't just sit there, like a stone; it has to be made, like bread, remade all the time, made new.

—Ursula K. LeGuin
The Lathe of Heaven

5 In our life there is a single color, as on an artist's palette, which provides the meaning of life and art. It is the color of love.

—Marc Chagall
Chagall

6 True love begins when nothing is looked for in return.

—Antoine de Saint-Exupéry
The Wisdom of the Sands

7 At the touch of love, everyone becomes a poet.

—Plato

8 This is the true measure of love: when we believe that we alone can love, that no one could ever have loved so before us, and that no one will ever love in the same way after us.

—Johann Wolfgang von Goethe

9 Love does not consist in gazing at each other, but in looking outward together in the same direction.

—Antoine de Saint-Exupéry

10 In the coldest February, as in every other month in every other year, the best thing to hold on to in this world is each other.

—Linda Ellerbee
Move On: Adventures in the Real World

11 Only discretion allows intimacy, which depends on shared reticence, on what is not said— unsolvable things that would leave the other person ill at ease.

—Hector Bianciotti
Sans La Misericorde Du Christ

12 We don't believe in rheumatism and true love until after the first attack.

—Marie von Ebner-Eschenbach

13 As soon go kindle fire with snow, as seek to quench the fire of love with words.

—William Shakespeare

1 I kissed my first woman and smoked my first cigarette on the same day. I have never had time for tobacco since.

—ARTURO TOSCANINI

2 All our loves are first loves.

—SUSAN FROMBERG
Schaeffer, Mainland

3 Two things only a man cannot hide: that he is drunk and that he is in love.

—ANTIPHANES

4 Is it not strange that love, so fickle, is ranked above friendship, almost always so worthy?

—GABRIELLE ROY
La Detresse et L'enchantement

5 Love is a game that two can play and both win.

—EVA GABOR

6 The giving of love is an education in itself.

—ELEANOR ROOSEVELT

7 We English have sex on the brain, which is not the most satisfactory place for it.

—MALCOLM MUGGERIDGE
in *The Observer* (London)

8 So many catastrophes in love are only accidents of egotism.

—HECTOR BIANCIOTTI
Sans La Misericorde Du Christ

9 Sometimes I wonder if men and women really suit each other. Perhaps they should live next door and just visit now and then.

—KATHARINE HEPBURN

10 You can't put a price tag on love, but you can on all its accessories.

—MELANIE CLARK

11 It is possible that blondes also prefer gentlemen.

—MAMIE VAN DOREN

12 Love is like quicksilver in the hand. Leave the fingers open, and it stays. Clutch it, and it darts away.

—DOROTHY PARKER

13 In true love the smallest distance is too great, and the greatest distance can be bridged.

—HANS NOUWENS

14 Love letters are the campaign promises of the heart.

—ROBERT FRIEDMAN

15 Only love can be divided endlessly and still not diminish.

—ANNE MORROW LINDBERGH

16 Love and time—those are the only two things in all the world and all of life that cannot be bought, but only spent.

—GARY JENNINGS
Aztec

1 It's easy to halve the potato where there's love.

—IRISH PROVERB

2 So long as we love we serve; so long as we are loved by others, I would almost say that we are indispensable.

—ROBERT LOUIS STEVENSON

3 The best proof of love is trust.

—JOYCE BROTHERS

4 Love is proud of itself. It leaks out of us even with the tightest security.

—MERRIT MALLOY
Things I Meant to Say to You When We Were Old

5 Let there be spaces in your togetherness / And let the winds of the heavens dance between you.

—KAHLIL GIBRAN

6 Familiarity, truly cultivated, can breed love.

—JOYCE BROTHERS

7 Love is what you've been through with somebody.

—Quoted by JAMES THURBER in *Life*

8 Love is a fruit in season at all times, and within the reach of every hand.

—MOTHER TERESA OF CALCUTTA

9 Love is an image of God, and not a lifeless image, but the living essence of the all divine nature which beams full of all goodness.

—MARTIN LUTHER

10 Where there is great love, there are always miracles.

—WILLA CATHER
Death Comes for the Archbishop

11 The Bible tells us to love our neighbors, and also to love our enemies; probably because they are generally the same people.

—G. K. CHESTERTON

12 No disguise can long conceal love where it is, nor feign it where it is not.

—FRANÇOIS DE LA ROCHEFOUCAULD

13 We are shaped and fashioned by what we love.

—JOHANN WOLFGANG VON GOETHE

14 Him that I love, I wish to be free—even from me.

—ANNE MORROW LINDBERGH

15 No one worth possessing can be quite possessed.

—SARA TEASDALE

16 The ultimate test of a relationship is to disagree but to hold hands.

—Quoted by ALEXANDRA PENNEY in *Self*

1 The love of our neighbor in all its fullness simply means being able to say to him: "What are you going through?"

—SIMONE WEIL
Waiting for God

2 The worst prison would be a closed heart.

—POPE JOHN PAUL II

3 I love you, not only for what you are, but for what I am when I am with you.

—ROY CROFT

4 Tell me whom you love, and I'll tell you who you are.

—CREOLE PROVERB

5 Love at first sight is easy to understand. It's when two people have been looking at each other for years that it becomes a miracle.

—SAM LEVENSON

6 Love is not measured by how many times you touch each other but by how many times you reach each other.

—CATHY MORANCY

7 Nobody has ever measured, even the poets, how much a heart can hold.

—ZELDA FITZGERALD

8 Love is a great beautifier.

—LOUISA MAY ALCOTT

9 The purest affection the heart can hold is the honest love of a nine-year-old.

—HOLMAN F. DAY
Up in Maine

10 If only one could tell true love from false love as one can tell mushrooms from toadstools.

—KATHERINE MANSFIELD

11 Four be the things I'd have been better without: love, curiosity, freckles and doubt.

—DOROTHY PARKER

12 It is often hard to bear the tears that we ourselves have caused.
—*The Maxims of MARCEL PROUST*

13 Never close your lips to those to whom you have opened your heart.

—CHARLES DICKENS

14 To love and be loved is to feel the sun from both sides.
—DAVID VISCOTT, MD
How to Live With Another Person

15 Seek not every quality in one individual.

—CONFUCIUS

16 Love doesn't make the world go round. Love is what makes the ride worthwhile.

—FRANKLIN P. JONES

1 When one loves somebody, everything is clear—where to go, what to do—it all takes care of itself and one doesn't have to ask anybody about anything.

—MAXIM GORKY
The Zykovs

2 Love is like a violin. The music may stop now and then, but the strings remain forever.

—JUNE MASTERS BACHER
Diary of a Loving Heart

3 Love is an act of faith, and whoever is of little faith is also of little love.

—ERICH FROMM

4 Love endures only when the lovers love many things together and not merely each other.

—WALTER LIPPMANN

5 When a woman says, "Ah, I could love you if . . ."—fear not, she already loves you.

—WALTER PULITZER

6 A woman can say more in a sigh than a man can say in a sermon.

—ARNOLD HAULTAIN
Colombo's Canadian Quotations

7 We love because it's the only true adventure.

—NIKKI GIOVANNI

8 Love can achieve unexpected majesty in the rocky soil of misfortune.

—TONY SNOW
in Detroit *News*

9 Love is the magician that pulls man out of his own hat.

—BEN HECHT

10 There is no surprise more magical than the surprise of being loved. It is God's finger on man's shoulder.

—CHARLES MORGAN
The Fountain

11 To love is to admire with the heart; to admire is to love with the mind.

—THÉOPHILE GAUTIER

12 What the world really needs is more love and less paper work.

—PEARL BAILEY

13 Never look for a worm in the apple of your eye.

—LANGSTON HUGHES

14 Anything will give up its secrets if you love it enough.

—GEORGE WASHINGTON CARVER

15 Love talked about can be easily turned aside, but love demonstrated is irresistible.

—W. STANLEY MOONEYHAM
Come Walk the World

1 The whole worth of a kind deed lies in the love that inspires it.

—THE TALMUD

2 A baby is born with a need to be loved—and never outgrows it.

—FRANK A. CLARK

3 I have enjoyed the happiness of the world; I have loved.

—SCHILLER

A MARRIED COUPLE . . .

4 A married couple that plays cards together is just a fight that hasn't started yet.

—GEORGE BURNS
Gracie: A Love Story

5 Marriage resembles a pair of shears, so joined that they cannot be separated; often moving in opposite directions, yet always punishing anyone who comes between them.

—SYDNEY SMITH

6 It isn't tying himself to one woman that a man dreads when he thinks of marrying; it's separating himself from all the others.

—HELEN ROWLAND
Violets and Vinegar

7 Marriage should be a duet—when one sings, the other claps.

—JOE MURRAY

8 The value of marriage is not that adults produce children, but that children produce adults.

—PETER DE VRIES
The Tunnel of Love

9 Whoever thinks marriage is a 50–50 proposition doesn't know the half of it.

—FRANKLIN P. JONES
in *Quote Magazine*

10 A marriage without conflicts is almost as inconceivable as a nation without crises.

—ANDRÉ MAUROIS
The Art of Living

11 A happy home is one in which each spouse grants the possibility that the other may be right, though neither believes it.

—DON FRASER

12 More marriages might survive if the partners realized that sometimes the better comes after the worse.

—DOUG LARSON

13 One advantage of marriage is that, when you fall out of love with him or he falls out of love with you, it keeps you together until you fall in again.

—JUDITH VIORST
in *Redbook*

1 Marriage is a covered dish.
—SWISS PROVERB

2 Love, honor and negotiate.
—ALAN LOY MCGINNIS
The Romance Factor

3 Almost no one is foolish enough to imagine that he automatically deserves great success in any field of activity; yet almost everyone believes that he automatically deserves success in marriage.
—SYDNEY J. HARRIS

4 Marriage has teeth, and him bite very hot.
—JAMAICAN PROVERB

5 Getting married is easy. Staying married is more difficult. Staying happily married for a lifetime should rank among the fine arts.
—ROBERTA FLACK

6 Marriage is like vitamins: we supplement each other's minimum daily requirements.
—KATHY MOHNKE

7 Never marry for money. Ye'll borrow it cheaper.
—SCOTTISH PROVERB

8 A wedding anniversary is the celebration of love, trust, partnership, tolerance and tenacity. The order varies for any given year.
—PAUL SWEENEY

9 A good marriage is like an incredible retirement fund. You put everything you have into it during your productive life, and over the years it turns from silver to gold to platinum.
—WILLARD SCOTT
The Joy of Living

10 In every marriage more than a week old, there are grounds for divorce. The trick is to find, and continue to find, grounds for marriage.
—ROBERT ANDERSON
Solitaire & Double Solitaire

11 If you made a list of reasons why any couple got married, and another list of the reasons for their divorce, you'd have a lot of overlapping.
—MIGNON MCLAUGHLIN

12 The concept of two people living together for 25 years without a serious dispute suggests a lack of spirit only to be admired in sheep.
—A. P. HERBERT

13 Story writers say that love is concerned only with young people, and the excitement and glamour of romance end at the altar. How blind they are. The best romance is inside marriage; the finest love stories come after the wedding, not before.
—IRVING STONE

1 It takes a loose rein to keep a marriage tight.

—JOHN STEVENSON

2 The great thing about marriage is that it enables one to be alone without feeling loneliness.

—GERALD BRENAN
Thoughts in a Dry Season

3 A happy marriage is the world's best bargain.

—O. A. BATTISTA

4 Marrying for love may be a bit risky, but it is so honest that God can't help but smile on it.

—JOSH BILLINGS

5 The particular charm of marriage is the duologue, the permanent conversation between two people who talk over everything and everyone.

—CYRIL CONNOLLY
The Unquiet Grave

6 In marriage, being the right person is as important as finding the right person.

—WILBERT DONALD GOUGH

7 In a successful marriage, there is no such thing as one's way. There is only the way of both, only the bumpy, dusty, difficult, but always mutual path.

—PHYLLIS McGINLEY
The Province of the Heart

8 Chains do not hold a marriage together. It is threads, hundreds of tiny threads, which sew people together through the years.

—SIMONE SIGNORET

9 All that a husband or wife really wants is to be pitied a little, praised a little, appreciated a little.

—OLIVER GOLDSMITH

10 Marriage should, I think, always be a little hard and new and strange. It should be breaking your shell and going into another world, and a bigger one.

—ANNE MORROW LINDBERGH

11 A happy marriage is a long conversation that always seems too short.

—ANDRÉ MAUROIS
Memoires

12 The difference between courtship and marriage is the difference between the pictures in a seed catalogue and what comes up.

—JAMES WHARTON

13 The greatest of all arts is the art of living together.

—WILLIAM LYON PHELPS
Marriage

14 A sound marriage is not based on complete frankness; it is based on a sensible reticence.

—MORRIS L. ERNST

1 A successful marriage requires falling in love many times, always with the same person.

—MIGNON MCLAUGHLIN
in *The Atlantic*

2 You don't marry one person; you marry three: the person you think they are, the person they are, and the person they are going to become as the result of being married to you.

—RICHARD NEEDHAM
You and All the Rest

3 Marriage is like twirling a baton, turning handsprings or eating with chopsticks. It looks easy until you try it.

—HELEN ROWLAND

4 The goal in marriage is not to think alike, but to think together.

—ROBERT C. DODDS

5 Married life teaches one invaluable lesson: to think of things far enough ahead not to say them.

—JEFFERSON MACHAMER

6 The marriages we regard as the happiest are those in which each of the partners believes that he or she got the best of it.

—SYDNEY J. HARRIS

7 Matrimony is the only game of chance the clergy favor.

—EMILY FERGUSON MURPHY

Nobody will ever win the battle of 8 the sexes. There's too much fraternizing with the enemy.

—HENRY KISSINGER

THE GREAT GIFT OF FAMILY LIFE . . .

The great gift of family life is to 9 be intimately acquainted with people you might never even introduce yourself to, had life not done it for you.

—KENDALL HAILEY
The Day I Became an Autodidact

A family vacation is one where you arrive with five bags, four 10 kids and seven I-thought-you-packed-its.

—IVERN BALL

Family faces are magic mirrors. 11 Looking at people who belong to us, we see the past, present and future. We make discoveries about ourselves.

—GAIL LUMET BUCKLEY
The Hornes: An American Family

Parentage is a very important pro- 12 fession; but no test of fitness for it is ever imposed in the interest of the children.

—BERNARD SHAW
Everybody's Political What's What?

1 A happy family is but an earlier heaven.

—JOHN BOWRING

2 Other things may change us, but we start and end with family.

—ANTHONY BRANDT
in *Esquire*

3 No matter how many communes anybody invents, the family always creeps back.

—MARGARET MEAD

4 Heredity is what sets the parents of a teenager wondering about each other.

—LAURENCE J. PETER
Peter's Quotations

5 Heredity is a splendid phenomenon that relieves us of responsibility for our shortcomings.

—DOUG LARSON

6 Adolescence is perhaps nature's way of preparing parents to welcome the empty nest.

—KAREN SAVAGE AND PATRICIA ADAMS
The Good Stepmother

7 Few things are more satisfying than seeing your children have teenagers of their own.

—DOUG LARSON

8 Even a family tree has to have some sap.

—Los Angeles Times Syndicate

9 Oh, to be only half as wonderful as my child thought I was when he was small, and only half as stupid as my teenager now thinks I am.

—REBECCA RICHARDS

10 We never know the love of the parent until we become parents ourselves.

—HENRY WARD BEECHER

11 He that has no fools, knaves nor beggars in his family was begot by a flash of lightning.

—THOMAS FULLER

12 If you don't believe in ghosts, you've never been to a family reunion.

—ASHLEIGH BRILLIANT

13 Before most people start boasting about their family tree, they usually do a good pruning job.

—O. A. BATTISTA

14 There is no king who has not had a slave among his ancestors, and no slave who has not had a king among his.

—HELEN KELLER

15 The family fireside is the best of schools.

—ARNOLD H. GLASOW

1 Making the decision to have a child—it's momentous. It is to decide forever to have your heart go walking around outside your body.

—ELIZABETH STONE

2 When you are a mother, you are never really alone in your thoughts. A mother always has to think twice, once for herself and once for her child.

—SOPHIA LOREN
Women and Beauty

3 Mothers are the most instinctive philosophers.

—HARRIET BEECHER STOWE

4 Instant availability without continuous presence is probably the best role a mother can play.

—LOTTE BAILYN
The Woman in America

5 The three most beautiful sights: a potato garden in bloom, a ship in sail, a woman after the birth of her child.

—IRISH PROVERB

6 Every parent is at some time the father of the unreturned prodigal, with nothing to do but keep his house open to hope.

—JOHN CIARDI

7 You never get over being a child, long as you have a mother to go to.

—SARAH ORNE JEWETT

8 A good father is a little bit of a mother.

—LEE SALK

9 The most important thing a father can do for his children is to love their mother.

—THEODORE HESBURGH

10 One father is more than a hundred schoolmasters.

—GEORGE HERBERT

11 My father didn't tell me how to live; he lived, and let me watch him do it.

—CLARENCE BUDINGTON KELLAND

12 You don't raise heroes; you raise sons. And if you treat them like sons, they'll turn out to be heroes, even if it's just in your own eyes.

—WALTER SCHIRRA SR.

13 The beauty of "spacing" children many years apart lies in the fact that parents have time to learn the mistakes that were made with the older ones—which permits them to make exactly the opposite mistakes with the younger ones.

—SYDNEY J. HARRIS

1 The thorn from the bush one has planted, nourished and pruned, pricks most deeply and draws more blood.

—MAYA ANGELOU
All God's Children Need Traveling Shoes

2 It doesn't matter who my father was; it matters who I remember he was.

—ANNE SEXTON

3 Parenthood remains the greatest single preserve of the amateur.

—ALVIN TOFFLER
Future Shock

4 The word no carries a lot more meaning when spoken by a parent who also knows how to say yes.

—JOYCE MAYNARD
in *Parenting*

5 Lucky parents who have fine children usually have lucky children who have fine parents.

—JAMES A. BREWER

6 Grandchildren are God's way of compensating us for growing old.

—MARY H. WALDRIP

7 Few things are more delightful than grandchildren fighting over your lap.

—DOUG LARSON

8 A grandmother is a person with too much wisdom to let that stop her from making a fool of herself over her grandchildren.

—PHIL MOSS
in *National Enquirer*

9 I have often thought what a melancholy world this would be without children—and what an inhuman world, without the aged.

—SAMUEL TAYLOR COLERIDGE

10 There's nothing like having grandchildren to restore your faith in heredity.

—DOUG LARSON

11 The simplest toy, one which even the youngest child can operate, is called a grandparent.

—SAM LEVENSON
You Don't Have to Be in "Who's Who" to Know What's What

12 Nobody can do for little children what grandparents do. Grandparents sort of sprinkle stardust over the lives of little children.

—ALEX HALEY
in *The Maroon*

13 I don't know who my grandfather was. I am much more concerned to know what his grandson will be.

—ABRAHAM LINCOLN

CHILDREN ARE THE LIVING MESSAGES . . .

1 Children are the living messages we send to a time we will not see.
—JOHN W. WHITEHEAD
The Stealing of America

2 My best creation is my children.
—DIANE VON FURSTENBERG

3 Every child comes with the message that God is not yet discouraged of man.
—RABINDRANATH TAGORE

4 Children are the anchors that hold a mother to life.
—SOPHOCLES

5 It is not easy to be crafty and winsome at the same time, and few accomplish it after the age of six.
—JOHN W. GARDNER AND
FRANCESCA GARDNER REESE
in *Know or Listen to Those Who Know*

6 Perhaps parents would enjoy their children more if they stopped to realize that the film of childhood can never be run through for a second showing.
—EVELYN NOWN

7 Cherishing children is the mark of a civilized society.
—JOAN GANZ COONEY

8 Human beings are the only creatures on earth that allow their children to come back home.
—BILL COSBY
Fatherhood

9 Life affords no greater responsibility, no greater privilege, than the raising of the next generation.
—C. EVERETT KOOP, MD

10 Children have more need of models than of critics.
—CAROLYN COATS
Things Your Dad Always Told You But You Didn't Want to Hear

11 The greatest natural resource that any country can have is its children.
—DANNY KAYE

12 Although today there are many trial marriages, there is no such thing as a trial child.
—GARY WILLS

13 Never worry about the size of your Christmas tree. In the eyes of children, they are all 30 feet tall.
—LARRY WILDE
The Merry Book of Christmas

14 In the little world in which children have their existence, whosoever brings them up, there is nothing so finely perceived and so finely felt as injustice.
—CHARLES DICKENS

1 Children are innocent and love justice, while most adults are wicked and prefer mercy.
—G. K. CHESTERTON

2 Children's talent to endure stems from their ignorance of alternatives.
—MAYA ANGELOU

3 When I was a child, love to me was what the sea is to a fish: something you swim in while you are going about the important affairs of life.
—P. L. TRAVERS

4 I still live in and on the sunshine of my childhood.
—CHRISTIAN MORGENSTERN

5 There are no seven wonders of the world in the eyes of a child. There are seven million.
—WALT STREIGHTIFF

6 The penalty for censoring what your children may be taught is children who are brighter than you.
—FRANK A. CLARK

7 If there is anything we wish to change in the child, we should first examine it and see whether it is not something that could better be changed in ourselves.
—CARL G. JUNG
The Development of Personality

8 Any child can tell you that the sole purpose of a middle name is so he can tell when he's really in trouble.
—DENNIS FAKES
Points with Punch

9 When I approach a child, he inspires in me two sentiments: tenderness for what he is, and respect for what he may become.
—LOUIS PASTEUR

10 We worry about what a child will be tomorrow, yet we forget that he is someone today.
—STACIA TAUSCHER

11 If children grew up according to early indications, we should have nothing but geniuses.
—JOHANN WOLFGANG VON GOETHE

12 A child is the root of the heart.
—CAROLINA MARÍA DE JESÚS

13 There never was a child so lovely but his mother was glad to get him asleep.
—RALPH WALDO EMERSON

14 Ask your child what he wants for dinner only if he's buying.
—FRAN LEBOWITZ
Social Studies

15 Telling a teenager the facts of life is like giving a fish a bath.
—ARNOLD H. GLASOW

1 Children have never been good at listening to their elders, but they have never failed to imitate them.
—JAMES BALDWIN

2 Oh, what a tangled web do parents weave when they think that their children are naive.
—OGDEN NASH

3 Babies are always more trouble than you thought—and more wonderful.
—CHARLES OSGOOD
"CBS Morning News"

4 The one thing children wear out faster than shoes is parents.
—JOHN J. PLOMP

5 Children aren't happy with nothing to ignore,
And that's what parents were created for.
—OGDEN NASH

6 Parents are the bones on which children cut their teeth.
—PETER USTINOV
in National Enquirer

7 Play is often talked about as if it were a relief from serious learning. But for children play is serious learning. Play is really the work of childhood.
—FRED ROGERS

8 Having a young child explain something exciting he has seen is the finest example of communication you will ever hear or see.
—BOB TALBERT

9 There's nothing that can help you understand your beliefs more than trying to explain them to an inquisitive child.
—FRANK A. CLARK

10 The greatest aid to adult education is children.
—CHARLIE T. JONES AND BOB PHILLIPS
Wit & Wisdom

11 Children are like wet cement. Whatever falls on them makes an impression.
—HAIM GINOTT

12 Children are not things to be molded, but are people to be unfolded.
—JESS LAIR

13 When everything is astonishing, nothing is astonishing; this is how the world is to children.
—ANTOINE RIVAROLI

14 You don't really understand human nature unless you know why a child on a merry-go-round will wave at his parents every time around—and why his parents will always wave back.
—WILLIAM D. TAMMEUS

1 A child is not a vase to be filled, but a fire to be lit.

—RABELAIS

2 Kids are always the only future the human race has.

—WILLIAM SAROYAN

3 The most important thing that parents can teach their children is how to get along without them.

—FRANK A. CLARK

4 We set standards for drugs, because bad drugs cross state lines. Well, badly educated children cross state lines, too.

—ADM. HYMAN G. RICKOVER

5 If you want your children to keep their feet on the ground, put some responsibility on their shoulders.

—ABIGAIL VAN BUREN

6 Loving a child doesn't mean giving in to all his whims; to love him is to bring out the best in him, to teach him to love what is difficult.

—NADIA BOULANGER

7 The best things you can give children, next to good habits, are good memories.

—SYDNEY J. HARRIS

8 A child, like your stomach, doesn't need all you can afford to give it.

—FRANK A. CLARK

9 The best security blanket a child can have is parents who respect each other.

—JAN BLAUSTONE
The Joy of Parenthood

10 The best inheritance a parent can give his children is a few minutes of his time each day.

—O. A. BATTISTA

11 Any kid who has two parents who are interested in him and has a houseful of books isn't poor.

—SAM LEVENSON

12 Sometimes the poorest man leaves his children the richest inheritance.

—RUTH E. RENKEL
in *National Enquirer*

13 The greatest gifts you can give your children are the roots of responsibility and the wings of independence.

—DENIS WAITLEY

14 A truly rich man is one whose children run into his arms when his hands are empty.

—*Spotlight* (Boise, Idaho)

15 I have found that the best way to give advice to your children is to find out what they want, and then advise them to do it.

—HARRY S. TRUMAN

1 If a child lives with approval, he learns to like himself.
—Dorothy Law Nolte

2 Parents need to fill a child's bucket of self-esteem so high that the rest of the world can't poke enough holes in it to drain it dry.
—Alvin Price

3 Every adult needs a child to teach; it's the way adults learn.
—Frank A. Clark

4 Children are likely to live up to what you believe of them.
—Lady Bird Johnson

5 If you can't hold children in your arms, please hold them in your heart.
—Mother Clara Hale

6 You cannot train a horse with shouts and expect it to obey a whisper.
—Dagobert D. Runes
Letters to My Son

7 What's done to children, they will do to society.
—Dr. Karl Menninger

8 What a father says to his children is not heard by the world; but it will be heard by posterity.
—Jean Paul Richter

9 Never fear spoiling children by making them too happy. Happiness is the atmosphere in which all good affections grow.
—Thomas Bray

10 The only thing worth stealing is a kiss from a sleeping child.
—Joe Houldsworth

MANNERS ARE THE HAPPY WAY . . .

11 Manners are the happy way of doing things.
—Ralph Waldo Emerson

12 Manners are a sensitive awareness of the feelings of others. If you have that awareness, you have good manners, no matter what fork you use.
—Emily Post

13 Most arts require long study and application, but the most useful of all, that of pleasing, requires only the desire.
—Lord Chesterfield

14 Life is not so short but that there is always time for courtesy.
—Ralph Waldo Emerson

15 Politeness is the art of selecting among one's real thoughts.
—Madame de Staël

1 To have a respect for ourselves guides our morals; to have a deference for others governs our manners.

—LAURENCE STERNE

2 Manners are like the zero in arithmetic; they may not be much in themselves, but they are capable of adding a great deal to the value of everything else.

—FREYA STARK
The Journey's Echo

3 Etiquette is getting sleepy in company and not showing it.

—HYMAN MAXWELL BERSTON

4 You can get through life with bad manners, but it's easier with good manners.

—LILLIAN GISH

5 Diplomacy gets you out of what tact would have kept you out of.

—BRIAN BOWLING

6 The point of tact is not sharp.

—COLLEEN CARNEY

7 People with tact have less to retract.

—ARNOLD H. GLASOW

8 Tact consists in knowing how far we may go too far.

—JEAN COCTEAU
A Call to Order

9 Tact is the knack of making a point without making an enemy.

—HOWARD W. NEWTON

10 Tact is the art of making guests feel at home when that's really where you wish they were.

—GEORGE E. BERGMAN
in *Good Housekeeping*

11 Tact is rubbing out another's mistake instead of rubbing it in.

—*Farmers' Almanac*

12 Tact is the art of recognizing when to be big and when not to belittle.

—BILL COPELAND

13 Tact is the ability to stay in the middle without getting caught there.

—FRANKLIN P. JONES

14 Tact is the art of convincing people that they know more than you do.

—RAYMOND MORTIMER

15 Tact is the art of building a fire under people without making their blood boil.

—FRANKLIN P. JONES

16 Never insult an alligator until after you have crossed the river.

—CORDELL HULL

1 The truly free man is he who knows how to decline a dinner invitation without giving an excuse.

—Jules Renard

2 Every generation is convinced there has been a deplorable breakdown of manners.

—Byron Dobell
in *American Heritage*

3 To be agreeable in society, you must consent to be taught many things which you already know.

—Talleyrand

4 It takes a lot of thought and effort and downright determination to be agreeable.

—Ray D. Everson

5 Praise is like champagne; it should be served while it is still bubbling.

—*Robins Reader*

6 Charm is the quality in others that makes us more satisfied with ourselves.

—Henri Frédéric Amiel

7 A gentleman is a man who uses a butter knife when dining alone.

—W. F. Dettle

8 Nothing prevents us from being natural so much as the desire to appear so.

—François de La Rochefoucauld

9 It is a great mistake for men to give up paying compliments, for when they give up saying what is charming, they give up thinking what is charming.

—Oscar Wilde

10 Politeness is to human nature what warmth is to wax.

—Arthur Schopenhauer

11 He who says what he likes, hears what he does not like.

—Leonard Louis Levinson

12 The manner in which it is given is worth more than the gift.

—Pierre Corneille

13 To receive a present handsomely and in a right spirit, even when you have none to give in return, is to give one in return.

—Leigh Hunt
Essays by Leigh Hunt

14 It is much easier to be a hero than a gentleman.

—Luigi Pirandello

15 Never claim as a right what you can ask as a favor.

—John Churton Collins

16 To err is human; to refrain from laughing, humane.

—Lane Olinghouse

OUR BETTER SIDE

Some people strengthen the society just by being the kind of people they are.

—JOHN W. GARDNER

A CONTINENT OF UNDIS-COVERED CHARACTER . . .

1 Every one of us has in him a continent of undiscovered character. Blessed is he who acts the Columbus to his own soul.

—Quoted in *Words of Life*, edited by Charles L. Wallis

2 Character is a strange blending of flinty strength and pliable warmth.

—ROBERT SHAFFER

3 No man knows his true character until he has run out of gas, purchased something on the installment plan, and raised an adolescent.

—EDNA MCCANN
The Heritage Book 1985

4 Character may be manifested in the great moments, but it is made in the small ones.

—PHILLIPS BROOKS

5 Nearly all men can stand adversity, but if you want to test a man's character, give him power.

—ABRAHAM LINCOLN

6 Everyone journeys through character as well as through time. The person one becomes depends on the person one has been.

—DICK FRANCIS
A Jockey's Life: The Biography of Lester Piggott

7 Character consists of what you do on the third and fourth tries.

—JAMES MICHENER
Chesapeake

8 You can measure a man by the opposition it takes to discourage him.

—ROBERT C. SAVAGE
Life Lessons

9 We know what a person thinks not when he tells us what he thinks, but by his actions.

—ISAAC BASHEVIS SINGER
in *The New York Times Magazine*

10 Another flaw in the human character is that everybody wants to build and nobody wants to do maintenance.

—KURT VONNEGUT
Hocus Pocus

11 Men are men before they are lawyers, or physicians, or merchants, or manufacturers; and if you make them capable and sensible men, they will make themselves capable and sensible lawyers or physicians.

—JOHN STUART MILL

12 The severest test of character is not so much the ability to keep a secret as it is, when the secret is finally out, to refrain from disclosing that you knew it all along.

—SYDNEY J. HARRIS

1 Show me the man you honor, and I will know what kind of man you are.

—THOMAS CARLYLE

2 People need responsibility. They resist assuming it, but they cannot get along without it.

—JOHN STEINBECK
in *Saturday Review*

3 If anyone thinks he has no responsibilities, it is because he has not sought them out.

—MARY LYON

4 Duty is a very personal thing. It is what comes from knowing the need to take action and not just a need to urge others to do something.

—MOTHER TERESA OF CALCUTTA

5 Our concern is not how to worship in the catacombs, but rather how to remain human in the skyscrapers.

—RABBI ABRAHAM JOSHUA HESCHEL
The Insecurity of Freedom

6 The treacherous, unexplored areas of the world are not in continents or the seas; they are in the minds and hearts of men.

—ALLEN E. CLAXTON

7 The truth about a man is, first of all, what it is that he keeps hidden.

—ANDRÉ MALRAUX

8 Men show their character in nothing more clearly than by what they think laughable.

—JOHANN WOLFGANG VON GOETHE

9 You can discover more about a person in an hour of play than in a year of conversation.

—PLATO

10 There are two insults no human being will endure: that he has no sense of humor, and that he has never known trouble.

—SINCLAIR LEWIS

11 Sports do not build character. They reveal it.

—HEYWOOD HALE BROUN

12 How a man plays the game shows something of his character; how he loses shows all of it.

—*Tribune* (Camden County, Georgia)

13 In our play we reveal what kind of people we are.

—OVID

14 You can tell more about a person by what he says about others than you can by what others say about him.

—LEO AIKMAN

15 Character is what you know you are, not what others think you are.

—MARVA COLLINS AND CIVIA TAMARKIN
Marva Collins' Way

1 You can easily judge the character of a man by how he treats those who can do nothing for him.
—JAMES D. MILES

2 Character is much easier kept than recovered.
—THOMAS PAINE

3 The way to gain a good reputation is to endeavor to be what you desire to appear.
—SOCRATES

4 A good reputation is better than fame.
—LOUIS DUDEK
Epigrams

5 Reputation is character minus what you've been caught doing.
—MICHAEL IAPOCE
A Funny Thing Happened on the Way to the Boardroom

6 Life is for one generation; a good name is forever.
—JAPANESE PROVERB

7 To have lost your reputation is to be dead among the living.
—S. H. SIMMONS

8 Modesty is to merit what shade is to figures in a picture; it gives it strength and makes it stand out.
—JEAN DE LA BRUYÈRE

9 Modesty is the clothing of talent.
—PIERRE VERON

10 He who is slowest in making a promise is most faithful in its performance.
—JEAN JACQUES ROUSSEAU

11 The only way to make a man trustworthy is to trust him.
—HENRY L. STIMSON
in *Harper's Magazine*

12 Willpower is being able to eat just one salted peanut.
—PAT ELPHINSTONE

13 The best discipline, maybe the only discipline that really works, is self-discipline.
—WALTER KIECHEL III
in *Fortune*

14 You can find on the outside only what you possess on the inside.
—ADOLFO MONTIEL BALLESTEROS
La Honda y La Flor

15 In great matters men show themselves as they wish to be seen; in small matters, as they are.
—GAMALIEL BRADFORD

16 What lies behind us and what lies before us are small matters compared to what lies within us.
—RALPH WALDO EMERSON

1 I see God in every human being.
—MOTHER TERESA OF CALCUTTA

2 Men may be divided almost any way we please, but I have found the most useful distinction to be made between those who devote their lives to conjugating the verb "to be," and those who spend their lives conjugating the verb "to have."
—SYDNEY J. HARRIS

3 There is more simplicity in the man who eats caviar on impulse than in the man who eats Grape Nuts on principle.
—G. K. CHESTERTON

4 One of the best ways to measure people is to watch the way they behave when something free is offered.
—ANN LANDERS

5 Say not you know a man entirely till you have divided an inheritance with him.
—JOHANN KASPAR LAVATER

6 Not what I have but what I do is my kingdom.
—THOMAS CARLYLE

7 The reputation of a thousand years may be determined by the conduct of one hour.
—JAPANESE PROVERB

8 Fame is the perfume of heroic deeds.
—SOCRATES

9 Dollars have never been known to produce character, and character will never be produced by money.
—W. K. KELLOGG
I'll Invest My Money in People

10 One isn't born one's self. One is born with a mass of expectations, a mass of other people's ideas— and you have to work through it all.
—V. S. NAIPAUL

11 Don't laugh at a youth for his affectations; he is only trying on one face after another to find a face of his own.
—LOGAN PEARSALL SMITH

12 It has amazed me that the most incongruous traits should exist in the same person and, for all that, yield a plausible harmony.
—W. SOMERSET MAUGHAM

13 We spend our time searching for security and hate it when we get it.
—JOHN STEINBECK
America and Americans

14 Without heroes, we are all plain people and don't know how far we can go.
—BERNARD MALAMUD
The Natural

1 The great man is he who does not lose his child-heart.

—MENCIUS

2 No great scoundrel is ever uninteresting.

—MURRAY KEMPTON
in *Newsday* (Long Island, New York)

3 Characters live to be noticed. People with character notice how they live.

—NANCY MOSER

4 Man is harder than iron, stronger than stone and more fragile than a rose.

—TURKISH PROVERB

5 He is ill clothed that is bare of virtue.

—BENJAMIN FRANKLIN

6 All of us are experts at practicing virtue at a distance.

—THEODORE M. HESBURGH

7 To err is human; to blame it on the other guy is even more human.

—BOB GODDARD

8 Man is the only kind of varmint sets his own trap, baits it, then steps in it.

—JOHN STEINBECK
Sweet Thursday

9 There's man all over for you, blaming on his boots the faults of his feet.

—SAMUEL BECKETT
Waiting for Godot

AN OPTIMIST STAYS UP UNTIL MIDNIGHT . . .

10 An optimist stays up until midnight to see the new year in. A pessimist stays up to make sure the old year leaves.

—BILL VAUGHAN
in Kansas City *Star*

11 Perpetual optimism is a force multiplier.

—COLIN POWELL

12 I will say this about being an optimist—even when things don't turn out well, you are certain they will get better.

—FRANK HUGHES

13 An optimist thinks this is the best of all worlds. A pessimist fears the same may be true.

—DOUG LARSON

14 Things will probably come out all right, but sometimes it takes strong nerves just to watch.

—HEDLEY DONOVAN

1 The optimist already sees the scar over the wound; the pessimist still sees the wound underneath the scar.

—ERNST SCHRODER

2 The point of living, and of being an optimist, is to be foolish enough to believe the best is yet to come.

—PETER USTINOV

3 It doesn't hurt to be optimistic. You can always cry later.

—LUCIMAR SANTOS DE LIMA

4 Cheerfulness, like spring, opens all the blossoms of the inward man.

—JEAN PAUL RICHTER

5 An optimist is the human personification of spring.

—SUSAN J. BISSONETTE

6 I always prefer to believe the best of everybody—it saves so much trouble.

—RUDYARD KIPLING

7 A positive attitude may not solve all your problems, but it will annoy enough people to make it worth the effort.

—HERM ALBRIGHT

8 Optimism is an intellectual choice.

—DIANA SCHNEIDER

9 Optimism is a cheerful frame of mind that enables a teakettle to sing though in hot water up to its nose.

—Quoted by HAROLD HELFER in *The Optimist*

10 An optimist is a person who starts a new diet on Thanksgiving Day.

—IRV KUPCINET in *Kup's Column*

11 The average pencil is seven inches long, with just a half-inch eraser—in case you thought optimism was dead.

—ROBERT BRAULT

12 Both optimists and pessimists contribute to our society. The optimist invents the airplane and the pessimist the parachute.

—GIL STERN

13 A pessimist? That's a person who has been intimately acquainted with an optimist.

—ELBERT HUBBARD

14 Pessimism never won any battle.

—DWIGHT D. EISENHOWER

15 The nice part about being a pessimist is that you are constantly being either proven right or pleasantly surprised.

—GEORGE F. WILL *The Leveling Wind*

1 I don't believe in pessimism. If something doesn't come up the way you want, forge ahead. If you think it's going to rain, it will.

—CLINT EASTWOOD

2 No one really knows enough to be a pessimist.

—NORMAN COUSINS

3 The optimist is the kind of person who believes a housefly is looking for a way out.

—GEORGE JEAN NATHAN

4 The pessimist complains about the wind; the optimist expects it to change; the realist adjusts the sails.

—WILLIAM ARTHUR WARD

5 A pessimist sees only the dark side of the clouds, and mopes; a philosopher sees both sides, and shrugs; an optimist doesn't see the clouds at all—he's walking on them.

—LEONARD LOUIS LEVINSON

6 An idealist believes the short run doesn't count. A cynic believes the long run doesn't matter. A realist believes that what is done or left undone in the short run determines the long run.

—SYDNEY J. HARRIS

MORALITY IS ITS OWN ADVOCATE . . .

Morality is its own advocate; it is never necessary to apologize for it. 7

—EDITH L. HARRELL

The three hardest tasks in the world are neither physical feats nor intellectual achievements, but moral acts: to return love for hate, to include the excluded, and to say, "I was wrong." 8

—SYDNEY J. HARRIS
Pieces of Eight

Moral excellence comes about as a result of habit. We become just by doing just acts, temperate by doing temperate acts, brave by doing brave acts. 9

—ARISTOTLE

It is much easier to repent of sins that we have committed than to repent of those we intend to commit. 10

—JOSH BILLINGS

The biggest threat to our well-being is the absence of moral clarity and purpose. 11

—RICK SHUMAN
in *Time*

We laugh at honor and are shocked to find traitors in our midst. 12

—C. S. LEWIS
The Abolition of Man

1 While an original is always hard to find, he is easy to recognize.
—JOHN L. MASON
An Enemy Called Average

2 The courage to imagine the otherwise is our greatest resource, adding color and suspense to all our life.
—DANIEL J. BOORSTIN

3 Discoveries are often made by not following instructions, by going off the main road, by trying the untried.
—FRANK TYGER
in *Forbes* magazine

4 It is by logic that we prove, but by intuition that we discover.
—HENRI POINCARÉ

5 Don't expect anything original from an echo.
—Quoted in "The 365 Great Quotes-a-Year Calendar"

6 Truth always originates in a minority of one, and every custom begins as a broken precedent.
—WILL DURANT

7 Eventually it comes to you: the thing that makes you exceptional, if you are at all, is inevitably that which must also make you lonely.
—LORRAINE HANSBERRY

8 If you're strong enough, there are no precedents.
—F. SCOTT FITZGERALD
The Crack-Up, edited by Edmund Wilson

9 The more original a discovery, the more obvious it seems afterward.
—ARTHUR KOESTLER
The Act of Creation

10 To go against the dominant thinking of your friends, of most of the people you see every day, is perhaps the most difficult act of heroism you can perform.
—THEODORE H. WHITE

11 Every society honors its live conformists and its dead troublemakers.
—MIGNON McLAUGHLIN

12 Everyone has talent; what is rare is the courage to follow the talent to the dark place where it leads.
—ERICA JONG

13 To do what others cannot do is talent. To do what talent cannot do is genius.
—WILL HENRY

14 When there is an original sound in the world, it wakens a hundred echoes.
—JOHN A. SHEDD
Salt from My Attic

1 The cynic says, "One man can't do anything." I say, "Only one man can do anything." One man interacting creatively with others can move the world.

—JOHN W. GARDNER

2 Everything has been thought of before, but the difficulty is to think of it again.

—JOHANN WOLFGANG VON GOETHE

3 Inspiration is never genuine if it is known as inspiration at the time. True inspiration always steals on a person, its importance not being fully recognized for some time.

—SAMUEL BUTLER

4 The work of the individual still remains the spark that moves mankind forward.

—IGOR SIKORSKY

5 The most powerful weapon on earth is the human soul on fire.

—FERDINAND FOCH

6 Whatever comes from the heart carries the heat and color of its birthplace.

—OLIVER WENDELL HOLMES SR.

7 We might define an eccentric as a man who is a law unto himself, and a crank as one who, having determined what the law is, insists on laying it down to others.

—LOUIS KRONENBERGER

8 No two men are alike, and both of them are happy for it.

—MORRIS MANDEL
in *The Jewish Press*

9 Some people march to a different drummer—and some people polka.

—Los Angeles Times Syndicate

THE REAL SECRET OF PATIENCE . . .

10 The real secret of patience is to find something else to do in the meantime.

—*Dell Pencil Puzzles and Word Games*

11 I endeavor to be wise when I cannot be merry, easy when I cannot be glad, content with what cannot be mended and patient when there be no redress.

—ELIZABETH MONTAGU

12 If you are patient in one moment of anger, you will escape a hundred days of sorrow.

—CHINESE EPIGRAM

13 He that can have patience can have what he will.

—BENJAMIN FRANKLIN

14 The key to everything is patience. You get the chicken by hatching the egg, not by smashing it.

—ARNOLD H. GLASOW

1 Patience! The windmill never strays in search of the wind.
—ANDY J. SKLIVIS

2 Nothing valuable can be lost by taking time.
—ABRAHAM LINCOLN

3 In any contest between power and patience, bet on patience.
—W. B. PRESCOTT

4 Beware the fury of a patient man.
—JOHN DRYDEN

5 Patience is bitter, but its fruit is sweet.
—JEAN JACQUES ROUSSEAU

6 Patience is the art of hoping.
—VAUVENARGUES

7 Be patient with everyone, but above all with yourself.
—ST. FRANCIS DE SALES

8 Patience is the ability to put up with people you'd like to put down.
—ULRIKE RUFFERT

9 There is a limit at which forbearance ceases to be a virtue.
—EDMUND BURKE

10 Patience is something you admire in the driver behind you and scorn in the one ahead.
—MAC MCCLEARY

11 Waiting is worse than knowing. Grief rends the heart cleanly, that it may begin to heal; waiting shreds the spirit.
—MORGAN LLYWELYN
The Wind from Hastings

12 There's a fine line between fishing and standing on the shore like an idiot.
—STEVEN WRIGHT

13 Regardless of how much patience we have, we would prefer never to use any of it.
—JAMES T. O'BRIEN

14 A man without patience is a lamp without oil.
—ANDRÉS SEGOVIA

15 Impatience can be a virtue, if you practice it on yourself.
—ROD MCKUEN
1985 Book of Days

16 He who is impatient waits twice.
—MACK MCGINNIS

17 One of the great disadvantages of hurry is that it takes such a long time.
—G. K. CHESTERTON

18 We may be willing to tell a story twice but we are never willing to hear it more than once.
—WILLIAM HAZLITT

1 How can a society that exists on instant mashed potatoes, packaged cake mixes, frozen dinners, and instant cameras teach patience to its young?

—PAUL SWEENEY

2 Patience often gets the credit that belongs to fatigue.

—FRANKLIN P. JONES

THE DIFFERENCE BETWEEN A HERO AND A COWARD . . .

3 The difference between a hero and a coward is one step sideways.

—GENE HACKMAN

4 Life shrinks or expands in proportion to one's courage.

—*The Diary of Anaïs Nin*
edited by Gunther Stuhlmann

5 Real courage is when you know you're licked before you begin, but you begin anyway and see it through no matter what.

—HARPER LEE
To Kill a Mockingbird

6 Courage is being scared to death—and saddling up anyway.

—JOHN WAYNE

7 It is often easier to fight for principles than to live up to them.

—ADLAI E. STEVENSON

8 Courage is the art of being the only one who knows you're scared to death.

—EARL WILSON

9 Facing it—always facing it—that's the way to get through. Face it!

—JOSEPH CONRAD

10 Pain nourishes courage. You can't be brave if you've only had wonderful things happen to you.

—MARY TYLER MOORE

11 Success is never final and failure never total. It's courage that counts.

—*Success Unlimited*

12 Courage is the ladder on which all the other virtues mount.

—CLARE BOOTHE LUCE

13 It's when you run away that you're most liable to stumble.

—CASEY ROBINSON

14 Curiosity will conquer fear even more than bravery will.

—JAMES STEPHENS

15 Courage is often lack of insight, whereas cowardice in many cases is based on good information.

—PETER USTINOV

16 Bravery never goes out of fashion.

—WILLIAM MAKEPEACE THACKERAY

1 There is a time to take counsel of your fears, and there is a time to never listen to any fear.
—GEN. GEORGE S. PATTON

2 Keep your fears to yourself, but share your courage.
—ROBERT LOUIS STEVENSON

3 You can't test courage cautiously.
—ANNIE DILLARD
An American Childhood

4 Courage is not the towering oak that sees storms come and go; it is the fragile blossom that opens in the snow.
—ALICE MACKENZIE SWAIM

5 Courage is contagious. When a brave man takes a stand, the spines of others are stiffened.
—REV. BILLY GRAHAM

6 The way you overcome shyness is to become so wrapped up in something that you forget to be afraid.
—LADY BIRD JOHNSON

A LITTLE KINDNESS . . .

7 A little kindness from person to person is better than a vast love for all humankind.
—RICHARD DEHMEL

8 The everyday kindness of the back roads more than makes up for the acts of greed in the headlines.
—CHARLES KURALT
On the Road With Charles Kuralt

9 A profusion of pink roses bending ragged in the rain speaks to me of all gentleness and its enduring.
—*The Collected Later Poems of William Carlos Williams*

10 Resolve to be tender with the young, compassionate with the aged, sympathetic with the striving, and tolerant with the weak and the wrong. Sometime in life you will have been all of these.
—BOB GODDARD

11 The heart is the toughest part of the body. Tenderness is in the hands.
—CAROLYN FORCHÉ
The Country Between Us

12 You cannot do a kindness too soon, for you never know how soon it will be too late.
—RALPH WALDO EMERSON

13 Life is short and we never have enough time for gladdening the hearts of those who travel the way with us. Oh, be swift to love! Make haste to be kind.
—HENRI FRÉDÉRIC AMIEL

1 There is nothing stronger in the world than gentleness.

—HAN SUYIN
A Many-Splendored Thing

2 How sweet it is when the strong are also gentle!

—LIBBIE FUDIM

3 Kindness consists in loving people more than they deserve.

—JOSEPH JOUBERT

4 Kindness is never wasted. If it has no effect on the recipient, at least it benefits the bestower.

—S. H. SIMMONS

5 Write injuries in sand, kindnesses in marble.

—FRENCH PROVERB

6 Ask any decent person what he thinks matters most in human conduct: five to one his answer will be "kindness."

—KENNETH CLARK

7 Two important things are to have a genuine interest in people and to be kind to them. Kindness, I've discovered, is everything in life.

—ISAAC BASHEVIS SINGER

8 Always try to be a little kinder than is necessary.

—JAMES M. BARRIE

9 Kindness is more important than wisdom, and the recognition of this is the beginning of wisdom.

—THEODORE ISAAC RUBIN, MD
One to One

10 When I was young, I admired clever people. Now that I am old, I admire kind people.

—ABRAHAM JOSHUA HESCHEL

11 Praise can give criticism a lead around the first turn and still win the race.

—BERN WILLIAMS
in *National Enquirer*

12 How beautiful a day can be when kindness touches it.

—GEORGE ELLISTON

13 One kind word can warm three winter months.

—JAPANESE PROVERB

14 Kind words can be short and easy to speak, but their echoes are truly endless.

—MOTHER TERESA OF CALCUTTA

15 Tenderness is passion in repose.

—JOSEPH JOUBERT

16 Kindness is a language which the deaf can hear and the blind can read.

—MARK TWAIN

1 Kindness can become its own motive. We are made kind by being kind.

—Eric Hoffer
The Passionate State of Mind

2 A pat on the back, though only a few vertebrae removed from a kick in the pants, is miles ahead in results.

—Bennett Cerf

3 A warm smile is the universal language of kindness.

—William Arthur Ward
"Reward Yourself"

4 When we put ourselves in the other person's place, we're less likely to want to put him in his place.

—*Farmer's Digest*

5 He best can pity who has felt the woe.

—John Gay

6 Could a greater miracle take place than for us to look through each other's eyes for an instant?

—Henry David Thoreau

7 You never really understand a person until you consider things from his point of view.

—Harper Lee
To Kill a Mockingbird

8 Feelings are everywhere—be gentle.

—J. Masai

9 Never does the human soul appear so strong and noble as when it forgoes revenge and dares to forgive an injury.

—E. H. Chapin

10 One of the most lasting pleasures you can experience is the feeling that comes over you when you genuinely forgive an enemy— whether he knows it or not.

—O. A. Battista
in *Quote Magazine*

11 A forgiveness ought to be like a canceled note, torn in two and burned up, so that it can never be shown against the man.

—Henry Ward Beecher

12 Forgiving and being forgiven are two names for the same thing. The important thing is that a discord has been resolved.

—C. S. Lewis

13 He who cannot forgive others destroys the bridge over which he himself must pass.

—George Herbert

14 When a deep injury is done us, we never recover until we forgive.

—Alan Paton

1 Forgiveness is a gift of high value. Yet its cost is nothing.

—BETTY SMITH
A Tree Grows in Brooklyn

2 One of the secrets of a long and fruitful life is to forgive everybody everything every night before you go to bed.

—ANN LANDERS

3 Forgiveness is a funny thing. It warms the heart and cools the sting.

—WILLIAM ARTHUR WARD

4 Forgive your enemies—if you can't get back at them any other way.

—FRANKLIN P. JONES

GOODNESS IS THE ONLY INVESTMENT . . .

5 Goodness is the only investment that never fails.

—HENRY DAVID THOREAU

6 On the whole, human beings want to be good, but not too good, and not quite all the time.

—GEORGE ORWELL

7 All that is worth cherishing in this world begins in the heart, not the head.

—Quoted by SUZANNE CHAZIN in *The New York Times*

8 Ten thousand bad traits cannot make a single good one any the less good.

—ROBERT LOUIS STEVENSON

9 The line separating good and evil passes not through states, nor between political parties either— but right through every human heart.

—ALEKSANDR I. SOLZHENITSYN
The Gulag Archipelago

10 Some people strengthen the society just by being the kind of people they are.

—JOHN W. GARDNER

11 Those who bring sunshine to the lives of others cannot keep it from themselves.

—JAMES MATTHEW BARRIE

12 It's not true that nice guys finish last. Nice guys are winners before the game even starts.

—ADDISON WALKER

13 Sincerity resembles a spice. Too much repels you and too little leaves you wanting.

—BILL COPELAND

14 If you haven't any charity in your heart, you have the worst kind of heart trouble.

—BOB HOPE

1 The work of an unknown good man is like a vein of water flowing hidden underground, secretly making the ground greener.

—THOMAS CARLYLE

2 Generosity always wins favor, particularly when accompanied by modesty.

—JOHANN WOLFGANG VON GOETHE

3 People want to know how much you care before they care how much you know.

—JAMES F. HIND
in *The Wall Street Journal*

4 Goodwill is earned by many acts; it can be lost by one.

—DUNCAN STUART

GRATITUDE IS A SOMETIME THING . . .

5 Gratitude is a sometime thing in this world. Just because you've been feeding them all winter, don't expect the birds to take it easy on your grass seed.

—BILL VAUGHAN
in Kansas City *Star*

6 Gratitude is the memory of the heart.

—J. B. MASSIEU

7 Swift gratitude is the sweetest.

—GREEK PROVERB

The hardest arithmetic to master is 8 that which enables us to count our blessings.

—ERIC HOFFER
Reflections On The Human Condition

Silent gratitude isn't very much 9 use to anyone.

—G. B. STERN
Robert Louis Stevenson

Feeling gratitude and not expressing it is like wrapping a present 10 and not giving it.

—WILLIAM ARTHUR WARD

One must be poor to know the 11 luxury of giving.

—GEORGE ELIOT

To know the value of generosity, 12 it is necessary to have suffered from the cold indifference of others.

—EUGENE CLOUTIER

Sometimes we need to remind 13 ourselves that thankfulness is indeed a virtue.

—WILLIAM J. BENNETT
The Moral Compass

Appreciation is like an insurance 14 policy. It has to be renewed every now and then.

—DAVE MCINTYRE

PERSEVERANCE IS NOT A LONG RACE . . .

1 Perseverance is not a long race; it is many short races one after another.

—WALTER ELLIOTT
The Spiritual Life

2 Fall seven times, stand up eight.

—JAPANESE PROVERB

3 Let me tell you the secret that has led me to my goal. My strength lies solely in my tenacity.

—LOUIS PASTEUR

4 Great works are performed, not by strength, but by perseverance.

—SAMUEL JOHNSON

5 Vitality shows not only in the ability to persist but in the ability to start over.

—F. SCOTT FITZGERALD

6 By perseverance the snail reached the ark.

—CHARLES HADDON SPURGEON

7 In the confrontation between the stream and the rock, the stream always wins—not through strength but by perseverance.

—H. JACKSON BROWN
A Father's Book of Wisdom

8 What counts is not necessarily the size of the dog in the fight—it's the size of the fight in the dog.

—DWIGHT D. EISENHOWER

9 A professional is someone who can do his best work when he doesn't feel like it.

—ALISTAIR COOKE

10 The man who removes a mountain begins by carrying away small stones.

—CHINESE PROVERB

11 If you can find a path with no obstacles, it probably doesn't lead anywhere.

—FRANK A. CLARK

12 Perseverance is the hard work you do after you get tired of doing the hard work you already did.

—NEWT GINGRICH

13 Go the extra mile. It's never crowded.

—*Executive Speechwriter Newsletter*

14 Lord, give me the determination and tenacity of a weed.

—MRS. LEON R. WALTERS

FOR BETTER OR WORSE

It has been my experience that folks who have no vices have very few virtues.

—ABRAHAM LINCOLN

WE ALL KNOW A FOOL . . .

1 We all know a fool when we see one—but not when we are one.
—ARNOLD H. GLASOW

2 It is wise to remember that you are one of those who can be fooled some of the time.
—LAURENCE J. PETER
Peter's Almanac

3 There is a foolish corner in the brain of the wisest man.
—ARISTOTLE

4 You will do foolish things, but do them with enthusiasm.
—COLETTE

5 April 1 is the day upon which we are reminded what we are on the other 364.
—MARK TWAIN

6 Only a fool tests the depth of the water with both feet.
—AFRICAN PROVERB

7 Anyone can make a mistake. A fool insists on repeating it.
—ROBERTINE MAYNARD

8 A fool judges people by the presents they give him.
—CHINESE SAYING

Astrology proves one scientific fact, and one only; there's one born every minute.
—PATRICK MOORE ... 9

Only a fool argues with a skunk, a mule or the cook.
—HARRY OLIVER
Desert Rat Scrap Book ... 10

The ultimate result of shielding men from the effects of folly is to fill the world with fools.
—HERBERT SPENCER
Essays ... 11

The surprising thing about young fools is how many survive to become old fools.
—DOUG LARSON ... 12

Self-delusion is pulling in your stomach when you step on the scales.
—PAUL SWEENEY ... 13

Any fool can criticize, condemn and complain—and most do.
—DALE CARNEGIE
How to Win Friends and Influence People ... 14

Anybody with money to burn will easily find someone to tend the fire.
—*Pocket Crossword Puzzles* ... 15

1 Follies change their type but foolishness remains.

—ERICH KASTNER

2 I'm not denyin' the women are foolish: God Almighty made 'em to match the men.

—GEORGE ELIOT

3 Let us be thankful for the fools. But for them the rest of us could not succeed.

—MARK TWAIN

4 Everybody has the right to express what he thinks. That, of course, lets the crackpots in. But if you cannot tell a crackpot when you see one, then you ought to be taken in.

—HARRY S. TRUMAN

5 Some people get lost in thought because it's such unfamiliar territory.

—G. BEHN

6 A fanatic is someone who can't change his mind and won't change the subject.

—WINSTON CHURCHILL

7 While intelligent people can often simplify the complex, a fool is more likely to complicate the simple.

—GERALD W. GRUMET, MD
in *Readings*

8 There are 40 kinds of lunacy, but only one kind of common sense.

—AFRICAN PROVERB

9 A bore is someone who persists in holding his own views after we have enlightened him with ours.

—MALCOLM S. FORBES

10 Bores bore each other, too, but it never seems to teach them anything.

—DON MARQUIS

11 Some people can stay longer in an hour than others can in a week.

—WILLIAM DEAN HOWELLS

12 A healthy male adult bore consumes each year one-and-a-half times his own weight in other people's patience.

—JOHN UPDIKE
Assorted Prose

13 Everyone is a bore to someone. That is unimportant. The thing to avoid is being a bore to oneself.

—GERALD BRENAN

14 A bore is a fellow talker who can change the subject to his topic of conversation faster than you can change it back to yours.

—LAURENCE J. PETER
Peter's Quotations

1 People who insist on telling their dreams are among the terrors of the breakfast table.

—MAX BEERBOHM

2 Don't approach a goat from the front, a horse from the back or a fool from any side.

—YIDDISH PROVERB

3 Human reason is like a drunken man on horseback; set it up on one side, and it tumbles over on the other.

—MARTIN LUTHER

LOST BY INDIFFERENCE . . .

4 More good things in life are lost by indifference than ever were lost by active hostility.

—ROBERT GORDON MENZIES

5 Apathy is the glove into which evil slips its hand.

—BODIE THOENE

6 Love me or hate me, but spare me your indifference.

—LIBBIE FUDIM

7 I have a very strong feeling that the opposite of love is not hate— it's apathy.

—LEO BUSCAGLIA
Love

8 It is a perplexing and unpleasant truth that when men have something worth fighting for, they do not feel like fighting.

—ERIC HOFFER
The True Believer

9 There is nothing harder than the softness of indifference.

—JUAN MONTALVO

10 The tragedy of modern man is not that he knows less and less about the meaning of his own life but that it bothers him less and less.

—VACLAV HAVEL

11 Crime expands according to our willingness to put up with it.

—BARRY FARBER

GROW ANGRY SLOWLY . . .

12 Grow angry slowly—there's plenty of time.

—RALPH WALDO EMERSON

13 Anger is a wind which blows out the lamp of the mind.

—ROBERT G. INGERSOLL

14 Anger is not only inevitable, it is necessary. Its absence means indifference, the most disastrous of all human failings.

—ARTHUR PONSONBY

1 Anger is a symptom, a way of cloaking and expressing feelings too awful to experience directly—hurt, bitterness, grief and, most of all, fear.

—JOAN RIVERS
Still Talking

2 Getting angry can sometimes be like leaping into a wonderfully responsive sports car, gunning the motor, taking off at high speed and then discovering the brakes are out of order.

—MAGGIE SCARF
in *The New York Times Magazine*

3 Anyone can become angry. That is easy. But to be angry with the right person, to the right degree, at the right time, for the right purpose and in the right way—that is not easy.

—ARISTOTLE

4 Anger is a bad counselor.

—FRENCH PROVERB

5 Resentment is an extremely bitter diet, and eventually poisonous. I have no desire to make my own toxins.

—NEIL KINNOCK

6 There's a bit of ancient wisdom that appeals to us: it's a saying that a fight starts only with the second blow.

—HUGH ALLEN

7 I will permit no man to narrow and degrade my soul by making me hate him.

—BOOKER T. WASHINGTON

8 My life is in the hands of any fool who makes me lose my temper.

—JOSEPH HUNTER

9 It is only our bad temper that we put down to being tired or worried or hungry; we put our good temper down to ourselves.

—C. S. LEWIS
Mere Christianity

10 Temper, if ungoverned, governs the whole man.

—ANTHONY SHAFTESBURY

11 Temper is a quality that at a critical moment brings out the best in steel and the worst in people.

—WILLIAM P. GROHSE

12 Revenge has no more quenching effect on emotions than salt water has on thirst.

—WALTER WECKLER

13 Violence is the last refuge of the incompetent.

—ISAAC ASIMOV

14 A man that studieth revenge keeps his own wounds green.

—FRANCIS BACON

1 Getting even throws everything out of balance.

—JOE BROWNE
in *Post-Gazette*
(Pittsburgh, Pennsylvania)

2 If a small thing has the power to make you angry, does that not indicate something about your size?

—SYDNEY J. HARRIS

3 I imagine one of the reasons people cling to their hates so stubbornly is because they sense, once hate is gone, they will be forced to deal with pain.

—JAMES BALDWIN

4 To carry a grudge is like being stung to death by one bee.

—WILLIAM H. WALTON

5 Nothing lowers the level of conversation more than raising the voice.

—STANLEY HOROWITZ

6 Not the fastest horse can catch a word spoken in anger.

—CHINESE PROVERB

7 Speak when you are angry and you will make the best speech you will ever regret.

—AMBROSE BIERCE

Hot words make a real cool friendship. 8

—FLO ASHWORTH
in *Advertiser & News* (Dawsonville, Georgia)

The best remedy for a short temper is a long walk. 9

—JACQUELINE SCHIFF
in *National Enquirer*

GOSSIP NEEDN'T BE FALSE . . .

Gossip needn't be false to be evil—there's a lot of truth that shouldn't be passed around. 10

—FRANK A. CLARK

There is nothing busier than an idle rumor. 11

—HERBERT V. PROCHNOW
The New Speaker's Treasury of Wit and Wisdom

In our appetite for gossip, we tend to gobble down everything before us, only to find, too late, that it is our ideals we have consumed, and we have not been enlarged by the feasts but only diminished. 12

—PICO IYER
in *Time*

Knowledge is power, if you know it about the right person. 13

—ETHEL WATTS

1 A gossip is a person who creates the smoke in which other people assume there's fire.

—DAN BENNETT

2 Gossip is that which no one claims to like—but everybody enjoys.

—JOSEPH CONRAD

3 Bad news goes about in clogs, good news in stockinged feet.

—WELSH PROVERB

4 The gossip of the future may not be a backbiting, nosy, tongue-wagging two-face but a super-megabyte, random-access, digital interface.

—RONALD B. ZEH

5 Some people will believe anything if it is whispered to them.

—PIERRE DE MARIVAUX

6 Men gossip less than women, but mean it.

—MIGNON MCLAUGHLIN

7 Scandal is the coin of contemporary celebrity. It keeps the public interested.

—RICHARD CORLISS

8 He who is caught in a lie is not believed when he tells the truth.

—SPANISH PROVERB

9 Gossip, unlike river water, flows both ways.

—MICHAEL KORDA

10 Trying to squash a rumor is like trying to unring a bell.

—SHANA ALEXANDER

11 A rumor without a leg to stand on will get around some other way.

—JOHN TUDOR
in *Omni*

12 Just because a rumor is idle doesn't mean it isn't working.

—MAURICE SEITTER

13 To speak ill of others is a dishonest way of praising ourselves.

—WILL DURANT

WHEN FLATTERERS MEET . . .

14 When flatterers meet, the devil goes to dinner.

—ENGLISH PROVERB

15 Of all music, that which most pleases the ear is applause. But it has no score. It ends and is carried off by the wind. Nothing remains.

—ENRIQUE SOLARI

16 Flattery is counterfeit money which, but for vanity, would have no circulation.

—FRANÇOIS DE LA ROCHEFOUCAULD

17 Beware the flatterer: he feeds you with an empty spoon.

—COSINO DEGREGRIO

1 A detour is a straight road which turns on the charm.

—ALBERT BRIE
Le Devoir

2 Flatterers look like friends, as wolves like dogs.

—GEORGE CHAPMAN

3 The punishment for vanity is flattery.

—WILHELM RAABE

4 We protest against unjust criticism, but we accept unearned applause.

—JOSÉ NAROSKY
Si Todos Los Sueños

5 I have yet to be bored by someone paying me a compliment.

—OTTO VAN ISCH

6 Flattery is all right—if you don't inhale.

—ADLAI E. STEVENSON

7 Praise, if you don't swallow it, can't hurt you.

—MORT WALKER

8 Praise can be your most valuable asset as long as you don't aim it at yourself.

—O. A. BATTISTA

9 Fish for no compliments; they are generally caught in shallow water.

—D. SMITH

10 Praise is warming and desirable. But it is an earned thing. It has to be deserved, like a hug from a child.

—PHYLLIS MCGINLEY
in *The Saturday Evening Post*

11 Sometimes we deny being worthy of praise, hoping to generate an argument we would be pleased to lose.

—CULLEN HIGHTOWER

12 He who praises everybody praises nobody.

—SAMUEL JOHNSON

FORBIDDEN FRUIT . . .

13 While forbidden fruit is said to taste sweeter, it usually spoils faster.

—ABIGAIL VAN BUREN

14 A compulsion is a highbrow term for a temptation we're not trying too hard to resist.

—HUGH ALLEN

15 Most people want to be delivered from temptation but would like it to keep in touch.

—ROBERT ORBEN

16 Those who flee temptation generally leave a forwarding address.

—LANE OLINGHOUSE

1 Temptation usually comes in through a door that has deliberately been left open.

—Arnold H. Glasow

2 Temptations, unlike opportunities, will always give you many second chances.

—O. A. Battista

3 There is no original sin; it has all been done before.

—Louis Dudek

4 Be cautious. Opportunity does the knocking for temptation too.

— Al Batt

5 Being virtuous is no feat once temptation ceases.

—Danish proverb

6 Nothing makes it easier to resist temptation than a proper bringing-up, a sound set of values—and witnesses.

—Franklin P. Jones

7 In this era of rapid change, one thing remains constant: it's easier to pray for forgiveness than to resist temptation.

—Sol Kendon

8 About the only time losing is more fun than winning is when you're fighting temptation.

—Tom Wilson

9 Come good times or bad, there is always a market for things nobody needs.

—Kin Hubbard

10 When there's a lot of it around, you never want it very much.

—Peg Bracken
The I Hate to Cook Almanack

LAZINESS HAS MANY DISGUISES . . .

11 Laziness has many disguises. Soon "winter doldrums" will become "spring fever."

—Bern Williams
in *National Enquirer*

12 He who is carried on another's back does not appreciate how far off the town is.

—African proverb

13 If you get a reputation as an early riser, you can sleep till noon.

—Irish proverb

14 Cultivate the habit of early rising. It is unwise to keep the head long on a level with the feet.

—Henry David Thoreau

15 Laziness may appear attractive, but work gives satisfaction.

—Anne Frank
The Diary of a Young Girl

1 The safest road to hell is the gradual one—the gentle slope, soft underfoot, without sudden turnings, without milestones, without signposts.

—C. S. LEWIS
The Screwtape Letters

2 Laziness is nothing more than resting before you get tired.

—JULES RENARD

3 A lot of what passes for depression these days is nothing more than a body saying that it needs work.

—GEOFFREY NORMAN

4 Beware of the man who won't be bothered with details.

—WILLIAM FEATHER SR.

5 It is better to have loafed and lost than never to have loafed at all.

—JAMES THURBER

6 The day will happen whether or not you get up.

—JOHN CIARDI

7 I'm lazy. But it's the lazy people who invented the wheel and the bicycle because they didn't like walking or carrying things.

—LECH WALESA

8 About the only thing that comes to us without effort is old age.

—GLORIA PITZER

9 I can do only one thing at a time, but I can avoid doing many things simultaneously.

—ASHLEIGH BRILLIANT

10 What a fearful object a long-neglected duty gets to be!

—CHAUNCEY WRIGHT

11 A life of ease is a difficult pursuit.

—WILLIAM COWPER

12 Most of our so-called reasoning consists in finding arguments for going on believing as we already do.

—JAMES HARVEY ROBINSON
The Mind in the Making

13 No one ever excused his way to success.

—DAVE DEL DOTTO
How to Make Nothing But Money

14 Excuses are the nails used to build a house of failure.

—DON WILDER AND BILL RECHIN

15 Whoever wants to be a judge of human nature should study people's excuses.

— FRIEDRICH HEBBEL

16 Don't tell me how hard you work. Tell me how much you get done.

—JAMES LING
in *Newsweek*

1 To be idle requires a strong sense of personal identity.

—ROBERT LOUIS STEVENSON

2 There are no shortcuts to any place worth going.

—BEVERLY SILLS

3 The older generation thought nothing of getting up at five every morning—and the younger generation doesn't think much of it either.

—JOHN J. WELSH

THE FAULTS OF OTHERS . . .

4 Rare is the person who can weigh the faults of others without putting his thumb on the scales.

—BYRON J. LANGENFIELD

5 Only God is in a position to look down on anyone.

—SARAH BROWN

6 The unforgiving man assumes a judgment that not even the theologians has [sic] given to God.

—SYDNEY J. HARRIS

7 I have never for one instant seen clearly within myself. How then would you have me judge the deeds of others?

—MAURICE MAETERLINCK

8 Moral indignation is jealousy with a halo.

—H. G. WELLS

9 Other people's faults are like bees — if we don't see them, they don't harm us.

—LUIS VIGIL
Pensamientos y Observaciónes

10 Make no judgments where you have no compassion.

—ANNE MCCAFFREY
Dragonquest

11 How much easier it is to be critical than to be correct.

—BENJAMIN DISRAELI

12 What we all tend to complain about most in other people are those things we don't like about ourselves.

—WILLIAM WHARTON
Tidings

13 I don't like a man to be efficient. He's likely to be not human enough.

—FELIX FRANKFRUTER

14 When a man points a finger at someone else, he should remember that three of his fingers are pointing at himself.

—ANONYMOUS

15 Ought is not a word we use to other people. It is a word we should reserve for ourselves.

—SISTER WENDY BECKETT

1 Perhaps no phenomenon contains so much destructive feeling as "moral indignation," which permits envy or hate to be acted out under the guise of virtue.

—ERICH FROMM

2 If you judge people, you have no time to love them.

—MOTHER TERESA OF CALCUTTA

3 Speak not against anyone whose burden you have not weighed yourself.

—MARION BRADLEY
Black Trillium

4 Puritanism is the haunting fear that someone, somewhere, may be happy.

—H. L. MENCKEN

5 This is a do-it-yourself test for paranoia: you know you've got it when you can't think of anything that's your fault.

—ROBERT M. HUTCHINS

6 That which we call sin in others is experiment for us.

—RALPH WALDO EMERSON

7 We all have weaknesses. But I have figured that others have put up with mine so tolerantly that I would be less than fair not to make a reasonable discount for theirs.

—WILLIAM ALLEN WHITE

8 We are all inclined to judge ourselves by our ideals; others, by their acts.

—HAROLD NICOLSON

9 Distrust all in whom the impulse to punish is powerful.

—FRIEDRICH NIETZSCHE

10 Nothing so needs reforming as other people's habits.

—MARK TWAIN

11 Our faults irritate us most when we see them in others.

—PENNSYLVANIA DUTCH PROVERB

12 The enthusiastic, to those who are not, are always something of a trial.

—ALBAN GOODIER

13 There is little room left for wisdom when one is full of judgment.

—MALCOLM HEIN

14 Nothing in the world is so rare as a person one can always put up with.

—GIACOMO LEOPARDI

15 When nobody around you seems to measure up, it's time to check your yardstick.

—BILL LEMLEY

1 It has been my experience that folks who have no vices have very few virtues.

—ABRAHAM LINCOLN

2 There are certain small faults that offset great virtues. There are certain great faults that are forgotten in small virtues.

—GRANTLAND RICE WATTS

3 Accept me as I am—only then will we discover each other.

—FROM FEDERICO FELLINI'S *8 1/2*

4 The less secure a man is, the more likely he is to have extreme prejudices.

—CLINT EASTWOOD

5 Nothing dies so hard, or rallies so often, as intolerance.

—HENRY WARD BEECHER

6 Prejudices are the chains forged by ignorance to keep men apart.

—COUNTESS OF BLESSINGTON

7 Prejudice is a disease characterized by hardening of the categories.

—WILLIAM ARTHUR

8 A prejudice is a vagrant opinion without visible means of support.

—AMBROSE BIERCE

9 It is never too late to give up our prejudices.

—HENRY DAVID THOREAU

10 Every bigot was once a child free of prejudice.

—SISTER MARY DE LOURDES

11 Too many of our prejudices are like pyramids upside down. They rest on tiny, trivial incidents, but they spread upward and outward until they fill our minds.

—WILLIAM MCCHESNEY MARTIN

STUPIDITY WON'T KILL YOU . . .

12 Stupidity won't kill you, but it can make you sweat.

—ENGLISH PROVERB

13 Ignorance is not bliss—it is oblivion.

—PHILIP WYLIE

14 I am patient with stupidity but not with those who are proud of it.

—EDITH SITWELL

15 The greatest obstacle to discovering the shape of the earth, the continents and the ocean was not ignorance but the illusion of knowledge.

—DANIEL J. BOORSTIN
The Discoverers

16 Ignorance is bold, and knowledge reserved.

—THUCYDIDES

1 The trouble with most folks isn't so much their ignorance, as knowing so many things that ain't so.

—JOSH BILLINGS

2 Sometimes the best way to convince someone he is wrong is to let him have his way.

—RED O'DONNELL

3 Everybody is ignorant, only on different subjects.

—WILL ROGERS

4 Nothing will divide this nation more than ignorance, and nothing can bring us together better than an educated population.

—JOHN SCULLEY
in *The Atlantic*

5 Preconceived notions are the locks on the door to wisdom.

—MERRY BROWNE
in *National Enquirer*

6 Fears are educated into us and can, if we wish, be educated out.

—KARL A. MENNINGER, MD
The Human Mind

7 The intelligent man who is proud of his intelligence is like the condemned man who is proud of his large cell.

—SIMONE WEIL

IF MALICE OR ENVY WERE TANGIBLE . . .

8 It is never wise to seek or wish for another's misfortune. If malice or envy were tangible and had a shape, it would be the shape of a boomerang.

—CHARLEY REESE

9 Spite is never lonely; envy always tags along.

—MIGNON MCLAUGHLIN

10 Envy is the art of counting the other fellow's blessings instead of your own.

—HAROLD COFFIN

11 Do not believe those persons who say they have never been jealous. What they mean is that they have never been in love.

—GERALD BRENAN

12 Love looks through a telescope; envy, through a microscope.

—JOSH BILLINGS

13 Jealousy is all the fun you think they had.

—ERICA JONG

14 I'd never try to learn from someone I didn't envy at least a little. If I never envied, I'd never learn.

—BETSY COHEN
The Snow White Syndrome

THE CHAINS OF HABIT . . .

1 The chains of habit are generally too small to be felt until they are too strong to be broken.
　　　　　　　—SAMUEL JOHNSON

2 Good habits are as easy to form as bad ones.
　　　　　　　—TIM MCCARVER

3 Habits are first cobwebs, then cables.
　　　　　　　—SPANISH PROVERB

4 Comfort comes as a guest, lingers to become a host and stays to enslave us.
　　　　　　　—LEE S. BICKMORE

5 Habit is habit, and not to be flung out of the window by any man, but coaxed downstairs a step at a time.
　　　　　　　—MARK TWAIN

6 A habit is a shirt made of iron.
　　　　　　　—HAROLD HELFER

7 Habits are like supervisors that you don't notice.
　　　　　　　—HANNES MESSEMER

8 We can often endure an extra pound of pain far more easily than we can suffer the withdrawal of an ounce of accustomed pleasure.
　　　　　　　—SYDNEY J. HARRIS

Habit, if not resisted, soon becomes necessity. 9
　　　　　　　—ST. AUGUSTINE

It is easy to assume a habit; but when you try to cast it off, it will take skin and all. 10
　　　　　　　—JOSH BILLINGS

A habit is something you can do without thinking—which is why most of us have so many of them. 11
　　　　　　　—FRANK A. CLARK

The best way to break a habit is to drop it. 12
　　　　　　　—LEO AIKMAN

A bad habit never disappears miraculously; it's an undo-it-yourself project. 13
　　　　　　　—ABIGAIL VAN BUREN

NEVER BE HAUGHTY . . .

Never be haughty to the humble. Never be humble to the haughty. 14
　　　　　　　—JEFFERSON DAVIS

None are so empty as those who are full of themselves. 15
　　　　　　　—BENJAMIN WHICHCOTE

The louder he talked of his honor, the faster we counted our spoons. 16
　　　　　　　—RALPH WALDO EMERSON

1 He who truly knows has no occasion to shout.
—LEONARDO DA VINCI

2 The question we do not see when we are young is whether we own pride or are owned by it.
—JOSEPHINE JOHNSON
The Dark Traveler

3 If you are all wrapped up in yourself, you are overdressed.
—*The Wedded Unmother*

4 A man wrapped up in himself makes a very small parcel.
—"Thought for the Day," BBC Radio

5 When someone sings his own praises, he always gets the tune too high.
—MARY H. WALDRIP

6 Vanity is the result of a delusion that someone is paying attention.
—PAUL E. SWEENEY

7 Oh, for a pin that would puncture pretension!
—ISAAC ASIMOV
Buy Jupiter and Other Stories

8 Men often mistake notoriety for fame, and would rather be remarked for their vices and follies than not be noticed at all.
—HARRY S. TRUMAN

9 It is far more impressive when others discover your good qualities without your help.
—JUDITH S. MARTIN

10 A modest man is usually admired—if people ever hear of him.
—ED HOWE

11 Lord, where we are wrong, make us willing to change; where we are right, make us easy to live with.
—REV. PETER MARSHALL

12 The nice thing about egotists is that they don't talk about other people.
—LUCILLE S. HARPER

13 The egotist always hurts the one he loves—himself.
—BERNICE PEERS

14 The only cure for vanity is laughter. And the only fault that's laughable is vanity.
—HENRI BERGSON

15 Pride makes some men ridiculous but prevents others from becoming so.
—CHARLES CALEB COLTON

16 Too great a sense of identity makes a man feel he can do no wrong. And too little does the same.
—DJUNA BARNES

WHEN WE ACT

" Life is a great big canvas, and you should throw all the paint on it you can.

—Danny Kaye

THE VERY ESSENCE OF LEADERSHIP . . .

1 The very essence of leadership is that you have to have a vision. You can't blow an uncertain trumpet.

—THEODORE HESBURGH

2 High sentiments always win in the end. The leaders who offer blood, toil, tears and sweat always get more out of their followers than those who offer safety and a good time. When it comes to the pinch, human beings are heroic.

—George Orwell
Collected Essays, Journalism and Letters

3 Consensus is the negation of leadership.

—MARGARET THATCHER

4 You do not lead by hitting people over the head. That's assault, not leadership.

—DWIGHT D. EISENHOWER

5 Lots of folks confuse bad management with destiny.

—KIN HUBBARD

6 Never tell people how to do things. Tell them what to do and they will surprise you with their ingenuity.

—GEN. GEORGE S. PATTON JR.

7 Rules are made for people who aren't willing to make up their own.

—CHUCK YEAGER AND CHARLES LEERHSEN
Press On!

8 A leader knows what's best to do; a manager knows merely how best to do it.

—KEN ADELMAN

9 Leadership is a potent combination of strategy and character. But if you must be without one, be without the strategy.

—GEN. H. NORMAN SCHWARZKOPF

10 A leader who keeps his ear to the ground allows his rear end to become a target.

—ANGIE PAPADAKIS

11 One measure of leadership is the caliber of people who choose to follow you.

—DENNIS A. PEER

12 The person who knows how will always have a job. But the person who knows why will be his boss.

—CARL C. WOOD

13 Anyone can hold the helm when the sea is calm.

—PUBLILIUS SYRUS

14 Nothing great was ever achieved without enthusiasm.

—RALPH WALDO EMERSON

1 Knowledge cannot make us all leaders, but it can help us decide which leader to follow.
—*Management Digest*

2 Wise are those who learn that the bottom line doesn't always have to be their top priority.
—William Arthur Ward

3 The mark of a true professional is giving more than you get.
—Robert Kirby

4 Rank does not confer privilege or give power. It imposes responsibility.
—Peter Drucker
in *Fortune*

5 A man who enjoys responsibility usually gets it. A man who merely likes exercising authority usually loses it.
—Malcolm S. Forbes

6 Few things are harder to put up with than the annoyance of a good example.
—Mark Twain

7 He that would be a leader must be a bridge.
—Welsh proverb

8 Life is like a dog-sled team. If you ain't the lead dog, the scenery never changes.
—Lewis Grizzard

9 The speed of the leader determines the rate of the pack.
—Wayne Lukas

10 If you want truly to understand something, try to change it.
—Kurt Lewin

11 We still think of a powerful man as a born leader and a powerful woman as an anomaly.
—Margaret Atwood

12 Asking "Who ought to be boss?" is like asking "Who ought to be the tenor in the quartet?" Obviously, the man who can sing tenor.
—Henry Ford

13 A great leader is the one who can show people that their self-interest is different from that which they perceived.
—Barney Frank

14 No person can be a great leader unless he takes genuine joy in the successes of those under him.
—W. A. Nance

15 First-rate men hire first-rate men; second-rate men hire third-rate men.
—Leo Rosten

16 It's easy to make a buck. It's a lot tougher to make a difference.
—Tom Brokaw

1 The things we fear most in organizations—fluctuations, disturbances, imbalances—are the primary sources of creativity.

—MARGARET J. WHEATLEY
Leadership and the New Science

2 Change starts when someone sees the next step.

—WILLIAM DRAYTON
in *Esquire*

3 I am more afraid of an army of 100 sheep led by a lion than an army of 100 lions led by a sheep.

—TALLEYRAND

4 It's better to be a lion for a day than a sheep all your life.

—SISTER KENNY

WHAT GREAT THING WOULD YOU ATTEMPT . . .

5 What great thing would you attempt if you knew you could not fail?

—ROBERT H. SCHULLER

6 Why not upset the apple cart? If you don't, the apples will rot anyway.

—FRANK A. CLARK

7 Determine that the thing can and shall be done, and then we shall find the way.

—ABRAHAM LINCOLN

8 When a man's willing and eager, the gods join in.

—AESCHYLUS

9 Trust in God and do something.

—MARY LYON

10 Action may not always be happiness, but there is no happiness without action.

—BENJAMIN DISRAELI

11 There is a close correlation between getting up in the morning and getting up in the world.

—RON DENTINGER
in *Chronicle* (Dodgerville, Wisconsin)

12 Noble deeds and hot baths are the best cures for depression.

—DODIE SMITH
I Capture The Castle

13 My view is that to sit back and let fate play its hand out and never influence it is not the way man was meant to operate.

—JOHN GLENN

14 People judge you by your actions, not your intentions. You may have a heart of gold, but so has a hard-boiled egg.

—*Good Reading*

15 Let him that would move the world, first move himself.

—SOCRATES

1 All glory comes from daring to begin.

—Eugene F. Ware

2 Everything comes to he who hustles while he waits.

—Thomas A. Edison

3 Well done is better than well said.

—Benjamin Franklin

4 You can't build a reputation on what you are going to do.

—Henry Ford

5 In life, as in a football game, the principle to follow is: hit the line hard.

—Theodore Roosevelt

6 If you never budge, don't expect a push.

—Malcolm S. Forbes

7 You must get involved to have an impact. No one is impressed with the won-lost record of the referee.

—John H. Holcomb
The Militant Moderate

8 Swing hard, in case they throw the ball where you're swinging.

—Duke Snider

9 Life is a great big canvas, and you should throw all the paint on it you can.

—Danny Kaye

10 Success is a ladder that cannot be climbed with your hands in your pockets.

—American proverb

11 Few wishes come true by themselves.

—June Smith
in *Sentinel* (Orlando, Florida)

12 Dig the well before you are thirsty.

—Chinese proverb

13 Have you considered that if you "don't make waves," nobody, including yourself, will know that you are alive?

—Theodore Isaac Rubin, MD

14 Many a man with no family tree has succeeded because he branched out for himself.

—Leo Aikman

15 God gives every bird his worm, but he does not throw it into the nest.

—Swedish proverb

16 Ask God's blessing on your work, but don't ask him to do it for you.

—Dame Flora Robson
on *Friends*, BBC

17 It is easy to sit up and take notice. What is difficult is getting up and taking action.

—Al Batt

1 Not everything that is faced can be changed. But nothing can be changed until it is faced.

—James Baldwin

2 Our dilemma is that we hate change and love it at the same time; what we really want is for things to remain the same but get better.

—Sydney J. Harris

3 Just as iron rusts from disuse, even so does inaction spoil the intellect.

—Leonardo da Vinci

4 Men may doubt what you say, but they will believe what you do.

—Lewis Cass

5 If your ship doesn't come in, swim out to it!

—Jonathan Winters

6 Sow an act, and you reap a habit. Sow a habit, and you reap a character. Sow a character, and you reap a destiny.

—Charles Reade

BE BOLD IN WHAT YOU STAND FOR . . .

7 Be bold in what you stand for and careful what you fall for.

—Ruth Boorstin
in *The Wall Street Journal*

8 Don't believe that winning is really everything. It's more important to stand for something. If you don't stand for something, what do you win?

—Lane Kirkland

9 Never give in—in nothing, great or small, large or petty—except to convictions of honor and good sense.

—Winston Churchill

10 The quality of a man's life is in direct proportion to his commitment to excellence, regardless of his chosen field of endeavor.

—Vince Lombardi

11 A good resolution is like an old horse which is often saddled but rarely ridden.

—Mexican proverb

12 Compromise makes a good umbrella, but a poor roof.

—James Russell Lowell

13 A thing moderately good is not so good as it ought to be. Moderation in temper is always a virtue; but moderation in principle is always a vice.

—Thomas Paine

14 He that always gives way to others will end in having no principles of his own.

—Aesop

1 Middleness is the very enemy of the bold.

—CHARLES KRAUTHAMMER

2 You've got to stand for somethin' or you're gonna fall for anything.

—JOHN COUGAR MELLENCAMP
"You've Got to Stand for Somethin'"

3 Learn to say no. It will be of more use to you than to be able to read Latin.

—CHARLES HADDON SPURGEON

4 One-half the troubles of this life can be traced to saying yes too quickly and not saying no soon enough.

—JOSH BILLINGS

5 It's important that people should know what you stand for. It's equally important that they know what you won't stand for.

—MARY H. WALDRIP

6 Standing in the middle of the road is very dangerous; you get knocked down by the traffic from both sides.

—MARGARET THATCHER

7 The main discomfort in being a middle-of-the-roader is that you get sideswiped by partisans going in both directions.

—SYDNEY J. HARRIS

8 The most prominent place in hell is reserved for those who are neutral on the great issues of life.

—REV. BILLY GRAHAM

9 Never "for the sake of peace and quiet" deny your own experience or convictions.

—DAG HAMMARSKJOLD

10 When something important is going on, silence is a lie.

—A. M. ROSENTHAL
in *The New York Times*

11 Please all and you please none.

—AESOP

12 He who turns the other cheek too far gets it in the neck.

—H. HERT

13 You can lean over backward so far that you fall flat on your face.

—BEN H. BAGDIKIAN

14 In the end it will not matter to us whether we fought with flails or reeds. It will matter to us greatly on what side we fought.

—G. K. CHESTERTON

15 A man's judgment is best when he can forget himself and any reputation he may have acquired and can concentrate wholly on making the right decisions.

—ADM. RAYMOND A. SPRUANCE

OPPORTUNITIES ARE NEVER LOST . . .

1 Opportunities are never lost. The other fellow takes those you miss.

—ANONYMOUS

2 Not many sounds in life, and I include all urban and all rural sounds, exceed in interest a knock at the door.

—CHARLES LAMB

3 The world is before you, and you need not take it or leave it as it was when you came in.

—JAMES BALDWIN

4 Opportunity is often difficult to recognize; we usually expect it to beckon us with beepers and billboards.

—WILLIAM ARTHUR WARD

5 If opportunity doesn't knock, build a door.

—MILTON BERLE

6 It is often hard to distinguish between the hard knocks in life and those of opportunity.

—FREDERICK PHILLIPS

7 Life is always walking up to us and saying, "Come on in, the living's fine," and what do we do? Back off and take its picture.

—RUSSELL BAKER

8 Opportunity is sometimes hard to recognize if you're only looking for a lucky break.

—MONTA CRANE

9 Opportunity's favorite disguise is trouble.

—FRANK TYGER
in Rotary "Scandal Sheet" (Graham, Texas)

10 Opportunities are often things you haven't noticed the first time around.

—CATHERINE DENEUVE

11 Wherever we look upon this earth, the opportunities take shape within the problems.

—NELSON A. ROCKEFELLER

12 If a window of opportunity appears, don't pull down the shade.

—TOM PETERS
The Pursuit of Wow!

13 A problem is a chance for you to do your best.

—DUKE ELLINGTON

14 Jumping at several small opportunities may get us there more quickly than waiting for one big one to come along.

—HUGH ALLEN

1 Problems are only opportunities with thorns on them.
—HUGH MILLER
Snow on the Wind

2 Opportunity is a bird that never perches.
—CLAUDE McDONALD

3 One of the secrets of life is to make stepping stones out of stumbling blocks.
—JACK PENN

4 Today's opportunities erase yesterday's failures.
—GENE BROWN
in *News-Times* (Danbury, Connecticut)

5 I make the most of all that comes and the least of all that goes.
—SARA TEASDALE
"The Philosopher," in *Poems That Touch the Heart*, edited by A. L. Alexander

OUT ON A LIMB . . .

6 Why not go out on a limb? Isn't that where the fruit is?
—FRANK SCULLY

7 All growth, including political growth, is the result of risk-taking.
—JUDE WANNISKI

8 What isn't tried won't work.
—CLAUDE McDONALD
in *The Christian Word*

9 What is more mortifying than to feel that you have missed the plum for want of courage to shake the tree?
—LOGAN PEARSALL SMITH

10 It is not because things are difficult that we do not dare; it is because we do not dare that they are difficult.
—SENECA

11 What would life be if we had no courage to attempt anything?
—VINCENT van GOGH

12 A coward meets his fate in his own hideout.
—JORGE SALVADOR LARA
El Comercio

13 All serious daring starts from within.
—EUDORA WELTY
One Writer's Beginnings

14 If you risk nothing, then you risk everything.
—GEENA DAVIS

15 Worry is like a rocking chair. It will give you something to do, but it won't get you anywhere.
—*The United Church Observer*

16 Progress always involves risks. You can't steal second base and keep your foot on first.
—FREDERICK B. WILCOX

1 Yes, risk-taking is inherently failure-prone. Otherwise, it would be called sure-thing-taking.
—Tim McMahon

2 Take a chance! All life is a chance. The man who goes furthest is generally the one who is willing to do and dare.
—*Dale Carnegie's Scrapbook*, edited by Dorothy Carnegie

3 People wish to learn to swim and at the same time to keep one foot on the ground.
—Marcel Proust
Remembrance of Things Past

4 High expectations are the key to everything.
—Sam Walton

5 If you're never scared or embarrassed or hurt, it means you never take any chances.
—Julia Sorel

6 When you're skating on thin ice, you may as well tap-dance.
—Bryce Courtenay

7 It's better to plunge into the unknown than to try to make sure of everything.
—Gerald Lescarbeault

8 Take calculated risks. That is quite different from being rash.
—Gen. George S. Patton Jr.

9 We cannot become what we need to be by remaining what we are.
—Max De Pree
Leadership Is an Art

10 When you reach for the stars, you may not quite get one, but you won't come up with a handful of mud either.
—Leo Burnett

11 In skating over thin ice, our safety is in our speed.
—Ralph Waldo Emerson

12 You are permitted in time of great danger to walk with the devil until you have crossed the bridge.
—Bulgarian proverb

13 If you don't place your foot on the rope, you'll never cross the chasm.
—Liz Smith

14 Necessity is the mother of taking chances.
—Mark Twain

15 If necessity is the mother of invention, discontent is the father of progress.
—David Rockefeller

16 Sometimes the fool who rushes in gets the job done.
—Al Bernstein

1 A man sits as many risks as he runs.
—HENRY DAVID THOREAU

2 A ship in harbor is safe—but that is not what ships are for.
—JOHN A. SHEDD

A ROAD TWICE TRAVELED . . .

3 A road twice traveled is never as long.
—ROSALIE GRAHAM

4 The meaning of life cannot be told; it has to happen to a person.
—IRA PROGOFF
The Symbolic & the Real

5 The winds and waves are always on the side of the ablest navigators.
—EDWARD GIBBON

6 The person who has had a bull by the tail once has learned 60 or 70 times as much as a person who hasn't.
—MARK TWAIN

7 The work will teach you how to do it.
—ESTONIAN PROVERB

8 Sometimes you earn more doing the jobs that pay nothing.
—TODD RUTHMAN

9 When you fall in a river, you're no longer a fisherman; you're a swimmer.
—GENE HILL
in *Field & Stream*

10 Believe one who has tried it.
—VIRGIL

11 Information's pretty thin stuff unless mixed with experience.
—CLARENCE DAY
The Crow's Nest

12 Only the wearer knows where the shoe pinches.
—PROVERB

13 A man begins cutting his wisdom teeth the first time he bites off more than he can chew.
—HERB CAEN

14 The value of experience is not in seeing much, but in seeing wisely.
—SIR WILLIAM OSLER

15 One thing about experience is that when you don't have very much you're apt to get a lot.
—FRANKLIN P. JONES
in *Quote*

16 Experience is a wonderful thing; it enables you to recognize a mistake every time you repeat it.
—The Associated Press

1 We learn to walk by stumbling.
—BULGARIAN PROVERB

2 I have never let my schooling interfere with my education.
—MARK TWAIN

3 People learn something every day, and a lot of times it's that what they learned the day before was wrong.
—BILL VAUGHAN

4 Just when you think you've graduated from the school of experience, someone thinks up a new course.
—MARY H. WALDRIP

5 Experience is what you get when you don't get what you want.
—DAN STANFORD

6 Anybody who profits from the experience of others probably writes biographies.
—FRANKLIN P. JONES

7 If we could sell our experiences for what they cost us, we'd all be millionaires.
—ABIGAIL VAN BUREN

8 Half, maybe more, of the delight of experiencing is to know what you are experiencing.
—JESSAMYN WEST
Hide and Seek

Perhaps the angels who fear to tread where fools rush in used to be fools who rushed in. 9
—FRANKLIN P. JONES

HE WHO HESITATES . . .

He who hesitates is last. 10
—*The Wit and Wisdom of Mae West*
edited by Joseph Weintraub

He who hesitates is sometimes 11
saved.
—JAMES THURBER
Fables for Our Time

These things are good in little 12
measure and evil in large: yeast, salt and hesitation.
—*THE TALMUD*

The man who insists upon seeing 13
with perfect clearness before he decides, never decides.
—HENRI FRÉDÉRIC AMIEL

A man would do nothing if he 14
waited until he could do it so well that no one could find fault.
—JOHN HENRY CARDINAL NEWMAN

It's better to be boldly decisive and 15
risk being wrong than to agonize at length and be right too late.
—MARILYN MOATS KENNEDY
Across the Board

1 If all difficulties were known at the outset of a long journey, most of us would never start out at all.
—DAN RATHER WITH PETER WYDEN
I Remember

2 Decision is a sharp knife that cuts clean and straight. Indecision is a dull one that hacks and tears and leaves ragged edges behind.
—JAN MCKEITHEN

3 The chief danger in life is that you may take too many precautions.
—ALFRED ADLER

4 You have to be careful about being too careful.
—BERYL PFIZER

5 If you wait, all that happens is that you get older.
—LARRY MCMURTRY
Some Can Whistle

6 If you take too long in deciding what to do with your life, you'll find you've done it.
—PAM SHAW

7 To think too long about doing a thing often becomes its undoing.
—EVA YOUNG

8 When you have to make a choice and don't make it, that is in itself a choice.
—WILLIAM JAMES

9 Half the failures in life arise from pulling in one's horse as he is leaping.
—JULIUS CHARLES HARE AND AUGUSTUS WILLIAM HARE

10 Give me the benefit of your convictions, if you have any; but keep your doubts to yourself, for I have enough of my own.
—JOHANN WOLFGANG VON GOETHE

11 Throughout history, the most common debilitating human ailment has been cold feet.
—*Country*

12 Calculation never made a hero.
—JOHN HENRY CARDINAL NEWMAN

13 He who hesitates is interrupted.
—FRANKLIN P. JONES

IF YOU CAN'T MAKE A MISTAKE . . .

14 If you can't make a mistake, you can't make anything.
—MARVA N. COLLINS

15 Never let the fear of striking out get in your way.
—BABE RUTH

16 The greatest mistake you can make in life is continually to be fearing you will make one.
—ELBERT HUBBARD

1 A stumble may prevent a fall.

—ENGLISH PROVERB

2 He who never made a mistake never made a discovery.

—SAMUEL SMILES

3 A mistake proves that someone stopped talking long enough to do something.

—PHOENIX FLAME

4 Mistakes are the usual bridge between inexperience and wisdom.

—PHYLLIS THEROUX
Night Lights

5 Better to ask twice than to lose your way once.

—DANISH PROVERB

6 We're all proud of making little mistakes. It gives us the feeling we don't make any big ones.

—ANDREW A. ROONEY
Not That You Asked . . .

7 To err is human; to admit it, superhuman.

—DOUG LARSON

8 Admit your errors before someone else exaggerates them.

—ANDREW V. MASON, MD

9 There is no saint without a past— no sinner without a future.

—ANCIENT PERSIAN MASS

10 Once we realize that imperfect understanding is the human condition, there is no shame in being wrong, only in failing to correct our mistakes.

—GEORGE SOROS
Soros on Soros

11 One of the most dangerous forms of human error is forgetting what one is trying to achieve.

—PAUL NITZE

12 It is very easy to forgive others their mistakes; it takes more grit and gumption to forgive them for having witnessed your own.

—JESSAMYN WEST

13 The worst part is not in making a mistake but in trying to justify it, instead of using it as a heaven-sent warning of our mindlessness or our ignorance.

—SANTIAGO RAMÓN Y CAJAL
Charlas de Cafe

14 Always acknowledge a fault frankly. This will throw those in authority off their guard and give you opportunity to commit more.

—MARK TWAIN

15 To obtain maximum attention, it's hard to beat a good, big mistake.

—DAVID D. HEWITT

16 Justifying a fault doubles it.

—FRENCH PROVERB

1 Your worst humiliation is only someone else's momentary entertainment.

—KAREN CROCKETT

2 He who is afraid to ask is ashamed of learning.

—DANISH PROVERB

3 The only nice thing about being imperfect is the joy it brings to others.

—DOUG LARSON

4 Nine times out of ten, the first thing a man's companion knows of his shortcomings is from his apology.

—OLIVER WENDELL HOLMES SR.

5 If all else fails, immortality can always be assured by spectacular error.

—JOHN KENNETH GALBRAITH
Money: Whence It Came, Where It Went

I'D RATHER BE A FAILURE . . .

6 I'd rather be a failure at something I enjoy than be a success at something I hate.

—GEORGE BURNS

7 You never conquer a mountain. You stand on the summit a few moments; then the wind blows your footprints away.

—ARLENE BLUM

8 Victory is in the quality of competition, not the final score.

—MIKE MARSHALL

9 Laurels don't make much of a cushion.

—DOROTHY RABINOWITZ

10 Success covers a multitude of blunders.

—BERNARD SHAW

11 Failure is the condiment that gives success its flavor.

—TRUMAN CAPOTE

12 Success and failure. We think of them as opposites, but they're really not. They're companions— the hero and the sidekick.

—LAURENCE SHAMES

13 Don't confuse fame with success. Madonna is one; Helen Keller is the other.

—ERMA BOMBECK

14 The hero reveals the possibilities of human nature; the celebrity reveals the possibilities of the media.

—DANIEL J. BOORSTIN
The Image

15 Oh, the difference between nearly right and exactly right.

—HORACE J. BROWN

1 Success is never final, but failure can be.

—BILL PARCELLS
Finding a Way to Win

2 I couldn't wait for success . . . so I went ahead without it.

—JONATHAN WINTERS

3 There is no comparison between that which is lost by not succeeding and that which is lost by not trying.

—FRANCIS BACON

4 You may be disappointed if you fail, but you are doomed if you don't try.

—BEVERLY SILLS

5 Use what talents you possess: the woods would be very silent if no birds sang there except those that sang best.

—HENRY VAN DYKE

6 Ability is what you're capable of doing. Motivation determines what you do. Attitude determines how well you do it.

—LOU HOLTZ

7 True success is overcoming the fear of being unsuccessful.

—PAUL SWEENEY

8 If at first you do succeed—try to hide your astonishment.

—Los Angeles Times Syndicate

9 If you're not failing now and again, it's a sign you're playing it safe.

—WOODY ALLEN

10 You're never as good as everyone tells you when you win, and you're never as bad as they say when you lose.

—LOU HOLTZ WITH JOHN HEISLER
The Fighting Spirit

11 It takes as much courage to have tried and failed as it does to have tried and succeeded.

—ANNE MORROW LINDBERGH

12 It isn't failing that spells one's downfall; it's running away, giving up.

—MICHEL GRECO

13 If at first you don't succeed, try, try again. Then give up. There's no use in being a damn fool about it.

—W. C. FIELDS

14 Being defeated is often a temporary condition. Giving up is what makes it permanent.

—MARILYN VOS SAVANT

15 On this earth, in the final analysis, each of us gets exactly what he deserves. But only the successful recognize this.

—GEORGES SIMENON

1 If at first you don't succeed, you are running about average.
—M. H. ALDERSON

2 Success is not forever, and failure's not fatal.
—DON SHULA WITH KEN BLANCHARD
Everyone's a Coach

3 Failure is an event, never a person.
—WILLIAM D. BROWN
Welcome Stress!

4 Do not let what you cannot do interfere with what you can do.
—JOHN WOODEN
They Call Me Coach

5 Defeat may serve as well as victory to shake the soul and let the glory out.
—EDWIN MARKHAM

THE REWARD FOR WORK WELL DONE . . .

6 The reward for work well done is the opportunity to do more.
—JONAS SALK, MD

7 The reward of a thing well done is to have done it.
—RALPH WALDO EMERSON

8 Work is something you can count on, a trusted, lifelong friend who never deserts you.
—MARGARET BOURKE-WHITE

9 The biggest mistake you can make is to believe that you are working for someone else.
—*Bits & Pieces*

10 The work praises the man.
—IRISH PROVERB

11 One of the greatest sources of energy is pride in what you are doing.
—SPOKES

12 Do the best you can in every task, no matter how unimportant it may seem at the time. No one learns more about a problem than the person at the bottom.
—SANDRA DAY O'CONNOR

13 Manual labor to my father was not only good and decent for its own sake but, as he was given to saying, it straightened out one's thoughts.
—MARY ELLEN CHASE
A Goodly Fellowship

14 There's no labor a man can do that's undignified—if he does it right.
—BILL COSBY

15 Happiness, I have discovered, is nearly always a rebound from hard work.
—DAVID GRAYSON
Adventures in Contentment

1 There are no menial jobs, only menial attitudes.

—WILLIAM J. BENNETT
The Book of Virtues

2 Just as there are no little people or unimportant lives, there is no insignificant work.

—ELENA BONNER
Alone Together

3 There is a kind of victory in good work, no matter how humble.

—JACK KEMP

4 Thinking is the hardest work there is, which is probably the reason so few engage in it.

—HENRY FORD

5 Accomplishments have no color.

—LEONTYNE PRICE

6 The best preparation for work is not thinking about work, talking about work, or studying for work: it is work.

—WILLIAM WELD

7 Look at a day when you are supremely satisfied at the end. It's not a day when you lounge around doing nothing. It's when you've had everything to do, and you've done it.

—MARGARET THATCHER

The more I want to get something 8 done, the less I call it work.

—RICHARD BACH
Illusions: The Adventures of a Reluctant Messiah

Nothing is work unless you'd 9 rather be doing something else.

—GEORGE HALAS

My father always told me, "Find a 10 job you love and you'll never have to work a day in your life."

—JIM FOX

When we do the best that we can, 11 we never know what miracle is wrought in our life or in the life of another.

—HELEN KELLER

Ability will never catch up with 12 the demand for it.

—MALCOLM S. FORBES

What you have inherited from 13 your fathers, earn over again for yourselves, or it will not be yours.

—JOHANN WOLFGANG VON GOETHE

Not only is woman's work never 14 done, the definition keeps changing.

—BILL COPELAND
in *Herald-Tribune* (Sarasota, Florida)

We work to become, not to 15 acquire.

—ELBERT HUBBARD

1 Blessed is the person who is too busy to worry in the daytime and too sleepy to worry at night.

—LEO AIKMAN
in *Journal-Constitution* (Atlanta, Georgia)

2 Perfection is finally attained, not when there is no longer anything to add, but when there is no longer anything to take away.

—ANTOINE DE SAINT-EXUPÉRY

3 If you have a job without any aggravations, you don't have a job.

—MALCOLM S. FORBES

4 Work keeps us from three evils: boredom, vice and need.

—VOLTAIRE

5 It's strange how unimportant your job is when you're asking for a raise, but how important it can be when you want to take a day off.

—EARL A. MATHES
in *Tri-County Record* (Kiel, Wisconsin)

6 I don't know what liberation can do about it, but even when the man helps, woman's work is never done.

—BERYL PFIZER

7 The man who didn't want his wife to work has been succeeded by the man who asks about her chances of getting a raise.

—EARL WILSON

There is no such thing as a non-working mother. 8

—HESTER MUNDIS
Powermom

Work consists of whatever a body 9 is obliged to do, and play consists of whatever a body is not obliged to do.

—MARK TWAIN
The Adventures of Tom Sawyer

Retirement, we understand, is 10 great if you are busy, rich and healthy. But then, under those conditions, work is great too.

—BILL VAUGHAN

Retirement should be based on 11 the tread, not the mileage.

—ALLEN LUDDEN

I don't want to achieve immortality 12 through my work. I want to achieve immortality through not dying.

—WOODY ALLEN

It proves, on close examination, 13 that work is less boring than amusing oneself.

—CHARLES BAUDELAIRE

EVERYWHERE IS WALKING DISTANCE . . .

Everywhere is walking distance if 14 you have the time.

—STEVEN WRIGHT

1 The perfect journey is circular—
the joy of departure and the joy of
return.

—DINO BASILI
in *Il Tempe* (Rome, Itlay)

2 What is traveling? Changing your
place? By no means! Traveling is
changing your opinions and your
prejudices.

—ANATOLE FRANCE

3 The world is a book, and those
who do not travel read only one
page.

—ST. AUGUSTINE

4 There ain't no surer way to find
out whether you like people or
hate them than to travel with
them.

—MARK TWAIN

5 The rule for traveling abroad is to
take our common sense with us,
and leave our prejudices behind.

—WILLIAM HAZLITT

6 A good traveler is one who does
not know where he is going. A
perfect traveler does not know
where he came from.

—LIN YUTANG

7 Be careful going in search of
adventure—it's ridiculously easy to
find.

—WILLIAM LEAST HEAT MOON
Blue Highways: A Journey into America

8 Most travel is best of all in the
anticipation or the remembering;
the reality has more to do with
losing your luggage.

—REGINA NADELSON
in *European Travel & Life*

9 Thanks to the Interstate Highway
System, it is now possible to travel
across the country from coast to
coast without seeing anything.

—CHARLES KURALT
On the Road With Charles Kuralt

10 The average tourist wants to go to
places where there are no tourists.

—SAM EWING

11 Men travel faster now, but I do
not know if they go to better
things.

—WILLA CATHER
Death Comes for the Archbishop

12 Each year it seems to take less
time to fly across the ocean and
longer to drive to work.
—*The Globe and Mail* (Totonto, Ontario)

13 For travel to be delightful, one
must have a good place to leave
and return to.

—FREDERICK B. WILCOX

14 Traveling is like falling in love; the
world is made new.

—JAN MYRDAL

THE ART OF CONVERSATION

Words can sometimes, in moments of grace, attain the quality of deeds.

—Elie Wiesel

IT'S A STRANGE WORLD OF LANGUAGE . . .

1 It's a strange world of language in which skating on thin ice can get you into hot water.
—FRANKLIN P. JONES
in *Quote*

2 If the English language made any sense, lackadaisical would have something to do with a shortage of flowers.
—DOUG LARSON

3 Words are vehicles that can transport us from the drab sands to the dazzling stars.
—M. ROBERT SYME

4 Words are like diamonds. Polish them too much, and all you get are pebbles.
—BRYCE COURTENAY

5 All words are pegs to hang ideas on.
—HENRY WARD BEECHER

6 Words can sometimes, in moments of grace, attain the quality of deeds.
—ELIE WIESEL

7 Words without ideas are like sails without wind.
—*Courier-Record* (Blackstone, Virginia)

8 A cliché is only something well said in the first place.
—BILL GRANGER
There Are No Spies

9 To "coin a phrase" is to place some value upon it.
—E. H. EVENSON

10 A different language is a different vision of life.
—FEDERICO FELLINI

11 Learn a new language and get a new soul.
—CZECH PROVERB

12 He who does not know foreign languages does not know anything about his own.
—JOHANN WOLFGANG VON GOETHE

13 It is often wonderful how putting down on paper a clear statement of a case helps one to see, not perhaps the way out, but the way in.
—A. C. BENSON

14 In certain trying circumstances, urgent circumstances, desperate circumstances, profanity furnishes a relief denied even to prayer.
—MARK TWAIN

15 Words, like eyeglasses, blur everything that they do not make more clear.
—JOSEPH JOUBERT

1 The two words "information" and "communication" are often used interchangeably, but they signify quite different things. Information is giving out; communication is getting through.

—SYDNEY J. HARRIS

2 Mincing your words makes it easier if you have to eat them later.

—FRANKLIN P. JONES

3 Man does not live by words alone, despite the fact that sometimes he has to eat them.

—ADLAI STEVENSON

4 When a man eats his words, that's recyling.

—FRANK A. CLARK

5 By inflection you can say much more than your words do.

—MALCOLM S. FORBES

6 Brevity may be the soul of wit, but not when someone's saying, "I love you."

—JUDITH VIORST

7 Words of comfort, skillfully administered, are the oldest therapy known to man.

—LOUIS NIZER

8 Be careful of your thoughts; they may become words at any moment.

—IARA GASSEN

Words, once they're printed, have a life of their own. 9

—CAROL BURNETT

Everything becomes a little different as soon as it is spoken out loud. 10

—HERMANN HESSE

If you wouldn't write it and sign it, don't say it. 11

—EARL WILSON

Among my most prized possessions are words that I have never spoken. 12

—ORSON REGA CARD

Words are as beautiful as wild horses, and sometimes as difficult to corral. 13

—TED BERKMAN
in *Christian Science Monitor*

Look out how you use proud words. When you let proud words go, it is not easy to call them back. 14

—CARL SANDBURG
Slabs of the Sunburnt West

North Americans communicate through buttons, T-shirts and bumper stickers the way some cultures use drums. 15

—TIM MCCARTHY

A spoken word is not a sparrow. Once it flies out, you can't catch it. 16

—RUSSIAN PROVERB

1 If you would be pungent, be brief; for it is with words as with sunbeams. The more they are condensed, the deeper they burn.
—ROBERT SOUTHEY

2 You can suffocate a thought by expressing it with too many words.
—FRANK A. CLARK

3 If it takes a lot of words to say what you have in mind, give it more thought.
—DENNIS ROTH

4 Say what you have to say, not what you ought.
—HENRY DAVID THOREAU

5 Why doesn't the fellow who says "I'm no speechmaker" let it go at that instead of giving a demonstration?
—KIN HUBBARD

6 The reason we make a long story short is so that we can tell another.
—SHARON SHOEMAKER

7 The most valuable of all talents is that of never using two words when one will do.
—THOMAS JEFFERSON

8 It's all right to hold a conversation, but you should let go of it now and then.
—RICHARD ARMOUR

To base thought only on speech is 9 to try nailing whispers to the wall. Writing freezes thought and offers it up for inspection.
—JACK ROSENTHAL
in *New York Times Magazine*

When the mouth stumbles, it is 10 worse than the foot.
—WEST AFRICAN PROVERB

One way to prevent conversation 11 from being boring is to say the wrong thing.
—FRANK SHEED

The first requirement of good con- 12 versation is that nobody should know what is coming next.
—HAVILAH BABCOCK

Conversation means being able 13 to disagree and still continue the discussion.
—DWIGHT MacDONALD

Candor is a compliment; it implies 14 equality. It's how true friends talk.
—PEGGY NOONAN
What I Saw at the Revolution

The genius of communication is 15 the ability to be both totally honest and totally kind at the same time.
—JOHN POWELL

Fine words butter no parsnips. 16
—ENGLISH PROVERB

1 To speak of "mere words" is much like speaking of "mere dynamite."

—C. J. DUCASSE
in *The Key Reporter*

2 Words must surely be counted among the most powerful drugs man ever invented.

—LEO ROSTEN

3 Sticks and stones may break our bones, but words will break our hearts.

—ROBERT FULGHUM
All I Really Need to Know I Learned in Kindergarten

4 The bitterest tears shed over graves are for words left unsaid and deeds left undone.

—HARRIET BEECHER STOWE

5 Do not the most moving moments of our lives find us all without words?

—MARCEL MARCEAU

6 In prayer it is better to have a heart without words than words without a heart.

—JOHN BUNYAN

7 Sometimes good intentions and feelings are of greater moment than the awkwardness of their expression.

—JONATHAN YARDLEY

8 Too much agreement kills a chat.

—ELDRIDGE CLEAVER
Soul on Ice

9 To touch a child's face, a dog's smooth coat, a petaled flower, the rough surface of a rock is to set up new orders of brain motion. To touch is to communicate.

—JAMES W. ANGELL
Yes Is a World

10 What a wonderful thing is the mail, capable of conveying across continents a warm human handclasp.

—Quoted by Ranjan Bakshi

11 A letter is a soliloquy, but a letter with a postscript is a conversation.

—LIN YUTANG

12 There is nothing like sealing a letter to inspire a fresh thought.

—AL BERNSTEIN

13 It is a damned poor mind indeed that can't think of at least two ways of spelling any word.

—ANDREW JACKSON

14 Parents can plant magic in a child's mind through certain words spoken with some thrilling quality of voice, some uplift of the heart and spirit.

—ROBERT MacNEIL
Wordstruck

1 A pun is a pistol let off at the ear; not a feather to tickle the intellect.

—CHARLES LAMB

SKILLFUL LISTENING IS THE BEST REMEDY . . .

2 Skillful listening is the best remedy for loneliness, loquaciousness and laryngitis.

—WILLIAM ARTHUR WARD
in *Tribune* (San Diego, California)

3 The greatest gift you can give another is the purity of your attention.

—RICHARD MOSS, MD

4 Listening, not imitation, may be the sincerest form of flattery.

—JOYCE BROTHERS

5 There is no greater loan than a sympathetic ear.

—FRANK TYGER
in *National Enquirer*

6 In order that all men may be taught to speak truth, it is necessary that all likewise should learn to hear it.

—SAMUEL JOHNSON

7 The less you talk, the more you're listened to.

—ABIGAIL VAN BUREN

8 Talk to a man about himself and he will listen for hours.

—BENJAMIN DISRAELI

9 Give every man thy ear but few thy voice.

—WILLIAM SHAKESPEARE

10 The most important thing in communication is to hear what isn't being said.

—PETER F. DRUCKER

11 Good communication is as stimulating as black coffee, and just as hard to sleep after.

—ANNE MORROW LINDBERGH
Gift From the Sea

12 There is always hope when people are forced to listen to both sides.

—JOHN STUART MILL

13 A good listener is not only popular everywhere, but after a while he knows something.

—WILSON MIZNER

14 Listen, or thy tongue will keep thee deaf.

—NATIVE AMERICAN PROVERB

15 No one really listens to anyone else. Try it for a while, and you'll see why.

—MIGNON MCLAUGHLIN

1 Listening to both sides of a story will convince you that there is more to a story than both sides.

—FRANK TYGER

2 Sainthood emerges when you can listen to someone's tale of woe and not respond with a description of your own.

—ANDREW V. MASON, MD

3 Most people would rather defend to the death your right to say it than listen to it.

—ROBERT BRAULT

4 To entertain some people all you have to do is listen.

—BERNARD EDINGER

5 Two great talkers will not travel far together.

—SPANISH PROVERB

SILENCES MAKE THE REAL CONVERSATIONS . . .

6 Silences make the real conversations between friends. Not the saying but the never needing to say is what counts.

—MARGARET LEE RUNBECK
Answer Without Ceasing

7 Hospitality consists in a little fire, a little food and an immense quiet.

—RALPH WALDO EMERSON

In quiet places, reason abounds. 8

—ADLAI E. STEVENSON

Well-timed silence is the most commanding expression. 9

—MARK HELPRIN
in *The Wall Street Journal*

There are times when silence has 10 the loudest voice.

—LEROY BROWNLOW
Today Is Mine

The time to stop talking is when 11 the other person nods his head affirmatively but says nothing.

—HENRY S. HASKINS
Meditations in Wall Street

The right word may be effective, 12 but no word was ever as effective as a rightly timed pause.

—MARK TWAIN

He approaches nearest to the gods 13 who knows how to be silent, even though he is in the right.

—CATO

Silence is the unbearable repartee. 14

—G. K. CHESTERTON

Silence is one of the hardest 15 arguments to refute.

—JOSH BILLINGS

Silence, along with modesty, is a 16 great aid to conversation.

—MONTAIGNE

1 Silence is the safety zone of
conversation.
—Arnold H. Glasow

2 Silence is still a marvelous
language that has few initiates.
—Roger Duhamel
Lettres à une Provinciale

3 The most difficult thing in the
world is to know how to do a
thing and to watch someone else
doing it wrong, without comment.
—Theodore H. White
in *The Atlantic*

4 Tact is the rare ability to keep
silent while two friends are arguing, and you know both of them
are wrong.
—Hugh Allen

5 Fools live to regret their words,
wise men to regret their silence.
—Will Henry

6 Some people talk because they
think sound is more manageable
than silence.
—Margaret Halsey

7 Blessed are they who have nothing to say and who cannot be
persuaded to say it.
—James Russell Lowell

8 If you really want to keep a secret
you don't need any help.
—O. A. Carping

9 Isn't it strange that we talk least
about the things we think about
most!
—Charles A. Lindbergh

10 A secret is what you tell someone
else not to tell because you can't
keep it to yourself.
—Leonard Louis Levinson

11 The vanity of being known to
be entrusted with a secret is generally one of the chief motives to
disclose it.
—Samuel Johnson

12 None are so fond of secrets as
those who do not mean to keep
them.
—C. C. Colton

13 The knowledge that a secret exists
is half of the secret.
—Joshua Meyrowitz
No Sense of Place

14 He who has a secret should not
only hide it, but hide that he has
it to hide.
—Thomas Carlyle

15 If you reveal your secrets to the
wind, you should not blame the
wind for revealing them to the
trees.
—Kahlil Gibran
Sand and Foam

1 No one keeps a secret better than he who ignores it.

—Louis-N. Fortin

2 Another person's secret is like another person's money: you are not as careful with it as you are with your own.

—E. W. Howe

3 Have you noticed that these days even a moment of silence has to be accompanied by background music?

—*Funny Funny World*

4 My personal hobbies are reading, listening to music and silence.

—Edith Sitwell

5 I like the silent church before the service begins better than any preaching.

—Ralph Waldo Emerson

By expert opinion . . .

6 You can't always go by expert opinion. A turkey, if you ask a turkey, should be stuffed with grasshoppers, grit and worms.

—*Changing Times*

7 The man who never alters his opinion is like standing water, and breeds reptiles of the mind.

—William Blake

8 Opinions should be formed with great caution—and changed with greater.

—Josh Billings

9 A leading authority is anyone who has guessed right more than once.

—Frank A. Clark

10 It is only about things that do not interest one that one can give a really unbiased opinion, which is no doubt the reason why an unbiased opinion is always valueless.

—Oscar Wilde

11 We tolerate differences of opinion in people who are familiar to us. But differences of opinion in people we do not know sound like heresy or plots.

—Brooks Atkinson

12 The function of the expert is not to be more right than other people, but to be wrong for more sophisticated reasons.

—David Butler

13 An expert is someone called in at the last minute to share the blame.

—Sam Ewing
in *Mature Living*

14 Even when the experts all agree, they may well be mistaken.

—Bertrand Russell
The Skeptical Essays

1 Every man has a right to be wrong in his opinions. But no man has a right to be wrong in his facts.

—BERNARD BARUCH
The Public Years

2 It is easy enough to hold an opinion, but hard work to actually know what one is talking about.

—PAUL F. FORD
Companion to Narnia

3 Too often we enjoy the comfort of opinion without the discomfort of thought.

—JOHN F. KENNEDY

4 The fewer the facts, the stronger the opinion.

—ARNOLD H. GLASOW

5 The only thing worse than an expert is someone who thinks he's an expert.

—ALY A. COLON

6 A public-opinion poll is no substitute for thought.

—WARREN BUFFETT

7 Public opinion is like the castle ghost; no one has ever seen it, but everyone is scared of it.

—SIGMUND GRAFF

8 Every conviction was a whim at birth.

—HEYWOOD BROUN

Refusing to have an opinion is a way of having one, isn't it? 9

—LUIGI PIRANDELLO
Each in His Own Way

Saying what we think gives a wider range of conversation than saying what we know. 10

—CULLEN HIGHTOWER

To disagree, one doesn't have to be disagreeable. 11

—BARRY M. GOLDWATER WITH JACK CASSERLY
Goldwater

There's a difference between opinion and conviction. My opinion is something that is true for me personally; my conviction is something that is true for everybody—in my opinion. 12

—SYLVIA CORDWOOD

Every new opinion, at its starting, is precisely in a minority of one. 13

—THOMAS CARLYLE

ADMIRABLE ADVICE . . .

I sometimes give myself admirable advice, but I am incapable of taking it. 14

—MARY WORTLEY MONTAGU

To profit from good advice requires more wisdom than to give it. 15

—JOHN CHURTON COLLINS

1 You don't need to take a person's advice to make him feel good—just ask for it.

—LAURENCE J. PETER
Peter's Almanac

2 A knife of the keenest steel requires the whetstone, and the wisest man needs advice.

—ZOROASTER

3 Advice is an uncertain gift.

—WHITNEY JEFFERY

4 Expert advice is a great comfort, even when it's wrong.

—Quoted by ELLEN CURRIE
in *The New York Times*

5 When we ask for advice, we are usually looking for an accomplice.

—MARQUIS DE LA GRANGE

6 Advice is what we ask for when we already know the answer but wish we didn't.

—ERICA JONG

7 Most of us ask for advice when we know the answer but want a different one.

—IVERN BALL
in *National Enquirer*

8 Express an opinion, but send advice by freight.

—CHARLES CLARK MUNN

9 Good advice usually works best when preceded by a bad scare.

—AL BATT

10 Of the few innocent pleasures left to men past middle life, the jamming of common sense down the throats of fools is perhaps the keenest.

—T. H. HUXLEY

11 When we are well, we all have good advice for those who are ill.

—TERENCE

12 We are never so generous as when giving advice.

—FRANÇOIS DE LA ROCHEFOUCAULD

13 People who have what they want are fond of telling people who haven't what they want that they really don't want it.

—OGDEN NASH

14 We give advice by the bucket but take it by the grain.

—WILLIAM ALGER

15 The thing to do with good advice is to pass it on. It is never any good to oneself.

—OSCAR WILDE

16 Advice should always be consumed between two thick slices of doubt.

—WALT SCHMIDT
in *Parklabrea News*

1 The best advice yet given is that you don't have to take it.
—LIBBIE FUDIM

2 Don't be troubled if the temptation to give advice is irresistible; the ability to ignore it is universal.
—*Planned Security*

USE SOFT WORDS . . .

3 Use soft words and hard arguments.
—ENGLISH PROVERB

4 A good indignation makes an excellent speech.
—RALPH WALDO EMERSON

5 There is nothing in the world like a persuasive speech to fuddle the mental apparatus.
—MARK TWAIN

6 If you have an important point to make, don't try to be subtle or clever. Use a pile driver. Hit the point once. Then come back and hit it again. Then hit it a third time a tremendous whack.
—WINSTON CHURCHILL

7 Charm is a way of getting the answer yes without asking a clear question.
—ALBERT CAMUS
The Fall

8 Praise, like gold and diamonds, owes its value only to its scarcity.
—SAMUEL JOHNSON

9 Sandwich every bit of criticism between two layers of praise.
—MARY KAY ASH
Mary Kay on People Management

10 One thought driven home is better than three left on base.
—JAMES LITER
in *National Enquirer*

11 Example is not the main thing in influencing others. It is the only thing.
—ALBERT SCHWEITZER

THE GREAT CHARM IN ARGUMENT . . .

12 The great charm in argument is really finding one's own opinions, not other people's.
—EVELYN WAUGH

13 It is better to debate a question without settling it than to settle a question without debating it.
—JOSEPH JOUBERT

14 Nothing can keep an argument going like two persons who aren't sure what they're arguing about.
—O. A. BATTISTA

1 A single fact will often spoil an interesting argument.
—*Selected Cryptograms III*

2 You have not converted a man because you have silenced him.
—JOHN MORLEY

3 It is impossible to defeat an ignorant man in an argument.
—WILLIAM G. MCADOO

4 In quarreling, the truth is always lost.
—PUBLILIUS SYRUS

5 Never answer an angry word with an angry word. It's the second one that makes the quarrel.
—W. A. NANCE

6 People generally quarrel because they cannot argue.
—G. K. CHESTERTON
More Quotable Chesterton

7 The difficult part in an argument is not to defend one's opinion but rather to know it.
—ANDRÉ MAUROIS

8 Quarrels would not last long if the fault were on one side only.
—FRANÇOIS DE LA ROCHEFOUCAULD

9 Violence in the voice is often only the death rattle of reason in the throat.
—JOHN F. BOYES

10 Whether on the road or in an argument, when you see red it's time to stop.
—JAN MCKEITHEN

11 Anybody who thinks there aren't two sides to every argument is probably in one.
—*The Cockle Bur*

12 An apology is the superglue of life. It can repair just about anything.
—LYNN JOHNSTON

13 The man who offers an insult writes it in sand, but for the man who receives it, it's chiseled in bronze.
—GIOVANNI GUARESCHI

14 An ounce of apology is worth a pound of loneliness.
—JOSEPH JOUBERT

15 An apology is a good way to have the last word.
—*Dell Crossword Puzzles*

PRAYER IS WHEN YOU TALK TO GOD . . .

16 Prayer is when you talk to God; meditation is when you listen to God.
—Quoted by DIANA ROBINSON in *The People's Almanac*

1 Prayer is the key of the morning and the bolt of the evening.
—MOHANDAS K. GANDHI

2 The greatest prayer is patience.
—GAUTAMA BUDDHA

3 What we usually pray to God is not that His will be done, but that He approve ours.
—HELGA BERGOLD GROSS

4 The object of most prayers is to wangle an advance on good intentions.
—ROBERT BRAULT

5 Certain thoughts are prayers. There are moments when, whatever be the attitude of the body, the soul is on its knees.
—VICTOR HUGO

6 If you begin to live life looking for the God that is all around you, every moment becomes a prayer.
—FRANK BIANCO

7 Our prayers are answered not when we are given what we ask but when we are challenged to be what we can be.
—MORRIS ADLER

8 Any concern too small to be turned into a prayer is too small to be made into a burden.
—CORRIE TEN BOOM
Clippings from My Notebook

If we could all hear one another's 9 prayers, God might be relieved of some of his burden.
—ASHLEIGH BRILLIANT

Serving God is doing good to 10 man. But praying is thought an easier service and is therefore more generally chosen.
—BENJAMIN FRANKLIN

God is like a mirror. The mirror 11 never changes but everybody who looks at it sees something different.
—Quoted by RABBI HAROLD KUSHNER
in *Ultimate Issues*

Prayer is less about changing the 12 world than it is about changing ourselves.
—DAVID J. WOLPE
Teaching Your Children About God

Get down on your knees and 13 thank God you are on your feet.
—IRISH SAYING

Never trust someone who has to 14 change his tone to ask something of the Lord.
—ROBERTA A. EVERETT

Call on God, but row away from 15 the rocks.
—ROBERT M. YOUNG

Trust in God—but tie your camel 16 tight.
—PERSIAN PROVERB

CIVILATION'S GIFT

Civilization is a movement and not a condition, tion, a voyage and not a harbor.

—ARNOLD TOYNBEE

GREAT IDEAS NEED LANDING GEAR . . .

1 Great ideas need landing gear as well as wings.

—C. D. JACKSON

2 The history of mankind is the history of ideas.

—LUDWIG VON MISES
Socialism: An Economic and Sociological Analysis

3 A man is but a product of his thoughts; what he thinks, that he becomes.

—MOHANDAS K. GANDHI

4 An invasion of armies can be resisted, but not an idea whose time has come.

—VICTOR HUGO

5 It is useless to send armies against ideas.

—GEORG BRANDES

6 Good ideas are not adopted automatically. They must be driven into practice with courageous impatience.

—ADM. HYMAN G. RICKOVER

7 A cup is useful only when it is empty; and a mind that is filled with beliefs, with dogmas, with assertions, with quotations is really an uncreative mind.

—J. KRISHNAMURTI

The man with a new idea is a crank until the idea succeeds. 8

—MARK TWAIN

The greatest discovery of my generation is that a human being can alter his life by altering his attitude. 9

—WILLIAM JAMES

Thought is action in rehearsal. 10

—SIGMUND FREUD

Change your thoughts and you change your world. 11

—REV. NORMAN VINCENT PEALE

He who cannot change the very fabric of his thought will never be able to change reality. 12

—ANWAR EL-SADAT

The mind is its own place, and in itself can make a heaven of hell, a hell of heaven. 13

—JOHN MILTON

If most of us are ashamed of shabby clothes and shoddy furniture, let us be more ashamed of shabby ideas and shoddy philosophies. 14

—ALBERT EINSTEIN

Civilization is a movement and not a condition, a voyage and not a harbor. 15

—ARNOLD TOYNBEE

1 Good thoughts bear good fruit, bad thoughts bear bad fruit—and man is his own gardener.

—JAMES ALLEN

2 Bring ideas in and entertain them royally, for one of them may be the king.

—MARK VAN DOREN

3 The test of a first-rate intelligence is the ability to hold two opposed ideas in the mind at the same time, and still retain the ability to function.

—F. SCOTT FITZGERALD

4 I like to have a man's knowledge comprehend more than one class of topics, one row of shelves. I like a man who likes to see a fine barn as well as a good tragedy.

—RALPH WALDO EMERSON

5 Learning is not attained by chance. It must be sought for with ardor and attended to with diligence.

—ABIGAIL ADAMS

6 What we learn with pleasure we never forget.

—ALFRED MERCIER

7 Most people are willing to pay more to be amused than to be educated.

—ROBERT C. SAVAGE
Life Lessons

8 Education is not training but rather the process that equips you to entertain yourself, a friend and an idea.

—WALLACE STERLING

9 Education is not the filling of a pail, but the lighting of a fire.

—WILLIAM BUTLER YEATS

10 There are two ways of spreading light: to be the candle or the mirror that reflects it.

—EDITH WHARTON

11 An education is like a crumbling building that needs constant upkeep with repairs and additions.

—LOUIS DUDEK

12 A master can tell you what he expects of you. A teacher, though, awakens your own expectations.

—PATRICIA NEAL WITH RICHARD DENEUT
As I Am: An Autobiography

13 A great teacher never strives to explain his vision—he simply invites you to stand beside him and see for yourself.

—REV. R. INMAN

14 If you would thoroughly know anything, teach it to others.

—TRYON EDWARDS

15 To teach is to learn twice.

—JOSEPH JOUBERT

CIVILIZATION'S GIFT

1 Good education is the essential foundation of a strong democracy.
—BARBARA BUSH
in a preface to *America's Country Schools* by Andrew Gulliford

2 Education is more than a luxury; it is a responsibility that society owes to itself.
—ROBIN COOK
Coma

3 Education is learning what you didn't even know you didn't know.
—DANIEL J. BOORSTIN
Democracy and Its Discontents

4 Without education, we are in a horrible and deadly danger of taking educated people seriously.
—G. K. CHESTERTON

5 It is not the business of science to inherit the earth, but to inherit the moral imagination; because without that, man and beliefs and science will perish together.
—JACOB BRONOWSKI

6 Science has made us gods even before we are worthy of being men.
—JEAN ROSTAND

7 An age is called Dark, not because the light fails to shine, but because people refuse to see it.
—JAMES A. MICHENER
Space

8 In every work of genius, we recognize our own rejected thoughts; they come back to us with a certain alienated majesty.
—RALPH WALDO EMERSON

9 If you are seeking creative ideas, go out walking. Angels whisper to a man when he goes for a walk.
—RAYMOND INMAN

10 An idea can turn to dust or magic, depending on the talent that rubs against it.
—WILLIAM BERNBACH

11 Be curious always! For knowledge will not acquire you; you must acquire it.
—SUDIE BACK

12 Curiosity is the wick in the candle of learning.
—WILLIAM A. WARD

13 The little I know, I owe to my ignorance.
—SACHA GUITRY

14 Curiosity is a willing, a proud, an eager confession of ignorance.
—S. LEONARD RUBINSTEIN
Writing: A Habit of Mind

15 A sense of curiosity is nature's original school of education.
—SMILEY BLANTON, MD
Love or Perish

1 The human mind is as driven to understand as the body is driven to survive.

—HUGH GILMORE
in *The Philadelphia Inquirer Magazine*

2 If a man had as many ideas during the day as he does when he has insomnia, he'd make a fortune.

—GRIFF NIBLACK
in *News* (Indianapolis, Indiana)

3 Ideas are like rabbits. You get a couple and learn how to handle them, and pretty soon you have a dozen.

—JOHN STEINBECK

4 All my best thoughts were stolen by the ancients.

—RALPH WALDO EMERSON

5 A new idea is delicate. It can be killed by a sneer or a yawn; it can be stabbed to death by a quip, and worried to death by a frown on the right man's brow.

—CHARLIE BROWER

6 Man's mind stretched to a new idea never goes back to its original dimensions.

—OLIVER WENDELL HOLMES

7 One should never spoil a good theory by explaining it.

—PETER MCARTHUR

8 Once a new idea springs into existence, it cannot be unthought. There is a sense of immortality in a new idea.

—EDWARD DE BONO
New Think: The Use of Lateral Thinking in the Generation of New Ideas

9 An open mind collects more riches than an open purse.

—WILL HENRY

10 A cold in the head causes less suffering than an idea.

—JULES RENARD

READING FURNISHES THE MIND . . .

11 Reading furnishes the mind only with materials of knowledge; it is thinking that makes what we read ours.

—JOHN LOCKE

12 Reading is to the mind what exercise is to the body.

—JOSEPH ADDISON

13 Books may well be the only true magic.

—ALICE HOFFMAN

14 Books are not made for furniture, but there is nothing else that so beautifully furnishes a house.

—HENRY WARD BEECHER

1 Reading makes immigrants of us all—it takes us away from home, but more important, it finds homes for us everywhere.
—HAZEL ROCHMAN
Against Borders

2 There are perhaps no days of our childhood we lived so fully as those we believe we left without having lived them: those we spent with a favorite book.
—MARCEL PROUST

3 From your parents you learn love and laughter and how to put one foot before the other. But when books are opened you discover that you have wings.
—HELEN HAYES WITH SANDFORD DODY
On Reflection

4 Books are the carriers of civilization. Without books, history is silent, literature dumb, science crippled, thought and speculation at a standstill.
—BARBARA W. TUCHMAN

5 Books had instant replay long before televised sports.
—BERN WILLIAMS

6 If you would understand your own age, read the works of fiction produced in it. People in disguise speak freely.
—ARTHUR HELPS
Thoughts in the Cloister and the Crowd

7 Books are more than books. They are the life, the very heart and core of ages past, the reason why men lived and worked and died, the essence and quintessence of their lives.
—AMY LOWELL

8 There are no faster or firmer friendships than those between people who love the same books.
—IRVING STONE

9 Every man who knows how to read has it in his power to magnify, to multiply the ways in which he exists, to make his life full, significant and interesting.
—ALDOUS HUXLEY

10 Fiction reveals truths that reality obscures.
—JESSAMYN WEST

11 Reading without reflecting is like eating without digesting.
—EDMUND BURKE

12 No one ever really paid the price of a book—only the price of printing it.
—LOUIS I. KAHN

13 A truly good book is something as wildly natural and primitive, mysterious and marvelous, ambrosial and fertile as a fungus or a lichen.
—HENRY DAVID THOREAU

1 I would rather be a poor man in a garret with plenty of books than a king who did not love reading.

—Thomas Babington Macaulay

2 My test of a good novel is dreading to begin the last chapter.

—Thomas Helm

3 A book is a success when people who haven't read it pretend they have.

—Los Angeles Times Syndicate

4 If you would know what nobody knows, read what everybody reads, just one year afterward.

—Ralph Waldo Emerson

5 I divide all readers into two classes: those who read to remember and those who read to forget.

—William Lyon Phelps

6 The wise man reads both books and life itself.

—Lin Yutang

7 The library is the temple of learning, and learning has liberated more people than all the wars in history.

—Carl Rowan

8 The real purpose of books is to trap the mind into doing its own thinking.

—Christopher Morley

Without libraries what have we? We have no past and no future. 9

—Ray Bradbury

Perhaps no place in any community is so totally democratic as the town library. The only entrance requirement is interest. 10

—Lady Bird Johnson

A book should serve as the ax for the frozen sea within us. 11

—Franz Kafka

A well-composed book is a magic carpet on which we are wafted to a world that we cannot enter in any other way. 12

—Caroline Gordon
How to Read a Novel

You know you've read a good book when you turn the last page and feel a little as if you have lost a friend. 13

—Paul Sweeney

Books support us in our solitude and keep us from being a burden to ourselves. 14

—Jeremy Collier

There is a wonder in reading braille that the sighted will never know: to touch words and have them touch you back. 15

—Jim Fiebig

1 A book, tight shut, is but a block of paper.

—CHINESE PROVERB

2 A great book should leave you with many experiences and slightly exhausted at the end. You live several lives while reading it.

—WILLIAM STYRON

3 A truly great book should be read in youth, again in maturity and once more in old age, as a fine building should be seen by morning light, at noon and by moonlight.

—ROBERTSON DAVIES
The Enthusiasms of Robertson Davies

4 "Tell me what you read and I'll tell you who you are" is true enough, but I'd know you better if you told me what you reread.

—FRANÇOIS MAURIAC

5 When something can be read without effort, great effort has gone into its writing.

—ENRIQUE JARDIEL PONCELA

6 Wherever they burn books they will also, in the end, burn human beings.

—HEINRICH HEINE

7 You don't have to burn books to destroy a culture. Just get people to stop reading them.

—RAY BRADBURY

8 An author retains the singular distinction of being the only person who can remain a bore long after he is dead.

—SYDNEY J. HARRIS

9 For a man to become a poet he must be in love, or miserable.

—GEORGE GORDON, LORD BYRON

10 You don't have to suffer to be a poet. Adolescence is enough suffering for anyone.

—JOHN CIARDI

11 In the end, the poem is not a thing we see; it is, rather, a light by which we may see—and what we see is life.

—ROBERT PENN WARREN

12 Poetry is language at its most distilled and most powerful.

—RITA DOVE

13 A poem begins in delight and ends in wisdom.

—ROBERT FROST

14 Poetry is an echo, asking a shadow to dance.

—CARL SANDBURG

15 The difference between reality and fiction? Fiction has to make sense.

—TOM CLANCY

1 Choose an author as you choose a friend.

—Wentworth Dillon

2 Fable is more historical than fact, because fact tells us about one man and fable tells us about a million men.

—G. K. Chesterton

3 Let us read and let us dance—two amusements that will never do any harm to the world.

—Voltaire

4 I cannot conceive how a novelist could fail to pity or love the smallest creation of his imagination; incomplete as these characters may be, they are the writer's bond with the real world, its suffering and heartbreak.

—Gabrielle Roy
The Fragile Lights Of Earth: Articles And Memories 1942–1970

5 When you take stuff from one writer, it's plagiarism; but when you take it from many writers it's research.

—Wilson Mizner

6 October is crisp days and cool nights, a time to curl up around the dancing flames and sink into a good book.

—John Sinor
in *Union-Tribune* (San Diego, California)

There's nothing to writing. All you 7 do is sit down at a typewriter and open a vein.

—Red Smith

When I want to read a novel, I 8 write one.

—Benjamin Disraeli

ART IS A STAPLE, LIKE BREAD . . .

Art is a staple, like bread or wine 9 or a warm coat in winter. Man's spirit grows hungry for art in the same way his stomach growls for food.

—Irving Stone
Depths of Glory

Art is the signature of civilization. 10

—Beverly Sills

Art extends each man's short time 11 on earth by carrying from man to man the whole complexity of other men's lifelong experience, with all its burdens, colors and flavor.

—Aleksandr Solzhenitsyn
One Word of Truth . . .

Every fragment of song holds 12 a mirror to a past moment for someone.

—Fanny Cradock
War Comes to Castle Rising

1 A room hung with pictures is a room hung with thoughts.
—SIR JOSHUA REYNOLDS

2 Anyone who says you can't see a thought simply doesn't know art.
—WYNETKA ANN REYNOLDS

3 No great artist ever sees things as they really are. If he did, he would cease to be an artist.
—OSCAR WILDE

4 Art is the demonstration that the ordinary is extraordinary.
—AMÉDÉE OZENFANT
Foundations of Modern Art

5 Art doesn't reproduce the visible but rather makes it visible.
—PAUL KLEE

6 It has been said that art is a tryst; for the joy of it maker and beholder meet.
—KOJIRO TOMITA

7 Art is the only way to run away without leaving home.
—TWYLA THARP

8 Half of art is knowing when to stop.
—ARTHUR WILLIAM RADFORD

9 The other arts persuade us, but music takes us by surprise.
—EDUARD HANSLICK

10 Without music, life is a journey through a desert.
—PAT CONROY
Beach Music

11 Country music is three chords and the truth.
—HARLAN HOWARD

12 Music is the way our memories sing to us across time.
—LANCE MORROW
in *Time*

13 After silence, that which comes nearest to expressing the inexpressible is music.
—ALDOUS HUXLEY
Music at Night and Other Essays

14 Music washes away from the soul the dust of everyday life.
—BERTHOLD AUERBACH

15 Music is the shorthand of emotion.
—LEO TOLSTOY

16 Where words fail, music speaks.
—HANS CHRISTIAN ANDERSEN

17 Music is a higher revelation than philosophy.
—LUDWIG VAN BEETHOVEN

18 People who make music together cannot be enemies, at least not while the music lasts.
—PAUL HINDEMITH

1 He who sings frightens away his ills.
—Miguel de Cervantes Saavedra

2 God respects me when I work, but he loves me when I sing.
—Rabindranath Tagore

3 If I may venture my own definition of a folk song, I should call it "an individual flowering on a common stem."
—Ralph Vaughn Williams

4 Learning music by reading about it is like making love by mail.
—Luciano Pavarotti

5 No one should be allowed to play the violin until he has mastered it.
—Jim Fiebig

6 Those move easiest who have learned to dance.
—Alexander Pope

7 The truest expression of a people is in its dances and its music. Bodies never lie.
—Agnes de Mille

8 Inside every man there is a poet who died young.
—Stephan Kanfer

9 There is no abstract art. You must always start with something. Afterward you can remove all traces of reality.
—Pablo Picasso

10 Every artist was first an amateur.
—Ralph Waldo Emerson

11 The greatest artist was once a beginner.
—Farmer's Digest

12 All art, like all love, is rooted in heartache.
—Alfred Stieglitz

13 What art offers is space—a certain breathing room for the spirit.
—John Updike

14 More important than a work of art itself is what it will sow. Art can die, a painting can disappear. What counts is the seed.
—Joan Miró

15 Art is the triumph over chaos.
—John Cheever

16 What is art but a way of seeing?
—Thomas Berger
Being Invisible

17 A great artist is never poor.
—Isak Dinesen
Anecdotes of Destiny

18 Talent is a flame. Genius is a fire.
—Bern Williams

19 No one can arrive from being talented alone. God gives talent; work transforms talent into genius.
—Anna Pavlova

1 Discipline is the refining fire by which talent becomes ability.

—Roy L. Smith

2 Perfectionism is the enemy of creation, as extreme self-solicitude is the enemy of well-being.

—John Updike
Odd Jobs

3 When love and skill work together, expect a masterpiece.

—John Ruskin

4 I created nothing; I invented nothing; I imagined nothing; I perverted nothing; I simply discovered drama in real life.

—Bernard Shaw

5 There's no need to believe what an artist says. Believe what he does; that's what counts.

—David Hockney

6 Every child is an artist. The problem is how to remain an artist once he grows up.

—Pablo Picasso

7 Really we create nothing. We merely plagiarize nature.

—Jean Baitaillon

8 A great city is one that handles its garbage and art equally well.

—Bob Talbert

9 A good snapshot stops a moment from running away.

—Eudora Welty

10 The cinema has no boundary; it is a ribbon of dream.

—Orson Welles

11 Of course, there must be subtleties. Just make sure you make them obvious.

—Billy Wilder

12 It pays to be obvious, especially if you have a reputation for subtlety.

—Isaac Asimov
Foundation

13 Simplicity, carried to an extreme, becomes elegance.

—Jon Franklin
Writing for Story

14 It is only by introducing the young to great literature, drama and music, and to the excitement of great science that we open to them the possibilities that lie within the human spirit — enable them to see visions and dream dreams.

—Eric Anderson

15 Man creates culture and through culture creates himself.

—Pope John Paul II
in *Osservatore Romano*

THE NATURE OF LIFE

The way I see it, if you want the rainbow,
you gotta put up with the rain.

—DOLLY PARTON

In the Long Eternity of Time . . .

1 It is easier to accept the message of the stars than the message of the salt desert. The stars speak of man's insignificance in the long eternity of time; the deserts speak of his insignificance right now.

—EDWIN WAY TEALE

2 Eternity is a terrible thought. I mean, where's it going to end?

—TOM STOPPARD

3 Forever is a long time, but not as long as it was yesterday.

—DENNIS H'ORGNIES

4 Time is but the stream I go a-fishing in.

—HENRY DAVID THOREAU

5 Time neither subtracts nor divides, but adds at such a pace it seems like multiplication.

—BOB TALBERT

6 The future is the past returning through another gate.

—ARNOLD H. GLASOW

7 Snatching the eternal out of the desperately fleeting is the great magic trick of human existence.

—TENNESSEE WILLIAMS
in *The New York Times*

8 Time is a versatile performer. It flies, marches on, heals all wounds, runs out and will tell.

—FRANKLIN P. JONES

9 Time goes, you say? Ah, no! Alas, Time stays, we go.

—AUSTIN DOBSON

10 Time marks us while we are marking time.

—THEODORE ROETHKE
Straw for the Fire

11 Time wastes our bodies and our wits, but we waste time, so we are quits.

—*Verse and Worse*

12 In rivers, the water that you touch is the last of what has passed and the first of that which comes: so with present time.

—LEONARDO DA VINCI

13 You don't get to choose how you're going to die. Or when. You can only decide how you're going to live. Now.

—JOAN BAEZ

14 The feeling of being hurried is not usually the result of living a full life and having no time. It is, rather, born of a vague fear that we are wasting our life.

—ERIC HOFFER

1 Yesterday is a canceled check; tomorrow is a promissory note; today is ready cash—use it.

—Kay Lyons

2 How you spend your time is more important than how you spend your money. Money mistakes can be corrected, but time is gone forever.

—David B. Norris

3 Those who make the worst use of their time are the first to complain of its shortness.

—Jean de La Bruyère

4 Half our life is spent trying to find something to do with the time we have rushed through life trying to save.

—Will Rogers

5 Today's greatest labor-saving device is tomorrow.

—Tom Wilson

6 Mañana is often the busiest day of the week.

—Spanish proverb

7 One of these days is none of these days.

—Henri Tubach

8 By the streets of "by and by" one arrives at the house of "never."

—Spanish proverb

9 Don't put off for tomorrow what you can do today, because if you enjoy it today you can do it again tomorrow.

—James A. Michener

10 Nothing adds to a person's leisure time like doing things when they are supposed to be done.

—O. A. Battista

11 For disappearing acts, it's hard to beat what happens to the eight hours supposedly left after eight of sleep and eight of work.

—Doug Larson

12 When we don't waste time, we always have enough.

—Jean Drapeau

13 As if we could kill time without injuring eternity!

—Henry David Thoreau

14 A man who has to be punctually at a certain place at five o'clock has the whole afternoon ruined for him already.

—Lin Yutang
The Importance of Living

15 The surest way to be late is to have plenty of time.

—Leo Kennedy

16 Normal day, let me be aware of the treasure you are.

—Mary Jean Irion

1 Butterflies count not months but moments, and yet have time enough.

—Rabindranath Tagore

2 Time, for all its smuggling in of new problems, conspicuously cancels others.

—Clara Winston
in *The Massachusetts Review*

3 Time has a wonderful way of weeding out the trivial.

—Richard Ben Sapir
Quest

4 I still find each day too short for all the thoughts I want to think, all the walks I want to take, all the books I want to read and all the friends I want to see.

—John Burroughs

5 Yesterday is experience. Tomorrow is hope. Today is getting from one to the other as best we can.

—John M. Henry

6 You must have been warned against letting the golden hours slip by; but some of them are golden only because we let them slip by.

—James M. Barrie

7 We are tomorrow's past.

—Mary Webb
Precious Bane

8 The present is the point at which time touches eternity.

—C. S. Lewis
Screwtape Letters

9 Life is uncharted territory. It reveals its story one moment at a time.

—Leo Buscaglia
in *Executive Health Report*

10 I never think of the future. It comes soon enough.

—Albert Einstein

11 There is no distance on this earth as far away as yesterday.

—Robert Nathan
So Love Returns

12 The past is really almost as much a work of the imagination as the future.

—Jessamyn West

13 He who believes that the past cannot be changed has not yet written his memoirs.

—Torvald Gahlin

14 There is a time to let things happen and a time to make things happen.

—Hugh Prather
Notes on Love and Courage

15 Every man regards his own life as the New Year's Eve of time.

—Jean Paul Richter

1 The best thing about the future is that it comes only one day at a time.

—DEAN ACHESON

2 I love best to have each thing in its season, doing without it at all other times.

—HENRY DAVID THOREAU

3 Life is not dated merely by years. Events are sometimes the best calendars.

—BENJAMIN DISRAELI

4 Time has no divisions to mark its passage; there is never a thunderstorm to announce the beginning of a new year. It is only we mortals who ring bells and fire off pistols.

—THOMAS MANN

5 Life is not a "brief candle." It is a splendid torch that I want to make burn as brightly as possible before handing it on to future generations.

—BERNARD SHAW

ALL THE ART OF LIVING . . .

6 All the art of living lies in a fine mingling of letting go and holding on.

—HAVELOCK ELLIS

God asks no man whether he will 7 accept life. That is not the choice. One must take it. The only choice is how.

—HENRY WARD BEECHER

If we live good lives, the times are 8 also good. As we are, such are the times.

—ST. AUGUSTINE

We are here to add what we can 9 to, not to get what we can from, life.

—SIR WILLIAM OSLER

Presence is more than just being 10 there.

—MALCOLM S. FORBES
The Further Sayings of Chairman Malcolm

There are three things that if a 11 man does not know, he cannot live long in this world: what is too much for him, what is too little for him and what is just right for him.

—SWAHILI PROVERB

You only live once. But if you 12 work it right, once is enough.

—FRED ALLEN

Besides the noble art of getting 13 things done, there is the noble art of leaving things undone. The wisdom of life consists in the elimination of non-essentials.

—LIN YUTANG

1 There is more to life than increasing its speed.

—MOHANDAS K. GANDHI

2 Everything should be made as simple as possible, but not simpler.

—ALBERT EINSTEIN

3 I believe the art of living consists not so much in complicating simple things as in simplifying things that are not.

—FRANÇOIS HERTEL

4 Simplicity is making the journey of this life with just baggage enough.

—CHARLES DUDLEY WARNER

5 Seize from every moment its unique novelty, and do not prepare your joys.

—ANDRÉ GIDE
Nourritures Terrestres

6 Excess on occasion is exhilarating. It prevents moderation from acquiring the deadening effect of a habit.

—W. SOMERSET MAUGHAM

7 If you can spend a perfectly useless afternoon in a perfectly useless manner, you have learned how to live.

—LIN YUTANG

8 He does not seem to me to be a free man who does not sometimes do nothing.

—CICERO

9 How we spend our days is, of course, how we spend our lives.

—ANNIE DILLARD
The Writing Life

10 A holiday gives one a chance to look backward and forward, to reset oneself by an inner compass.

—MAY SARTON
At Seventy (A Journal)

11 The time to relax is when you don't have time for it.

—SYDNEY J. HARRIS

12 A vacation is having nothing to do and all day to do it in.

—ROBERT ORBEN

13 The discovery of a new dish does more for human happiness than the discovery of a star.

—ANTHELME BRILLAT-SAVARIN

14 A good cook is like a sorceress who dispenses happiness.

—ELSA SCHIAPARELLI

15 There is no love sincerer than the love of food.

—BERNARD SHAW

1 We never repent of having eaten too little.

—THOMAS JEFFERSON

2 One of the very nicest things about life is the way we must regularly stop whatever it is we are doing and devote our attention to eating.

—LUCIANO PAVAROTTI WITH WILLIAM WRIGHT
Pavarotti, My Own Story

3 There is a sufficiency in the world for man's need but not for man's greed.

—MOHANDAS K. GANDHI

4 Whatever will satisfy hunger is good food.

—CHINESE PROVERB

5 'Tis an ill cook that cannot lick his own fingers.

—WILLIAM SHAKESPEARE

6 One must ask children and birds how cherries and strawberries taste.

—JOHANN WOLFGANG VON GOETHE

7 Never eat more than you can lift.
—*Miss Piggy's Guide to Life*,
as told to Henry Beard

8 There is only one difference between a long life and a good dinner: that, in the dinner, the sweets come last.

—ROBERT LOUIS STEVENSON

9 We are all mortal until the first kiss and the second glass of wine.

—EDUARDO GALEANO
The Book of Embraces

10 Be glad of life because it gives you the chance to love and to work and to play and to look up at the stars.

—HENRY VAN DYKE

11 The art of living is more like wrestling than dancing.

—MARCUS AURELIUS

12 Part of the art of living is knowing how to compare yourself with the right people. Dissatisfaction is often the result of unsuitable comparison.

—DR. HEINRICH SOBOTKA
Madame

13 Is not life a hundred times too short for us to bore ourselves?

—FRIEDRICH NIETZSCHE

14 Enjoy the little things, for one day you may look back and realize they were the big things.

—ROBERT BRAULT
in *National Enquirer*

15 Yes, there is a nirvana; it is in leading your sheep to a green pasture, and in putting your child to sleep, and in writing the last line of your poem.

—KAHLIL GIBRAN

1 When things start going your way, it's usually because you stopped going the wrong way down a one-way street.
—Los Angeles Times Syndicate

2 One ought, every day at least, to hear a little song, read a good poem, see a fine picture and, if possible, speak a few reasonable words.
—Johann Wolfgang von Goethe

IDEALS ARE LIKE THE STARS . . .

3 Ideals are like the stars. We never reach them but, like the mariners on the sea, we chart our course by them.
—Carl Schurz

4 The ideals which have lighted my way, and time after time have given me new courage to face life cheerfully, have been kindness, beauty and truth.
—Albert Einstein
Ideas and Opinions

5 When you teach your son, you teach your son's son.
—The Talmud

6 The true idealist pursues what his heart says is right in a way that his head says will work.
—Richard M. Nixon

7 If things were really as we wanted them to be, people would still complain that they were no longer what they used to be.
—Pierre Dac

8 I am an idealist. I don't know where I'm going, but I'm on my way.
—Carl Sandburg

SOME THINGS HAVE TO BE BELIEVED . . .

9 Some things have to be believed to be seen.
—Ralph Hodgson
The Skylark and Other Poems

10 One person with a belief is a social power equal to 99 who have only interests.
—John Stuart Mill

11 To believe with certainty, we must begin with doubting.
—Stanislaus I

12 Faith is building on what you know is here, so you can reach what you know is there.
—Cullen Hightower

13 Strike from mankind the principle of faith and men would have no more history than a flock of sheep.
—Mark Beltaire

1 Science is not only compatible with spirituality; it is a profound source of spirituality.

—CARL SAGAN
The Demon-Haunted World: Science as a Candle in the Dark

2 If we were logical, the future would be bleak indeed. But we are more than logical. We are human beings, and we have faith, and we have hope, and we can work.

—JACQUES COUSTEAU

3 We couldn't conceive of a miracle if none had ever happened.

—LIBBIE FUDIM

4 In faith there is enough light for those who want to believe and enough shadows to blind those who don't.

—BLAISE PASCAL

5 All I have seen teaches me to trust the Creator for all I have not seen.

—RALPH WALDO EMERSON

6 Faith is knowing there is an ocean because you have seen a brook.

—WILLIAM ARTHUR WARD

7 Faith is like radar that sees through the fog—the reality of things at a distance that the human eye cannot see.

—CORRIE TEN BOOM
Tramp for the Lord

8 Faith is the bird that sings when the dawn is still dark.

—RABINDRANATH TAGORE

9 What I admire in Columbus is not his having discovered a world but his having gone to search for it on the faith of an opinion.

—A. ROBERT TURGOT

10 If the stars should appear just one night in a thousand years, how would men believe and adore!

—RALPH WALDO EMERSON

11 Many of us look at the Ten Commandments as an exam paper: eight only to be attempted.

—MALCOLM MUGGERIDGE
Reality Ireland

12 The finest fruit of serious learning should be the ability to speak the word God without reserve or embarrassment.

—NATHAN M. PUSEY

13 Our rabbi once said, "God always answers our prayers, it's just that sometimes the answer is no."

—BARBARA FEINSTEIN

14 If you are not as close to God as you used to be, who moved?
—*St. Mathias' Church Bulletin*

15 Sorrow looks back, worry looks around, faith looks up.
—Quoted in *Guideposts Magazine*

1 It is good enough to talk of God while we are sitting here after a nice breakfast and looking forward to a nicer luncheon, but how am I to talk of God to the millions who have to go without two meals a day? To them God can only appear as bread and butter.

—MOHANDAS K. GANDHI

2 Real religion is a way of life, not a white cloak to be wrapped around us on the Sabbath and then cast aside into the six-day closet of unconcern.

—WILLIAM ARTHUR WARD
Think It Over

HOPE IS THE THING WITH FEATHERS . . .

3 Hope is the thing with feathers that perches in the soul.

—EMILY DICKINSON

4 Hope smiles on the threshold of the year to come, whispering that it will be happier.

—ALFRED, LORD TENNYSON

5 He who has health has hope, and he who has hope has everything.

—ARAB PROVERB

6 The natural flights of the human mind are not from pleasure to pleasure but from hope to hope.

—SAMUEL JOHNSON

7 Hope is not the conviction that something will turn out well but the certainty that something makes sense, regardless of how it turns out.

—VACLAV HAVEL
Disturbing the Peace

8 There is one thing which gives radiance to everything. It is the idea of something around the corner.

—G. K. CHESTERTON

9 Waiting is still an occupation. It is not having anything to wait for that is terrible.

—CESARE PAVESE
Il Mestiere di Vivere

10 We must learn to reawaken and keep ourselves awake, not by mechanical aids, but by an infinite expectation of the dawn.

—HENRY DAVID THOREAU

11 In every winter's heart there is a quivering spring, and behind the veil of each night there is a smiling dawn.

—KAHLIL GIBRAN

12 Sometimes our fate resembles a fruit tree in winter. Who would think that those branches would turn green again and blossom, but we hope it, we know it.

—JOHANN WOLFGANG VON GOETHE

1 A ship should not ride on a single anchor, nor life on a single hope.

—EPICTETUS

2 We must accept finite disappointment, but we must never lose infinite hope.

—REV. MARTIN LUTHER KING JR.

3 There are no hopeless situations; there are only people who have grown hopeless about them.

—CLARE BOOTHE LUCE

4 I have always been delighted at the prospect of a new day, a fresh try, one more start, with perhaps a bit of magic waiting somewhere behind the morning.

—J. B. PRIESTLEY

5 In the face of uncertainty, there is nothing wrong with hope.

—BERNIE SIEGEL
Love, Medicine and Miracles

6 When you say a situation or a person is hopeless, you are slamming the door in the face of God.

—REV. CHARLES L. ALLEN

7 There is no better or more blessed bondage than to be a prisoner of hope.

—ROY Z. KEMP

THE KIND OF BEAUTY I WANT . . .

8 The kind of beauty I want most is the hard-to-get kind that comes from within—strength, courage, dignity.

—RUBY DEE

9 Some people, no matter how old they get, never lose their beauty—they merely move it from their faces into their hearts.

—MARTIN BUXBAUM
in *National Enquirer*

10 Love beauty; it is the shadow of God on the universe.

—GABRIELA MISTRAL
Desolación

11 Though we travel the world over to find the beautiful, we must carry it with us or we find it not.

—RALPH WALDO EMERSON

12 Taking joy in living is a woman's best cosmetic.

—ROSALIND RUSSELL

13 Tell a girl she's beautiful, and she wouldn't believe you really mean it. Tell her she's more beautiful than another girl, and she would delightfully believe you're being true.

—HASNA HASSAN SIRAJEDDINE

1 People have the strength to over-come their bodies. Their beauty is in their minds.

—PETER GABRIEL CLARK-BROWN
in *Style* magazine

2 It is amazing how complete is the delusion that beauty is goodness.

—LEO TOLSTOY

3 I'm tired of all this nonsense about beauty being only skin-deep. That's deep enough. What do you want—an adorable pancreas?

—JEAN KERR
The Snake Has All the Lines

4 Nothing makes a woman more beautiful than the belief that she is beautiful.

—SOPHIA LOREN
Women & Beauty

5 Fashions fade; style is eternal.

—YVES SAINT LAURENT

6 The most beautiful thing we can experience is the mysterious. It is the source of all true art and science.

—ALBERT EINSTEIN

SPEAK THE TRUTH . . .

7 Speak the truth, but leave immediately after.

—SLOVENIAN PROVERB

8 Never assume the obvious is true.

—WILLIAM SAFIRE
Sleeper Spy

9 I have one request: may I never use my reason against truth.

—ELIE WIESEL
quoting from a Hasidic rabbi's prayer

10 Truth isn't always beauty, but the hunger for it is.

—NADINE GORDIMER

11 The truth is not always dressed for the evening.

—MARGARET LEWERTH
Stuyvesant Square

12 Truth has no special time of its own. Its hour is now—always.

—ALBERT SCHWEITZER
On the Edge of the Primeval Forest

13 Only the truth can still astonish people.

—JEAN-MARIE POUPART
Ma Tite Vache A Mal Aux Pattes

14 Some people so treasure the truth that they use it with great economy.

—H. RAY GOLENOR

15 A half truth is a whole lie.

—YIDDISH PROVERB

16 A half-truth is usually less than half of that.

—BERN WILLIAMS

1 A truth that's told with bad intent
beats all the lies you can invent.
—WILLIAM BLAKE

2 The most dangerous untruths are
truths moderately distorted.
—GEORG CHRISTOPH LICHTENBERG

3 Add one small bit to the truth and
you inevitably subtract from it.
—*Dell Crossword Puzzles*

4 Many people today don't want
honest answers insofar as honest
means unpleasant or disturbing.
They want a soft answer that
turneth away anxiety.
—LOUIS KRONENBERGER

5 The man who is brutally honest
enjoys the brutality quite as much
as the honesty. Possibly more.
—RICHARD J. NEEDHAM
in *The Globe and Mail* (Toronto)

6 We have to live today by what
truth we can get today and
be ready tomorrow to call it
falsehood.
—WILLIAM JAMES

7 Truth is tough. It will not break,
like a bubble, at a touch. Nay,
you may kick it about all day,
and it will be round and
full at evening.
—OLIVER WENDELL HOLMES SR.

8 Most of the change we think we
see in life is due to truths being in
and out of favor.
—ROBERT FROST

9 Truth hurts—not the searching
after; the running from!
—JOHN EYBERG

10 The truth will ouch.
—ARNOLD H. GLASOW

11 Of course, it's the same old
story. Truth usually is the same
old story.
—MARGARET THATCHER

12 The color of truth is gray.
—ANDRÉ GIDE

13 One of the most striking differences between a cat and a lie is
that a cat has only nine lives.
—MARK TWAIN

14 A lie has speed, but truth has
endurance.
—EDGAR J. MOHN

15 Every time you try to smother a
truth, two others get their breath.
—BILL COPELAND

16 What upsets me is not that you
lied to me, but that from now on
I can no longer believe you.
—FRIEDRICH NIETZSCHE

1 He who mistrusts most should be trusted least.

—THEOGNIS

2 I seem to have been like a child playing on the sea shore, finding now and then a prettier shell than ordinary, whilst the great ocean of truth lay undiscovered before me.

—ISAAC NEWTON

3 A paradox is a truth that bites its own tale.

—*American Farm & Home Almanac*

4 We always weaken whatever we exaggerate.

—JEAN-FRANÇOISE DE LA HARPE

5 Nothing lays itself open to the charge of exaggeration more than the language of naked truth.

—JOSEPH CONRAD

6 Always tell the truth. You may make a hole in one when you're alone on the golf course someday.

—FRANKLIN P. JONES

7 It takes two to speak truth—one to speak and another to hear.

—HENRY DAVID THOREAU

8 We do not err because truth is difficult to see. It is visible at a glance. We err because this is more comfortable.

—ALEXANDER SOLZHENITSYN

We lie loudest when we lie to ourselves. 9

—ERIC HOFFER

Men hate those to whom they have to lie. 10

—VICTOR HUGO

The most exhausting thing in life is being insincere. 11

—ANNE MORROW LINDBERGH
Gift from the Sea

When you stretch the truth, watch out for the snapback. 12

—BILL COPELAND

HAPPINESS LIES IN WAIT . . .

Happiness lies in wait; it comes upon suddenly, like a midnight thief at a turn up in the street, or in the midst of a dream, because a ray of light, a strain of music, a face, or a gesture has overcome the despair of living. 13

—HECTOR BIANCIOTTI
Sans la Misericorde du Christ

Happiness walks on busy feet. 14

—KITTE TURMELL

If only we'd stop trying to be happy, we could have a pretty good time. 15

—WILLARD R. ESPY

1 Man must search for what is right, and let happiness come on its own.

—JOHANN PESTALOZZI

2 Now and then it's good to pause in our pursuit of happiness and just be happy.

—Quoted in *The Cockle Bur*

3 To be without some of the things you want is an indispensable part of happiness.

—BERTRAND RUSSELL
The Conquest of Happiness

4 Before strongly desiring anything, we should look carefully into the happiness of its present owner.

—FRANÇOIS DE LA ROCHEFOUCAULD

5 It is an illusion to think that more comfort means more happiness. Happiness comes of the capacity to feel deeply, to enjoy simply, to think freely, to be needed.

—STORM JAMESON

6 Happiness is a way station between too little and too much.

—CHANNING POLLOCK
Mr. Moneypenny

7 Most people ask for happiness on condition. Happiness can be felt only if you don't set any conditions.

—ARTHUR RUBINSTEIN

8 Most men pursue pleasure with such breathless haste that they hurry past it.

—SOREN KIERKEGAARD

9 The foolish person seeks happiness in the distance; the wise person grows it under his feet.

—JAMES OPPENHEIM

10 Fortify yourself with contentment, for this is an impregnable fortress.

—EPICTETUS

11 The discontented man finds no easy chair.

—BENJAMIN FRANKLIN

12 Real elation is when you feel you could touch a star without standing on tiptoe.

—DOUG LARSON

13 The more the heart is nourished with happiness, the more it is insatiable.

—GABRIELLE ROY

14 Joy seems to me a step beyond happiness—happiness is a sort of atmosphere you can live in some-times when you're lucky. Joy is a light that fills you with hope and faith and love.

—ADELA ROGERS ST. JOHNS
Some Are Born Great

1 Happiness is good health and a bad memory.

—INGRID BERGMAN

2 The summit of happiness is reached when a person is ready to be what he is.

—ERASMUS

3 Don't wait around for other people to be happy for you. Any happiness you get you've got to make yourself.

—ALICE WALKER

4 Happiness is a thing to be practiced, like the violin.

—JOHN LUBBOCK

5 One filled with joy preaches without preaching.

—MOTHER TERESA OF CALCUTTA

6 Happiness is a conscious choice, not an automatic response.

—MILDRED BARTHEL
in *Ensign*

7 Happiness often sneaks in through a door you didn't know you left open.

—JOHN BARRYMORE

8 To show a child what once delighted you, to find the child's delight added to your own—this is happiness.

—J. B. PRIESTLEY

9 There can be no happiness if the things we believe in are different from the things we do.

—FREYA STARK
The Journey's Echo

10 Shared joy is double joy and shared sorrow is half-sorrow.

—SWEDISH PROVERB

11 Success is getting what you want. Happiness is liking what you get.

—H. JACKSON BROWN
A Father's Book of Wisdom

12 An ecstasy is a thing that will not go into words; it feels like music.

—MARK TWAIN

13 Great joys, like griefs, are silent.

—SHACKERLEY MARMION

14 For happiness one needs security, but joy can spring like a flower even from the cliffs of despair.

—ANNE MORROW LINDBERGH

15 If you want others to be happy, practice compassion. If you want to be happy, practice compassion.

—DALAI LAMA

16 Unhappiness is the ultimate form of self-indulgence.

—TOM ROBBINS
Jitterbug Perfume

HUMOR IS NOT A TRICK . . .

1 Humor is not a trick, not jokes. Humor is a presence in the world—like grace—and shines on everybody.

—GARRISON KEILLOR

2 Time spent laughing is time spent with the gods.

—JAPANESE PROVERB

3 Laughter is the shortest distance between two people.

—VICTOR BORGE

4 Laughter is the sun that drives winter from the human face.

—VICTOR HUGO

5 Laughter is a tranquilizer with no side effects.

—ARNOLD H. GLASOW

6 Like a welcome summer rain, humor may suddenly cleanse and cool the earth, the air and you.

—LANGSTON HUGHES
The Book of Negro Humor

7 Laughter is the brush that sweeps away the cobwebs of the heart.

—MORT WALKER

8 Laughter can be heard farther than weeping.

—YIDDISH PROVERB

9 Laughter translates into any language.

—*Graffiti*

10 The kind of humor I like is the thing that makes me laugh for five seconds and think for ten minutes.

—WILLIAM DAVIS

11 Good humor may be said to be one of the very best articles of dress one can wear in society.

—WILLIAM MAKEPEACE THACKERAY

12 Among those whom I like, I can find no common denominator; but among those whom I love, I can: all of them make me laugh.

—W. H. AUDEN

13 After God created the world, He made man and woman. Then, to keep the whole thing from collapsing, He invented humor.

—GUILLERMO MORDILLO

14 Imagination was given to man to compensate him for what he is not; a sense of humor, to console him for what he is.

—*The Wall Street Journal*

15 So many tangles in life are ultimately hopeless that we have no appropriate sword other than laughter.

—GORDON W. ALLPORT

1 Wit surprises, humor illuminates.

—ELI SCHLEIFER

2 It always hurts a bit when you strike your funny bone. That's the essence of humor.

—JIM FIEBIG

3 Someone who makes you laugh is a comedian. Someone who makes you think and then laugh is a humorist.

—GEORGE BURNS

4 We do have a zeal for laughter in most situations, give or take a dentist.

—JOSEPH HELLER

5 Nothing makes your sense of humor disappear faster than having somebody ask where it is.

—IVERN BALL
in *The Saturday Evening Post*

6 If you're going to be able to look back on something and laugh about it, you might as well laugh about it now.

—MARIE OSMOND

7 Anyone without a sense of humor is at the mercy of everyone else.

—WILLIAM ROTSLER

8 Beware of those who laugh at nothing or at everything.

—ARNOLD H. GLASOW

9 Next to power without honor, the most dangerous thing in the world is power without humor.

—ERIC SEVAREID

10 The love of truth lies at the root of much humor.

ROBERTSON DAVIES
in *Our Living Tradition*

11 I think the next best thing to solving a problem is finding some humor in it.

—FRANK A. CLARK

12 Humor is a hole that lets the sawdust out of a stuffed shirt.

—JAN MCKEITHEN

13 Humor is laughing at what you haven't got when you ought to have it.

—LANGSTON HUGHES

14 A humorist is a fellow who realizes, first, that he is no better than anybody else, and, second, that nobody else is either.

—HOMER MCLIN

15 Comedy has to be based on truth. You take the truth and you put a little curlicue at the end.

—SID CAESAR

16 Comedy is simply a funny way of being serious.

—PETER USTINOV

1 Always laugh at yourself first—
before others do.
—ELSA MAXWELL
R.S.V.P.: Elsa Maxwell's Own Story

2 A laugh at your own expense
costs you nothing.
—MARY H. WALDRIP
in *Advertiser* (Dawson County, Georgia)

3 Happy is the person who can
laugh at himself. He will never
cease to be amused.
—HABIB BOURGUIBA

4 Humor is a spontaneous, wonderful bit of an outburst that just
comes. It's unbridled, it's
unplanned, it's full of surprises.
—ERMA BOMBECK

5 Humor is a reminder that no matter how high the throne one sits
on, one sits on one's bottom.
—TAKI

6 You cannot hold back a good
laugh any more than you can the
tide. Both are forces of nature.
—WILLIAM ROTSLER

7 It has always seemed to me that
hearty laughter is a good way to
jog internally without having to go
outdoors.
—NORMAN COUSINS
Anatomy of an Illness

8 When the first baby laughed for
the first time, the laugh broke into
a thousand pieces and they all
went skipping about, and that was
the beginning of fairies.
—JAMES M. BARRIE

9 No symphony orchestra ever
played music like a two-year-old
girl laughing with a puppy.
—BERN WILLIAMS
in *National Enquirer*

10 A pun is the lowest form of
humor, unless you thought of it
yourself.
—DOUG LARSON

WIT OUGHT TO BE A GLORIOUS TREAT . . .

11 Wit ought to be a glorious treat,
like caviar. Never spread it about
like marmalade.
—NOËL COWARD

12 Wit has truth in it; wisecracking is
simply calisthenics with words.
—DOROTHY PARKER
in *The Paris Review*

13 Wit is the salt of conversation, not
the food.
—WILLIAM HAZLITT

14 Wit is educated insolence.
—ARISTOTLE

1 A caricature is always true only for an instant.

—CHRISTIAN MORGENSTERN

2 Wit penetrates; humor envelops. Wit is a function of verbal intelligence; humor is imagination operating on good nature.

—PEGGY NOONAN
What I Saw at the Revolution

3 The wit of conversation consists more in finding it in others than in showing a great deal yourself.

—JEAN DE LA BRUYÈRE

THE ONLY WAY TO KEEP YOUR HEALTH . . .

4 The only way to keep your health is to eat what you don't want, drink what you don't like, and do what you'd druther not.

—MARK TWAIN

5 The only way for a rich man to be healthy is, by exercise and abstinence, to live as if he were poor.

—PAUL DUDLEY WHITE

6 So many people spend their health gaining wealth, and then have to spend their wealth to regain their health.

—A. J. REB MATERI
Our Family

7 It would be a service to mankind if the pill were available in slot machines and the cigarette were placed on prescription.

—MALCOLM POTTS, MD
in *The Observer* (London)

8 The best cure for hypochondria is to forget about your own body and get interested in someone else's.

—GOODMAN ACE

9 Those who think they have not time for bodily exercise will sooner or later have to find time for illness.

—EDWARD STANLEY

10 It is part of the cure to wish to be cured.

—SENECA

11 You know you've reached middle age when a doctor, not a policeman, tells you to slow down, all you exercise are your prerogatives and it takes you longer to rest than to get tired.

—*Friends News Sheet*
(Royal Perth Hospital, Australia)

12 An early-morning walk is a blessing for the whole day.

—HENRY DAVID THOREAU

13 As with liberty, the price of leanness is eternal vigilance.

—GENE BROWN

1 Your body is the baggage you must carry through life. The more excess baggage, the shorter the trip.

—ARNOLD H. GLASOW

2 You can't lose weight by talking about it. You have to keep your mouth shut.

—*The Old Farmers Almanac*

3 You know it's time to diet when you push away from the table and the table moves.

—Quoted in *The Cockle Bur*

4 Probably nothing in the world arouses more false hopes than the first four hours of a diet.

—DAN BENNETT

5 If it weren't for the fact that the TV set and the refrigerator are so far apart, some of us wouldn't get any exercise at all.

—JOEY ADAMS

TAKING MY PROBLEMS ONE AT A TIME . . .

6 It's not easy taking my problems one at a time when they refuse to get in line.

—ASHLEIGH BRILLIANT

7 He who can't endure the bad will not live to see the good.

—YIDDISH PROVERB

8 It has been my philosophy of life that difficulties vanish when faced boldly.

—ISAAC ASIMOV
Foundation

9 When things are bad, we take comfort in the thought that they could always be worse. And when they are, we find hope in the thought that things are so bad they have to get better.

—MALCOLM S. FORBES
The Sayings of Chairman Malcolm

10 I don't think of all the misery but of the beauty that still remains.

—ANNE FRANK
The Diary of a Young Girl

11 Although the world is full of suffering, it is also full of the overcoming of it.

—HELEN KELLER

12 Nothing is more desirable than to be released from an affliction, but nothing is more frightening than to be divested of a crutch.

—JAMES BALDWIN

13 A certain amount of opposition is a great help to a man. Kites rise against, not with the wind.

—JOHN NEAL

14 What I'm looking for is a blessing that's not in disguise.

—KITTY O'NEILL COLLINS

1 People need resistance, for it is resistance which gives them their awareness of life.

—Karl Ritter

2 That some good can be derived from every event is a better proposition than that everything happens for the best, which it assuredly does not.

—James K. Feibleman

3 The worst thing in your life may contain seeds of the best. When you can see crisis as an opportunity, your life becomes not easier, but more satisfying.

—Joe Kogel

4 Storms make trees take deeper roots.

—Claude McDonald
in *The Christian Word*

5 Smooth seas do not make skillful sailors.

—African proverb

6 It is the wounded oyster that mends its shell with pearl.

—Ralph Waldo Emerson

7 The soul would have no rainbow had the eyes no tears.

—John Vance Cheney

8 Some people are always grumbling that roses have thorns; I am thankful that thorns have roses.

—Alphonse Karr

9 He knows not his own strength that hath not met adversity.

—Ben Jonson

10 Adversity is the trial of principle. Without it, a man hardly knows whether he is honest or not.

—Henry Fielding

11 You'll never find a better sparring partner than adversity.

—Walt Schmidt
in *Parklabrea News* (Los Angeles)

12 A gem is not polished without rubbing, nor a man perfected without trials.

—Chinese proverb

13 Drag your thoughts away from your troubles—by the ears, by the heels, or any other way you can manage it. It's the healthiest thing a body can do.

—Mark Twain

14 Borrow trouble for yourself if that's your nature, but don't lend it to your neighbors.

—Rudyard Kipling
Rewards and Fairies

15 Don't meet trouble halfway. It is quite capable of making the entire journey.

—Bob Edwards

16 Simple solutions seldom are.

—*Forbes* magazine

1 No one has completed his education who has not learned to live with an insoluble problem.
—EDMUND J. KIEFER

2 Keep your face to the sunshine and you cannot see the shadows.
—HELEN KELLER

3 When you can't solve the problem, manage it.
—REV. ROBERT H. SCHULLER

4 Most problems precisely defined are already partially solved.
—HARRY LORAYNE
Memory Makes Money

5 If the only tool you have is a hammer, you tend to see every problem as a nail.
—ABRAHAM MASLOW

6 Nothing lasts forever—not even your troubles.
—ARNOLD H. GLASOW
in *Rotary "Scandal Sheet"* (Graham, Texas)

7 People who drink to drown their sorrow should be told that sorrow knows how to swim.
—ANN LANDERS

8 The way I see it, if you want the rainbow, you gotta put up with the rain.
—DOLLY PARTON

9 The human capacity to fight back will always astonish doctors and philosophers. It seems, indeed, that there are no circumstances so bad and no obstacles so big that man cannot conquer them.
—JEAN TETREAU

10 How a person masters his fate is more important than what his fate is.
—WILHELM VON HUMBOLDT

11 All blessings are mixed blessings.
—JOHN UPDIKE

12 Most of the shadows of this life are caused by our standing in our own sunshine.
—RALPH WALDO EMERSON

13 Life would not be life if a sorrow were sad, and a joy merry, from beginning to end.
—GERMAINE GUEVREMONT
EN PLEINE TERRE

14 Night is the blotting paper for many sorrows.
—LITAUISCH

15 The darkest hour has only 60 minutes.
—MORRIS MANDEL

16 When you get to the end of your rope, tie a knot and hang on. And swing!
—LEO BUSCAGLIA

1 Every problem contains within itself the seeds of its own solution.
—EDWARD SOMERS
in *National Enquirer*

2 Worry often gives a small thing a big shadow.
—SWEDISH PROVERB

3 Little things console us because little things afflict us.
—BLAISE PASCAL

4 For every problem there is one solution which is simple, neat and wrong.
—H. L. MENCKEN
A Mencken Chrestomathy

5 Inside every small problem is a large problem struggling to get out.
—PAUL HUGHES

6 People in distress will sometimes prefer a problem that is familiar to a solution that is not.
—NEIL POSTMAN

7 The first step in solving a problem is to tell someone about it.
—JOHN PETER FLYNN

8 Some people suffer in silence louder than others.
—MORRIE BRICKMAN

Untold suffering seldom is. 9
—FRANKLIN P. JONES

Never bear more than one kind of 10 trouble at a time. Some people bear three—all they have had, all they have now, and all they expect to have.
—EDWARD EVERETT HALE

An adventure is an inconvenience 11 rightly considered. An inconvenience is an adventure wrongly considered.
—G. K. CHESTERTON

IT IS THE LOOSE ENDS . . .

It is the loose ends with which 12 men hang themselves.
—ZELDA FITZGERALD

Two dangers constantly threaten 13 the world: order and disorder.
—PAUL VALÉRY

Nothing is really lost. It's just 14 where it doesn't belong.
—SUZANNE MUELLER

One of the advantages of being 15 disorderly is that one is constantly making exciting discoveries.
—A. A. MILNE

More things grow in the garden 16 than the gardener sows.
—SPANISH PROVERB

1 Organizing is what you do before you do something, so that when you do it, it's not all mixed up.

—A. A. MILNE

2 When one finds himself in a hole of his own making, it is a good time to examine the quality of workmanship.

—JON REMMERDE
in *The Christian Science Monitor*

WHEN LUCK ENTERS . . .

3 When luck enters, give him a seat!

—JEWISH PROVERB

4 A person often meets his destiny on the road he took to avoid it.

—JEAN DE LA FONTAINE

5 Fortune brings in some boats that are not steered.

—WILLIAM SHAKESPEARE

6 Heaven goes by favor. If it went by merit, you would stay out and your dog would go in.

—MARK TWAIN

7 It's hard to detect good luck—it looks so much like something you've earned.

—FRANK A. CLARK

8 Luck is the residue of design.

—BRANCH RICKEY

The luck of having talent is not enough; one must also have a talent for luck. 9

—HECTOR BERLIOZ

Luck never gives; it only lends. 10

—SWEDISH PROVERB

Good luck is with the man who doesn't include it in his plan. 11

—*Graffiti*

Thorough preparation makes its own luck. 12

—JOE POYER
The Contra

Luck is a matter of preparation meeting opportunity. 13

—OPRAH WINFREY

Miracles sometimes occur, but one has to work terribly hard for them. 14

—CHAIM WEIZMANN

Luck is not chance, it's toil. Fortune's expensive smile is earned. 15

—EMILY DICKINSON

One half of life is luck; the other half is discipline—and that's the important half, for without discipline you wouldn't know what to do with your luck. 16

—CARL ZUCKMAYER

1 With money in your pocket, you are wise and you are handsome and you sing well, too.

—YIDDISH PROVERB

2 Some people have all the luck. And they're the ones who never depend on it.

—BOB INGHAM

3 There is no substitute for incomprehensible good luck.

—LYNNE ALPERN AND ESTHER BLUMENFELD
Oh, Lord, I Sound Just Like Mama

4 Serendipity is looking in a haystack for a needle and discovering the farmer's daughter.

—Quoted by JULIUS H. COMROE JR.
in *Retrospectroscope*

5 It is an all-too-human frailty to suppose that a favorable wind will blow forever.

—RICK BODE
First You Have to Row a Little Boat

6 It is perhaps a more fortunate destiny to have a taste for collecting shells than to be born a millionaire.

—ROBERT LOUIS STEVENSON

7 Superstition is foolish, childish, primitive and irrational—but how much does it cost you to knock on wood?

—JUDITH VIORST
Love & Guilt & the Meaning of Life, Etc.

THE LIMITS OF THE POSSIBLE . . .

The only way of discovering the limits of the possible is to venture a little way past them into the impossible. 8

—ARTHUR C. CLARKE
Profiles of the Future

I have learned to use the word impossible with the greatest caution. 9

—WERNHER VON BRAUN

What we need are more people who specialize in the impossible. 10

—THEODORE ROETHKE

The difference between the impossible and the possible lies in a person's determination. 11

—TOMMY LASORDA

The impossible is often the untried. 12

—JIM GOODWIN

All things are possible until they are proved impossible—and even the impossible may only be so, as of now. 13

—PEARL S. BUCK
A Bridge for Passing

Progress begins with the belief that what is necessary is possible. 14

—NORMAN COUSINS

1 Start by doing what's necessary, then what's possible and suddenly you are doing the impossible.
—St. Francis of Assisi

2 Everything looks impossible for the people who never try anything.
—Jean-Louis Etienne

3 The young do not know enough to be prudent, and therefore they attempt the impossible—and achieve it, generation after generation.
—Pearl S. Buck

4 Nothing ever built arose to touch the skies unless some man dreamed that it should, some man believed that it could, and some man willed that it must.
—Charles F. Kettering

5 Accomplishing the impossible means only that the boss will add it to your regular duties.
—Doug Larson

IF YOU WANT A PLACE IN THE SUN . . .

6 If you want a place in the sun, you've got to put up with a few blisters.
—Abigail Van Buren

7 Always bear in mind that your own resolution to succeed is more important than any one thing.
—Abraham Lincoln

8 Probably the most honest "self-made man" ever was the one we heard say: "I got to the top the hard way—fighting my own laziness and ignorance every step of the way."
—James Thom

9 You can't expect to make a place in the sun for yourself if you keep taking refuge under the family tree.
—Claude McDonald
in The Christian Word

10 The important thing in life is not to have a good hand but to play it well.
—Louis-N. Fortin
Pensées, Proverbes, Maximes

11 Striving for success without hard work is like trying to harvest where you haven't planted.
—David Bly
in Deseret News (Salt Lake City)

12 Showing up is 80 percent of life.
—Woody Allen

13 If you play to win, as I do, the game never ends.
—Stan Mikita
Journal (Edmonton, Alberta)

1 There are no secrets to success. It is the result of preparation, hard work, learning from failure.
—GEN. COLIN L. POWELL
in *The Black Collegian*

2 Success is how high you bounce when you hit bottom.
—GEN. GEORGE S. PATTON

3 Success is often the result of taking a misstep in the right direction.
—AL BERNSTEIN

4 Wherever you see a successful business, someone once made a courageous decision.
—PETER DRUCKER

5 Success is often just an idea away.
—FRANK TYGER

6 The only thing that ever sat its way to success was a hen.
—SARAH BROWN

7 Success has a simple formula: do your best, and people may like it.
—SAM EWING

8 As a general rule, the most successful man in life is the man who has the best information.
—BENJAMIN DISRAELI

9 You're never a loser until you quit trying.
—MIKE DITKA

10 There's no secret about success. Did you ever know a successful man who didn't tell you about it?
—KIN HUBBARD

11 Success is more a function of consistent common sense than it is of genius.
—AN WANG
Lessons: An Autobiography

12 Don't aim for success if you want it; just do what you love and believe in, and it will come naturally.
—DAVID FROST

13 Success isn't a result of spontaneous combustion. You must set yourself on fire.
—ARNOLD H. GLASOW

14 Success without honor is an unseasoned dish; it will satisfy your hunger, but it won't taste good.
—JOE PATERNO

15 Sports serve society by providing vivid examples of excellence.
—GEORGE F. WILL

16 Always do what you say you are going to do. It is the glue and fiber that binds successful relationships.
—JEFFRY A. TIMMONS
The Entrepreneurial Mind

THE NATURAL WORLD

When one tugs at a single thing in nature,
he finds it attached to the rest of the world.

—JOHN MUIR

A FINE LANDSCAPE IS LIKE A PIECE OF MUSIC . . .

1 There is nothing like walking to get the feel of a country. A fine landscape is like a piece of music; it must be taken at the right tempo. Even a bicycle goes too fast.

—PAUL SCOTT MOWRER
The House of Europe

2 When one tugs at a single thing in nature, he finds it attached to the rest of the world.

—JOHN MUIR

3 The universe is not required to be in perfect harmony with human ambition.

—CARL SAGAN

4 Our Creator would never have made such lovely days and have given us the deep hearts to enjoy them unless we were meant to be immortal.

—NATHANIEL HAWTHORNE

5 Climb the mountains and get their good tidings. Nature's peace will flow into you as sunshine flows into trees. The winds will blow their freshness into you, and the storms their energy, while cares will drop off like falling leaves.

—JOHN MUIR

6 There is no silence like that of the mountains.

—GUY BUTLER
A Local Habitation

7 I have seen the sea when it is stormy and wild; when it is quiet and serene; when it is dark and moody. And in all its moods, I see myself.

—MARTIN BUXBAUM

8 April hath put a spirit of youth in every thing.

—WILLIAM SHAKESPEARE

9 Our Lord has written the promise of resurrection, not in books alone but in every leaf of springtime.

—MARTIN LUTHER

10 Spring hangs her infant blossoms on the trees / Rock'd in the cradle of the western breeze.

—WILLIAM COWPER

11 Spring, thy name is color.

—LIBBIE FUDIM

12 Spring is nature's way of saying, "Let's party!"

—ROBIN WILLIAMS

13 A little madness in the spring is wholesome even for the king.

—EMILY DICKINSON

1 Springtime is the land awakening.
The March winds are the morning
yawn.
—Quoted by Lewis Grizzard
in *Kathy Sue Loudermilk, I Love You*

2 The first day of spring is one
thing, and the first spring day is
another. The difference between
them is sometimes as great as a
month.
—Henry Van Dyke

3 Spring is when you feel like
whistling even with a shoe full
of slush.
—Doug Larson

4 Summer afternoon—summer afternoon; to me those have always
been the two most beautiful
words in the English language.
—Henry James

5 If a June night could talk, it would
probably boast that it invented
romance.
—Bern Williams

6 Until you have heard the whip-
poorwill, either nearby or in the
faint distance, you have not
experienced summer night.
—Henry Beetle Hough
in *Vineyard Gazette* (Edgartown,
Massachusetts)

Oh, the summer night has a smile 7
of light, and she sits on a sapphire
throne.
—B. W. Procter

The experience of drought and 8
dust storms remains central to the
psychology of the prairie west;
more than the intermittent afflu-
ence of postwar decades, it tints
a westerner's outlook on life.
He continues to live in next year
country, where he smokes a pack
of hope a day.
—Mark Abley
Beyond Forget

For man, autumn is a time of 9
harvest, of gathering together.
For nature, it is a time of sowing,
of scattering abroad.
—Edwin Way Teale
Autumn Across America

Autumn is a second spring when 10
every leaf is a flower.
—Albert Camus

Autumn carries more gold in its 11
hand than all the other seasons.
—Jim Bishop

October's poplars are flaming 12
torches lighting the way to winter.
—Nova S. Bair
in *Capper's Weekly*

1 October, here's to you. Here's to the heady aroma of the frost-kissed apples, the winey smell of ripened grapes, the wild-as-the-wind smell of hickory nuts and the nostalgic whiff of that first wood smoke.

—KEN WEBER
in Providence, R.I., *Journal-Bulletin*

2 Autumn is a season followed immediately by looking forward to spring.

—DOUG LARSON

3 Winter is not a season; it's an occupation.

—SINCLAIR LEWIS

4 Few things are as democratic as a snowstorm.

—BERN WILLIAMS
in *The National Enquirer*

5 No winter lasts forever; no spring skips its turn.

—HAL BORLAND
Sundial of the Seasons

6 All sunshine makes a desert.

—ARABIC PROVERB

7 I am sure it is a great mistake always to know enough to go in when it rains. One may keep snug and dry by such knowledge, but one misses a world of loveliness.

—ADELINE KNAPP

8 When there is a river in your growing up, you probably always hear it.

—ANN ZWINGER
Run, River, Run

9 I like trees because they seem more resigned to the way they have to live than other things do.

—WILLA CATHER

10 A man has made at least a start on discovering the meaning of human life when he plants shade trees under which he knows full well he will never sit.

—D. ELTON TRUEBLOOD

11 I never knew how soothing trees are—many trees and patches of open sunlight, and tree presences; it is almost like having another being.

—D. H. LAWRENCE

12 The soil in return for her service keeps the tree tied to her, the sky asks nothing and leaves it free.

—RABINDRANATH TAGORE

13 Everything is blooming most recklessly; if it were voices instead of colors, there would be an unbelievable shrieking into the heart of the night.

—RAINER MARIA RILKE
Letters of Rainer Maria Rilke

1 A woodland in full color is awesome as a forest fire; but a single tree is like a dancing tongue of flame to warm the heart.

—HAL BORLAND
Sundial of the Seasons

2 He that plants trees loves others besides himself.

—ENGLISH PROVERB

3 Flowers always make people better, happier and more helpful; they are sunshine, food and medicine to the soul.

—LUTHER BURBANK

4 If we had a keen vision of all that is ordinary in human life, it would be like hearing the grass grow or the squirrel's heart beat, and we should die of that roar which is the other side of silence.

—GEORGE ELIOT

5 People from a planet without flowers would think we must be mad with joy the whole time to have such things about us.

—IRIS MURDOCH
A Fairly Honourable Defeat

6 The Pyramids will not last a moment compared with the daisy.

—D. H. LAWRENCE
D. H. Lawrence and Italy

7 I don't see why I am always asking for private, individual, selfish miracles when every year there are miracles like white dogwood.

—ANNE MORROW LINDBERGH
Bring Me a Unicorn

8 I don't ask for the meaning of the song of a bird or the rising of the sun on a misty morning. There they are, and they are beautiful.

—PETE HAMILL
in *Esquire*

9 A bird does not sing because it has an answer. It sings because it has a song.

—CHINESE PROVERB

10 Let us a little permit nature to take her own way; she better understands her own affairs than we.

—MONTAIGNE

11 I've always regarded nature as the clothing of God.

—ALAN HOVHANESS

12 The sky is the daily bread of the eyes.

—RALPH WALDO EMERSON

13 One touch of nature makes the whole world kin.

—WILLIAM SHAKESPEARE

14 Repetition is the only form of permanence that nature can achieve.

—GEORGE SANTAYANA

1 The repetition in nature may not be a mere recurrence. It may be a theatrical "encore."
—G. K. CHESTERTON

2 Everybody wants to go back to nature—but not on foot.
—WERNER MITSCH

3 Never a daisy grows but a mystery guides the growing.
—RICHARD REALF

4 I would rather live in a world where my life is surrounded by mystery than live in a world so small that my mind could comprehend it.
—HARRY EMERSON FOSDICK

5 If the human brain were so simple that we could understand it, we would be so simple that we couldn't.
—EMERSON M. PUGH

6 Science cannot answer the deepest questions. As soon as you ask why there is something instead of nothing, you have gone beyond science. I find it quite improbable that such order came out of chaos. There has to be some organizing principle. God to me is the explanation for the miracle of existence—why there is something instead of nothing.
—COSMOLOGIST ALLAN R. SANDAGE

Sometimes I think we're alone in the universe, and sometimes I think we're not. In either case, the idea is quite staggering. 7
—ARTHUR C. CLARKE

Unknowingly, we plow the dust of stars, blown about us by the wind, and drink the universe in a glass of rain. 8
—IHAB HASSAN

The universe is full of magical things patiently waiting for our wits to grow sharper. 9
—EDEN PHILLPOTTS
A Shadow Passes

The sun, with all those planets revolving around it and dependent on it, can still ripen a bunch of grapes as if it had nothing else in the universe to do. 10
—GALILEO

To define the universe would be to contain it, and that would be to limit existence. 11
—DAVID BERESFORD
in *The Weekly Mail & Guardian*
(Johannesburg, South Africa)

The universe is merely a fleeting idea in God's mind—a pretty uncomfortable thought, particularly if you've just made a down payment on a house. 12
—WOODY ALLEN

LEAVE A LANDSCAPE AS IT WAS . . .

1 There is nothing in which the birds differ more from man than the way in which they can build and yet leave a landscape as it was before.

—ROBERT LYND
The Blue Lion and Other Essays

2 Don't blow it—good planets are hard to find.

—Quoted in *Time*

3 What is the use of a house if you haven't got a tolerable planet to put it on?

—HENRY DAVID THOREAU

4 It is horrifying that we have to fight our own government to save the environment.

—ANSEL ADAMS

5 Growth for the sake of growth is the ideology of the cancer cell.

—EDWARD ABBEY

6 Progress might have been all right once, but it's gone on too long.

—OGDEN NASH

7 Progress is man's ability to complicate simplicity.

—THOR HEYERDAHL
Fatu-Hiva

8 You can tell all you need to about a society from how it treats animals and beaches.

—FRANK DEFORD
in *Sports Illustrated*

9 Since the beginning each generation has fought nature. Now, in the life-span of a single generation, we must turn around 180 degrees and become the protector of nature.

—JACQUES-YVES COUSTEAU

10 We haven't got too much time left to ensure that government of the earth, by the earth, for the earth, shall not perish from the people.

—C. P. SNOW

11 The activist is not the man who says the river is dirty. The activist is the man who cleans up the river.

—ROSS PEROT

12 I think God's going to come down and pull civilization over for speeding.

—STEVEN WRIGHT

13 Civilization no longer needs to open up wilderness; it needs wilderness to open up the still largely unexplored human mind.

—DAVID RAINS WALLACE
The Dark Range

1 If we do not permit the earth to produce beauty and joy, it will in the end not produce food either.

—Joseph Wood Krutch

2 We abuse land because we regard it as a commodity belonging to us. When we see land as a community to which we belong, we may begin to use it with love and respect.

—Aldo Leopold
A Sand County Almanac

3 A true conservationist is a man who knows that the world is not given by his fathers but borrowed from his children.

—*Audubon*

4 The other planets may not be able to support life, but it isn't easy on this one either.

—*Banking*

THERE'S NO DEALING WITH A CAT . . .

5 There's no dealing with a cat who knows you're awake.

—Brad Solomon
The Open Shadow

6 The only mystery about the cat is why it ever decided to become a domestic animal.

—Compton MacKenzie
Cats' Company

7 The cat could very well be man's best friend but would never stoop to admitting it.

—Doug Larson

8 Cats have it all—admiration and an endless sleep and company only when they want it.

—Rod McKuen
Book of Days

9 Cats don't caress us—they caress themselves on us.

—Rivarol

10 When dogs leap onto your bed, it's because they adore being with you. When cats leap onto your bed, it's because they adore your bed.

—Alisha Everett

11 You can keep a dog; but it is the cat who keeps people because cats find humans useful domestic animals. A dog will flatter you but you have to flatter a cat. A dog is an employee; the cat is a freelance.

—George Mikes
How to Be Decadent

12 When I play with my cat, who knows if I am not more of a pastime to her than she is to me?

—Montaigne

1 Ignorant people think it's the noise which fighting cats make that is so aggravating, but it ain't so; it's the sickening grammar they use.

—MARK TWAIN

2 No matter how much cats fight, there always seem to be plenty of kittens.

—ABRAHAM LINCOLN

3 It is impossible to keep a straight face in the presence of one or more kittens.

—CYNTHIA E. VARNADO

4 You can't look at a sleeping cat and be tense.

—JANE PAULEY

5 The idea of calm exists in a sitting cat.

—JULES RENARD

6 Cats seem to go on the principle that it never does any harm to ask for what you want.

—JOSEPH WOOD KRUTCH
The Twelve Seasons

7 Never try to outstubborn a cat.

—ROBERT A. HEINLEIN
The Notebooks of Lazarus Long

IF DOGS COULD TALK . . .

If dogs could talk, it would take a lot of fun out of owning one. 8

—ANDREW A. ROONEY
Not That You Asked . . .

One reason a dog can be such a comfort when you're feeling blue is that he doesn't try to find out why. 9

—*National Enquirer*

There is no psychiatrist in the world like a puppy licking your face. 10

—BERN WILLIAMS

To his dog, every man is Napoleon; hence the popularity of dogs. 11

—ALDOUS HUXLEY

The great pleasure of a dog is that you may make a fool of yourself with him and not only will he not scold you, but he will make a fool of himself too. 12

—SAMUEL BUTLER

The dog has got more fun out of Man than Man has got out of the dog, for the clearly demonstrable reason that Man is the more laughable of the two animals. 13

—JAMES THURBER
Thurber's Dogs

1 Dogs laugh, but they laugh with their tails.

—MAX EASTMAN
Enjoyment of Laughter

2 A dog wags its tail with its heart.

—MARTIN BUXBAUM
in *Table Talk*

3 A dog teaches a boy fidelity, perseverance, and to turn around three times before lying down.

—ROBERT BENCHLEY

4 Home computers are being called upon to perform many new functions, including the consumption of homework formerly eaten by the dog.

—DOUG LARSON

5 If you think dogs can't count, try putting three dog biscuits in your pocket and then giving Fido only two of them.

—PHIL PASTORET

6 Any time you think you have influence, try ordering around someone else's dog.

—*The Cockle Bur*

7 Door: What a dog is perpetually on the wrong side of.

—OGDEN NASH

8 We give them the love we can spare, the time we can spare. In return dogs have given us their absolute all. It is without a doubt the best deal man has ever made.

—ROGER CARAS
A Celebration of Dogs

THE WORLD OF NATIONS

To understand a man, you must know his memories. The same is true of a nation.

—ANTHONY QUAYLE

THE AMERICAN DREAM IS NOT OVER . . .

1 The American dream is not over. America is an adventure.

—THEODORE WHITE

2 There are those who will say that the liberation of humanity, the freedom of man and mind, is nothing but a dream. They are right. It is the American dream.

—ARCHIBALD MACLEISH
A Continuing Journey

3 It is a part of the American character to consider nothing as desperate.

—THOMAS JEFFERSON

4 What is the essence of America? Finding and maintaining that perfect, delicate balance between freedom "to" and freedom "from."

—MARILYN VOS SAVANT
in *Parade*

5 The saving grace of America lies in the fact that the overwhelming majority of Americans are possessed of two great qualities— a sense of humor and a sense of proportion.

—FRANKLIN DELANO ROOSEVELT

6 America is a religious nation, but only because it is religiously tolerant and lets every citizen pray, or not pray, in his own way.

—From an editorial in *The New York Times*

7 America is a place where Jewish merchants sell Zen love beads to agnostics for Christmas.

—JOHN BURTON BRIMER

8 America is great because America is good, and if America ever ceases to be good, America will cease to be great.

—ALEXIS DE TOCQUEVILLE

9 The things that have made America great are being subverted for the things that make Americans rich.

—LOU ERICKSON

10 How often we fail to realize our good fortune in living in a country where happiness is more than a lack of tragedy.

—PAUL SWEENEY

11 America did not invent human rights. In a very real sense, it is the other way around. Human rights invented America.

—JIMMY CARTER

12 What the people want is very simple—they want an America as good as its promise.

—BARBARA JORDAN

1 Being American is not a matter of birth. We must practice it every day, lest we become something else.
—MALCOLM WALLOP
in *Imprimis*

2 What's right with America is a willingness to discuss what's wrong with America.
—HARRY C. BAUER

3 America is not like a blanket—one piece of unbroken cloth. America is more like a quilt—many patches, many pieces, many colors, many sizes, all woven together by a common thread.
—REV. JESSE L. JACKSON

4 America is a tune. It must be sung together.
—GERALD STANLEY LEE
Crowds

5 In America nobody says you have to keep the circumstances somebody else gives you.
—AMY TAN
The Joy Luck Club

6 One of the fondest expressions around is that we can't be the world's policeman. But guess who gets called when suddenly someone needs a cop.
—GEN. COLIN POWELL

7 I thank God that I live in a country where dreams can come true, where failure sometimes is the first step to success and where success is only another form of failure if we forget what our priorities should be.
—HARRY LLOYD

8 Americans are optimists. They hope they'll be wealthy someday—and they're positive they can get one more brushful of paint out of an empty can.
—BERN WILLIAMS

9 Give the American people a good cause, and there's nothing they can't lick.
—JOHN WAYNE

10 The business of America is not business. Neither is it war. The business of America is justice and securing the blessings of liberty.
—GEORGE F. WILL
in *Newsweek*

11 If the American Revolution had produced nothing but the Declaration of Independence, it would have been worthwhile.
—SAMUEL ELIOT MORISON
The Oxford History of the American People

1 Whoever wants to know the heart and mind of America had better learn baseball.

—JACQUES BARZUN
God's Country and Mine

2 Highways have made tangible the conviction that the truth about America, its heart and soul, is always to be found somewhere just over the horizon, somewhere around the next bend.

—PHIL PATTON
Open Road

3 A frontier is never a place; it is a time and a way of life. Frontiers pass, but they endure in their people.

—HAL BORLAND
High, Wide and Lonesome

THE REAL ESSENCE OF CANADA . . .

4 To agree to disagree, to harness diversity, to respect dissent; perhaps this is the real essence of Canada.

—ROBERT L. PERRY
Peter's Quotations

5 The soul of Canada is a dual personality, and must remain only half-revealed to those who know only one language.

—FRANK OLIVER CALL
Canadian Quotations and Phrases

6 A Canadian is someone who drinks Brazilian coffee from an English teacup, and munches a French pastry while sitting on his Danish furniture, having just come home from an Italian movie in his German car. He picks up his Japanese pen and writes to his MP to complain about the American takeover of the Canadian publishing business.

—CAMPBELL HUGHES
in *Time*

7 "Liberty" sounds awkward on the Canadian tongue; we use "freedom," a more passive-sounding word. When I was a soldier applying for a three-day pass, I asked for "leave," a word that suggests permission. United States G.I.'s were granted "liberty," a word that implies escape.

—PIERRE BERTON
Why We Act Like Canadians

8 Freedom is to you, what the sun was for us. You take it for granted.

—MOHAMED MAGHJI
Vancouver Sun

9 Such a land [British Columbia] is good for an energetic man. It is also not so bad for the loafer.

—RUDYARD KIPLING

LIBERTY IS ALWAYS DANGEROUS . . .

1 Liberty is always dangerous—but it is the safest thing we have.

—HARRY EMERSON FOSDICK

2 Liberty, when it begins to take root, is a plant of rapid growth.

—GEORGE WASHINGTON

3 Let freedom reign. The sun never set on so glorious a human achievement.

—NELSON MANDELA

4 Free is not the same as free and easy.

—LARRY EISENBERG

5 Every generation of Americans needs to know that freedom consists not in doing what we like, but in having the right to do what we ought.

—POPE JOHN PAUL II

6 The cause of freedom, of the defense of man's conscience, is indivisible. By defending it in one country, we defend it everywhere in the world.

—VLADIMIR BUKOVSKY

7 Freedom is the right to be wrong, not the right to do wrong.

—JOHN G. DIEFENBAKER

8 There are two freedoms: the false where a man is free to do what he likes; the true where a man is free to do what he ought.

—CHARLES KINGSLEY

9 Your liberty to swing your arms ends where my nose begins.

—Quoted by STUART CHASE

10 The right to do something does not mean that doing it is right.

—WILLIAM SAFIRE
in *The New York Times*

11 My definition of a free society is a society where it is safe to be unpopular.

—ADLAI E. STEVENSON

12 Many politicians of our time are in the habit of laying down as self-evident the proposition that no people ought to be free until they are fit to use their freedom. The maxim is worthy of the fool in the old story, who had resolved not to go in the water until he had learnt to swim. If men are to wait for liberty until they become wise and good in slavery, they may indeed wait for ever.

—THOMAS BABINGTON MACAULAY, 1825

13 Liberty is the only thing you cannot have unless you are willing to give it to others.

—WILLIAM ALLEN WHITE

1 Freedom is a powerful animal that fights the barriers, and sometimes makes people wish for higher fences.

—LANCE MORROW
in *Time*

2 The function of freedom is to free somebody else.

—TONI MORRISON

3 It is easy to take liberty for granted, when you have never had it taken from you.

—DICK CHENEY

4 Those who expect to reap the blessings of freedom must undergo the fatigue of supporting it.

—THOMAS PAINE

5 Those who profess to favor freedom and yet depreciate agitation are men who want rain without thunder and lightning.

—FREDERICK DOUGLASS

6 Freedom never yet was given to nations as a gift, but only as a reward, bravely earned by one's own exertions.

—LAJOS KOSSUTH

7 The history of liberty is a history of the limitation of government power.

—WOODROW WILSON

8 They have rights who dare defend them.

—ROGER BALDWIN

9 The love of liberty is the love of others. The love of power is the love of ourselves.

—WILLIAM HAZLITT

10 Freedom is nothing else but a chance to be better.

—ALBERT CAMUS
Resistance, Rebellion and Death

11 Freedom is the right to choose the habits that bind you.

—RENATE RUBENSTEIN
Liefst Verliefd

12 If a nation values anything more than freedom, it will lose its freedom; and the irony of it is that if it is comfort or money that it values more, it will lose that too.

—W. SOMERSET MAUGHAM,
Strictly Personal

13 A country free enough to examine its own conscience is a land worth living in, a nation to be envied.

—PRINCE CHARLES

14 The clash of ideas is the sound of freedom.

—*Graffiti*

1 Where opinions, morals and politics are concerned, there is no such thing as objectivity. The best we can hope for is that freedom will enable subjective points of view to meet and complement each other.

—Jean D'Ormesson

2 A people that values its privileges above its principles soon loses both.

—Dwight D. Eisenhower

3 It is a seldom proferred argument as to the advantages of a free press that it has a major function in keeping the government itself informed as to what the government is doing.

—Walter Cronkite

4 A free press can be good or bad, but, most certainly, without freedom a press will never be anything but bad.

—Albert Camus

5 Where the press is free and every man able to read, all is safe.

—Thomas Jefferson

6 Censorship reflects a society's lack of confidence in itself.

—Potter Stewart

7 Every time we liberate a woman, we liberate a man.

—Margaret Mead

8 No man is free who is not master of himself.

—Epictetus

9 No woman can call herself free until she can choose consciously whether she will or will not be a mother.

—Margaret Sanger

10 Freedom always carries a burden of proof, always throws us back on ourselves.

—Shelby Steele
The Content of Our Character

11 Patriotism is not so much protecting the land of our fathers as preserving the land of our children.

—José Ortega y Gasset

12 If everything would be permitted to me, I would feel lost in this abyss of freedom.

—Igor Stravinsky

13 Freedom is the oxygen of the soul.

—Moshe Dayan

14 Timid men prefer the calm of despotism to the tempestuous sea of liberty.

—Thomas Jefferson

15 We are in bondage to the law in order that we may be free.

—Cicero

1 To live anywhere in the world today and be against equality because of race or color is like living in Alaska and being against snow.

—WILLIAM FAULKNER
Essays, Speeches and Public Letters

2 The defect of equality is that we desire it only with our superiors.

—HENRY BECQUE

3 It is often easier to become outraged by injustice half a world away than by oppression and discrimination half a block from home.

—CARL T. ROWAN

TO PREVENT INJUSTICE . . .

4 There may be times when we are powerless to prevent injustice, but there must never be a time when we fail to protest.

—ELIE WIESEL

5 History will have to record that the greatest tragedy of this period of social transition was not the strident clamor of the bad people, but the appalling silence of the good people.

—REV. MARTIN LUTHER KING JR.
Stride Toward Freedom

6 There is no happiness for people at the expense of other people.

—ANWAR EL-SADAT

Injustice anywhere is a threat to justice everywhere. 7

—REV. MARTIN LUTHER KING JR.

Equal rights for the sexes will be achieved only when mediocre women occupy high positions. 8

—FRANÇOISE GIROUD

To do injustice is more disgraceful than to suffer it. 9

—PLATO

A great many people in this country are worried about law-and-order. And a great many people are worried about justice. But one thing is certain: you cannot have either until you have both. 10

—RAMSEY CLARK

What is morally wrong cannot be politically right. 11

—WILLIAM GLADSTONE

In recognizing the humanity of our fellow beings, we pay ourselves the highest tribute. 12

—THURGOOD MARSHALL

As long as you keep a person down, some part of you has to be down there to hold him down, so it means you cannot soar as you otherwise might. 13

—MARIAN ANDERSON

1 One man cannot hold another man down in the ditch without remaining down in the ditch with him.

—BOOKER T. WASHINGTON

2 Justice may be blind, but she has very sophisticated listening devices.

—EDGAR ARGO
in *Funny Times*

3 Justice is the insurance we have on our lives, and obedience is the premium we pay for it.

—WILLIAM PENN

4 A minority group has "arrived" only when it has the right to produce some fools and scoundrels without the entire group paying for it.

—CARL T. ROWAN

5 We are not bitter, not because we have forgiven but because there is so much to be done that we cannot afford to waste valuable time and resources on anger.

—GOVAN MBEKI
Johannesburg Weekly Mail (South Africa)

6 Efficiency can never be substituted for due process. Is not a dictatorship the more "efficient" form of government?

—THURGOOD MARSHALL

7 It is better to risk saving a guilty man than to condemn an innocent one.

—VOLTAIRE

8 Most lawyers who win a case advise their clients that "we have won" and, when justice has frowned upon their cause, that "you have lost."

—LOUIS NIZER

9 Injustice is relatively easy to bear; what stings is justice.

—H. L. MENCKEN
Prejudices

10 That old law about "an eye for an eye" leaves everybody blind.

—REV. MARTIN LUTHER KING JR.
Stride Toward Freedom

11 I would uphold the law if for no other reason but to protect myself.

—THOMAS MORE

12 I sometimes wish that people would put a little more emphasis upon the observance of the law than they do upon its enforcement.

—CALVIN COOLIDGE

13 The ultimate solution to the race problem lies in the willingness of men to obey the unenforceable.

—REV. MARTIN LUTHER KING JR.

1 The worst form of injustice is
pretended justice.

—PLATO

THE REAL BEAUTY OF DEMOCRACY . . .

2 The real beauty of democracy is
that the average man believes he
is above average.

—MORRIE BRICKMAN

3 Man's capacity for justice makes
democracy possible, but man's
inclination to injustice makes
democracy necessary.

—REINHOLD NIEBUHR

4 Democracy's real test lies in its
respect for minority opinion.

—ELLERY SEDGWICK
in *Jersey Journal*

5 The test of courage comes when
we are in the minority. The test
of tolerance comes when we are
in the majority.

—RALPH W. SOCKMAN

6 Consensus means that lots of people say collectively what nobody
believes individually.

—ABBA EBAN
in *Montreal Gazette*

7 Democracy without morality is
impossible.

—JACK KEMP

8 Democracy does not guarantee
equality, only equality of
opportunity.

—IRVING KRISTOL

9 Democracy cannot survive without
the guidance of a creative minority.

—HARLAN F. STONE

10 One has the right to be wrong in
a democracy.

—CLAUDE PEPPER

11 Democracy is a small hard core of
common agreement, surrounded
by a rich variety of individual
differences.

—JAMES B. CONANT

12 Our political institutions work
remarkably well. They are designed
to clang against each other. The
noise is democracy at work.

—MICHAEL NOVAK

13 I like the noise of democracy.

—JAMES BUCHANAN

14 Democracy, like any noncoercive
relationship, rests on a shared
understanding of limits.

—ELIZABETH DREW
*Washington Journal: The Events of
1973–1974*

15 Democracy means that if the
doorbell rings in the early hours,
it is likely to be the milkman.

—WINSTON CHURCHILL

1 Democracy is not a matter of sentiment, but of foresight. Any system that doesn't take the long run into account will burn itself out in the short run.

—CHARLES YOST

2 I'm tired of hearing it said that democracy doesn't work. Of course it doesn't work. We are supposed to work it.

—ALEXANDER WOOLLCOTT

3 People often say that, in a democracy, decisions are made by a majority of the people. Of course, that is not true. Decisions are made by a majority of those who make themselves heard and who vote—a very different thing.

—WALTER H. JUDD

4 Democracy, like love, can survive any attack—save neglect and indifference.

—PAUL SWEENEY

5 There can be no daily democracy without daily citizenship.

—RALPH NADER

6 Democracy is the only system that persists in asking the powers that be whether they are the powers that ought to be.

—SYDNEY J. HARRIS

7 Every private citizen has a public responsibility.

—MYRA JANCO DANIELS
in *Newsweek*

8 We will all be better citizens when voting records of our Congressmen are followed as carefully as scores of pro-football games.

—LOU ERICKSON
in *Atlanta Journal*

9 The most important political office is that of private citizen.

—LOUIS BRANDEIS

10 Democracy is based upon the conviction that there are extraordinary possibilities in ordinary people.

—HARRY EMERSON FOSDICK

11 Democracy is not a mathematical deduction proved once and for all time. Democracy is a just faith fervently held, a commitment to be tested again and again in the fiery furnace of history.

—JACK KEMP

12 Democracy may not prove in the long run to be as efficient as other forms of government, but it has one saving grace: it allows us to know and say that it isn't.

—BILL MOYERS
in *Newsweek*

1 Democracy is like a raft. It won't sink, but you'll always have your feet wet.

—Quoted by RUSSELL LONG in *The Washingtonian*

2 Whenever you find yourself on the side of the majority, it is time to pause and reflect.

—MARK TWAIN

3 Sometimes a majority simply means that all the fools are on the same side.

—CLAUDE McDONALD

4 Democracy is the recurrent suspicion that more than half of the people are right more than half of the time.

—E. B. WHITE
in *The New Yorker*

5 It's not the hand that signs the laws that holds the destiny of America. It's the hand that casts the ballot.

—HARRY TRUMAN

6 It's not the voting that's democracy; it's the counting.

—TOM STOPPARD
Jumpers

7 Anything that keeps a politician humble is healthy for democracy.

—MICHAEL KINSLEY

Democracy is the art of disciplining oneself so that one need not be disciplined by others. 8

—GEORGES CLEMENCEAU

IN POLITICS . . .

In politics, what begins in fear usually ends in folly. 9

—SAMUEL TAYLOR COLERIDGE

The bedfellows politics makes are never strange. It only seems that way to those who have not watched the courtship. 10

—KIRKPATRICK SALE

Politics has got so expensive that it takes lots of money to even get beat with nowadays. 11

—WILL ROGERS

Politicians and journalists share the same fate in that they often understand tomorrow the things they talk about today. 12

—HELMUT SCHMIDT

Politics is like coaching a football team. You have to be smart enough to understand the game but not smart enough to lose interest. 13

—EUGENE McCARTHY

1 No man should enter politics unless he is either independently rich or independently poor.

—ROBERT JAMES MANION
Gentlemen, Players and Politicians

2 The idea that you can merchandise candidates for high office like breakfast cereal is the ultimate indignity to the democratic process.

—ADLAI E. STEVENSON

3 Politics is perhaps the only profession for which no preparation is thought necessary.

—ROBERT LOUIS STEVENSON

4 The truly skillful politician is one who, when he comes to a fork in the road, goes both ways.

—MARCO A. ALMAZAN
Píldoras Anticonceptistas

5 What's real in politics is what the voters decide is real.

—BEN J. WATTENBERG
Values Matter Most

6 Politics are too serious a matter to be left to the politicians.

—GEN. CHARLES DE GAULLE

7 Everything is changing. People are taking their comedians seriously and the politicians as a joke.

—WILL ROGERS

8 When things don't go well they like to blame presidents; and that's something that presidents are paid for.

—JOHN F. KENNEDY

9 Sincerity and competence is a strong combination. In politics, it's everything.

—PEGGY NOONAN
in *Catholic New York*

10 When a man assumes a public trust he should consider himself as public property.

—THOMAS JEFFERSON

11 Talk is cheap—except when Congress does it.

—CULLEN HIGHTOWER

12 A strong conviction that something must be done is the parent of many bad measures.

—DANIEL WEBSTER

13 Those who corrupt the public mind are just as evil as those who steal from the public purse.

—ADLAI E. STEVENSON

14 When the search for truth is confused with political advocacy, the pursuit of knowledge is reduced to the quest for power.

—ALSTON CHASE
In a Dark Wood

1 A statesman who keeps his ear permanently glued to the ground will have neither elegance of posture nor flexibility of movement.

—ABBA EBAN

2 Congress is continually appointing fact-finding committees, when what we really need are some fact-facing committees.

—ROGER ALLEN
in *Grand Rapids Press*

3 Asking an incumbent member of Congress to vote for term limits is a bit like asking a chicken to vote for Colonel Sanders.

—BOB INGLIS

4 A politician without a prepared text is like a Boris Becker without a tennis racket, a dog biscuit without a dog, or opera glasses without an opera.

—C. M. BOWRA

5 When buying and selling are controlled by legislation, the first things to be bought and sold are legislators.

—P. J. O'ROURKE

6 Now and then an innocent man is sent to the legislature.

—KIN HUBBARD

7 Election year is that period when politicians get free speech mixed up with cheap talk.

—J. B. KIDD

8 Politicians are like ships: noisiest when lost in a fog.

—BENNETT CERF

9 A politician is a person who can make waves and then make you think he's the only one who can save the ship.

—IVERN BALL
in *Modern Secretary*

10 Politicians say they're beefing up our economy. Most don't know beef from pork.

—HAROLD LOWMAN

11 Politicians are people who, when they see light at the end of the tunnel, go out and buy some more tunnel.

—JOHN QUINTON

12 It's extremely difficult to build a political platform that supports candidates without holding up taxpayers.

—HAROLD COFFIN

13 Washington is a place where politicians don't know which way is up and taxes don't know which way is down.

—ROBERT ORBEN
in *The Wall Street Journal*

1 Politics is the art of getting money from the rich and votes from the poor, with the pretext of protecting one from the other.

—*Muy Interesante*

2 Instead of giving a politician the keys to the city, it might be better to change the locks.

—DOUG LARSON

3 To create a housing shortage in a huge country, heavily wooded, with a small population—ah, that's proof of pure political genius.

—RICHARD J. NEEDHAM
The Globe and Mail (Toronto)

4 When they call the roll in the Senate, the Senators do not know whether to answer "Present" or "Not guilty."

—THEODORE ROOSEVELT

IF A GOVERNMENT COMMISSION HAD WORKED ON THE HORSE . . .

5 If a government commission had worked on the horse, you would have had the first horse that could operate its knee joint in both directions. The only trouble is it couldn't have stood up.

—PETER DRUCKER

6 Bureaucracy is the art of making the possible impossible.

—JAVIER PASCUAL SALCEDO

7 I don't make jokes. I just watch the government and report the facts.

—WILL ROGERS

8 Governing a large country is like frying a small fish. You spoil it with too much poking.

—LAO-TZU

9 A little government and a little luck are necessary in life, but only a fool trusts either of them.

—P. J. O'ROURKE
Parliament of Whores

10 Everyone wants to live at the expense of the state. They forget that the state wants to live at the expense of everyone.

—FRÉDÉRIC BASTIAT

11 Government can't give us anything without depriving us of something else.

—HENRY HAZLITT
in *The Freeman*

12 Everybody wants to eat at the government's table, but nobody wants to do the dishes.

—WERNER FINCK

1 When government accepts responsibility for people, then people no longer take responsibility for themselves.

—GEORGE PATAKI

2 The mistakes made by Congress wouldn't be so bad if the next Congress didn't keep trying to correct them.

—CULLEN HIGHTOWER

3 Useless laws weaken the necessary laws.

—MONTESQUIEU

4 Bad laws are the worst sort of tyranny.

—EDMUND BURKE

5 You are better off not knowing how sausages and laws are made.

—Washington, D.C., adage

6 A country is considered the more civilized the more the wisdom and efficiency of its laws hinder a weak man from becoming too weak or a powerful one too powerful.

—PRIMO LEVI
Survival In Auschwitz

7 Government never furthered any enterprise but by the alacrity with which it got out of its way.

—HENRY DAVID THOREAU

8 A government is the only vessel known to leak from the top.

—JAMES RESTON
in *The New York Times*

9 Knowing exactly how much of the future can be introduced into the present is the secret of a great government.

—VICTOR HUGO

10 It's every American's duty to support his government, but not necessarily in the style to which it has become accustomed.

—Quoted by Thomas Clifford

11 The best defense against usurpatory government is an assertive citizenry.

—WILLIAM F. BUCKLEY JR.
Windfall: The End of the Affair

12 We should know everything we can about government — and the first thing we should know is what we're paying for it.

—ROBERT FULFORD
Financial Times

13 Government investigations have always contributed more to our amusement than they have to our knowledge.

—WILL ROGERS

1 It's one thing to call a spade a spade, but I wish my local social security office hadn't called the maternity benefit a lump sum.

—JOHN WATTS

2 There's nothing wrong with waiting for your ship to come in, but you can be sure that if it ever does, the Receiver of Revenue will be right there to help you unload it.

—DAVID BIGGS
Cape Town Argus (South Africa)

3 What is the difference between a taxidermist and a tax collector? The taxidermist takes only your skin.

—MARK TWAIN

4 Tax reform is taking the taxes off things that have been taxed in the past and putting taxes on things that haven't been taxed before.

—ART BUCHWALD

5 The government deficit is the difference between the amount of money the government spends and the amount it has the nerve to collect.

—SAM EWING

FINANCE IS THE ART . . .

6 Finance is the art of passing currency from hand to hand until it finally disappears.

—ROBERT W. SARNOFF

7 Money still talks, but it has to catch its breath more often.

—*Parts Pups*

8 Money talks—but credit has an echo.

—BOB THAVES

9 A big disappointment in life is the discovery that the man who writes the finance company ads isn't the one who makes the loans.

—*The London Free Press* (Ontario)

10 Time was when the average person could pay as he goes. Nowadays he has to pay as he comes and goes.

—O. A. BATTISTA

11 An economist is an expert who will know tomorrow why the things he predicted yesterday didn't happen.

—EARL WILSON

12 Economics is extremely useful as a form of employment for economists.

—JOHN KENNETH GALBRAITH

1 The economy depends about as much on economists as the weather does on weather forecasters.

—JEAN-PAUL KAUFFMANN

2 An economist's guess is liable to be just as good as anybody else's.

—WILL ROGERS

3 Isn't it strange? The same people who laugh at Gypsy fortunetellers take economists seriously.

—*The Cincinnati Enquirer*

4 The only function of economic forecasting is to make astrology look respectable.

—EZRA SOLOMON

5 We have become, to some extent, economic hypochondriacs. You get a wiggle in a statistic, and everyone runs to get the thermometer.

—PAUL W. MCCRACKEN

6 Torture numbers, and they'll confess to anything.

—GREGG EASTERBROOK
in *The New Republic*

7 Although he may not always recognize his bondage, modern man lives under a tyranny of numbers.

—NICHOLAS EBERSTADT
*The Tyranny of Numbers:
Mismeasurement and Misrule*

8 It is not the employer who pays— he only handles the money. It is the product that pays wages.

—HENRY FORD

9 It would be nice if the poor were to get even half of the money that is spent in studying them.

—BILL VAUGHAN

10 To view poverty simply as an economic condition, to be measured by statistics, is simplistic, misleading and false; poverty is a state of mind, a matter of horizons.

—PATRICK J. BUCHANAN
Right from the Beginning

11 When economics gets important enough, it becomes political.

—PETER G. PETERSON

12 Statistics are human beings with the tears wiped off.

—PAUL BRODEUR
Outrageous Misconduct

13 When goods do not cross borders, soldiers will.

—FRÉDÉRIC BASTIAT

14 There are so many men who can figure costs, and so few who can measure values.

—*Tribune* (San Marino, California)

15 Only a fool thinks price and value are the same.

—ANTONIO MACHADO

1 The best cure for the national economy would be economy.
—ASHLEY COOPER
in *News and Courier* (Charleston, South Carolina)

2 People want economy, and they will pay any price to get it.
—LEE IACOCCA

3 The shortest recorded period of time lies between the minute you put some money away for a rainy day and the unexpected arrival of rain.
—JANE BRYANT QUINN

4 One thing I could never abide was the leaving of money to lie idle, or even to have credit and not use it.
—LORD THOMSON OF FLEET
After I Was Sixty

5 Measure wealth not by the things you have, but by the things you have for which you would not take money.
—ANONYMOUS

6 Money changes people just as often as it changes hands.
—AL BATT

7 The most efficient labor-saving device is still money.
—FRANKLIN P. JONES

8 Money does make all the difference. If you have two jobs and you're rich, you have diversified interests. If you have two jobs and you're poor, you're moonlighting.
—*Changing Times*

9 Money is better than poverty, if only for financial reasons.
—WOODY ALLEN

10 A rand goes a long way these days. You can carry it around for days without finding a thing it will buy.
—*Daily Dispatch*
(East London, South Africa)

11 I don't like money, actually, but it quiets my nerves.
—JOE LOUIS

12 Money is a good servant but a bad master.
—FRENCH PROVERB

13 The beauty of having a low income is that there is not enough money to buy what you don't really need.
—RAY INMAN

14 There is nothing so habit-forming as money.
—DON MARQUIS

15 When a man says money can do anything, that settles it; he hasn't any.
—ED HOWE

1 Bankruptcy stared me in the face, but one thought kept me calm; soon I'd be too poor to need an anti-theft alarm.

—GINA ROTHFELS

To LIVE IN SOCIETY . . .

2 To live in society doesn't mean simply living side by side with others in a more or less close cohesion; it means living through one another and for one another.

—PAUL-EUGENE ROY

3 Civilization is a process whose purpose is to combine single human individuals, and after that families, and then races, peoples and nations, into one great unity, the unity of mankind.

—*The Complete Psychological Works of* SIGMUND FREUD

4 We ought to think that we are one of the leaves of a tree, and the tree is all humanity. We cannot live without the others, without the tree.

—PABLO CASALS

5 A community is like a ship; everyone ought to be prepared to take the helm.

—HENRIK IBSEN

No one is rich enough to do without a neighbor. 6

—HAROLD HELFER

A school system without parents 7 at its foundation is just like a bucket with a hole in it.

—REV. JESSE L. JACKSON

If we cannot now end our differences, at least we can help make the world safe for diversity. 8

—JOHN F. KENNEDY

Aristide Briand, French statesman 9 and winner of the Nobel Peace Prize: "In order to have peace we must want it, and not always doubt it."

—MATTHIAS JAGGI
Schweizer Jugend

There's just no place you can go 10 any longer and escape the global problems, so one's thinking must become global.

—THEODORE ROSZAK

In every community, there is work 11 to be done. In every nation, there are wounds to heal. In every heart, there is the power to do it.

—MARIANNE WILLIAMSON
A Return to Love

1 A nation is a body of people who have done great things together in the past and who hope to do great things together in the future.

—F. H. UNDERHILL
Colombo's Little Book of Canadian Proverbs, Graffiti, Limericks and Other Vital Matters

2 I look to a time when brotherhood needs no publicity, to a time when a brotherhood award would be as ridiculous as an award for getting up each morning.

—DANIEL D. MICH

3 We should see the new world order as a building constructed brick by brick and be motivated by the fact that we have only got as far as building the ground floor.

—DOUGLAS HURD
Daily Telegraph (London)

4 I can think of no more stirring symbol of man's humanity to man than a fire engine.

—KURT VONNEGUT

WHOEVER DOESN'T KNOW THE PAST . . .

5 Whoever doesn't know the past must have little understanding of the present and no vision of the future.

—JOSEPH S. RAYMOND

History is the unfolding of miscalculation. 6

—BARBARA TUCHMAN

History doesn't pass the dishes again. 7

—LOUIS-FERDINAND CÉLINE

History is a vast early-warning system. 8

—NORMAN COUSINS

History is a better guide than good intentions. 9

—JEANE J. KIRKPATRICK

Once the game is over, the king and the pawn go back into the same box. 10

—ITALIAN PROVERB

A nation forgetful and disrespectful of its past has no future, and deserves none. 11

—*Daily Telegraph* (London)

Righteousness is easy in retrospect. 12

—ARTHUR SCHLESINGER JR.
in *Newsweek*

The history of every country begins in the heart of a man or a woman. 13

—WILLA CATHER

1 To understand a man, you must know his memories. The same is true of a nation.

—ANTHONY QUAYLE

2 It was the same with those old birds in Greece and Rome as it is now. The only thing new in the world is the history you don't know.

—HARRY S. TRUMAN

3 I look upon the whole world as my fatherland, and every war has to me the horror of a family feud.

—HELEN KELLER
in *New York Call*

4 Genuine tragedies in the world are not conflicts between right and wrong. They are conflicts between two rights.

—GEORG HEGEL

5 Nationalism is an infantile disease. It is the measles of mankind.

—ALBERT EINSTEIN

6 In individuals, insanity is rare; but in groups, parties, nations and epochs, it is the rule.

—FRIEDRICH NIETZSCHE

7 The great tragedies of history occur not when right confronts wrong but when two rights confront each other.

—HENRY A. KISSINGER

We have war when at least one of the parties to a conflict wants something more than it wants peace. 8

—JEANE J. KIRKPATRICK

In war, there are no unwounded soldiers. 9

—JOSÉ NAROSKY

The soldiers fight, and the kings are heroes. 10

—BARBARA MECHELS

When elephants fight, it's the grass that suffers. 11

—AFRICAN PROVERB

Might does not make right; it only makes history. 12

—JIM FIEBIG

In war there is no second prize for the runner-up. 13

—GEN. OMAR N. BRADLEY

As long as war is regarded as wicked, it will always have its fascination. When it is looked upon as vulgar, it will cease to be popular. 14

—OSCAR WILDE

You can build a throne with bayonets, but you can't sit on it for long. 15

—BORIS YELTSIN

1 A peace which depends upon fear is nothing but a suppressed war.
—HENRY VAN DYKE

2 Foreign relations are like human relations. They are endless. The solution of one problem usually leads to another.
—JAMES RESTON

3 Treaties are like roses and young girls. They last while they last.
—CHARLES DE GAULLE

4 Revolutions are built on empty bellies.
—WYNDHAM HARTLEY
Natal Witness (South Africa)

5 Who overcomes by force hath overcome but half his foe.
—JOHN MILTON

6 I like a little rebellion now and then. It is like a storm in the atmosphere.
—THOMAS JEFFERSON

7 No one is more surprised than a revolutionary rebelled against.
—PIERRE GAXOTTE

8 Every successful revolution puts on in time the robes of the tyrant it has deposed.
—BARBARA TUCHMAN

9 If we want things to stay as they are, things will have to change.
—GIUSEPPE TOMASI DI LAMPEDUSA
The Leopard

10 It is not necessary to imagine the world ending in fire or ice. There are two other possibilities: one is paper work, and the other is nostalgia.
—FRANK ZAPPA

11 Perhaps the rediscovery of our humanity, and the potential of the human spirit which we have read about in legends of older civilizations, or in accounts of solitary mystics, or in tales of science fiction writers— perhaps this will constitute the true revolution of the future. The new frontier lies not beyond the planets but within each one of us.
—PIERRE ELLIOT TRUDEAU
Biodynamics

List of Themes

Blue numbers indicate specific quotation on that page.

D

E

Q, R

S

Q, R

S

LIST OF THEMES

Y, Z

HUMOR in UNIFORM®

★ ★ ★ ★ ★ ★ ★

Funny True Stories
about Life in the Military

★ ★ ★ ★ ★ ★ ★ ★ ★ ★ ★ ★ ★ ★ ★ ★ ★

CONTENTs

★ ★ ★ ★ ★ ★ ★ ★ ★ ★ ★ ★ ★ ★ ★ ★ ★ ★

Introduction ★

Life in the military is no picnic. The U.S. services—Army, Navy, Marines, Air Force, Coast Guard, and National Guard—all require strict discipline in a rigid hierarchy. The training is diabolically tough, and that's just the beginning. The pay isn't much, and living conditions can be primitive.

Assignments can be harsh. Baghdad, for example, routinely hits 120°F on summer days. Parts of Afghanistan are snowed in for most of the winter. Missions are often not only dangerous but potentially lethal. On the other hand, when duties are not life-threatening, they can be mind-numbingly tedious.

So, how do our military men and women survive? We think a well-developed sense of humor is a key to their equanimity. It lets these put-upon heroes relieve their tensions with laughter.

All of the anecdotes in this book were sent to Reader's Digest by men and women of the U.S. military and their families. There are more than 500 separate stories of contemporary life in uniform—with its contradictions, its foibles, and its ridiculous mixups and misunderstandings. We applaud these all-too-human people who are able to laugh at themselves while still bravely defending our country.

— THE EDITORS

BASiC
TRAINING ★

★ **A Word to the Wise**

★ **Meeting Expectations**

★ ★ ★ ★ ★ ★ ★ ★ ★ ★ ★ ★ ★ ★ ★ ★ ★

"Today, gentlemen, I have some good news and some bad news," said our platoon sergeant during our morning lineup. "First, the good news. Private Tomkins will be setting the pace on our run." The platoon began to hoot and holler, since the overweight Tomkins was the slowest guy in the group. "Now the bad news. Private Tomkins will be driving a truck."

— RICK STOVER

With his squad at attention, my father's drill sergeant began inspecting their rifles. Grabbing one soldier's M-1, he peered down the barrel only to be stared back at by a spider. "Two demerits," yelled the sergeant. "Why two?" asked the private. "One for keeping an unclean weapon," said the sergeant. "And one for keeping an unauthorized pet."

— KATHLEEN SHEEHY

"All you idiots, fall out!" shouted the sergeant at the soldiers standing in formation. As the rest of the squad dispersed, one soldier remained at attention. The sergeant stalked over and raised a single eyebrow. The private grinned.

"Sure was a lot of them, huh, sir?"

— MATTHEW HAWORTH

If he wasn't already aware of the dangers inherent in military life, things became pretty clear for my son with one look at his Marine boot camp itinerary. On one of the first days, Bayonet Techniques was scheduled for the morning. Following that: Beginning First Aid.

— TOMMY SISSON

★ ★ ★ ★ ★ ★ ★ ★ ★ ★ ★ ★ ★ ★ ★ ★ ★

Basic training for new Army recruits includes small arms instruction. One enlistee goes out to practice on the rifle range, where he fires 99 shots, missing the target every time. "You are the worst rifleman I've ever seen!" says his drill instructor. "What were you in civilian life?" "I repaired telephones," replies the recruit, "and I don't know why I can't hit the target. Let me see...."He gives his rifle the once-over, checks it again, and finally a third time. Then he places his hand in front of the muzzle, pulls the trigger—and blows off the tip of his finger. "Well, that answers that," says the phone guy, in obvious pain. "The bullets are leaving here fine. The trouble must be on the other end."

— SOURCE UNKNOWN

In Marine Corps basic training, I soon learned that everything we recruits used actually belonged to our drill instructor. For instance, she referred to the stuff in our footlockers as "my trash," and to the racks we slept in as "my racks." One time when we were all whispering in the bathroom while making "head calls," our drill instructor must have overheard us. To our surprise, she suddenly yelled, "Why do I hear voices in my head?!"

— KATHY VANDENBRINK

When my father was in boot camp, the troops were instructed to put their belongings in their footlockers, write their last names and first initials on the containers, and report back for inspection. A few minutes later, the commanding officer, after having seen my father's locker emblazoned with his last name "Locke" and his first initial "R," furiously bellowed, "Okay, who's the wise guy?"

— TOD LOCKE

★ ★ ★ ★ ★ ★ ★ ★ ★ ★ ★ ★ ★ ★ ★ ★ ★ ★

"Well," snarled the drill sergeant to the miserable recruit doing push-ups in the rain, "I suppose after you're discharged you'll just be waiting for me to die so you can spit on my grave." "Not me," replied the recruit. "Once I get out of the Marines, I'm never standing in line again."

— PETE E. MURPHY

Joining the Air Force was a dream come true. And when I sat in the copilot's seat during an introduction to the cockpit, I was eager to impress my instructor. I quickly made my way through the maze of dials and levers on the instrument panel, naming each one and describing what they did in great detail. Until, that is, I came to one with a bunch of numbers. "What's this?" I asked. "The clock," he answered.

— FAISAL MASOODI

A Word to the Wise

One of my fellow recruits at Marine boot camp looked extremely young. During inspection our drill instructor asked him, "Does your mother know you're in the Marine Corps?" "Yes, sir," replied the recruit. "Does she know you're staying overnight?"

— JAMIE WALKER

During basic training one lesson stood out from all the others: Keep your mouth shut unless given permission to talk. But I didn't realize how well our instructors had hammered this point home until one evening when we sat down to eat. My table mate started her evening prayer with, "God, request permission to pray."

— GAIL HAYES

Our first stop as new recruits was the barber's. "Want to keep your sideburns?" he asked. "Yes, that would be great," I said. "Okay, I'll get you a bag to put them in."

— JAMES MCGRUDER

Shortly after reporting to the 101st Airborne Division, we were ordered to fall out in our dress uniforms. Only problem was, I didn't know how to tie a necktie. So I asked the guy in the next bunk for help. "Sure," he said. "Lie down." Confused, I lay down on the bunk and he tied my tie. "Sorry, but this is the only way I know how," he said. "Comes from practicing on my father's clients." "What does your father do?"

"He's a mortician."

— HOWARD MARSHALL

★ ★ ★ ★ ★ ★ ★ ★ ★ ★ ★ ★ ★ ★ ★ ★ ★

One day in artillery instruction, a colonel came to inspect our class. First up was Private O'Malley. The colonel got in his face and asked him what reading he had on his 105 mm howitzer. "Two-nine-oh-seven, sir," was the reply.

"Soldier," said the colonel, "don't you know you never say "oh" in the artillery? You say "zero." What's your name, soldier?" "Zero Malley, sir," answered the private.

— JOHN MADSON

Short and baby-faced, my buddy Wiggins had trouble being taken seriously in the Army. A mustache, he assumed, would fix that. He was wrong. "Wiggins!" bellowed our drill instructor after spotting the growth during inspection.

"What's so special about your nose that it's got to be underlined?"

— K. TROTT

Basic training has a way of making a soldier feel that he or she is being worked like a dog. Now I have proof. While on KP duty at Fort Leonard Wood in Missouri, I was hauling containers of vegetables. On the side of one box was this: "FOR ANIMAL OR MILITARY USE ONLY."

— LORI MONTGOMERY

During a field exercise at Camp Lejeune, N.C., my squad was on a night patrol through some thick brush. Halfway through the exercise, we realized we had lost our map. The patrol navigator informed us, "Our odds are 1 in 359 that we'll get out of here." "How do you come up with that?" someone asked. "Well," he replied, "one of the degrees on the compass has to be right."

— K. S. MCGUIRE

★ ★ ★ ★ ★ ★ ★ ★ ★ ★ ★ ★ ★ ★ ★ ★ ★

While being transported to basic training as a new enlistee of the Air National Guard, I accidentally opened a parachute in the rear of the C-47. The plane was piloted by a major and a captain, and I felt intimidated as I opened the cockpit door to confess what I had done. Expecting to be severely chastised, I was surprised by the captain's calm response. "Well, son," he said, "if this plane goes down, that chute is yours."

— JAMES KUHNZ

My grandson, Will, called home from West Point one evening and complained about how difficult the training was. When his father told him to try to find something positive, Will mentioned how he liked to spit-shine his boots. "Really?" his father said. "Why?" "Because," Will replied, "that means my feet aren't in them."

— PAULINE CANDA

During basic training, my platoon was given a choice of going either to the gym or the PX. By a show of hands, we opted for the PX. "Uh-uh," said our sergeant. "You're all going to the gym." "But, Sarge," whined one recruit, "we took a vote." "Boys, let me explain," he said. "We're here to defend democracy, not practice it."

— WARREN PANSIRE

After enlisting in the Navy, a friend of mine found himself in basic training learning about firearms. He was aided by a sticker on his rifle with an arrow pointed toward the barrel. It read: "Point This End At Enemy."

— BRIANNA SCANLON

★ ★ ★ ★ ★ ★ ★ ★ ★ ★ ★ ★ ★ ★ ★ ★ ★

"Miserable" doesn't begin to describe how my troops and I felt during two weeks of maneuvers. Aside from grueling training, we camped outside under austere conditions, in often severe weather. So on our last Sunday morning, I was heartened to see many of the enlisted men standing single file waiting to enter a small local church. "A little of that old-time religion?" I remarked to the first sergeant. "No, sir," he said. "Flush toilets."

— MICHAEL CAMPO

Meeting Expectations

After enlisting in the 82nd Airborne Division, I eagerly asked my recruiter what I could expect from jump school. "Well," he replied, "it's three weeks long." "What else?" I inquired. "The first week they separate the men from the boys," he said. "The second week they separate the men from the fools." "And the third week?" I asked. "The third week the fools jump."

— TOD REJHOLEC

You've never seen two greener recruits than Fred and me the day we arrived for basic training. We were immediately assigned guard duty, and soon after, Fred was approached by an officer. "Halt! Who goes there?" Fred shouted. The officer identified himself and waited for a response. And waited … "What's wrong, soldier, don't you remember what comes next?" "No," Fred yelled back. "And you're not taking another step until I do."

— L. EDMOND WOLFE

★ ★ ★ ★ ★ ★ ★ ★ ★ ★ ★ ★ ★ ★ ★ ★

While in marine corps boot camp, we were taught to keep our heads if taken prisoner by the enemy. After all, methods used to extract information, we learned, might not be the ones we were expecting. "Imagine that the door to your cell opens and in walks a beautiful young woman in a revealing outfit," said our instructor. "The best thing to do is not to touch her." From the back of the room came the question, "Sir, what's the second best thing?"

— DAVID GRAVES

Being a career soldier was not in the cards for one particular recruit. Every time he took his turn at the rifle range, he'd lift his rifle, aim at the target, fire—and hit some tree way off in the distance. One day, despondent after claiming a number of trees but no targets, he said to the sergeant, "I think I'll just go and shoot myself." "Better take a couple of extra rounds," the sergeant shot back.

— MANUEL G. RODRIGUEZ

My brother and I arrived at boot camp together. On the first morning, our unit was dragged out of bed by our drill sergeant and made to assemble outside. "My name's Sergeant Jackson," he snarled. "Is there anyone here who thinks he can whip me?" My six-foot-three, 280-pound brother raised his hand and said, "Yes, sir, I do." Our sergeant grabbed him by the arm and led him out in front of the group. "Men," he said, "this is my new assistant. Now, is there anyone here who thinks he can whip both of us?"

— ROBERT NORRIS

No, Ferguson, the military does not have
Casual Fridays!

★ ★ ★ ★ ★ ★ ★ ★ ★ ★ ★ ★ ★ ★ ★ ★ ★

During flight school, our instructor noticed that a young pilot wasn't wearing her earplugs correctly. "If you don't fix your earplugs, you'll turn into a deaf old man like me," he warned over the roar of helicopter engines. She shot back, "If I turn into a deaf old man, I've got bigger problems than hearing loss."

— DEBORAH GATRELL

For some recruits, there is nothing basic about basic training. It was clear that one soldier in particular was not getting the hang of it when on guard duty one night, he cried out, "Halt! Don't shoot or I'll move!"

— TOM BIRDWELL

A recruit in Navy boot camp got on the wrong side of our company commander and was ordered to do push-ups. As he neared triple digits, an airliner flew overhead. "I bet you wish you were on that plane, don'tcha?" sneered the CC. "No, sir," said the unlucky recruit. "Why wouldn't you want to be on that plane?" "Because," the recruit grunted between push-ups, "that plane's landing. I want to be on one that's leaving."

— GENE DAMRON

After about three weeks in basic training, my husband's unit was not measuring up to expectations, and the sergeant threatened to send them all back three weeks to start over. Apparently, at least one new soldier was already reconsidering his career choice. As the sergeant's threat hung in the air, an anonymous voice called out, "How about sending us back four weeks?"

— DEBORAH FRANK

★ ★ ★ ★ ★ ★ ★ ★ ★ ★ ★ ★ ★ ★ ★ ★ ★

Shortly after joining the Army, I was in line with some other inductees when the sergeant stepped forward with that day's assignments. After handing over various tasks, he asked, "Does anyone here have experience with radio communications?" A longtime ham operator, I shouted, "I do!" "Good," he said. "You can dig the hole for the new telephone pole."

— DON KETCHUM

One month into Marine Corps training in San Diego, Calif., we were preparing for a ten-mile march in 100-degree weather when a jeep drove up with a large radio in the back. "Who knows anything about radios?" our drill instructor asked. Several hands went up, and anticipating a ride in the jeep, recruits began listing their credentials. Everything from a degree in communications to a part-time job in a repair shop was declared. The DI listened to all the contenders, then pointed to the most qualified. "You," he barked. "Carry the radio."

— JIM SAPAUGH

After a grueling day of training, which had included a ten-mile hike and completion of a difficult obstacle course, my son Eric's platoon of raw recruits quickly fell into bed. As Eric lay in the dark, he heard a voice recite a prayer: "Now I lay me down to sleep, I pray the Lord my soul to keep, if I should die before I wake, thank you, Lord." There was a brief pause and then several voices said in unison, "Amen."

— ROBERT MOORE

AT the FRONT

★ **Morale Building**

★ **Pride of the Corps**

★ ★ ★ ★ ★ ★ ★ ★ ★ ★ ★ ★ ★ ★ ★ ★ ★

As if being sent off to war-torn Somalia in the '90s weren't nerve-racking enough, there were also the bugs. "Sergeant," I called out during our orientation briefing, "is there a problem with scorpions here?" "No need to worry about scorpions, Captain," he assured me. "There are enough snakes around to eat most of them."

— CAPT. M. A. NIXON

In the final days before our massive ground attack on Iraq in Operation Desert Storm, my tank company was moved to a position 15 to 20 kilometers from the Iraqi border. It was a very flat, open area that left us vulnerable to Scud missile attacks. Therefore, every evening we repositioned one kilometer to make targeting more difficult. It meant tearing down tents, camouflage nets, communications gear, barbed wire and more, only to reassemble it ten minutes later in a new location. Since we had other units to our south, east, and west, the only direction we could move was north, closer to the border. As a young company commander, I knew that my soldiers hated this routine. One day I asked a small group of soldiers if they understood why we relocated every night. "Yes, sir," came the confident reply of one soldier. "We're sneaking up on them!"

— DAVID C. STADER

As we drove our refueling truck through a heavily bombed-out area of Iraq, I spotted an unexploded shell in the middle of the road. "Look out!" I yelled to my friend who was driving. But he wasn't the least bit concerned. "Don't worry," he said. "It's one of ours."

— SHAD ALEXANDER

★ ★ ★ ★ ★ ★ ★ ★ ★ ★ ★ ★ ★ ★ ★ ★ ★ ★

During the Persian Gulf War, my Marine Corps unit had to dig new foxholes every time we changed positions. Once, when a private was making his trench, he complained to our sergeant, "Why do we have to do this stupid digging?" Then there was a loud explosion a hundred feet away. "What was that?" asked the private. "That," replied the sergeant, "is called incentive."

— MICHAEL MERRELL

Our daily routine aboard the USS Trenton off the Somali coast, transporting Marines and their cargo to and from shore, was disrupted by a visit from an admiral. I was in charge of the ensign, a huge, 30-by-50-foot American flag. After the admiral gave his speech and left, the ensign was to be lowered. I had folded our national flag many times, but never one of this immense size. Fortunately, a group of Marines nearby was quick to help. One of them, Ramirez, immediately took charge, showing great pride with every meticulous fold. "Where did you master the art of folding a flag this size?" I asked. "Are you on a special flag detail?" "Actually," said Ramirez, "I learned this while working at McDonald's."

— SAM RICKABAUGH

Western Iraq is a dangerous place, so the arrival of my flak jacket was a welcome sight. What was less welcome was the sight of these words someone had written on the ceramic plates that made up the inside of the jacket:

"Fragile! Handle with Care."

— NIC EVANSO

★ ★ ★ ★ ★ ★ ★ ★ ★ ★ ★ ★ ★ ★ ★ ★ ★

A few years ago I worked as a radio operator with the Second Infantry Division in Korea. Traffic over the radio came fast and furious, and it became apparent early on that handling it all was a special skill. During one particularly hectic day I took a break and walked past another unit, where an operator calmly manned three radios while flawlessly taking down messages. Later I ran into the soldier and remarked how impressed I was with his cool efficiency. "What's your secret?" I asked. "I had training as a civilian," he responded. "I worked the McDonald's drive-through."

— GREGORY LIPE

Morale Building

Serving in Afghanistan is, as might be expected, very stressful. So another soldier and I built a horseshoe pit to help ease the tension. When our sergeant came by to play, everything was in place except for one thing. "Aren't you going to put in the stakes?" he asked. "Nope," I answered. "Fine, I'll do it myself." "Okay," I said. "But remember, this is one of the most heavily land-mined countries in the world." "You're right!" he said, gingerly stepping out of the pit. "I'll get the new lieutenant."

— JASON GARDNER

Our division had to repaint our Humvees to a sand color for Desert Storm. The result was a pinkish hue, and the jokes began. One wag renamed us the Pink Panzer Division. But the best was the Humvee bumper sticker "Ask me about Mary Kay."

— DAVID K. DRURY

★ ★ ★ ★ ★ ★ ★ ★ ★ ★ ★ ★ ★ ★ ★ ★

Okay, we'll meet back here at 1600 hours. Synchronize your

BlackBerries.

★ ★ ★ ★ ★ ★ ★ ★ ★ ★ ★ ★ ★ ★ ★ ★ ★

My cousin was attached to a Marine air squadron that was deployed with an Air Force fighter unit flying missions over Bosnia. When the Marines arrived at the air base in Italy, they were ordered to move into a camp in a field near the runway. The Air Force unit soon followed, but their pilots checked into a hotel. Shortly afterward an Air Force colonel drove to the Marine camp. "Hey, Marines," he called out, "start breaking camp." "Are we moving into the hotel with you?" the Marines asked. "No," the Air Force colonel joked. "We need you to move your tents off of what's going to be our golf course."

— W. C. GRAHAM

At the end of a tough day in Iraq, my daughter the airman collapsed onto the first seat in the transport truck, forcing everyone else to climb over her. "Private!" hollered the sergeant. "Skinny girls get in the back so when we men get on with our weapons and equipment, we don't have to climb over you. Have I made myself clear?" Suddenly my daughter perked up, responding, "Do you really think I'm skinny?"

— MARGARET CULBERTSON

The boyfriend of a co-worker is serving in Iraq. Naturally, she can't wait for him to come home. "How's it going over there?" I asked her. "He e-mailed me last night," she said. "It's quiet where he is." Knowing that doesn't make it any less scary, I asked, "What outfit is he serving in?" "Desert camouflage."

— GEORGE COVELES

★ ★ ★ ★ ★ ★ ★ ★ ★ ★ ★ ★ ★ ★ ★ ★ ★ ★

To mail a big package of cookies to my two Air Force sons, both of whom were serving in Saudi Arabia, I was required to attach a label describing the contents. I carefully marked the box "Cookies" and sent it off, but after a month my sons said they had yet to receive my package. Suspicious, I baked another batch, only this time I labeled the contents "Health Food." Within a week my sons reported they had received the goodies.

— WANDA HAMEISTER

While serving in Korea, I took a course in rappelling. As the only noninfantryman in the group, I felt pressure to perform as well as the "ground pounders." In our first class we were told to hook up to a rope and jump off a 50-foot tower. As each student nervously went over the edge, we were encouraged to shout morale-building slogans. Ahead of me I heard cries of "Geronimo," "Airborne" and "Air Assault." Being a postal clerk, I got a round of laughs when I jumped from the tower and shouted, "Airmail!"

— PHILIP PETERS

Before shipping out to Europe with the Army Air Corps during World War II, my father loancd his buddy $20. The two were assigned to different units and lost contact. Months later, my father's plane was shot down. Bleeding from shrapnel wounds, he bailed out and was greeted by German soldiers, who took him as a prisoner. After a long train ride, little food and days of forced marching, he arrived at his assigned stalag. As he entered the compound, he heard a familiar voice. "You cheapskate! You followed me all the way here for a measly $20?"

— BRUCE EY

★ ★ ★ ★ ★ ★ ★ ★ ★ ★ ★ ★ ★ ★ ★ ★ ★

Since I'm at a base in Korea, my family has to stay behind in the States. Every package I get from them comes with a customs form listing the contents and their value. Once, I got a box from home. The contents listed on the form read: "Homemade chocolate chip cookies." In the space marked "Value," my wife wrote: "Priceless."

— JON SUTTERFIELD

Using sand from quarries in Kuwait, Navy Seabees stationed in Al Jaber Air Base were building concrete aircraft parking ramps before the start of Operation Iraqi Freedom. When the quarries were closed temporarily, our stockpiles were exhausted in three days. The fourth day the following report was issued: "Kuwait has run out of sand."

— JOHN LAMB

Pride of the Corps

I was participating in a U.N. peacekeeping mission outside Skopje, Macedonia. We were required to stay on post at all times, so I hadn't been off base for six weeks when a general came to boost morale. Speculation ran high over who would be invited to the general's dinner at a top restaurant in Skopje. The afternoon of the big event, my commander called me over and said, "Captain Adams, you know the dinner we're having for the general?" "Yes, sir!" I replied, expectantly. "Well, the general forgot to bring civilian clothes," he said. "You're about his size. Can he borrow a pair of pants?"

— THOMAS R. ADAMS, JR.

★ ★ ★ ★ ★ ★ ★ ★ ★ ★ ★ ★ ★ ★ ★ ★ ★ ★

As he prepared to leave for the Gulf, my husband was complaining to a friend about his uniform. Military men are taught to care about their appearance, and the Air National Guard would be wearing desert camouflage but not the matching sand-colored utility belt. "I get it," said his friend. "You always want to look your best, even when you don't want to be seen."

— LISA RAINO

When the Second Division set up shop in South Korea, it did so with its slogan proudly displayed at the front gate: "Second to None." A few months later, a South Korean base opened two miles down the road. The sign greeting visitors read "You are now entering the famed sector of the South Korean ROK Division, better known as 'The None Division.' "

— LUCION CLEMONS

We were asleep in our cots at Bagram Air Base in Afghanistan when exploding enemy rockets woke us up. My platoon and I threw on our fatigues, grabbed our weapons and ran to the bunker for protection. Inside the bunker, one nervous soldier lit up. "Put that cigarette out!" I ordered. "Yeah, forget the rockets," said another soldier as more rounds rocked the bunker. "That secondhand smoke'll kill ya."

— SSG JAMES KELLERT

★ ★ ★ ★ ★ ★ ★ ★ ★ ★ ★ ★ ★ ★ ★ ★ ★ ★

At an air force symposium, a colonel gave a briefing on military activity in the Persian Gulf. "The first slide shows the area in which we were operating," the colonel began. Then he realized the slide was in backward. There was a pause as the projectionist flipped the map around. "As you can see," the colonel continued dryly, "our first and constant concern was the region's instability."

— ANDY SMITH

In Korea, a number of fellow Marines who were raised in the country told those of us from the city how delicious roasted pheasant was. They even persuaded our cook to make the dish, should we be lucky enough to find a few birds. Driving in the countryside soon afterward, I spotted one of them in a tree about 200 yards away. I immediately shot the bird, jumped over a fence and ran across the field to retrieve it. When I got back to my jeep, there were two military policemen waiting for me. I explained what I had done and why, but the sergeant still scowled. "You made two mistakes, son," he said. "First, that's a hawk, not a pheasant. Second, you just ran through a minefield."

— LAWRENCE L. VOYER

BEATING the SYSTeM

★ **A Matter of Wits If not Wisps**

★ ★ ★ ★ ★ ★ ★ ★ ★ ★ ★ ★ ★ ★ ★ ★ ★

Impressed by how well Airman Jones gets recruits to sign up for GI insurance, the captain listens in on his sales pitch. "If you have insurance and are killed in battle, the government pays $50,000 to your beneficiaries," explains Jones. "If you don't have insurance and get killed, the government pays nothing. Now," he concludes, "who do you think gets sent into battle first?"

— SGT. KENNETH J. ALMODOVAR

A few years ago, with the Fourth of July approaching, it was my job as safety officer of my Marine Corps unit to develop a slogan and to put up posters discouraging drinking over the holiday weekend. We had no accidents that year, and I attribute it partly to our slogan: "He who comes forth with a fifth on the Fourth may not come forth on the fifth."

— ROBERT ABNEY

I was stationed at Sheppard Air Force Base in Texas when I was told I would have to qualify to use a .38-caliber pistol. Having only held a gun on two other occasions, I was apprehensive. When I fired my first shot, the loud bang and the gun's kick startled me so much I almost dropped the pistol. Worst of all, in my panic I forgot to keep the gun pointed down range and drew a stern reprimand from my sergeant. When I retrieved my targets, however, I was amazed to see that I had qualified with flying colors. The sergeant looked at my scores with disbelief and commented that he had been certain I would fail. Smiling, I held up my index finger and thumb in a mock gun position and said, "Nintendo."

— PEGGY ALSTON

★ ★ ★ ★ ★ ★ ★ ★ ★ ★ ★ ★ ★ ★ ★ ★ ★

Some pet peeves with soldiers: Finding out the "C" in C rations stands for "cat." You're on amphibious maneuvers and you just can't stop giggling. Marching with fixed bayonets and the guy behind you doesn't hear "halt!" Mediocre in-flight magazine on troop transports. Whenever you screw up, somebody starts singing that "Be All That You Can Be" song real sarcastically.

— SOURCE UNKNOWN

A friend whose husband was stationed at Fort Bliss, in Texas, actually got a letter addressed to "Fort Ignorance." "How did you know where to deliver it?" she asked the mailman. "We were stumped at first," he admitted. "But then I remembered, "Ignorance is bliss."

— WILLIAM DE GRAF

The guard in Air Force basic training must check the ID of everyone who comes to the door. A trainee was standing guard when he heard a pounding on the door and the order "Let me in!" Through the window he saw the uniform of a lieutenant colonel and immediately opened up. He quickly realized his mistake. "Airman! Why didn't you check for my authority to enter?" Thinking fast, the airman replied, "Sir, you'd have gotten in anyway." "What do you mean?" "Uh ... the hinges on the door ... they're broken, sir." "What? Show me!" With a twinkle in his eye, the airman opened the door, let the officer step out and slammed the door shut. "Airman! Open up immediately!" "Sir, may I see your authority to enter?" The airman was rewarded for outsmarting his commanding officer.

— ROSS BALFOUR

In the early '90s, when I was stationed at Caserma Carlo Ederle in Italy, it was very common to see soldiers riding bicycles back and forth to work. So it came as no big surprise that, after a series of painfully comic accidents, a new policy was announced, saying in summary, "Soldiers shall no longer salute officers who are engaged in the riding of a bicycle."

— MICHAEL TEAS

My boss is a public-affairs manager who is called at all hours of the day to solve various problems for clients. But as a Naval Reservist, he was summoned to the Persian Gulf War for an extended time, leaving me to explain that he was serving his country halfway around the world and therefore could not be reached. Most callers understood, but one was indignant. "Can he be paged?" the man inquired. "I don't think you understand," I said in my most patient voice. "He's serving on a ship in a war zone." "I see," the man said. "Do you think he will be calling in for messages?"

— SUSAN HULL

Fifteen years of blissful civilian life ended when I re-upped with the Air National Guard recently. It took time getting back into the swing of things, and after a particularly rough day I missed chow, which meant dinner would be a dreaded MRE: Meal Ready to Eat. As I sat on my bunk staring at "dinner," I said to a far younger airman, "Well, I guess we just have to get used to roughing it." "Dude, tell me about it," he said. "We only get basic cable!"

— KINGSLEY SLONE

★ ★ ★ ★ ★ ★ ★ ★ ★ ★ ★ ★ ★ ★ ★ ★ ★ ★

My husband and I were stationed at Marine Corps Air Station, Cherry Point, N.C., where he worked with top-secret communications equipment. One afternoon I watched as he and three other Marines struggled to set up a huge screen that looked like a television. After they finished, I asked my husband if he was permitted to tell me what the screen was for. He said that it would be used for communications, but that the higher ranks couldn't know its intended use. Confused, I asked, "Is it that top secret?" "No," he replied, "we're gonna use it to watch football games."

— J. L. SABIN

★ ★ ★ ★ ★ ★ ★ ★ ★ ★ ★ ★ ★ ★ ★ ★ ★ ★

Soon after graduating from the Primary Leadership Development Course at Fort Campbell in Kentucky, I bragged to my first sergeant about how well I did in the land-navigation exercise. Looking at me skeptically, the first sergeant handed me a map of the base, a compass and a set of coordinates. Then he ordered me to find his designated point and call in. When I reached the coordinates, it turned out to be the PX. I found a pay phone and contacted the first sergeant. "Great job!" he declared. "Now that you're there, could you bring me some lunch?"

— ROBERT WIDO

A Matter of Wits If not Wisps

How do you stop a thief? This was the question that vexed my brother-in-law, a rugged Marine. Every morning he picked up coffee from Starbucks, and every morning that cup of coffee mysteriously disappeared from his desk. Although he never caught the bandit, he did resolve the matter. One morning, when all personnel were gathered for a staff meeting, he popped out the partial plate from his mouth and swished it around in his coffee before placing it back. His coffee was never stolen again.

— JEAN SHORT

A senior in the high school class I taught was always in trouble, both at home and at school, and he was getting fed up. "That's it! I'm tired of people telling me what to do," he announced one day. "As soon as I graduate, I'm joining the Marines."

— DENNIS BRESNAHAN

★ ★ ★ ★ ★ ★ ★ ★ ★ ★ ★ ★ ★ ★ ★ ★ ★

While delivering a motivational lecture to a group of young Navy men, I spoke in great detail about why I joined the military and how much it meant to me. Finishing my story, I pointed to a young, sharp-looking sailor and asked him why he decided to go to sea. "Well, Chief," he said, "When my old man put lights on the tractor, I knew it was time to leave the farm."

— BILL CROCKETT

My husband, a U.S. Coast Guard pilot, was on an exchange tour with the Royal Navy in England. Everyone who drove through the base's gates was required to hold an official ID card up to the windshield for inspection by the guards. As a friendly competition, my husband's squadron started flashing different forms of ID, such as a driver's license, just to see how far they could go to fool the busy guards. The winner? The fellow who breezed past waving a piece of toast.

— ELIZABETH M. LANGE

I served with a guy who did a strange thing: He bounced an imaginary basketball wherever he went. Eventually, a psychiatrist labeled him unfit for duty, which led to a medical discharge. After the proceedings, he addressed the officer in charge. "Sir, may I approach?" With permission granted, he went through the motion of putting something on the officer's desk. "What is this?" asked the officer. "My basketball. I don't need it anymore."

— SOURCE UNKNOWN

★ ★ ★ ★ ★ ★ ★ ★ ★ ★ ★ ★ ★ ★ ★ ★ ★ ★

When a ship enters a port, special permission must be given for sailors to begin their liberty early. My friend had a good reason for getting a head start. "I have to go to the bus station," he told a superior officer. "I have a one-armed uncle coming to town with two suitcases." Permission was granted.

— N. U. TURPEN

One of the fighter pilots at my base in England, tired of being kidded about his baldness, tried one worthless miracle cure after another. Finally he settled for growing his remaining hair long and combing it over the top of his head. The taunts continued, however, until the day they were overheard by a visiting general. Walking up to the pilot, the general soberly commended him for adopting the official Air Force solution to his problem. Then, turning to the tormentors, the general removed his hat to reveal three wispy strands of hair carefully combed over an otherwise bald pate. "This, gentlemen," he said with a smile, "is what we call tactical redeployment of available forces."

— FRANCESCA BARTHOLOMEW

I was talking on the phone with my son, who was stationed in Hawaii with the Air Force. He was explaining how the troops were learning to scuba dive. They used the buddy system, he said, and occasionally dived into shark-infested waters. Listening on the extension, my daughter asked, "What do you do when you see a shark?" Said my son, "Swim faster than my buddy."

— JOAN NOZKOWSKI

ALL in the FAMILY

★ **From the Peanut Gallery**

★ **Parental Pride**

★ **Family Matters**

★ **Service Adjustments**

★ **Love 'em As They Are**

★ ★ ★ ★ ★ ★ ★ ★ ★ ★ ★ ★ ★ ★ ★ ★ ★ ★

My husband was a Navy chaplain deployed to the Persian Gulf at the end of Desert Storm. I did everything possible to ensure that our three young children wouldn't be worried about their father being in danger. It wasn't always easy, but I knew I'd succeeded when someone at church asked our three-year-old where his dad was. My son replied, "He's in Persia, golfing."

— MARSHA HANSEN

When I tell people that I am an explosive ordinance disposal technician, I usually need to go into further detail about what I do. Once I was with my eight-year-old son when I was explaining my job to someone. "I defuse live bombs," I said. "Yeah," my son added. "If you see him running, you'd better catch up!"

— THOMAS LIGON

I knew I had been in the military too long when my five-year-old daughter sang her version of "Silent Night." It went like this: "Silent night, holy night, all is calm, all is bright, Round yon virgin mother and child, Holy infantry, tender and mild .... "

— MIKE ADAMS

Since I grew up in the civilian world, I knew my daughter's childhood as a military brat would be drastically different from my own. This became quite apparent one day when a playmate arrived and asked my daughter, "Wanna play commissary?"

— LORI A. BURDETTE

★ ★ ★ ★ ★ ★ ★ ★ ★ ★ ★ ★ ★ ★ ★ ★ ★

One day while stationed at Fort Stewart, Ga., I drove onto the base with my five-year-old son, Michael. It was approaching 5:00 p.m., and traffic came to a halt because it was time for taps. We stopped right in front of the field where the flag ceremony was taking place. The bugler played, the cannon boomed and the flag came down. "Mom," Michael said with surprise, "the only way they can get the flag down is to shoot it?"

— CRYSTAL D. FRANQUEZ

As a woman in the Marines, I often don't feel as feminine as when I had a civilian job in which I wore dresses and left my hair down. One day I was feeling especially depressed about this and couldn't wait to get home to change. When I arrived, I found that my friend and her 18-month-old daughter had been waiting for me. My friend is married to a Marine, and my worries about appearing less than feminine only increased when her little girl glanced up at me and yelled happily, "Daddy's home!"

— TIFFANY EVANS

Just before I was deployed to Iraq, I sat my eight-year-old son down and broke the news to him. **"I'm going to be away for a long time,"** I told him. **"I'm going to Iraq." "Why?"** he asked. **"Don't you know there's a war going on over there?"**

— THOMAS CIOPPA

Not bad kid, but you'd be vulnerable **to attacks** here and here.

★ ★ ★ ★ ★ ★ ★ ★ ★ ★ ★ ★ ★ ★ ★ ★ ★

Teaching second graders at our base school, I showed photos of Greek ruins, including the Acropolis, Mycenae and Corinth. "Any questions?" I asked afterward. One boy raised his hand. "Who bombed them?"

— KATHLEEN CORMACK

One day a fellow Coast Guard Auxiliary member delivered a water-safety speech to a group of Brownies. Having served a career in the Air Force before joining the auxiliary, he wore a chestful of award ribbons. After his talk a little girl in the front row raised her hand and asked him how he had gotten so many medals. My friend pointed to the top half and said, "The Air Force gave me these." Then he pointed to the lower half and said, "The Coast Guard gave me these." The little girl paused, frowned and replied, "In the Brownies, we have to earn them."

— SOURCE UNKNOWN

From the Peanut Gallery

My son-in-law, Carlos, stationed at March AFB in California, was deployed to Saudi Arabia for three months. Before leaving his wife and three young children, he sat down with four-year-old Andrew. "I'm going to be gone a long time, he said. "While I'm away, you're going to have to be the man in the family. You'll have to take care of your younger brother and sister. There are lots of things you can do around the house." The more he talked, the bigger Andrew's eyes got. Finally Andrew turned to his mother and said, "You'll have to help."

— JOSEPH P. MCPARLAN

★ ★ ★ ★ ★ ★ ★ ★ ★ ★ ★ ★ ★ ★ ★ ★ ★ ★

We had just moved to an Army post from an Air Force base and my young son, an avid fan of GI Joe toys, was excited to see the troops marching in cadence. An even bigger thrill came when he passed the motor pool with its tanks, jeeps and trucks. "Look!" he squealed with delight. "They have the whole collection!"

— JEREMY THORNTON

An Army intelligence officer, I took my four-year-old daughter into the office, and before long she spotted a man whose uniform was covered in ribbons, badges and medals. "Is he a general?" my daughter asked. "No, honey," I replied. "He's the first sergeant." With a quizzical look she asked, "Ever?"

— ROBERT H. MILLER

My seven-year-old grandson from New York was in New Orleans visiting when he noticed a photo of me from World War II in a Navy WAVES uniform. He later remarked to my daughter that he was impressed I had served during the war, but was sorry that my side lost. "What do you mean?" my daughter asked. "Well," my grandson replied, "Isn't she from the South?"

— VIOLET Y. WALSH

Our 15-year-old daughter, Melanie, had to write a report for school about World War II, specifically D-Day and the invasion of the Normandy beaches. "Isn't there a movie about that?" she asked me. I told her there was, but that I couldn't think of the name. Then it came to her.
"Oh, I remember," she said. "Isn't it something like 'Finding Private Nemo'?"

— REBECCA DEMAURO

★ ★ ★ ★ ★ ★ ★ ★ ★ ★ ★ ★ ★ ★ ★ ★ ★

While my husband was stationed at Fort Sill, Okla., our children attended a private school. One day my daughter came home with enrollment papers that needed to be filled out for the following school year. "Dad," she announced proudly as she handed over the forms, "here are my re-enlistment papers."

— SANDIE WEBSTER

When I re-enlisted as a Marine, my family came to the ceremony, in which I stood face to face with a lieutenant colonel, our right hands raised. A few weeks later, as I was showing photographs of the big day to my children, my nine-year-old daughter was unimpressed. "Look at Dad," she said. "He thinks he's so cool giving this guy a high-five."

— MICHAEL N. RUSSELL

Parental Pride

I overheard my father telling a family friend about my newly assigned mission in the U.S. Coast Guard. I work on a cutter that escorts all cruise ships and international vessels under the bridges in California's Bay Area. But what my father told his friend was, "She's involved in some sort of an escort service."

— ADRIENNE BLODGETT

As a public-affairs officer in the Air Force, I accompany members of the media while they pursue stories at area bases. But I realized I hadn't explained my job clearly enough to my mother when I overheard her tell a friend, "My daughter provides escort service to television reporters."

— JAMIE S. ROACH

★ ★ ★ ★ ★ ★ ★ ★ ★ ★ ★ ★ ★ ★ ★ ★ ★ ★

A distraught driver was grateful when our Marine son, Jim, stopped to help put out a fire in her car. "I prayed 'please let the next car stop,' and it was you," the woman gushed. Jim's mother was also pleased when she heard the story. "Who would have thought," she told him, "that you would be the answer to any girl's prayers?"

— RICHARD BELL

When my son, Tom, came home from the Army medical school at Fort Sam Houston on his first leave, I proudly watched him disembark from the plane. He looked so much more mature with his close haircut and immaculate uniform, and I was very impressed that he was carrying a briefcase. I gave Tom a big hug, and, pointing to the briefcase, I asked if he had much studying to do. "No, Dad," Tom replied. "This is my Sony PlayStation!"

— THOMAS W. TOBIN

Family Matters

During the Persian Gulf War, I was assigned to go to Saudi Arabia. As I was saying good-bye to my family, my three-year-old son, Christopher, was holding on to my leg and pleading with me not to leave. "No, Daddy, please don't go!" he kept repeating. We were beginning to make a scene when my wife, desperate to calm him, said, "Let Daddy go and I'll take you to get pizza." Immediately, Christopher loosened his death grip, stepped back and in a calm voice said, "'Bye, Daddy."

— CRAIG S. KUNISHIGE

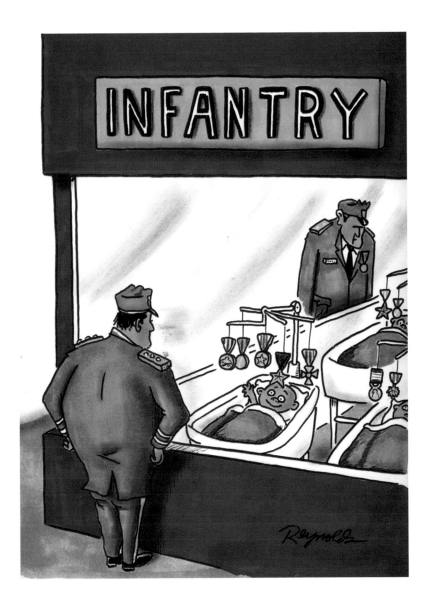

While conducting inspection one morning, I entered the quarters of a young enlisted man. His room was spotless, but **I** knew something wasn't right. Then I noticed his pants were cuffed, not hanging straight as service regulations demand. "Airman," I snapped, "have you decided to change the Air Force dress code?" "No, sir," he replied. "My mother did. She thought the uniform looked better this way."

— COL. RON COX (RET.)

★ ★ ★ ★ ★ ★ ★ ★ ★ ★ ★ ★ ★ ★ ★ ★ ★ ★

Sixteen years is a long time. That's how far the photo of my husband—looking slim and fit in his Marine Reserve uniform—goes back. Today, he's about 100 pounds heavier, so it was understandable when my friend's son asked who it was. "That's my father," my daughter told him. Looking at my husband, then at the photo, he asked, "Your first father?"

— MELE KOLOKIHAKAUFISI

When my brother, Jarrett, was trying to decide which branch of the military to join, he sought advice from our two uncles, one an Air Force reservist, the other a Marine. After Jarrett had decided on the Corps and left for boot camp, my Air Force uncle told a friend, "I must not be a very good salesman." "I guess not," replied his friend. "But I bet right now you're his favorite uncle."

— AMANDA YOUNG

I was leaving the grocery store with my three young sons when I spotted an Army tank loaded onto a flatbed truck with soldiers standing nearby. Knowing how my boys love anything that has to do with the military, I remarked, "Ooohhh, soldiers!" One of the men gave me a sheepish but somewhat flirtatious grin. Only then did I realize I was standing there alone. My boys had stopped at the gumball machine inside the store.

— TINA COOMES

Soon after we arrived at my husband's new duty station in Groton, Conn., I took our young son to the base hospital to take care of our health records. A Marine wearing a green, brown and black camouflage uniform, along with heavy combat boots, sat at his keyboard, entering our information.

★ ★ ★ ★ ★ ★ ★ ★ ★ ★ ★ ★ ★ ★ ★ ★ ★ ★

My son stared at him in awe, then turned to me and asked, "Mommy, does he think he's hiding?"

— CAROL KING

At his first parade as a Naval Academy midshipman, my brother, A.J., and the others drilled for hours. Finally, they lined up in columns and were assigned commanders who issued further orders. Many of the mids were anxious and repeatedly made mistakes. But my brother seemed confident and never missed a beat. "Mister," his commander asked, "have you any previous experience?" "Yes, ma'am," A.J. replied. "I have three older sisters!"

— JAYME BARDIN

Service Adjustments

Just after my father, who was a career Air Force NCO, passed away, all my brothers and sisters returned home to be with Mom. As we reminisced about my dad, we found ourselves floating from sorrow to laughter as we brought up fond memories of our nomadic military lifestyle. One morning we were discussing what music should be played at the funeral and several hymns were suggested. "But, Mom," my older sister said, "since Daddy was in the Air Force, shouldn't we request the Air Force song?" "No, dear," my mother said with a smile. "We are not playing a song with the words 'Off we go into the wild blue yonder' at your father's funeral!"

— JOHN H. WILLIAM

★ ★ ★ ★ ★ ★ ★ ★ ★ ★ ★ ★ ★ ★ ★ ★ ★ ★

Some friends were hoping their second child would be a girl, and they even had a name picked out. The ultrasound didn't reveal the baby's sex, though, and since the expectant father had orders from the Navy to ship out before the due date, he told his wife, "We'd better pick out a boy's name, just in case." But when it was time for him to report for duty, they still hadn't decided. At sea a few weeks later, he got notification that his son, Justin Kase, had been born.

— RICH ELKINS

When my husband joined the Coast Guard, I knew there would be some adjustments. Not only did I have to get accustomed to his short haircut, but also to his new sailor lingo. I eventually got used to him saying aye instead of yes, but nothing prepared me for the night when I was seven months pregnant and trying to roll over in bed. In his sleep, with a very military-sounding voice, my husband shouted at the top of his lungs, "She's comin' in on the port side!"

— CHRISTINE BERG

When I worked for the credit union at Fort Sill, Okla., a woman came in twice a month to cash her husband's pay-check, with four boys in tow. The kids didn't misbehave, but they kept their mother busy. One rainy payday, as the woman came with her brood, she dropped a piece of paper. I went over and picked it up for her. "On a day like today," I said, "you should've gotten your husband to take care of this." "Oh, he couldn't," the young mother replied. "He's on vacation in Korea."

— MARI COUCH

★ ★ ★ ★ ★ ★ ★ ★ ★ ★ ★ ★ ★ ★ ★ ★ ★ ★ ★

At a reception following my son Mark's graduation from basic training, he was given the duty of manning a small lemonade stand. A box was placed nearby to collect donations, and a scattering of dollar bills lay at the bottom. After one man put in a $50 bill, Mark sought him out and offered to return the money, convinced the man had put the large bill there by mistake. "Son," the man replied, "my grandson has a job and short hair, and he just called me 'sir.' That's worth fifty bucks any day."

— KATIE NYE

 When you say 'quagmire with no exit strategy,' you're talking about our relationship, right?

★ ★ ★ ★ ★ ★ ★ ★ ★ ★ ★ ★ ★ ★ ★ ★ ★ ★

After our son, Vincent, left for a year's stint with the Air Force in Korea, we decided to send him a string of letters from friends and family taped together to form a banner. Vincent's grandmother had done the same when her brother was in World War II, and she was proud that the banner she'd sent off had measured 18 feet long. My husband and I were determined to match that length, so we feverishly sought out friends and relatives to contribute to the chain. Weeks later we had the banner finished, but it was barely 17 feet long. Still, we sent it off to Korea, happy with our efforts, although a little disappointed that we didn't quite measure up. Shortly afterward my son called to say he had received the banner. "I can't believe how long it is!" he said excitedly. "But why didn't you two write?"

— LOUISE AND RICHARD JONES

When my husband, Bill, was stationed in Germany, our four-year-old son, Darren, would often help me think of gifts to send him. So on learning that Bill would be coming home in late fall, I told Darren we should have a Christmas surprise waiting for him. But I was taken aback by the gift Darren requested for his father from the mall's Santa Claus. "Please, Santa," he asked, "bring me a little brother so we'll have a surprise for Daddy when he comes home."

— JUNE B. SCHUH

Sign posted in the Army recruiting office:
Marry a veteran, girls. He can cook, make beds, sew and is already used to taking orders.

— BRIAN DION

★ ★ ★ ★ ★ ★ ★ ★ ★ ★ ★ ★ ★ ★ ★ ★ ★

I attended airborne training, where I spent three weeks learning how to pack parachutes and land without hurting myself. I completed five jumps and received my wings. After I returned home, my wife had done a load of laundry and I was helping her fold it. "I can't believe it," she said, after watching me for a while. "You made five jumps with chutes you packed yourself, and you can't even fold a fitted sheet!"

— COL. JAMES T. CURRIE

Love 'em As They Are

A retired navy admiral, my father began a second career working in a bank. One morning, while he prepared his desk for the day, he was approached by a young officer from the nearby naval base. "Sorry, but the department isn't open yet," Dad said. "But, it's nine o'clock!" protested the officer. My father didn't look at his watch. Instead, he surveyed his customer's uniform. "Ensign," he snapped, "I'll decide when it's nine o'clock!"

— SUSAN N. BOLINGER

My daughter, then a member of the Oregon Air National Guard, and I were waiting for the driver who would take her to the airport, where she would catch a flight for an overseas assignment. There she stood, punk hair style, three earrings in one ear, bulky sweater, bright red pants, and brass-toed boots. Turning to me, she said, "I'm sure glad they didn't make us wear our uniforms on this trip. I hate to look conspicuous."

— MARY BENTLY-GARDNER

★ ★ ★ ★ ★ ★ ★ ★ ★ ★ ★ ★ ★ ★ ★ ★ ★

On a shopping trip with my daughter, a Navy flight surgeon, I noticed that one item on her list was Snoopy bandages. She said that they were for some of her patients who were unnecessarily upset by their minor scratches and routine shots. Beaming with maternal pride, I told her how thoughtful she was to make the officers' children so happy. "Children?" She said, "Mother, these are for the pilots."

— FRAN SOLOMON SMITH

I spent several years as a submariner, and while at sea we would have a celebration halfway through a patrol. On one such night, the captain, who was serving dinner to the crew, tried to put some vegetables on a recruit's plate. The young seaman wouldn't take them. "With all due respect, sir, " the recruit said, "I don't eat them for my mother, and she outranks you."

— MARK WIDMAN

When I was at Fort Dix, N.J. for army basic training, my father, an air force master sergeant, was stationed at Dover Air Force Base in Delaware. I got a weekend pass, and Dad picked me up Friday evening so we could drive home to Massachusetts. On the way, we stopped at a diner. I was wearing my dress greens and Dad was in dress blues. The waitress looked puzzled as she took our order. "Is something wrong, Ma'am?" I asked. "It's unusual to see men in different services traveling together," she explained. "That's nothing," Dad replied. "He's taking me home to sleep with his mother!"

— DOUGLAS MOORE

★ ★ ★ ★ ★ ★ ★ ★ ★ ★ ★ ★ ★ ★ ★ ★

When my best friend, James, came home on his first army leave, my little brother asked him what he did in the service. "I do calisthenics, shoot guns, and follow orders," James replied. Walking in town that day, James and I ran into a buddy who also asked him what he did in the service. James gave the same reply, "I do calisthenics, shoot guns, and follow orders." A while later, we met a former classmate, an attractive woman, and she asked the same question. This time James said, "I'm studying communications, learning foreign languages, and traveling around the world."

— JAMES D. ANGLETON

While we stood at attention during a parade, the private next to me waved to someone in the audience. "Jones, never do that again!" our drill instructor sternly whispered. But a few minutes later, the soldier waved a second time. Back in the barracks after the parade, the DI barreled in and barked for Jones to come front and center. "Son, you knew I was going to see you," he screamed. "You knew it was wrong. Aren't you afraid of me?" "Yes, sir!" replied Jones. "But you don't know my mother!"

— ANDREW G. RAMON

I didn't think I had been gone that long. After 20 months overseas, my ship arrived in San Diego and, as soon as I got ashore, I phoned home. **"Hi, Mom!"** I said. **"Who is this?"** she answered. **"Hello! I'm an only child."**

— JOHN NEDDERMAN

★ ★ ★ ★ ★ ★ ★ ★ ★ ★ ★ ★ ★ ★ ★ ★ ★

I was chatting with a woman about my husband, Marryl, a marine stationed at Parris Island Recruit Training Depot. "What does he do there ?" she asked. "He teaches at the drill instructors' school, " I replied. She said, puzzled, "I figured they just got the meanest marines they could find and put them to work."

— HOLLY BRISBIN

My husband Brent, our four-month-old baby and I were shopping when Brent remembered he had to take care of some paper work at his army reserve unit. We stopped there near the baby's feeding time, and as we waited for Brent, our little one became increasingly fussy. I sat and rocked him, vainly trying to quiet his cries. Several officers peeked in to check on the commotion. "I know just how he feels," one lieutenant consoled. "I cried my first day in the army, too."

— THERESA MELLOR

I spent my 22nd birthday at the MP school in Fort Gordon, Ga., drilling in the extreme heat. Cleaning up for chow, I was ordered to report to the telegraph center "on the double!" Panting breathlessly after running two miles in the sweltering humidity, I opened the wire that had been sent to me: "HAPPY BIRTHDAY, SON. LOVE, MOM AND DAD."

— ANTHONY ANDRIANO

OOPS!

★ It's Inevitable

★ And So It Goes...

★ ★ ★ ★ ★ ★ ★ ★ ★ ★ ★ ★ ★ ★ ★ ★ ★ ★

Two female privates are ordered to paint the general's office. They are warned not to get paint on their uniforms. So they lock the door, strip off their clothes and get to work. An hour later, there's a knock at the door. "Who is it?" they ask. "Blind man." Thinking nothing of it, the privates open up. "Hi," says the man. "Where do you want the blinds?"

— SOURCE UNKNOWN

While serving in the Persian Gulf, I was living in one of the tent cities that housed many of the troops. The tents were pitched so close together that the ropes crisscrossed. As I was heading back from chow, rifle slung over my shoulder, I decided to take a shortcut between the tents. Soldiers living there had hung their laundry on the outstretched ropes, but I deftly ducked under them. As I emerged from this tangle and continued down another pathway, a pair of soldiers pointed and laughed at me. Puzzled, I turned around to find a pair of men's underwear swinging from the muzzle of my rifle.

— KATHY EVANSON

Loading my jeep with a generator, gas and other necessary items for flood victims in Warren, Minn., I drove to a National Guard checkpoint and flashed my fire department badge to get past. The Guardsman waved me through with a picture-perfect salute, and my chest swelled with pride at the show of respect. On my way back out, I stopped to talk to the soldier and thanked him for the salute. "That wasn't a salute, sir," he told me. "I was just showing you how deep the water was."

— PAT COLLINS

★ ★ ★ ★ ★ ★ ★ ★ ★ ★ ★ ★ ★ ★ ★ ★ ★

While in the field one night on Army maneuvers, my husband, Francisco, came under fire by "opposing" forces. Fortunately, he was using night-vision goggles. Crawling low through the woods, Francisco followed another soldier who was really making time as he moved through the bushes. My husband drew closer to his unusually speedy comrade just in time to realize he was not a soldier at all. Francisco had been trying to keep pace with a porcupine.

— REBECCA LLENAS

On leave after a yearlong tour of duty in Korea, my friend's first craving back home in the States was a meal at McDonald's. Much to his surprise, the cashier took one look at his uniform and refused his money. "Thanks," he said. "Sure," she replied. "We never charge bus drivers."

— LEESA BRAUN

My air national guard unit in Virginia Beach, Va., had a change-of-command ceremony, and a high-ranking general came to deliver a speech. He was given VIP treatment and even received some press coverage. The day after the big ceremony, the general took his wife to the movies at a local cinema. When he entered the small theater, he was given a standing ovation. Flattered by the response to his arrival, he acknowledged the applause with a wave of his hand and a big grin. Later, after the movie, one of the patrons approached him. "Gee," remarked the fan, "we are so lucky you came." "Oh, really?" the general replied, obviously pleased. "Yes, they weren't going to start the movie unless they got 15 paying customers. We only had 13 until you two showed up."

— BRADLEY D. STEELE

★ ★ ★ ★ ★ ★ ★ ★ ★ ★ ★ ★ ★ ★ ★ ★ ★

As new Naval reservists, my friends and I were proud to wear our uniforms to an armed-forces parade in New York City. After leaving the subway, we were walking the short distance to the assembly point when we noticed the green coat, gold buttons and double bars of an approaching officer. We quickly straightened up and presented him with sharp salutes. Our wonder over why the Army captain had not returned our salutes quickly turned to embarrassment when we realized he was a foreman for the New York City sanitation department.

— EDWARD T. ZAREK

On the heels of a massive storm, our supervisor visited headquarters to be briefed. When the major had concluded his rundown, the supervisor pointed to the map, where colored pins indicated affected towns, generators and so on. "What are the red pins at the top for?" he asked. "Those," said the major, "hold up the map."

— MAJ. RYAN JESTIN

During my Army Reserve unit's annual training at Fort Ord, Calif., our battalion commander was upset that evening chow was late. He called the mess hall, and the mess sergeant explained that because their vehicle broke down, they couldn't deliver the field rations to our bivouac site. The commander immediately yelled to his driver, "Private! Drive to the mess hall and get chow!" The private took off on the 15-minute trip. Over an hour later, we were dismayed to see him return empty-handed. "Private!" demanded the commander. "What about chow?" "It was delicious, sir," replied the driver. "I got there right before the mess hall closed, so I got seconds."

— VINCE GILKEY

★ ★ ★ ★ ★ ★ ★ ★ ★ ★ ★ ★ ★ ★ ★ ★ ★

It's Inevitable!

During Operation Desert Storm, I was a legislative affairs officer for Gen. Norman Schwarzkopf. Often I was required to transport gifts, sent to him from patriotic Americans, from Washington, D.C., to his home base in Florida. On one trip I "escorted" a four-foot teddy bear dressed in fatigues with a name tag reading "Bear," General Schwarzkopf's nick-name. As I boarded the plane, I explained my mission to the flight attendant and asked if she could store the bear in first class. She was honored to do so, and I disappeared into the coach section. Then, just before takeoff, an announcement came over the intercom: "Colonel Preast, would you please come up to first class? We have an extra seat here for you to sit next to your teddy bear."

— DAVID R. PREAST

★ ★ ★ ★ ★ ★ ★ ★ ★ ★ ★ ★ ★ ★ ★ ★ ★ ★

During Army basic training, our first lieutenant took us on a march and asked each of us where our home was. After everyone had answered, he sneered and said, "You're all wrong. The Army is now your home." Back at the barracks, he read our evening duties, then asked our first sergeant if he had anything to say. "You bet I do," the sergeant replied. "Men, while you were gone today, I found beds improperly made, clothes not hanging correctly, shoes not shined and footlockers a mess. Where do you think you are? Home?"

— JACK HEAVEY

Jimmy, our son, is an Army ROTC cadet at Northern Arizona University in Flagstaff. During a field exercise, he was assigned to "attack" a designated bunker, but also instructed not to strike if he was outnumbered by more than three soldiers. As Jimmy made his approach, he saw a crowd of people around his target, some in civilian clothes. Since he was vastly outnumbered, he set off a smoke grenade for cover and conducted a by-the-book retreat. Jimmy's captain intercepted him. "Cadet, do you know what you've done?" Unbeknownst to my son, a group of reporters was covering the event. He had just retreated from the press.

— CHUCK BEVAN

> Two green recruits found three hand grenades on the road and decided to take them back to the base. "What if one of them explodes?" asked one young private. "No problem," said his buddy. **"We'll say we only found two."**
>
> — SOURCE UNKNOWN

★ ★ ★ ★ ★ ★ ★ ★ ★ ★ ★ ★ ★ ★ ★ ★ ★

Our unit stood at attention one morning as the officer in charge presented a shipmate with a Good Conduct Award. The officer read from the certificate, "in recognition of faithful, zealous and obedient naval service." As the certificate was handed over, we heard a voice from the ranks say, "They make it sound like you should wag your tail and bark."

— SUSAN AVILA

"I feel sorry for this soldier," joked my husband as he handed me a flier he'd found in our mailbox. It read: Lost Cat/Black and white/Answers to Nate/Belongs to a soldier/Recently neutered.

— SONDRA GILBERTSON

In the Army during Operation Desert Storm, I found myself in a world that had changed little since Biblical times. With so few creature comforts available, packages from home containing cookies and canned goods were received with great anticipation. When I got a box from my sister, I happily tore into it, only to discover just how far from home I really was. She had filled it with packages of microwave popcorn.

— ROBERT T. SIMS

I was in a Novocain fog following a visit to the dentist when I found myself lost on a deserted highway. Within minutes, I was surrounded by security officers who escorted me home. Later that day, my Air Force pilot husband came home, fuming. "You won't believe what happened!" he said, shaking his head. "Some idiot was driving around the runway and we had to circle until the police could get the car off!"

— PAMELA ISOM

★ ★ ★ ★ ★ ★ ★ ★ ★ ★ ★ ★ ★ ★ ★ ★

 I'd like to stop saluting, Sir, but my hair is **stuck** in my watchband.

★ ★ ★ ★ ★ ★ ★ ★ ★ ★ ★ ★ ★ ★ ★ ★ ★

Tiring of the same old buzz cut from the base barber at Fort Dix, New Jersey, I went into town to get my haircut. The hairdresser noticed my accent and asked where I was from. "Trinidad," I said. "Is that in Arabia?" "The Caribbean." She laughed, "I never was good at geometry."

— GERARD D'ORNELLAS

The trip aboard the transport ship that brought my Air Force father and mother to Japan promised to be a long, tedious one. But the Navy, trying to liven things up for the couples, posted this sign by the galley for all to see when they dined: "Officers may mess with their wives between 1100-1200 and 1800-1900."

— LESLIE MATHES

And So It Goes ...

When my sister was considering joining the Army, she was showered with attention from recruiters. Cars with drivers were made available to take her to meetings, and every door was opened and held for her. She enjoyed the special treatment and signed up. On the day she left for boot camp, an impeccably dressed sergeant arrived to pick her up. As she got ready to leave, she asked, "Aren't you going to help me with these bags?" "Get them yourself," the man replied. "You're in the Army now!"

— DOROTHY GLENDORA GIBBS

Decal on the door of a military base: "Freedom's Door Is Open to Everyone." Below it, another decal: "Authorized Personnel Only!"

— HEATHER HARRIS

★ ★ ★ ★ ★ ★ ★ ★ ★ ★ ★ ★ ★ ★ ★ ★ ★ ★

Patrolling the streets of Baghdad is a tense job. But one thing that lightens the mood is sharing treats with the kids. One day, I leaned out of our Humvee and tossed some goodies to the children. I was enjoying the laughter and smiles when I noticed a man glowering at me after some candy landed at his feet. "What's wrong with that guy?" I asked our gunner. "He was pouring cement," he explained.

— JENNIFER TWITCHELL

Nights in England are coal black, making parachute jumps difficult and dangerous. So we attach small lights called chemlites to our jumpsuits to make ourselves visible to the rest of our team. Late one night, lost after a practice jump, we knocked on the door of a small cottage. When a woman answered, she was greeted by the sight of five men festooned in glowing chemlites. "Excuse me," I said. "Can you tell me where we are?" In a thick English accent, the woman replied, "Earth."

— BILL BLACK

I was in the band at Ellsworth Air Force Base, South Dakota. Our group was required to play for all generals who arrived on base. So one morning, when our commanding officer heard on the radio that a General Frost was expected just after noon, he sent us scrambling to the flight line with our instruments. Turns out one of the musicians had also heard the radio announcement. He took the C.O. aside For a whispered conference. When they returned, the officer told us the performance was canceled. There was no arriving general—we had almost played for the weather forecast.

— DAVID YOST

★ ★ ★ ★ ★ ★ ★ ★ ★ ★ ★ ★ ★ ★ ★ ★ ★ ★

One morning a helicopter crew from my squadron got an order to pick up a mental patient and deliver him to an aircraft carrier. The passenger boarded the copter unescorted, but when it landed on the carrier, four Marines charged in, restrained the bewildered passenger and unceremoniously delivered him to the ship's doctor. Then the flight crew received another message: "Replace mental patient with dental patient." The poor guy had a toothache.

— MICHAEL KVICALA

When my father, a retired Marine, and I were visiting the PX at Camp Lejeune, N.C., we saw his friend, a retired sergeant major, who was continually looking up from his wristwatch. "What are you up to?" my father asked him. "I've been standing here for twenty-eight minutes," his buddy replied, "and not one Marine has come through these doors in full uniform. I'll give fifty dollars to the first Marine who comes in dressed with spit and polish." Within seconds, a private walked into the PX decked out in his full uniform. Pleased, the sergeant major presented him with the money and asked him about his impeccable appearance. The private lowered his eyes and replied, "I've just come from my court-martial, sir."

— TERRY MCGUIRE

During reservists' training, my commanding officer was briefing his colleagues on the battalion's mission. While he was highlighting the key objectives, of our task—serious business, aimed at motivating the troops—he was suddenly interrupted by a ringing cell phone. The tune? "Mission Impossible."

— SAMUEL HENRY

★ ★ ★ ★ ★ ★ ★ ★ ★ ★ ★ ★ ★ ★ ★ ★ ★ ★

There was a high volume of new recruits when I joined the Army. Instead of using our names, we were called by ID numbers. On the second day of reception, a group of new privates awaited instructions. Suddenly a sergeant burst into the room and yelled, "Hey, you, Private!" We all stared, unsure whom he was talking to. Annoyed, the sergeant stepped up to the intended private and shouted, "You!" "Hey," she protested, "I have a number!"

— KAMI HOLLIDAY

During basic training at Lackland AFB in Texas, our flight crew marched back to the barracks after receiving our coveted dress-blue uniforms. Our boots were tied to the duffel bags strapped to our backs. As we marched, one airman called out to the drill instructor, "Sir, permission to adjust. My boots keep kicking me in the butt." "Permission denied," the instructor replied. "Those boots are doing exactly what I've been dying to do since day one!"

— ANTHONY MCCORD

My father, an Army major, was conducting a field test when communications went dead. Immediately, he jumped into a jeep and ordered a sergeant to speed to the command station. When my father and the sergeant ran in, the group there cheered their arrival. The commanding officer then stepped forward and shook my father's hand. "Don't congratulate me, sir," my father said modestly as he pointed to his driver. "It was all the sergeant's doing." The commanding officer nodded and turned to the sergeant. "Congratulations," he said. "The major's wife just had a baby girl."

— DIANE DUDMAN

The HOME FRONT

- ★ Can You Cope?
- ★ We Do Our Best
- ★ It's Really Okay
- ★ Homecoming
- ★ Supportive Spouses?

★ ★ ★ ★ ★ ★ ★ ★ ★ ★ ★ ★ ★ ★ ★ ★ ★ ★

While my husband was stationed overseas, our four-year-old daughter decided that she needed a baby brother. "Good idea," I told her. "But don't you think we should wait till your father's home?" Lori had a better idea. "Why don't we just surprise him?"

— KAY SCHMIDT

Few people know what a quartermaster does. So during my aircraft carrier's Family Day, I demonstrated a procedure called semaphore—I grabbed my flags and signaled an imaginary boat. When finished, I pointed to a little girl in front and asked, "Now do you know what I do?" "Yes," she said. "You're a cheerleader."

— DANNY SULLIVAN

Early in my marriage, I found it hard to get used to the strict rules of Marine life. One time my husband's sergeant suggested he have me wake up at 5:00 a.m., then drive him to another base to pick up a truck they needed. Ashamed to admit it, Steven told his superior that I'd probably be unwilling to help. "She's not a team player, is she?" his sergeant asked. "No," Steven replied. "She's not even a fan."

— KELLY DAVIS KING

Our son, who's in the Army stationed in Georgia, invited my husband and me for a visit. After driving endlessly through unfamiliar streets in search of an entrance to Fort Stewart, my husband, suddenly said, "We're getting close." "How do you know?" I asked. He pointed to a sign that read: "Sonny's Bar-B-Q. Tank Parking Available."

— WILMA J. FLEMING

My family and I had just arrived at a Naval air station in Texas after a tour in Japan. We met another new couple at the base who had been staying in a hotel with their six kids. Since we had already rented a large home, we told them they could stay with us for a few days. "And don't worry about the kids," my wife said. "We have futons for them." "Oh, don't go to any trouble," the wife said. "They eat anything."

— ROBERT J. DOUGHER

As a young married couple, my husband and I lived in a cheap housing complex near the base where he was stationed. Our chief complaint was that the walls were paper-thin and that we had no privacy. This was painfully obvious one morning when my husband was upstairs and I was downstairs on the telephone. I was interrupted by the doorbell and went to greet my neighbor. "Give this to Lieutenant Gridley," he said, thrusting a roll of toilet paper into my hands. "He's been yelling for it for 15 minutes."

— GAIL GRIDLEY

I once lived in Arizona near Fort Huachuca, an Army installation. Our street consisted mainly of mobile homes with small yards, but grass was difficult to grow in that climate, especially with the many children and dogs romping through the neighborhood. One lawn stood out, however. It was green and lush with neat rows of flowers. I was puzzled how the owner managed to do it until I noticed a sign in the yard. It read: "Danger—Minefield."

— ELLEN ZRELAK

★ ★ ★ ★ ★ ★ ★ ★ ★ ★ ★ ★ ★ ★ ★ ★ ★ ★

My brother, Tim, and I were both college students at Texas A & M University, where he was enrolled as a member of the Corps of Cadets, our school's version of ROTC. One day while we were walking through our student center together, I saw an Air Force officer. Noting the eagle on his insignia, I asked Tim, who had not seen the officer, what you call a man with a bird on his shoulder. With a puzzled look, he replied, "A pirate?"

— LINDA EVAN

I had been married for only a week and was just learning about life as a military spouse when I went to the hospital at Randolph Air Force Base near San Antonio for a dental checkup. After the appointment, I took out my checkbook and asked the sergeant behind the counter to whom I should make the check payable. "Honey, this is the military," she said. "We don't take your money, we just take your husband."

— KATHY A. HEDRICK

When faced with overseas duty, I tried to soften the blow of my departure by telling my children we'd be able to buy special things with the extra money I'd earn for the assignment, such as a new car or a vacation. After I'd been in Asia for about six months, I received a tape recording from my children. When my oldest son spoke, he recounted the promise I'd made and then added, "Dad, can you stay a little longer so we can get a new television set, too?"

— LOWELL C. MULLINS

★ ★ ★ ★ ★ ★ ★ ★ ★ ★ ★ ★ ★ ★ ★ ★ ★

My son, a private first class in the Army, was stationed in Bosnia. He called home from his camp one day in good spirits. He said he had just finished a softball game and they didn't even have to chase after the foul balls. "Why not?" I asked. "Because," came a response no mother would want to hear, "the foul line is where the minefield begins."

— KAREN POND

Last Halloween a civilian friend had me pick up his son from day care on the way home from my base. Signing him out, I felt something press against my back. I turned to see him painting on my camouflage uniform. "What are you doing?" I cried. "I like your tree costume," the boy replied innocently. "But you need some red and yellow leaves."

— ADAM CARROLL

Can You Cope?

As a sergeant stationed at Andrews Air Force Base in Washington, D.C., I dated a communications sergeant for the 89th Airlift Wing. Frequently, because of last-minute mission requirements, our personal plans had to be changed. One day before my boyfriend and I were to attend a wedding, I came home to an interesting message on my answering machine: "Ma'am," said a male voice, "this is the Andrews Command Post relaying a message from Sergeant Smith, who is traveling with the Secretary of State. He says he's sorry, but he's out of the country, and so the wedding is off." After a pause, the operator continued in a concerned, unofficial tone, "I hope that's okay, ma'am."

— BARBARA WEBER

I was visiting my parents with my new husband, a Navy frogman, when he drew me aside. "I don't think your mother likes me," he said. "I was explaining that I can't wear my wedding ring when I dive because barracudas are attracted to shiny things and might bite off my finger. And she said, 'Well, can't you wear it on a chain around your neck?' "

— MARJORIE MANSON TELFORD

 I can't **heeear you!**

According to my mother, she and Dad decided to start a family soon after he became an officer in the Air Force. When months went by without success, they consulted the base physician, who chose to examine Mom right then and there. "Please disrobe," he told her. "With him in the room?" she yelled, pointing to my father. Turning to Dad, the doctor said, "Captain, I think I found the problem."

— WINDLEY HOFLER WALDEN

When my brother, John, joined the Marines about a year ago, friends and family told my mother not to worry, reassuring her that "at least it's during peacetime." On September 11, when terrorists attacked our country, John was stationed in Japan. My mother, upon hearing the news, didn't panic. Instead, she headed to the nearest recruiting office. When a recruiter came to the desk and asked if she needed help, she responded, "Yes—I need to hug a Marine!"

— JULIANNE STARE

My father, an engineer on a submarine, was often out at sea for family occasions. As a result, he sometimes forgot about them. One year he missed my mother's birthday. Unfortunately, it was impossible for her to tell him how furious she was since the Navy screened all messages, editing out anything that could be considered disturbing to the men on board. However, my mother was not so easily defeated. She sent my dad a message, thanking him profusely for the lovely birthday present he so kindly remembered to send her. Mom went on about how special Dad had made her feel by his thoughtfulness, and how grateful she was for his generosity.

— ALEXIS ANDREWS

★ ★ ★ ★ ★ ★ ★ ★ ★ ★ ★ ★ ★ ★ ★ ★ ★ ★

I work on a navy base in Maryland, across the Patuxent River from my home. When the bridge was closed for repairs, the base provided ferryboats for personnel. After I got to work one morning, my wife, pregnant with twins, called to say that she had forgotten her house key and was locked out. I told her I'd give my key to a sailor working on the ferry, and he could bring it to her at the Navy annex across the river. I explained the situation to a sailor at the marina and told him he'd have no problem recognizing my wife. "She's short, blond and very pregnant," I said. "Buddy," the sailor exclaimed, "this is a Navy base. You'll have to be more specific!"

— PIERRE CONLEY

Marine boot camp was a learning experience for my son. Among the more gruesome skill sets he picked up, he wrote in a letter to the family, was how you can kill a man 12 ways using only your bare hands. This prompted my nephew to wonder aloud, "How does he practice?"

— KELLY SCHACKMAN

A couple of summers ago, our son Scott and his family relocated to Eielson Air Force Base near Fairbanks, Alaska. In awe of the state's wildlife and natural beauty, they looked forward to their four-year tour. That December we received an e-mail from our 11-year-old granddaughter that stated her opinion pretty clearly. It read "Dear Grandma and Grandpa: It is 24 degrees below zero here today. We have three years and eight months left. I love and miss you. Leah."

— BEVERLY BAHNUB

★ ★ ★ ★ ★ ★ ★ ★ ★ ★ ★ ★ ★ ★ ★ ★ ★ ★

My wife was sitting in the cockpit of my fighter jet— her head spinning as I pointed to the myriad buttons, levers and switches on the control panel. "Do you really know what each one of these buttons does?" she asked. "Yep," I said proudly. Scowling, she then asked, "And I'm supposed to believe you can't figure out how to run the washing machine?"

— MATT DIETZ

Feeling thoroughly sorry for myself after being transferred clear across the continent to Spokane, Washington, I reached out to the one person I knew would sympathize: my mother. "Dear Mom," I wrote, "I have no money and no friends." "Dear Bill," she wrote back. "Make friends."

— WILLIAM SOLOMON

When my father enlisted in the Air Force, he left his church in the capable hands of my mother. Nevertheless, one member of his flock took it upon herself to put Dad's mind at ease. "Pastor, the church is doing well," she wrote. "Your wife is carrying on with the deacons."

— LORA MAE MILLER

During Desert Storm, one of our co-workers was called to serve in Iraq. Upon his safe return and arrival back at work, we tied yellow ribbons around numerous trees and hung a huge sign that read:

"We missed you... thank God the Iraqis did, too!"

— BILLIE MCCRACKEN

★ ★ ★ ★ ★ ★ ★ ★ ★ ★ ★ ★ ★ ★ ★ ★ ★ ★

We Do Our Best

If I say so myself, I looked pretty brawny in my Navy summer whites. And as I stood in line at the Long Beach Naval Hospital pharmacy, I wasn't the only one who thought so—a young boy kept staring at my arms. Eventually, he whispered something to his mother, who, in turn, leaned over to me. "My son wants to know," she said, "if you have a can of spinach in your shirt."

— LOY MCDONALD

After spending a wonderful week together, my fiancé dropped me off at the airport and returned to his base. I didn't realize how much I'd miss him until I reached the plane and burst into tears. "What's the matter?" asked the unlucky woman seated next to me. Between sobs I told her the sad story of my long-distance relationship. "If you truly love him, it will work," she said. "I know. My ex-husband was in the Army."

— ABBY KIESER

As a member of the organization that installs computer systems aboard Navy ships, I am mindful of how important the off-ship e-mail capabilities are to sailor morale, especially when some vessels are deployed for up to six months. One day while shopping at the base commissary, I realized another crucial aspect of my job. I was trailing a frazzled mother with two active children, and I watched as she stalked over to where her young son had perched himself on the rail of the freezer case. "If you don't get off there right now," she commanded, "I'm going to e-mail your father!"

— GREGORY MARTIN

★ ★ ★ ★ ★ ★ ★ ★ ★ ★ ★ ★ ★ ★ ★ ★ ★

It was a very emotional time for me—my youngest son was about to leave for basic training. I took the day off so we could spend his last day as a civilian together. My son likes to pass himself off as a tough guy, but as we climbed into the car, he blurted out in a halting, sad voice, "I'm going to miss you." Well, I just about lost it. The tears flowed from my eyes as I turned to say how much I was going to miss him too. That's when I saw that he was addressing a can of Pepsi he'd just opened.

— SUE STRUTHERS

My husband wore his Army uniform with pride. One day, coming home from the base and dressed in his olive drab fatigues, he stopped off at the grocery store to pick up a few things. While on line at the checkout counter, he noticed a little boy standing with his mother. The boy took one look at my husband in his uniform, and his eyes grew wide. My husband, in turn, gave the young man a crisp salute. The boy was so excited. He pointed at my husband and announced, "Look, Mom, a giant Boy Scout."

— BERNICE QUENTAL

My family wanted to do something to honor my nephew, a Ranger with the Army's 101st Airborne, who had been sent to Iraq. So, with the help of her four-year-old grandson, Chandler, my sister tied a yellow ribbon on the tree in her front yard. "Why are we doing this, Grandma?" Chandler asked. "It's for your uncle," she said. As he watched his grandmother attach the bow, Chandler remarked quietly, "A tree's not much of a present."

— DIANE L. OLWIN

During a promotion celebration for my husband, his father, an old Army colonel, introduced himself to the rear admiral in charge by saying, "I've never shaken hands with a rear admiral, and a female rear admiral at that!" He was stunned when she leaned forward and kissed him on the cheek, saying, "Betcha never been kissed by one either!"

— MARIANNE MANN

Reservists like myself always had a hard time parking on base, as most spaces were set aside for the brass. My wife never had this problem. I finally found out why after she drove me to the PX and parked in a space marked "Reserved." "See?" she said. "Just look at all the spaces they've set aside for you Reserves."

— JAMES KLEEMAN

My friend received a package from the Navy containing the civilian clothes her son was wearing when he left for boot camp. Not wanting to open the box, she put it away. This cracked up her husband, who accused her of being a sentimental old fool. "I'm not sentimental," she shot back. "I'm realistic. His shoes, socks and underwear have been inside that box for two weeks, and I'm not going to be the one to open it!"

— SUSAN STUCZYNSKI

★ ★ ★ ★ ★ ★ ★ ★ ★ ★ ★ ★ ★ ★ ★ ★ ★

It's Really Okay

One evening my new husband called to have me pick him up from work. Since I had never been on the military post before, I was a little reluctant, but I agreed to attempt the task. While I drove through the base, a young soldier in his camouflage uniform stepped out onto the street. I slammed on the brakes to avoid hitting him, and the screeching tires attracted the attention of a nearby MP. I was in tears as the officer approached my car. "I didn't see him!" I blurted out. " Well, ma'am," the MP remarked, grinning at me, "that's kind of the point."

— CHRISTIN SMITH

When our son, Jimmy, went to Navy boot camp, we waited impatiently for word from him. Finally we received a postcard telling us he was doing well and we shouldn't worry. It went on to say that he was being kept busy acclimating to a military lifestyle and that he would send a detailed letter in a couple of weeks. After reading his card a second time, however, we noticed that Jimmy had faintly underlined letters throughout the note. When the letters were combined, his hidden message read, "Help me!"

— DONNA GRIMES

Following an overnight flight to meet my father at his latest military assignment, my mother, eight noisy and shoving siblings, and I arrived at Rhein-Main Air Base in Germany. "Do you have any weapons or illegal drugs in your possession?" the customs agent asked my weary mother. "Sir," she said while separating my brother and me, "if I had either of those items, I would have used them by now."

— JIM RISDAL

★ ★ ★ ★ ★ ★ ★ ★ ★ ★ ★ ★ ★ ★ ★ ★ ★ ★

My husband is an Army helicopter pilot, and we never seem to live in one place for very long. Typically, during a move, we stay in a hotel until we can find a permanent place to have our things delivered. Our four children enjoy this greatly, although sometimes it can be a bit confusing for them. One recent day, as we were driving down an interstate and passed a Holiday Inn, our three-year-old squeaked in excitement from the back seat. " Look," he exclaimed. "There's our old house!"

— KIMBERLY O'DONNELL

I was in the perfume aisle of our base exchange and noticed an airman as she picked up a bottle and sniffed its contents. I told her that I particularly liked her selection. "Oh, I'm not buying any perfume," she responded. "When I get homesick for my mom, I always come here to smell her brand of cologne."

— JANE W. RANDO

I rarely talked to my daughter, Rita, about my military experience, so it surprised me when I overheard her mention it during a phone conversation with her boyfriend. Apparently he was having a hard time adjusting to Army boot camp, and had stolen a moment to call her and complain about his tough regimen. "Look," Rita admonished him, **"if my mother can do it, then you can, too."**

— F. O'GARA

★ ★ ★ ★ ★ ★ ★ ★ ★ ★ ★ ★ ★ ★ ★ ★

My husband's cousin married a former Marine who now works for United Parcel Service. They bought their four-year-old son two stuffed bears—one in a UPS uniform and the other in Marine garb. When the boy seemed confused, his father brought out a picture of himself in full Marine dress. "See, Connor?" he explained, pointing to the photo and then to the bear. "That's Daddy." Connor's eyes went from one to the other, and then he asked in a puzzled voice, "You used to be a bear?"

— ROBIN YEDLOCK

While my brother was stationed overseas, his wife wrote to him daily. For an added touch, she'd always scribble little abbreviated notes on the outside of the envelopes. One day my brother received a letter with the familiar "SWL" (sealed with love) message on the envelope. He noticed that the letter was sealed with tape and chuckled as he read this notation written by a postal employee: "Love didn't stick—resealed in Seattle."

— MARY ANN DAVIS

My friend's wife returned from a tour of duty in the Middle East. To celebrate, he decided to take her out for a night on the town. Proud of her service record, he suggested she wear her uniform. Not only did a patriotic taxi driver refuse to accept money from them, but an appreciative citizen paid for her meal at the restaurant, and the theater manager upgraded their balcony seats to the orchestra. At the end of the evening, my friend turned to his wife. "I still get credit for taking you out, right?"

— JODIE STODDARD

★ ★ ★ ★ ★ ★ ★ ★ ★ ★ ★ ★ ★ ★ ★ ★ ★ ★

Homecoming

After an exhausting military maneuver, our colonel collected his officers and told us, "I intend to go home now, open a bottle of wine and sit with my wife in front of the fireplace. I suggest you all do the same." "Okay, sir," shot back one officer. "If you don't think your wife will mind."

— STEVEN W. CHAPMAN

An Air Force pilot, I was taking a fighter jet from Utah back home to New York, so I called my wife to meet me at the base. Near the end of the flight visibility was poor, and as I began my descent my navigational electronics went dead along with my radio. I managed to find the beacon at the end of the runway and was barely able to make out the ground. Unsure of my situation, the control tower dispatched every emergency vehicle on the base to the runway with lights on and sirens blaring. Fortunately, I landed without incident and taxied to the ramp area. Having seen and heard all the commotion, my wife greeted me with a big hug and said, "Honey, you should have been here for all of the excitement!"

— TOM ROYSTON

After leaving the regulated life of the Navy, an old friend of mine, a retired officer, took a civilian job but had trouble getting to work on time. Finally his boss asked, "What would they have said to you in your previous job about being late?" My friend answered him, "Good morning, Admiral."

— SALVADOR SEPULVEDA, JR.

★ ★ ★ ★ ★ ★ ★ ★ ★ ★ ★ ★ ★ ★ ★ ★ ★ ★

Upon returning from Iraq, I received a number of commendations and medals, including the Bronze Star for meritorious achievement. Still, my daughter was unimpressed. "Who won the Silver and the Gold?" she asked.

— KEITH ANDERSON

My neighbor, Terry, a former high-school halfback, came home from combat duty in Afghanistan. He was excited to tell me that his unit had played a makeshift game of football. "Just don't tell my mom," he begged. "If she knew I was playing football she'd worry that I might reinjure my knee."

— MIKE CALLISON

My friend Herb was returning home after several months aboard a Navy submarine. His wife and a crowd of people anxiously awaited the arrival of the vessel at a San Diego dock. She was so excited that she parked their car near the edge of the dock in a no-parking zone. The sub finally appeared. But it came in too fast and slammed into the end of the wharf. Fortunately no one was injured. Unfortunately, Herb and his wife had to explain to their insurance company that their car had been damaged by a runaway submarine.

— DONALD L. HEFLIN

My father was often away on lengthy tours of duty, leaving my mother to manage five kids by herself. While he was away we used to sneak into their room to sleep. So before shipping out one time, Dad reminded us to respect Mom's space and sleep in our own rooms. Upon his return, as he disembarked the plane with the rest of his unit, my brother ran up to him, jumped into his arms and loudly announced, "Dad, you're going to be so happy. While you were gone this time, nobody slept with Mom."

— KATHLEEN HODGE

My husband, a war-movie buff, and my six-year-old daughter sat in front of the TV watching actual World War II footage of the unconditional surrender that ended the war with Japan. As General Douglas MacArthur and

★ ★ ★ ★ ★ ★ ★ ★ ★ ★ ★ ★ ★ ★ ★ ★ ★

Japan's General Umeza stood on the deck of the USS Missouri and signed documents—under the watchful gaze of Allied troops—my daughter was confused. "What's wrong?" asked my husband. Pointing to the set, she said, "Which one is John Wayne?"

— JENNIE KELLER

My son arrived back in the United States after fighting with the First Marine Division in Iraq. But I still couldn't help reacting like a mom when I saw him on the base running over to some buddies to return a bayonet. "Kevin!" I shouted halfway across the base, before I could stop myself. "Don't run with that knife in your hands!"

— PAM HODGSKIN

I was driving one day when I noticed a car behind me flashing its lights repeatedly. Alarmed, I pulled over, and the other vehicle stopped behind me. Thinking there must be something wrong with my car, I was shocked when an old Army buddy I hadn't seen in 20 years stepped up and shook my hand. We reminisced for a while and then, just before we parted company, I asked him how he knew it was me driving ahead of him. "I marched behind you for years," he said. "I'd recognize the back of your head anywhere!"

— BEN KENT

Supportive Spouses?

Before my husband left for a military-training class one day, he asked me to iron his dress whites for an important inspection the next evening. Having just been married, I ironed the uniform with great zeal, keen to prove my capabilities as a Navy wife and eager for my husband to make a good impression on his superiors. When he came home the following night, he told me that he had passed his inspection and that the commanding officer had said to congratulate me. "Why?" I asked, mystified. "For ironing out the permanent creases that were supposed to be in my uniform!" he replied.

— LYNN MUCICA

Not long ago, a friend in the Army married a woman who was also in the service. The ceremony went splendidly, but my friend's rather domineering mother looked grim throughout the proceedings. At the reception I remarked on this to a major, who also happened to be the couple's commanding officer. "Have you met the bride?" he asked. After I told him I had not, he smiled, drew closer and whispered, "That was no wedding. That was a change-of-command ceremony."

— CHRISTOPHER WIST

Halfway through dinner one night, our friend Jim told us of his days playing football in college as a defensive lineman. "Did you play sports in college, Mike?" his wife then asked me. "Yes," I answered. "I was on West Point's shooting team." "That's great," she said, appropriately impressed. "Offense or defense?"

— MIKE MALONEY

★ ★ ★ ★ ★ ★ ★ ★ ★ ★ ★ ★ ★ ★ ★ ★ ★

One fall, my husband and I attended the San Diego State–Navy football game in San Diego. During halftime I went to a pay phone to check in with my kids but found a sailor in the nearest booth having a teary conversation with his sweetheart. Being a Navy wife, I knew how hard it was being separated from loved ones, so I gladly gave him room for his conversation. My sympathy subsided, however, when I heard his last heartfelt statement: "You know I'd be there with you, honey," he said emotionally, "but I'm stuck here in Virginia."

— TERESA CHRISTENSON

At Fort Riley, Kan., the soldiers' wives were asked to bake treats for a party. My brownies did not turn out well, and I told my husband I would be embarrassed if no one ate them. As a group of soldiers filed in, however, I noticed they bypassed other goodies in favor of mine. I was flattered until I heard one soldier ask my husband, "Hey, Sarge, are these the brownies you told us we better eat, or else?"

— ELIZABETH RADDATZ

Faced with yet another change of bases, I had the unenviable task of packing up our two young children and all our household goods and moving to a new home—without the help of my Air Force husband. One day, after a week of complete chaos as I unpacked and made the other necessary arrangements, I heard the doorbell. When I opened the door, I found a dozen red roses and a small card from my husband. The card said, "Honey, you still move me."

— AUDREY L. MURPHY

This one?
That's my cell phone.

★ ★ ★ ★ ★ ★ ★ ★ ★ ★ ★ ★ ★ ★ ★ ★ ★ ★ ★

As a sergeant stationed at Fort Meade, Md., I was recommended for a promotion. I had to appear before a promotion board as part of the process, and answer questions about everything from current events to military history. Just when I thought I had successfully completed the interrogation, one first sergeant asked me, "What is the significance of March 9?" My mind raced through the possibilities, but after several tense minutes I gave up and replied, "First Sergeant, I do not know the significance of March 9." "Too bad," he said. "I'm sure your wife would be pleased to hear that you forgot her birthday."

— CWO2 THOMAS M. KANNENBERG

When I entered the Marine Corps, we were authorized to wear only white crewneck T-shirts with our uniforms. While I didn't always keep mine neatly folded and put away, I did separate them by quality. The newest T-shirts were used when I wore my service uniforms, the next best were for wear with utilities or flight suits, and the oldest were for sweaty jobs like mowing the grass. When I got married, my wife began to do my laundry and although she did a much better job, she didn't separate my T-shirts. One day, after I complained that I could not find the "right" T-shirt, I came home to find them neatly folded in three stacks. They were labeled "The Good," "The Bad" and "The Ugly."

— ROY D. BRYANT

My husband, Douglas, and I were driving around Luke Air Force Base in Arizona where we had recently been stationed. In front of us was a blue military truck bearing the letters S.W.A.T. and a sign advising people to stay at a safe distance. Suddenly the truck stopped, and several soldiers jumped out. I commented to Douglas that something exciting must have happened—and we were about to witness a dramatic scene. Douglas looked at me and laughed. He explained that S.W.A.T stands for "seeds, weeds and trash." The soldiers were assigned to keep the base clean.

— WENDY MOORE

During our preparation for Operation Desert Storm, I had to make sure the entire crew received immunizations. Our commanding officer, a macho guy, was the most difficult to get to sick bay. He finally showed up late one Friday afternoon. I explained to him that the shots might make him slightly feverish and cranky. "I'll come back on Monday, then," he replied. "Why?" I asked. "Would you rather be irritable to the crew or your wife?" "Doc," he declared, "I'm not afraid of the crew."

— DAVID L. KING

At the completion of our week-long training seminar, 40 of us Naval Reserve chaplains went to Los Angeles International Airport to catch flights home. Dressed in my chaplain uniform, I was walking to the boarding gate when the ticket collector pulled me aside. "I've been watching chaplains get on flights out of Los Angeles all afternoon," she said. "Is something going on that I should know about?"

— WILLIAM W. GASSER

★ ★ ★ ★ ★ ★ ★ ★ ★ ★ ★ ★ ★ ★ ★ ★ ★

Soon after being transferred to a new duty station, my Marine husband called home to tell me he would be late—again. He went on to say that dirty magazines had been discovered in the platoon's quarters and they had to police the area. I launched into a tirade, arguing that many men had pictures hanging in their quarters at our previous post, so his new platoon should not be penalized for something trivial. My husband calmly listened to my gripes and then explained, "Kathy, dirty magazines: the clips from their rifles had not been properly cleaned."

— KATHY ROZINA

As a recruit nearing the completion of basic training at Fort Knox, I was looking forward to my leave home. After 13 weeks of sleeping on the ground, eating army food, and being tormented by drill sergeants, all I could think of was clean sheets, Mom's cooking and some relaxation. Arriving in Boston the day after graduation, I was greeted by my joyous family. "Just wait until you hear about the camping trip we've planned," exclaimed my mother.

— CURT J. CARLSON

Preparing for our wedding, I signed up for dance lessons with my fiancé, an Army sergeant at Fort Meade, Md. We were doing pretty well one day until we got to a complicated turn sequence. My fiancé lost his direction and we both stumbled. "My mistake," my fiancé apologized. **"As you were."**

— A. HICKS

★ ★ ★ ★ ★ ★ ★ ★ ★ ★ ★ ★ ★ ★ ★ ★ ★

My husband's two friends delivered a briefing while taking a course on tactical operations. When they were through, the instructor said the presentation was good, but it had failed to distinguish between engagements and battles. The teacher grew frustrated when no one in the class volunteered to explain that a battle is a series of smaller engagements. "Everyone was responsible for last night's reading assignment," he said. "Surely someone knows the difference." "I know," my husband finally offered. "An engagement is what precedes a wedding, and the battle is what follows."

— KAREN SOTO

I was stationed in Germany as a furniture-supply clerk. My duties included supervising civilian moving crews when an officer changed residences. On one job, a newly promoted Army major general was moving to larger quarters, and, although they weren't my regular men, the crew seemed to be doing well. One fellow, however, carried nothing but small items while the rest lugged the heavy furniture. I informed him in German that if he couldn't carry his fair share, he should sit in the truck and stay out of the way. "Specialist," the general cheerfully replied in English, "that is exactly what my wife told me."

— STEVE RIEPE

LaST ★
LAUGH

★ ★ ★ ★ ★ ★ ★ ★ ★ ★ ★ ★ ★ ★ ★ ★ ★ ★ ★

My unit at Fort Bliss in Texas was detailed with guard duty. However, since live ammunition was reserved for sensitive locations, our rifles were issued with unloaded magazines. One day while we stood at attention for inspection, the officer in charge confronted a private and barked, "What is the maximum effective range of your M-16, soldier?" The hapless private glanced down at his empty rifle and replied, "As far as I can throw it, sir."

— JAN GETTING

After a few rough years, my cousins and their son Jim decided it'd be best if he tried the rigid structure of the military. Since he'd never been one for following rules, we wondered how he'd adjust. It wasn't long before we got our answer. Once he'd completed basic training, he took a two-day drive across the country to his new assignment. Mid-morning on the second day, my cousin was surprised to receive a call from his son, who was still at his hotel. "Why aren't you on the road yet?" he asked. "Well, I'm all ready to go, Dad," Jim replied, "but the sign on the door says, 'Checkout at 11 a.m.'"

— KEN LYNCH

Our air national guard unit conducted weapons-qualifying at the firing range. We had been issued our last round of ammo and were firing at the silhouettes, when a gust of wind ripped the targets from their frames and they fluttered away. Firing stopped as we looked to the range officials. "Keep shooting, boys," a voice yelled. "We've got 'em on the run now!"

— CHRIS B. WITTEK

★ ★ ★ ★ ★ ★ ★ ★ ★ ★ ★ ★ ★ ★ ★ ★ ★

While stationed at Fort Rucker, Ala., where helicopter pilots are trained, I learned to identify the different copters by their sound alone. Early one morning, I was awakened when one buzzed my barracks. I ran through the possibilities, but couldn't identify it. Intrigued by what kind of helicopter it could be, I sprinted to the window just in time to see the single engine, twin-bladed main rotor lawn mower come into view.

— KAREN BOEHLER

We were using live ammunition during maneuvers in Germany when a phosphorus flare fell short, coming perilously close to me and some of my buddies. We did what most people do under such circumstances—we ran for our lives. "Get back to your weapons!" shouted the officer in charge. "Why are you men running?" As one private ran past him, he answered the officer, "Because we can't fly, sir."

— MYRON EPSTEIN

After completing medical officers basic training, I was assigned to a small Army post in a Boston suburb. I arrived after dark and was directed to my quarters. The next morning a noncommissioned officer escorted me to the commander's office. As we exited the barracks, I looked toward Massachusetts Bay and noticed the back of a large curved device supported by a labyrinth of steel girders. Anxious to impress the NCO with my new knowledge of the Army's air-defense system, I pointed to the structure and said, "So that's our primary target acquisition radar?" "No, sir," the sergeant replied. "That's the back of the drive-in movie screen."

— SOURCE UNKNOWN

★ ★ ★ ★ ★ ★ ★ ★ ★ ★ ★ ★ ★ ★ ★ ★ ★ ★ ★

A pair of night-vision goggles sets Uncle Sam back a pretty penny. So just before night maneuvers, as my son-in-law handed a pair to a young private with a reputation for losing things, he warned, "Hold on to these!" Afterward, my son-in-law ran into the private, who said, "I have good news and bad news." "You lost those goggles?" "No, of course not." "So what's the bad news?" "I lost the Humvee."

— CONNIE STACY

The Art of Communication

As a department head stationed on a Navy vessel, I was concerned about one of my senior enlisted men. He was a superb technician, but he had a problem taking orders. One day I took him aside and suggested he try something that had worked for me. "Whenever an officer gives you a directive that you think is stupid," I told him, "just say, 'Yes, sir.' But in your mind, think, 'You're an idiot!' Will this work for you?" He smiled at me and replied, "Yes, sir!"

— LEO KING

My thick Southern accent is often a source of miscommunication. One night while driving through base housing, I saw four skunks crossing the road. The next day I told my supervisor what I saw. "So did you get Tom Hanks' autograph?" he asked. "Excuse me?" I said, puzzled. "Didn't you say you saw Forrest Gump in base housing last night?"

— ERIC GRUBBS

★ ★ ★ ★ ★ ★ ★ ★ ★ ★ ★ ★ ★ ★ ★ ★ ★ ★ ★

The base's public-address system is the simplest way to call the troops—just shout out the soldiers' last names, tell them where they're needed, and they'll hustle right over. But there was some head-turning the day I summoned these two privates to assist the chaplain: "Pope, Paul, please report to the orderly room."

— GREG KNOBLOCK

My wife, Dolores, never quite got the hang of the 24-hour military clock. One day she called the orderly room and asked to speak with me. The person who answered told her to call me at the extension in the band rehearsal hall. "He can be reached at 4700, ma'am," the soldier advised. With a sigh of exasperation, my wife responded, "And just what time is that?"

— ERIC D. ERICKSON

★ ★ ★ ★ ★ ★ ★ ★ ★ ★ ★ ★ ★ ★ ★ ★ ★ ★

One night at McChord Air Force Base in Washington, I was dispatched to check out the security fence where an alarm had gone off. The fence was at the end of the base runway. When I got to the scene, I found that a raccoon was the culprit, so I ran around and flapped my arms to scare off the animal. Suddenly an air-traffic controller came over the public-address system and announced loudly, "Attention to the airman at the end of the runway. You are cleared for takeoff."

— CHAD BLAKE

As his destroyer entered fabled Pearl Harbor, my friend stood alongside a cocky lieutenant and the Hawaiian harbor pilot. "So tell me," said the lieutenant to the pilot, "is your state pronounced 'Huh-WI-ee' or 'Huh-VI-ee'?" "We say 'Huh-VI-ee,' " the pilot answered. "And that sign over there," asked the lieutenant, pointing ashore, "is it pronounced 'Pi-Pee-Lie-Nee'?" "You could say it that way," said the pilot. "But we Huh-VI-ans usually just say 'Pipeline.'"

— BRUCE CLARK

My helicopter aircrew was into its seventh hour of flying replenishment missions to Navy battle groups off the coast of Sicily when we approached a ship for landing, only to be told we had to circle overhead. Just as I was beginning to get nervous because we were running low on fuel, my crew chief asked me to fly down and hover alongside the ship's bridge. I obliged and I could see the captain of the ship look at us, then frantically pick up the phone. Within seconds we were given clearance to land. "What did you do?" I asked the crew chief, amazed. "Not much," he answered nonchalantly. "I just held their mailbag out the door."

— KIM SHELDON

★ ★ ★ ★ ★ ★ ★ ★ ★ ★ ★ ★ ★ ★ ★ ★ ★

Rocks and Other Difficulties

My parents scoffed, but I knew my college degree in geology would come in handy one day. It was during basic training, at Sheppard Field, Texas, and I was pulling KP duty. When the sergeant asked me what I did in civilian life, I proudly announced that I was a geologist. "Good. I'm looking for someone with your background," he said, while dropping a bulging sack onto the table. "You've got just the right qualifications to pick the rocks out of this hundred pounds of beans."

— RALPH NICHOLS

While a friend and I were visiting at Annapolis, we noticed there were several students on their hands and knees assessing the courtyard with pencils and clipboards in hand. "What are they doing?" I asked our tour guide. "Each year," he replied with a grin, "the upperclassmen ask the freshmen how many bricks it took to finish this courtyard." "So what's the answer?" my friend asked him when we were out of earshot of the freshmen. The guide replied simply, "One."

— GREGORY BOKENKAMP

While stationed with the Strategic Air Command,
I found a memo typed on official letterhead.
At the bottom of the letterhead was our motto:
"Peace is our profession." Beneath that, someone had added: "Bombing is only a hobby."

— DAVID FRENCH

★ ★ ★ ★ ★ ★ ★ ★ ★ ★ ★ ★ ★ ★ ★ ★ ★ ★

 Don't worry, these sand storms never last
more than an hour.

★ ★ ★ ★ ★ ★ ★ ★ ★ ★ ★ ★ ★ ★ ★ ★ ★

Out of the navy and ready to buy my own home, I filled out the veterans loan forms and mailed them away. But what I didn't realize was that I had placed the forms in the envelope containing a lock of hair from my two-year-old son's first haircut. Two weeks later I received this note: "Enclosed is your loan certificate. Regardless of what you were told, we really don't need a sample of your DNA."

— FRANCIS T. JIMMIS

The first thing I noticed when I picked up my clothes from the off-base laundry was that they reeked. So the next week, I sent my clothes over with a note complaining, "My laundry had a peculiar musty odor when I got it back." When my clothes were returned, I found the following appended to my note: "How do you think it smelled when we got it?"

— ROBERT EDDY

When I was stationed in Würzburg, Germany, I ran several miles every day along the beautiful Main River. Once, several fellow lieutenants, all men, joined me. For the first half of the run I was able to keep up with them. However, on the return I started to fall behind. "How are you doing back there?" one of the guys called. "Fine," I replied. I didn't want to admit I couldn't keep up with their fast pace, so looking past the river to the vineyard-covered hills, I said, "I'm just enjoying the view." One lieutenant, running easily in his skimpy nylon shorts, hollered back, "Thanks!"

— VIRGINIA B. TAYLOR

★ ★ ★ ★ ★ ★ ★ ★ ★ ★ ★ ★ ★ ★ ★ ★ ★

When my Navy Medical Reserve Unit was called up for Operation Desert Storm, I was awakened by a phone call at three o'clock on a Sunday morning with the order to report for duty in four hours for processing. After I hung up the phone, my husband groggily asked, "Who was that?" "Oh, honey," I moaned, thinking of our 15-month-old child, "I have to go to war!" "Don't worry," he said as he rolled over, "It's Sunday, and the traffic won't be bad."

— LINDA P. DEMARCHE

My former boyfriend, Duncan, was an officer in the Naval Reserve. One day while stopped at a red light, his car was rear-ended. As the other driver, a sailor, approached, his eyes widened when he saw the lieutenant's uniform. "It gets even better," Duncan said with a smirk. "I'm also a lawyer."

— BATYAH CHLIEK

Friends of ours were driving along the road one day when they collided with a camouflaged Army truck. Everyone was okay, but when asked by the soldiers what had happened, our friends told them, "We just never saw you coming."

— ANGIE MANSFIELD

Aboard the USS *Tarawa* for six months, my brother, Don, posted a picture of his beloved truck in his locker. Since his fellow Marines had pictures of their girlfriends up, they often ridiculed him for his object of adoration. "Laugh all you want," Don told them. "At least my truck will still be there when I get home!"

— SHERRY TOMBOC

★ ★ ★ ★ ★ ★ ★ ★ ★ ★ ★ ★ ★ ★ ★ ★ ★

As I guided an elderly safety inspector on a trip around an oil rig out at sea, I invited him to take the helm. "Turn to port," I said, adding, "that's left to you. Now, turn starboard—that means right." Having circled the rig, I joked, "Now, give the boat back to the driver." As he did so, I asked him about his career. "Navy," he said. "Twenty years. Submarines." Then he leaned in. "I was the driver."

— BRUCE MILLAR

Respectfully Submitted

I was sending out military recruitment pitches when I found one addressed to a guy named "Lord." When I filled in the form letter, it read, thanks to some strange computer glitch, "Dear Lord, I need to speak to you as soon as possible regarding your service to your country." I laughed and mailed it off. Weeks later, the letter was returned with a note: "The Lord doesn't live here. If you find his address, let me know. I also need to speak with him."

— MATTHEW WELDY

During basic training, our drill sergeant asked all Jewish personnel to make themselves known. Six of us tentatively raised our hands. Much to our relief, we were given the day off for Rosh Hashanah. A few days later, in anticipation of Yom Kippur, the sergeant again asked for all Jewish personnel to identify themselves. This time, every soldier raised his hand. "Only those who were Jewish last week can be Jewish this week," declared the sergeant.

— ALLEN ISRAEL

★ ★ ★ ★ ★ ★ ★ ★ ★ ★ ★ ★ ★ ★ ★ ★ ★ ★

I was on board the USS *Kitty Hawk* when we docked in the Sri Lankan capital, Colombo. One morning, as the local fishing fleet passed by on its way out to sea, a boat came too close to our ship. A Marine held up a sign warning the captain to stay away, and he complied. But the next day, the boat was back. This time, the fisherman held something. The nervous Marine pointed to his rifle. The fisherman lifted the object and unfurled it, revealing a sign of his own. In perfect English it read "Your Sign Is Upside Down."

— KEVIN MELIA

The sweat dripping off my brow gave away my secret: I dreaded giving blood. "This'll only take 15 minutes," said the nurse on our base. Pointing to a judge advocate general also donating a pint, I said, "She's been here longer than that." Another donor interjected, "That's because she's used to taking blood, not giving it."

— NATE SMITH

Our bomb squad commander at Fort Lewis, Washington, was testifying in court about a traffic accident. When the prosecutor began questioning her, the captain suddenly lost her voice. "I'm sorry," she said to the judge. "I guess I'm nervous." "You're nervous?" laughed the judge. **"And what exactly is it you do again?"**

— LT. DIANA MANCIA

★ ★ ★ ★ ★ ★ ★ ★ ★ ★ ★ ★ ★ ★ ★ ★ ★ ★

Although I knew our commanding officer hated doling out weekend passes, I thought I had a good reason. "My wife is pregnant and I want to be with her," I told the CO. Much to my surprise, he said, albeit curtly, "Permission granted." Inspired by my success, a fellow soldier also requested a weekend pass. His wife wasn't pregnant. So when the CO asked why he should grant him permission, my friend responded, "My wife is getting pregnant this weekend and I want to be with her."

— DOUG LADLE

My father, a retired Air Force pilot, often sprinkles his conversation with aviation jargon. I didn't realize what flying had meant to him, however, until the day he showed me the folder with his last will and testament. It was labeled "Cleared for departure."

— CHERYL E. DRAKE

As the commander made his way up front to speak, tension was high. Plans to move the Camp Lejeune Marines north for cold-weather exercises could all be for naught. "General," an officer spoke up, "there's no snow in the forecast." The general called out to a member of his battle staff. "Chaplain, I believe that's your department." "With all due respect, sir," said the chaplain, "I'm in sales, not production."

— BO RUSSELL

★ ★ ★ ★ ★ ★ ★ ★ ★ ★ ★ ★ ★ ★ ★ ★ ★

Getting Real

Some people are extremely impressed when you tell them you're a Navy SEAL. Case in point: my grandson's pre-kindergarten class. It was career day, and I was regaling them with stories of my exploits in the military. After I finished, hands shot up in the air. The kids were fascinated and eager to ask questions. "So," asked one little girl, "can you balance a ball on your nose?"

— G. A. DAVIS

I was working at the base exchange one busy day when the line grew quite long. There was much grumbling among those waiting, but one man made light of the situation. He approached a woman who was obviously very pregnant and tapped her on the shoulder. "Would you mind my asking a personal question?" he said. "Were you pregnant when you got in this line?"

— JAN BOILEAU

My father, an Air Force Academy graduate, still retains a strict military code of ethics as well as a quick wit. One day I mentioned that I was thinking about getting my bellybutton pierced. "No way!" my father fired back. "This is an Air Force family—no navel destroyers are allowed!"

— SARAH BLOMQUIST

On the wall of the mess hall of one Marine Corps base:
"This food must be good.
Ten thousand flies can't be wrong!"
— JOE TURMAN

★ ★ ★ ★ ★ ★ ★ ★ ★ ★ ★ ★ ★ ★ ★ ★ ★

I was golfing with a soldier who had just returned from Afghanistan. His plans included becoming a greens keeper once he was discharged in a few months. He applied to a local college for its golf course superintendent program, but the department chair worried that he might not be up for the job. "It's stressful," he said. "You have to fight the weather, insects and demanding club members." "Will anyone be shooting at me while I mow the grass?" asked the soldier. "Of course not." "I'll take the job."

— BILL BAILEY

Upon retiring from the service, my husband, Don, needed a new ID card showing he had gone from active duty to retirement status. But the photo taken of him was not particularly good. And he wasn't at all quiet about it. "If I have to carry that ID around with me for the rest of my life," he complained to the photographer, "I want a better picture!" "Want a better picture?" asked the photographer defiantly. "Then bring a better face."

— NANCY WALLIS

Flying into a Middle East Airport, my copilot and I reviewed our flight plan for the trip back to the USS Enterprise. We were to pick up a Navy captain, and experience had taught me that even seasoned vets turn white-knuckled during carrier landings. Once the captain was strapped in, I turned around to welcome him on board. "Sir," I asked, "will this be your first carrier landing?" Looking at me with disdain, he opened his inflatable vest to display gold wings above five rows of ribbons. "Son," he said, "I have over 500 carrier landings in jet fighters." "That's good to hear," my copilot said, winking at me, "because this will be our first."

— KENNETH J. TONELLI

★ ★ ★ ★ ★ ★ ★ ★ ★ ★ ★ ★ ★ ★ ★ ★ ★ ★

I recently returned to work after a year abroad with the Army Reserve. On my first day back, a visitor from headquarters took me aside. "How are you?" he asked, looking concerned. "Do you feel all right?" "I'm fine," I replied, nonplussed. "Great!" he said. "I heard that you were away from work for a year because you were in a wreck." It took a minute before it dawned on me what he meant. "Iraq," I said finally. "I've just come back from I-raq."

— DEREK SCHNEIDER

Eager to speak military English the way the pros do? Then remember this simple rule—the most basic word comes first. For example: Trousers, Green, Male; Truck, Cargo, 4x4. On a recent trip to the Air Force Academy commissary, I saw, written on the side of a large carton, yet another example: Melon, Water.

— JOSEPH R. SIMKINS

My office collects care packages of snack food and reading materials to be sent to the Army Reserve stationed in the Middle East. Among the suggestions for gifts was rat poison, apparently to deal with a persistent problem in their housing units. "That's a first," I said to my coworkers. "Now we're sending packages to Afghanistan containing weapons of mouse destruction."

— JOHN ALBRIGHT

At the canteen on base, we sold snacks, coffee and soda for 25 cents. One night, we decided to charge officers 50 cents. It was explained away as a "Sir charge."

— ROBERT P. THORNE

In the Navy much of our time is spent at sea, drilling for emergencies. Once when our ship was conducting simulated combat exercises, a message came over the loudspeaker: "This is a drill, torpedo hit to starboard, all hand prepare to abandon ship—land bears 090 degrees, 11 miles. Running to my abandon-ship station, I was stopped by a young seaman, apparently on his first sea tour. "Excuse me," he drawled,"but if we really had to swim for it, how would we deal with those bears?"

— RANDOLPH HERROLD

★ ★ ★ ★ ★ ★ ★ ★ ★ ★ ★ ★ ★ ★ ★ ★ ★

Our new commander was the gung-ho type, determined to shake things up on the base. No detail was too small, not even the IN and OUT trays on his desk. "Get rid of them," he told me. "I don't want them on my desk." As the supply sergeant, I knew that the company clerks relied on those trays to process work. So I offered him an alternative, which he liked. After that, one tray read CHALLENGES and the other CONQUESTS.

— ALAN ANDERSON

Like many American soldiers stationed in Saudi Arabia, I had my picture taken as I sat on a camel. I figured it would be a good souvenir to send home. A few days later, some buddies and I were visiting a local town. When we returned to our vehicle, we found two young Saudis taking each other's picture—sitting on our jeep.

— TOBIE W. JOHNSON

I didn't realize how deep the inter-service rivalry between the Navy and the Marine Corps ran until just before my son's birth. At a prenatal checkup, I asked my obstetrician, a Navy officer, what type of anesthesia he was planning to use. "You're a marine officer's wife, aren't you?" he said. "Yes," I answered. "Well, then," he replied, "You get to bite on a silver bullet."

— DALE EMKEN

ON the JOB

★ **From the Mess**

★ **In Flight**

★ ★ ★ ★ ★ ★ ★ ★ ★ ★ ★ ★ ★ ★ ★ ★ ★ ★

While my son, Cliff, was on board the Navy carrier USS *George Washington*, the air wing was busy with training missions. After talking to a pilot, one air-traffic controller accidentally left his microphone on and remarked to a nearby buddy, "That guy sounded just like Elmer Fudd." The airwaves got strangely quiet as everyone listening realized the pilot had also heard the comment. After about ten seconds, the pilot broke the silence by announcing, "Be vewy, vewy quiet. We are hunting submawenes."

— WAYNE ROBERTSON

Life on board an aircraft carrier is noisy, with jets, mechanical equipment and the dull roar of blowers circulating air. One night the ship had a massive power failure, and our berthing compartment became abruptly quiet. Everyone woke up with a start. One half-asleep seaman shouted, "What the heck was that!" From across the dark room came a voice, "That was silence, you idiot!"

— JAMES TODHUNTER

My job on our combat store ship was to make sure that the 21 three-ton forklifts on board were firmly secured and positioned to keep the ship on an even keel. One night I was told to report to the captain's stateroom. After I knocked and entered, the captain silently folded his arms, lifted his feet, then pushed himself away from his desk on his chair, which was equipped with wheels. He slowly coasted across the room to the starboard side, then said, "Dismissed." I took the hint and moved six forklifts to the port side.

— RICHARD E. KOONS

Doing tech support for the Navy, my husband is used to dealing with frustrated clients. So when a woman proceeded to spit out every curse word she'd ever heard, it didn't faze Craig. Eventually she calmed down. "Pardon my French," she said. Craig was sympathetic. "I've worked here a long time," he said, "and the one thing I've noticed about the Navy is that everyone is fluent in French."

— JENNIE PAGE

I was serving on a destroyer when we passed an old frigate off the coast of Bermuda. Looking through my binoculars, I was startled to see that the other ship was drifting into our path. Clearly it had come untethered from its anchor. I alerted my captain, who immediately contacted the frigate. "Have you lost your anchor?" he asked. The other captain responded, "No, sir. I know exactly where it is. It's five miles back."

— R. J. M. HARDY

While scrubbing the decks of our Coast Guard cutter on a scorching summer day, a few shipmates and I decided to break the rules and go for a swim. With no officers in sight, I scrambled atop a railing 40 feet above the water. Just as I leaned forward, I could see the captain step out on the bridge. Too late to stop, I did a picture-perfect dive into the ocean. When I had clambered back aboard, the captain was there to greet me. Fearing the worst, I was greatly relieved when he said, "I'll give you a ten." "Thanks, Captain," I said. "I used to dive in college." "I don't mean a score of ten," he spat back. "I mean ten days of restriction."

— RUSTY JACKSON

The crew of a fast frigate was practicing the man overboard drill by "rescuing" a bright orange fluorescent dummy dubbed Oscar. The captain watched as a young lieutenant nervously stopped the ship, turned it and maneuvered into place. Unfortunately, he ran right over Oscar. Surveying the remains of Oscar scattered around the ship, the captain told the lieutenant, "Son, do me a favor. If I ever fall overboard, just drop anchor and I'll swim to you."

— ANTHONY WATSON

We were on our destroyer's bridge when the captain noticed something wrong with our course. "I believe you're out of position," he told the junior officer. "Please come to the left a little." So the officer took a step to the left. "I don't think that's far enough," said the captain. So the officer stepped left again. "Perfect," the captain said. "Now bring the ship with you."

— FRANK COLLINS

The commander of the C-141 was in a hurry to fly out of the U.S. air base in Thule, Greenland. But everything was working against him. The truck to pump the sewage from the plane was late, and then the airman pumping out the tank was taking his time. The commander berated the lowly airman, threatening to have him punished. Turning to the officer, the airman said, "I have no stripes, it's 40 degrees below zero, I'm stationed in Thule, and I'm pumping sewage out of airplanes. Just how do you plan on punishing me?"

— JAMES STILWELL

★ ★ ★ ★ ★ ★ ★ ★ ★ ★ ★ ★ ★ ★ ★ ★ ★

My daughter, Michelle, is the commander of a Coast Guard cutter. When she gave my husband, Bob, a tour of her ship, he was impressed with the neatness of all decks. However, when Michelle brought Bob to her house, he couldn't believe the disorganization. "Why is everything in its place on your ship," he asked, "but your house is such a mess?" Michelle replied, "My house doesn't take 30-degree rolls."

— MARY ANN SCHALLIP

Dead ahead, through the pitch-black night, the captain sees a light on a collision course with his ship. He sends a signal: "Change your course ten degrees east." "Change yours ten degrees west," comes the reply. The captain responds, "I'm a United States Navy captain! Change your course, sir!" "I'm a seaman second class," the next message reads. "Change your course, sir." The captain is furious. "I'm a battleship! I'm not changing course!" "I'm a lighthouse. Your call."

— SOURCE UNKNOWN

As a retired Air Force officer vacationing in Florida, I was playing a round of golf at Pensacola Naval Air Station with three Navy officers. I marveled at the splendid course, which included a tall white stake placed in each fairway to mark 150 yards to the green. At first I feared these markers would be distracting, but I soon found they helped me aim my shots. I mentioned to my companions that distance indicators at Air Force golf courses are flush to the ground, along the edges of the fairway. "Well," one of my Navy friends remarked, "sailors play their best when they can see a mast on the horizon."

— STEVE FISH

A shore-based officer, I had the opportunity to go aboard a Navy vessel for a week of training. On the first day we were pivoting into a slip on the pier, and the commanding officer patiently explained a variety of technical terms. Wanting to increase my shipboard vocabulary, I commented on the way we were pulling into port and asked the CO if there was a term to describe our maneuver. "Yes," he answered. "We call it 'backing up.'"

— TANYA L. WALLACE

While on patrol with the Coast Guard, we stopped to help a sailor whose boat was hung up on a sandbar. I asked the owner what had happened. He gave us a lengthy description of his boating experience, then explained that his navigational chart failed to show the sandbar. Skeptical, I asked to see the chart. It was actually a place mat from a seafood restaurant.

— LANCE HANNA

The seas were rough the day the transport ship carried us to Europe. As we pitched up and down, there wasn't one soldier onboard who didn't feel seasick. To take our minds off the bleak conditions, we were invited to see a movie. What film did the captain choose to calm our frayed nerves? *The Caine Mutiny.*

— ROGER COBURN

As a seaman aboard an aircraft carrier, it was my duty to make the morning coffee for my department. After a year of this, I felt a rush of relief when, on the day before my promotion, my department chief put his arm around my shoulder and said, "Rhodes, this will be the last day you'll be making coffee as a seaman." My heart sank, however, when he added, "Tomorrow will be your first day making it as a petty officer."

— JOHN R. RHODES

After spending a few years on shore duty, I found myself back at sea trying to remember what all of the signal bells and whistles piped over the ship's intercom meant. I was beginning to catch on again when I heard an unfamiliar beeping in the chief's mess. "What's that one?" I asked. When my coworkers finally stopped laughing, they informed me it was the microwave.

— MELANIE M. PATTERSON

P. BYRNES.

 Don't worry, ma'am.
He left a **trail.**

From the Mess

Once a week we were served steak at my base's mess hall. The meat was so tough you could hardly chew it. When we complained to our colonel, he agreed to come to dinner with us to see for himself. Sure enough, the steak was tough as usual, but after the meal the colonel said nothing. A few days later he sent a memo to the sergeant in charge of the mess. It read: "Sharpen all knives immediately."

— JOHN G. DAVIS

I wanted to make my mark as the new food-service officer at a recruit training center. The menu was loaded with red meat, so I devised a new one to reduce cholesterol. I substituted chicken for beef, and awaited comments from the suggestion box. The first one summed up the recruits' feelings. It read simply, "Let the chickens live."

— RAWLINS LOWNDES

Soon after our son's ship returned to base after a six-month deployment, friends and family of the crew were given permission to tour the vessel. Lunch was served in the mess, and since I had never eaten Navy food, I decided to try a little taste of everything. As I approached some soggy-looking spinach, I pointed out to the sailor standing behind the counter, "There's no serving spoon in the spinach." "Ma'am," he responded quite apologetically, "no one's ever asked for the spinach before."

— PATRICIA K. DOYLE

★ ★ ★ ★ ★ ★ ★ ★ ★ ★ ★ ★ ★ ★ ★ ★ ★ ★ ★

I was dishing out chow to the Marines at Cherry Point, North Carolina, when an irate gunnery sergeant slammed his tray on the counter and pointed to a cooked grasshopper sitting on top of his spinach. "Look at that!" he barked. Motioning to the other Marines waiting in line, my boss, the mess sergeant, leaned over. "Keep it down, Sarge," he whispered, "or else they'll all want one."

— RON PIRKLE

"Chow looks wonderful," I told the mess sergeant, a large, intimidating man. "I'd love seconds." "You'll get the same as everyone else," he growled as he chucked food on my tray. "Now move it!" After finishing the edible portion of my meal, I dumped the rest in the garbage, accidentally tossing out my silverware. While leaning into the trash can to look for my knife and fork, I felt a tap on my shoulder. It was the mess sergeant. "It's all right, son," he said. "You can grab seconds."

— SCOTT POPE

A sign posted on the wall of an Army mess hall read: "Don't Waste Food—Food Will Win the War." Beneath these words someone had scrawled: **"That's fine, but how do we get the enemy to eat here?"**

— IRVING SCHIFF

★ ★ ★ ★ ★ ★ ★ ★ ★ ★ ★ ★ ★ ★ ★ ★ ★

While dining in the officers club at an air base in the Philippines, my wife and I lost our appetites when a rat scurried past us. "Waiter!" I said, pointing to the rodent. "What are you going to do about that?" "It's all right, sir," he said unfazed. "I've already confirmed he's a club member."

— KIRBY HUNOLT

I am a grocer's nightmare. I pinch and squeeze each piece of fruit before making my choice. One day, at the base commissary, I was in my element, manhandling all the melons before finally settling on a perfect specimen. "Excuse me," I heard, as I started for the tomatoes. It was my husband's commanding officer. "Mind showing me which one was your second choice?"

— JACKI KECK

Distrustful of Army chefs' culinary talents, my father quizzed the top cook at his base. How did he know when the food was ready to be served? Dad asked. "Easy," said the sergeant, glaring back.

"When it's burning, it's cooking. When it's smoking, it's done."

— BRIAN HENDRICKS

★ ★ ★ ★ ★ ★ ★ ★ ★ ★ ★ ★ ★ ★ ★ ★ ★ ★ ★ ★

In Flight

As he reviewed pilot crash reports, my Air Force military science professor stumbled upon this understated entry: "After catastrophic engine failure, I landed long. As I had no power, the landing gear failed to deploy and no braking was available. I bounced over the stone wall at the end of the runway, struck the trailer of a truck while crossing the perimeter road, crashed through the guardrail, grazed a large pine tree, ran over a tractor parked in the adjacent field, and hit another tree. Then I lost control."

— JOHN D. MILLARD

My uncle was a flight surgeon in the Air Force Reserve. Part of his training included practice runs with jet-fighter pilots. Sometimes they would have fun at his expense, performing aerial maneuvers in an attempt to make him sick. In the middle of one hair-raising turn, the pilot asked him how he was handling all of the flips and twists. "I'm fine," replied my uncle calmly. "Just don't forget, your physical is tomorrow."

— DREW SMITH

I was proud and excited on my first day of Air Force pilot training as I walked toward the instruction facility. From a distance I could see large letters looming over the entrance: "Through these doors pass the best pilots in the world." My pride was quickly deflated, however, as I reached the threshold and read the small, scribbled cardboard sign that had been taped to the glass by a maintenance worker. It said "Please use other door."

— JAMES BIERYLA

Military guys can't help debating which branch is the best. A friend was asked why he chose the Air Force over the Navy. "Simple, really," he said. "Whatever goes up must come down. But whatever goes down doesn't necessarily have to come up."

— JESSE DAVIS

Riding in a jet trainer for the first time was exhilarating. It was also frightening, especially when I began to think, What if we crash? "Excuse me," I said to the pilot. "Is there anything I should know in case we need to eject?" "Yes," he said. "If I say 'Go' and you say 'What?' you'll be talking to yourself."

— HARRY FOSTER

Listening to a lecture about jumping out of airplanes in an emergency made my son-in-law's classmate uneasy. "We only get one parachute?" he asked the instructor. "Where's our reserve?" "Son, you're a pilot. You're supposed to land the airplane," came the answer. "That means the parachute is your reserve."

— BARBARA GRAYDON

The topic of the day at Army Airborne School was what you should do if your parachute malfunctions. We had just gotten to the part about reserve parachutes when another student raised his hand. "If the main parachute malfunctions," he asked, "how long do we have to deploy the reserve?" Looking the trooper square in the face, the instructor replied, "The rest of your life."

— KENNETH RAUENS

★ ★ ★ ★ ★ ★ ★ ★ ★ ★ ★ ★ ★ ★ ★ ★ ★ ★ ★

My boyfriend, Tim, a mechanic, does work for the Air Force Academy. One day, a guard asked, "Mind if our new guard dog practices sniffing your truck?" Tim obliged and the dog went to work. Almost immediately, it latched onto a scent and jumped into the truck bed, sniffing furiously. Tim grew nervous. There were no drugs, no weapons. What could the dog be after? A few minutes later, the guard approached Tim. "Sorry," he said sheepishly. "Our dog ate your lunch."

— CHRISTI LIGHTCAP

The team of guys who packed our parachutes at Bitburg Air Base in Germany were a proud and cocky bunch. So much so, they posted this sign outside their shop: Depend on Us to Let You Down.

— STEVE JURACKA

After enlisting in the 82nd Airborne Division, I eagerly asked my recruiter what I could expect from jump school. "It's three weeks long," he said. "What else?" I asked. "The first week they separate the men from the boys," he said. "The second week, they separate the men from the fools." "And the third week?" I asked. "The third week, the fools jump."

— ROBERT GARDINIER

One of my first assignments for my college newspaper was to cover weekend maneuvers with the Air Force ROTC. When I boarded an ancient C-119 cargo plane for a training flight—my first time ever on a plane—a gruff sergeant strapped me into a parachute. "What do I do with this?" I asked nervously. "If we're going down," he said, "jump out of the plane and pull the rip cord." "When do I pull the rip cord?" I yelled as he walked away. "Before you hit the ground," he called back.

— JOHN H. STENGER

Following a few frantic minutes, air-traffic controllers finally made radio contact with the lost young pilot. "What was your last known position?" they asked. "When I was No. 1 for takeoff," came the reply.

— PHYLLIS NIELSON

★ ★ ★ ★ ★ ★ ★ ★ ★ ★ ★ ★ ★ ★ ★ ★ ★

During the second Gulf War, I was an Air Force colonel. I routinely flew on different aircraft to familiarize myself with their capabilities. One day I was aboard an intelligence aircraft where each crew member was surrounded by complex gear. A young major showed me his computer screen. "That's a chat screen, sir," the soldier said. "We use it to relay enemy information to the crew—like instant messaging." Nodding, I moved down the line. Flashing on an airman's screen several feet away was the warning: "Heads up—the colonel is on his way!"

— JAMES MOSCHGAT

What's the difference between a fighter pilot and a jet engine?

A jet engine stops whining when the plane shuts down.

— SOURCE UNKNOWN

One month into Marine Corps training in San Diego, Calif., we were preparing for a ten-mile march in 100-degree weather when a jeep drove up with a large radio in the back. "Who knows anything about radios?" our drill instructor asked. Several hands went up, and anticipating a ride in the jeep, recruits began listing their credentials. Everything from a degree in communications to a part-time job in a repair shop was declared. The DI listened to all the contenders, then pointed to the most qualified. "You," he barked. "Carry the radio."

— JIM SAPAUGH

★ ★ ★ ★ ★ ★ ★ ★ ★ ★ ★ ★ ★ ★ ★ ★ ★ ★ ★

As a flight instructor, one of my duties was to check out pilots who had been involved in aircraft accidents to ensure that they were proficient in emergency procedures. After completing one ride with a helicopter pilot whose engine had failed, the engine on my own helicopter suddenly gave out. As I initiated an emergency landing, I instructed my student to put out a mayday call on the radio. "Would you rather I take the controls?" he suggested. "After all, I've done this before."

— DANIEL M. JUNEAU

ONE UP

★ **The Right Stuff**

★ **Military "Maneuvers"**

★ ★ ★ ★ ★ ★ ★ ★ ★ ★ ★ ★ ★ ★ ★ ★ ★

While in the 101st Airborne Division at Fort Campbell, Ky., my husband would often pass the base mascot, an eagle in a large cage. The bird's name, Sergeant Glory, was even engraved on a nearby plaque. One morning my husband saw Sergeant Glory give his handler a nasty bite while being fed. The next day a new plaque appeared on the bird's enclosure. It read "Private Glory."

— ELISE DWOREK

At a tea for officers and their wives, the commanding general of a base delivered a seemingly endless oration. A young lieutenant grumbled to the woman sitting beside him, "What a pompous and unbearable old windbag that slob is!" The woman turned to him, her face red with rage. "Excuse me, Lieutenant. Do you have any idea who I am?" "No, ma'am," the man fumbled. "I am the wife of the man you just called an unbearable old windbag." "Oh," said the lieutenant. "And do you have any idea who I am?" "No," said the general's wife. "Thank God," said the lieutenant, getting up from his seat and disappearing into the crowd.

— MATT PARKER

My wife, Anita, worked at the Navy exchange dry cleaners while I was stationed at the submarine base in Groton, Conn. One evening a familiar-looking man in civilian clothes came to pick up his dry cleaning. Anita was sure he was on my crew and that she had met him at the "Welcome Aboard" family briefing a few weeks earlier. As she handed him his change, she said, "Excuse me, but aren't you on my husband's boat?" "No, ma'am," my commanding officer replied, "I believe your husband is on my boat."

— MICHAEL GORIUP

★ ★ ★ ★ ★ ★ ★ ★ ★ ★ ★ ★ ★ ★ ★ ★ ★ ★

When my friend Brian was at a Marine Corps boot camp, a member of his unit was having little success on the firing range with his M-16 rifle—the poor guy couldn't hit targets at any distance. He was already frustrated when an angry drill instructor jumped in his face and berated him for poor marksmanship. "You can't hit a target at 50 yards!" the instructor bellowed. "Why, I'll bet you couldn't hit a target two inches in front of your face." "Of course I could," the recruit said. "But first you'll have to back up."

— J. L. SABIN

I knew my new golfing friend, Bill, had been in the Army, so after he arrived late for three tee times, I offered a good-natured jab at his tardiness. "Bill," I said, "I wonder what they used to say in the service when you were late for roll call?" "They always said the same thing whether I was late or not," he replied. " 'Good morning, Colonel.' "

— SOURCE UNKNOWN

While checking in for a short stay at Keesler Air Force Base in Biloxi, Miss., I overheard another visiting serviceman complaining about his accommodations. He had already had a confrontation with one person, a sergeant, but was not satisfied, so he moved over to a clerk and began to grill her for information. The clerk tried her best to remain calm, but the serviceman wouldn't let up. Finally, wishing to speak to a higher authority, he asked, "Who would the sergeant call if the building were on fire?" She eyed him coolly and said, "The fire department."

— BILLY CRESWELL

★ ★ ★ ★ ★ ★ ★ ★ ★ ★ ★ ★ ★ ★ ★ ★ ★ ★

 And these are for
keeping my pants up.

My son regaled me with stories about how they do things in the modern Air Force. Being an old Air Force man myself, I scoffed at their complicated methods. "That's not the way we did it when I was in the service," I said. "Yeah," he shot back. "But when you were in, there were only two pilots, Wilbur and Orville."

— TED SHIRLEY

★ ★ ★ ★ ★ ★ ★ ★ ★ ★ ★ ★ ★ ★ ★ ★ ★

The lieutenant wanted to use a pay phone but didn't have change for a dollar. He saw a private mopping the floors and asked him, "Soldier, do you have change for a dollar?" "I sure have, buddy," the private answered. Giving him a mean stare, the lieutenant said, "That's no way to address an officer. Let's try it again. Private, do you have change for a dollar?" "No, sir," the private replied.

— GEORGE MELLO

The Right Stuff

While on a Coast Guard cutter in Narragansett Bay, Rhode Island, my radar-room staff was being tested on navigating by radar. We were able to tell the bridge what course to steer, based on the land, buoys and other ships spotted on the screen. But we could never tell what type of ships they were—all we saw were blips. At one point, our radar operator identified a target as the Newport ferry, supplying its course and speed. After he received a top score, with extra credit for identifying the ship, I asked him how he had known what it was. He took the ferry schedule out of his pocket.

— DONALD J. KAYTON

Conducting a study of sexual behavior, a researcher poses this question to an older Air Force pilot: "When did you last make love?" "Nineteen fifty-nine," he answers. "That's an awfully long time," she says. "I suppose," says the pilot, glancing at his watch. "But it's only twenty-one fifteen now."

— JOHN CLEESE, in *Life and How to Survive It*

★ ★ ★ ★ ★ ★ ★ ★ ★ ★ ★ ★ ★ ★ ★ ★ ★

On one of our ROTC field-training exercises we were required to fire flares. A fellow cadet and I managed to misfire and start a brush fire. We immediately called range control, and they promptly responded with fire-fighting equipment to put out the blaze. I had to set off a second flare and it, too, misfired, causing another fire. Once again, I called range control. Two weeks later our unit received a commendation for quick fire reporting.

— CLAYTON AHLFIELD

Stopping for a light at a Florida intersection, I noticed the car in front of me was stalled. Another motorist had stopped to help the woman push her car out of the way, but they were getting nowhere. A white van pulled alongside the disabled vehicle. Out jumped six Marines in full dress uniform. They jogged in unison, three to each side of the car, and without breaking cadence rolled the vehicle around the corner and into a parking lot. They then saluted the driver and leapt back into their van, never missing a beat. The door closed, and the van rolled on.

— GAIL W. KEISLER

Docked in St. Thomas in the Caribbean, the first thing I noticed was graffiti that screamed, "Yankees, Go Home."
Underneath, a sailor had scrawled,
"Red Sox, Free Drinks at the Bar."
— JASON CAIN

★ ★ ★ ★ ★ ★ ★ ★ ★ ★ ★ ★ ★ ★ ★ ★ ★

A new Navy wife, my sister, Gina, drove to Millington, Tenn., to join her husband. After an exhausting 18-hour drive, she pulled up to the gate and told the guard that her husband was stationed there. "Do you have a sticker?" the guard asked. "Ummm, yes, I do," she said, confused. "It's on the back." The sentry was skeptical as he walked to the rear of her car. But when he bent down to have a look, he smiled and waved her on. The sticker read "Go Navy."

— JAN ROLLYSON

Military "Maneuvers"

Everyone in my Army Reserve unit is required to complete an annual physical-fitness test. As my group neared the halfway point of our 2 1/2-mile run last year, one of the monitors shouted, "It helps to focus on a point far out ahead of you!" "Yeah," agreed one of the veterans, "like my retirement."

— SFC. DAVID GRANT

I run sophisticated weather programs on multimillion-dollar supercomputers at a Navy center for environmental predictions. On the morning Hurricane Opal was heading for the Florida coast, my boss, a Navy commander, gave me detailed reports on the hurricane's status to pass along to a friend who has family in the area. Fascinated by his ability to summon up-to-date reports so quickly, I asked him how to do it. He gave me a puzzled look and said, "Simple. Go turn on the television and watch the Weather Channel."

— JOANNE MILLER

While I was attending an advanced infantry training class, the MPs decided to stage a drug raid in our barracks to break in the post's newest search dog. When I returned to my quarters later that evening, the sergeant informed me of the search. Alarmed at the tone of her voice, I became increasingly nervous as she described how the dog, straining at the leash, led the MPs to the bottom drawer of my dresser. A variety of scenarios raced through my mind, but none explained why the dog would behave that way. Finally the sergeant put me out of my misery. "Why," she asked, "did you have a ham sandwich in your dresser?"

— CAROL A. COOPER

Our new elementary school was raising the American flag for the first time. To make the day special, we invited a Marine Corps color guard to come out and perform the duty for us. The day before the ceremony, the Marine in charge of the unit called to confirm directions to the school. After doing so, he was asked by our secretary whether he was sending Marines who like children. There was a brief pause on the other end of the line before the man replied, "Ma'am, if I tell them to like children, they will like children."

— ANN CUNNINGHAM

I was a young, hard-charging Marine corporal stationed in Okinawa when I took a course in map reading. After completing it, I reported my success to the company office. The commanding officer, a crusty Vietnam veteran, congratulated me. Knowing the major was strict about haircuts, though, I braced myself for a reprimand because I had missed my weekly trim. Instead, he asked if I could help him out using my new map-reading skills. Saying it would be a career-enhancing opportunity, he gave me precise coordi-

★ ★ ★ ★ ★ ★ ★ ★ ★ ★ ★ ★ ★ ★ ★ ★ ★ ★ ★

nates and told me to report back to him with what I found. Eagerly I pulled out the map and a compass and followed it while daydreaming about a promotion to sergeant. And then I arrived at my destination—a barbershop.

— CHARLES B. BROWN, JR.

One night at Coast Guard boot camp, a talented shipmate entertained our barracks with uncanny impressions of various officers. While most of us were in stitches, our recruit company commander warned the comic to stop his antics. When he was ignored, the overzealous recruit snitched. The following morning, our resident comedian was summoned to the commander's office, where he was confronted by the three subjects of his impressions and ordered to imitate them to their faces. They found his performance hilarious and sent him on his way with one proviso: he tell the "bootlicker" to report to the commander's office immediately. That afternoon we had a new recruit company commander when our aspiring comedian was promoted to the "recently vacated position."

— MICHAEL C. CORSEN

I was loading our aircraft carrier with supplies when an ensign saw one of my friends spit on the hangar floor, which was already covered with oil and refuse. The officer was appalled. "Sailor," he demanded, "would you spit on your floor at home?" "No, sir," my friend replied. "But I wouldn't land airplanes on my roof either."

— MICKEY HOMAN

★ ★ ★ ★ ★ ★ ★ ★ ★ ★ ★ ★ ★ ★ ★ ★ ★ ★

Soon after graduating from the Primary Leadership Development Course at Fort Campbell in Kentucky, I bragged to my first sergeant about how well I did in the land-navigation exercise. Looking at me skeptically, the first sergeant handed me a map of the base, a compass and a set of coordinates. Then he ordered me to find his designated point and call in. When I reached the coordinates, it turned out to be the PX. I found a pay phone and contacted the first sergeant. "Great job!" he declared. "Now that you're there, could you bring me some lunch?"

— SGT. KENNETH J. ALMODOVAR

When I was in Bosnia, a group of Marines returned from a four-day patrol in five beat-up Chevy pickups and ten Humvees. After receiving a box meal and a cup of coffee, the men wanted to shower at camp five miles away. A group headed for camp in the pickups. I was surprised to see the others wait in the rain for the pickups to return rather than drive the Humvees. I asked a gunnery sergeant why no one wanted to ride in the Humvees. Swallowing a gulp of coffee, he replied, "Humvees don't have cup holders."

— LT. G.A. KILLINGBECK

While my wife and I were vacationing in Hawaii, we went to see the USS *Arizona* Memorial but got lost and ended up at a gate manned by a young Marine. After he gave me directions to the memorial, I thanked him and said, "Have a nice day." As I was about to leave he said, "Sir, I'm 20 years old, single and stationed in Hawaii. Every day is a nice day."

— MICHAEL CRAIN

★ ★ ★ ★ ★ ★ ★ ★ ★ ★ ★ ★ ★ ★ ★ ★ ★ ★

Excellence First was the motto of my Army company at Fort Gordon, Ga., and we were required to repeat it every time we greeted an officer. One afternoon, however, I met a second lieutenant at the entrance of the building where I work and forgot to recite the motto. After receiving a scolding for my breach of protocol, I reached out to open the door for him, but he said, "No, allow me." As I walked through the open door, I nodded to him and said without thinking, "Excellence First!"

— JEFFREY A. HURSEY

As an Army media analyst for a military press information center in Sarajevo, one of our more monotonous tasks was editing the transcripts of our daily briefings and press conferences. During one conference, however, it was driven home to me how important this job was. After a British general had referred to snipers in the area as the "lunatic fringe" during a press conference, one of our young officers was reading the transcript when he piped up, "Sir, the transcribers apparently know who the snipers are!" "Who?" I asked with great interest. "The lunatic French!"

— CHESTER A. KROKOSKI, JR.

Going over our weekly training schedule one morning at our small Army garrison, we noticed that our annual trip to the rifle range had been canceled for the second time, but that our semiannual physical-fitness test was still on as planned. "Does it bother anyone else," one soldier asked, "that the Army doesn't seem concerned with how well we can shoot, yet is extremely interested in how fast we can run?"

— THOMAS L. HAMMOND

★ ★ ★ ★ ★ ★ ★ ★ ★ ★ ★ ★ ★ ★ ★ ★ ★ ★

In officer's training at the Army's Aberdeen, Md., Proving Ground, our class received instruction on sophisticated equipment. During one class, I was fascinated by an expensive-looking computer. The instructor bragged that it was able to withstand nuclear and chemical attacks. I was duly impressed. But then the instructor abruptly stopped his lecture and turned to me. "Lieutenant, there will be no eating or drinking in my class," he snapped. "You'll have to get rid of that coffee!" "Sure ... but why?" I inquired meekly. "Because," he scolded, "a coffee spill could ruin the keyboard."

— JEANNE T. WHITAKER

MILITARY WiSDOM

★ **Just a Little Red Tape**

★ **Reading the Signals**

★ ★ ★ ★ ★ ★ ★ ★ ★ ★ ★ ★ ★ ★ ★ ★ ★ ★ ★

The military leaves nothing to chance, as shown by a Department of Defense manual that includes the definition of what a first page is: "If the document has no front cover, the first page will be the front page. If it has a cover, the first page is defined as the first page you see when you open the cover. In some documents, the title page and the first page may be the same."

— ELEUTERIO EVANGELISTA

Soldiers' combat clothing is not supposed to be ironed, according to an unwritten rule. That, however, did not prevent one sergeant from slightly massaging the regulation. "Gentlemen," said the sergeant to his troops, "I cannot order you to press your combat dress. Nevertheless, for tomorrow's parade, uniforms will be allowed only four wrinkles, with one wrinkle running directly down the center and rear of each leg."

— CAPT. JAMES FISHER

With several years of Army National Guard duty under his belt, my roommate applied for officer training. But his lifelong dreams were dashed after he failed the eye exam. "That's too bad," I sympathized. "Does that mean you now have to quit the Guard entirely?" "No, I get to keep my old job," he said. "Driving trucks."

— DIANE HASTINGS

Our bulletin announced the upcoming Secretary of the Army Awards, given to those who "reduce consumption of printed material. Submit nominations using DA Form 1256 (include six copies) plus all documentation."

— WILLIAM PAQUIN

★ ★ ★ ★ ★ ★ ★ ★ ★ ★ ★ ★ ★ ★ ★ ★ ★

I've concluded that the military has more rules than bullets. What convinced me? A simple memo. "To whom it may concern," it began innocently enough. "This memo was misdirected to my department and I am forwarding it on to you. I have erased my initials and initialed my erasure."

— BRUCE CARNAHAN

When his jeep got stuck in the mud during a war game, our commanding officer pointed to some men lounging around and told them to help. "Sorry, sir," said one. "We've been classified dead." "Okay," said the CO. Turning to his driver, he ordered, "Throw those dead bodies under the wheels to give us traction."

— CATHERINE MOUNT

It took forever, but dog tags for my new chief petty officer arrived just days before we were shipping out. Trouble was, the tags listed him as Catholic, not Protestant. "I really should get them replaced," he said. "Don't bother," I told him. "It'll be faster and easier to convert."

— LESTER E. STILLWELL

My father, a Navy man, had the good fortune to be stationed in Hawaii—but the bad fortune to have fair skin. One day, after spending many hours under the hot sun, he reported back to duty with a terrible sunburn. Expecting sympathy, he was, instead, reprimanded by his superiors and then written up for **"destruction of government property."**

— LORA TEBBETTS

I was charged by the Coast Guard to buy a house near Station Rockland in Maine to be converted into military housing. But after many delays on our part, the owners' lawyer got antsy. "I don't like working with the government," the man said. "I'm not sure I'd even trust one of your checks." "I wouldn't worry," I replied. "Not only do we print our own checks, we also print the money to back them up."

— BRUCE HERMAN

While trying to order an Air Force publication online, I stumbled upon a unique way the staff had found to deal with their back-order troubles. They had resolved the problems processing back orders, they said. "However, in order to implement the solution, we will have to cancel all back orders before we resume operations."

— JAMES WITMER

Just a Little Red Tape

My friend's husband, responsible for the overall closing of a military base, was reviewing voluminous files. He found some old records that were of no possible value, and sent a letter to Washington requesting permission to destroy them. The reply he received read as follows: "Permission is given to destroy the records, but please make triplicate copies of them first."

— JEANIE L. SORENSEN

"Working on nuclear submarines is not hazardous," a military lecturer insisted. The soldiers in the audience were skeptical, but he persisted. "For example," he said, "some seamen stay on board for three to four years. And at the same time, their wives give birth to perfectly healthy babies."

— DONCHO KAROVV

My son, Barry, came home from a three-month deployment aboard his submarine, and told us that one of the ways the sailors kept up morale was to make wooden cars out of kits and run derby races. "What do you do for a ramp?'" my husband inquired. "Don't need one," Barry said. "We just put the cars on the floor and then tilt the sub."

— MARY C. RYAN

★ ★ ★ ★ ★ ★ ★ ★ ★ ★ ★ ★ ★ ★ ★ ★ ★

I was scrubbing the bulkhead on the USS *Kitty Hawk* one Sunday when the loudspeaker announced: "Religious services. Maintain silence about the decks. Knock off all unnecessary work." An hour later, the opinion many of us held regarding our daily routine was confirmed with the announcement: "Resume all unnecessary work."

— KENNETH BOOKS

Reading the Signals

The military is known for two things: secrets and acronyms. When my husband's public-affairs unit was reorganized, these office names were proposed—News Operations, News Operations Technology, and News Operation Web. Or, in military acronym-speak, "NO, NOT, NOW."

— MONICA YACENDA

One of my jobs in the Army is to give service members and their families tours of the demilitarized zone in South Korea. Before taking people to a lookout point to view North Korea, we warn visitors to watch their heads climbing the stairs, as there is a low overhang. The tour guide, first to the top, gets to see how many people have not heeded his advice. On one tour I watched almost an entire unit hit their heads one after another as they came up the stairs. Curious, I asked their commander what unit they were from. "Military intelligence," he replied.

— EDWARD RAMIREZ

★ ★ ★ ★ ★ ★ ★ ★ ★ ★ ★ ★ ★ ★ ★ ★ ★ ★

As I drove past the Post Exchange one afternoon, the pickup truck in front of me suddenly stopped. The driver shouted to a private on the sidewalk, "How do I get to the gym?" The PFC pointed ahead and instructed the driver to make several turns. The man in the truck didn't understand, so the PFC repeated his directions. Still confused, the truck driver shook his head. Finally I decided to help. I leaned out my window and yelled, "Left, right, left!" A wide grin appeared on the driver's face. "Thanks, Sarge," he called. "Now I've got it!"

— SFC BILL ROCHE

Before we could go on leave, my division had to endure a safety briefing from the base commander. As you can imagine, the Army is very thorough, and she left nothing to chance. "If you find that you are going to be delayed," said the commander, "you need to call 555-1234. If you are arrested, call 555-1235. And finally, call 555-1236 if you are a fatality."

— SGT. SHAWN BOIKO

A maxim of war is to confuse the enemy. This job description from the Army Handbook for Joint Actions proves that our military is on the leading edge of confusion. OPSDEP: Short for Operations Deputy. By JCS charter, the Army representative is the DCSOPS. However, the ADSOPS (JA), who is the DEPOPSDEP, may act for the OPSDEP on all joint matters. The use of the term OPSDEP also includes DEPOPSDEP. OPSDEPs, or DEPOPSDEPs, can approve papers for the JCS.

— ROSS AND KATHRYN PETRAS, *THE LEXICON OF STUPIDITY*

★ ★ ★ ★ ★ ★ ★ ★ ★ ★ ★ ★ ★ ★ ★ ★ ★ ★

Living near the Army's Yakima Training Center in Washington, I often see tanks and other military vehicles perform maneuvers in the nearby hills. One day I noticed a whole crowd of tanks and jeeps, along with tents and personnel, camped in a valley just off the freeway. The vehicles and tents were painted with camouflage colors, and also covered with nets and brush in order to conceal them from view. The scene would never have caught my eye—if it weren't for the brightly colored outhouses scattered across the entire camp.

— BEN HODGE

During my first night flight, I asked my instructor what to do if the engine failed. "Get the plane gliding in a controlled descent, attempt to restart the engine and make a Mayday call," he explained. "The difference between day and night flying is that the terrain below will not be clearly visible, so turn on the landing light when you get close to the ground, and if you like what you see, land." "All right, but what if I don't like what I see?" I asked. "Turn off the landing light."

— SOURCE UNKNOWN

During his re-enlistment interview, the first sergeant asked my friend if he'd considered re-upping in the Air Force. "I wouldn't re-enlist if you made me a four-star general, gave me a million dollars and Miss America for a roommate!" he seethed. On the form, the first sergeant wrote, "Airman is undecided."

— BILL BACHMAN

★ ★ ★ ★ ★ ★ ★ ★ ★ ★ ★ ★ ★ ★ ★ ★ ★

Tax day—April 15—was looming when an elderly woman showed up at my desk at the IRS. She said she required a thick stack of tax forms. "Why so many?" I asked. "My son is stationed overseas," she said. "He asked me to pick up forms for the soldiers on the base." "You shouldn't have to do this," I told her. "It's the base commander's job to make sure that his troops have access to the forms they need." "I know," said the woman. "I'm the base commander's mother."

— DONNA BELL

In army basic training, we were required to crawl face-down on the ground under barbed-wire fencing with machine guns firing blank ammunition above us. Since I am six feet, six inches tall, however, it was impossible for me to accomplish this without my rear end sticking up in the air. No matter how hard I tried or how loudly the sergeant yelled, I couldn't keep my behind down. "Well, Private Olson," the sergeant said after I finally completed one obstacle course, "one thing's for sure—you'll never take a bullet in the head!"

— ANDRA M. OLSON

During inspection, I was hoping—praying—that our gnarly-looking sergeant would find nothing wrong with my sleeping area. He did. But much to my surprise, he was quite philosophical about it. "Son, when you're born you come from dust, and when you die you return to dust," he intoned. "Now, someone is either coming or going underneath your bed and you better get him cleaned up."

— WILLIAM GERBER

★ ★ ★ ★ ★ ★ ★ ★ ★ ★ ★ ★ ★ ★ ★ ★ ★

"**W**ho here speaks French?" demanded our sergeant. Three guys raised their hands. "Good," he said. "You get to clean the latrine. That's a French word."

— JAMES CONAHAN

A senior in high school, and a few years away from becoming a U.S. citizen, I received a recruiting call from the Army. After listening intently to how I would have my college tuition paid for, not to mention the many benefits of serving my country, I told the officer that while I was very interested, there was one problem: I was Libyan. "That's okay," he answered understandingly. "We take liberals too."

— KOLOUD TARAPOLSI

Go FIGURE

★ **Think Again**

★ **Don't Ask**

★ **Getting By**

★ ★ ★ ★ ★ ★ ★ ★ ★ ★ ★ ★ ★ ★ ★ ★ ★ ★

I was standing on the shore of a lake in Fort Polk, La., showing some soldiers how to use a compass, when I heard a collective gasp from the group. I quickly wheeled around only to catch sight of a huge alligator crouching in the mud no more than five feet away. Before I could flee for my life, one of my guys let me know I should take my time. "Don't worry, Sarge, he ain't movin'," he shouted. "He fell asleep listening to you, too."

— LARRY THOMPSON

Because of the constant movement in the military, our headquarters command marked parking spaces with acronyms representing the various job titles worthy of reserved spots. A new staff sergeant was immediately struck by the variety of vehicles owned by the person assigned one particularly choice slot—it seemed a different model was parked there each day. Curious, he looked through the base phone book to find out who was in charge of "FCFS," as the space was marked. Finally, unable to come up with the answer, he asked his coworkers if they knew. That's when he learned the acronym stood for "First Come, First Served."

— CAPT. JAMEY CIHAK

Sitting in basic communications training, we were having trouble understanding some concepts of satellite technology. "Come on, guys," the instructor said, "this isn't rocket science." After an uncomfortable pause, a courageous trainee raised his hand and said, "Sir, I'm no genius, but since we are dealing with launching satellites, I believe this actually is rocket science."

— JON REINSCH

★ ★ ★ ★ ★ ★ ★ ★ ★ ★ ★ ★ ★ ★ ★ ★ ★

As a professor at Southwest Baptist University in Bolivar, Mo., I often begin class by telling a story about my son who attends the U.S. Naval Academy. Last December, one ingenious student left me a note on the blackboard, wishing me a merry Christmas with the following words: "Feliz Navydad!"

— BING B. BAYER

There were tons of vending machines on base, and as the supply sergeant, I was responsible for all of them. So I pulled in a private and had him count the money. An hour later, he was finished. "Good," I said. "What's the count?" He replied, "I have 210 quarters, 180 dimes and 35 nickels."

— DAVID MORRIS

A friend was visiting me at Davis-Montham Air Force Base and asked me to explain various acronyms. I told him PCS means permanent change of station, NCOIC stands for noncommissioned officer in charge, and TDY is used for temporary duty. Later, we were visiting the ruins of an old fort. I mentioned that an assignment there must have been very tedious. My friend asked, "What's TDS?"

— ROBERT WIDO

Think Again

One day a young Air Force enlisted man walked into the base newspaper office where I work and said he'd like to place an advertisement. "Classified?" I asked. "No, ma'am," he replied with great seriousness. "It's unclassified."

— MONICA COSTELLO

 Talk about service.

While attending a formal military dinner with my boyfriend, an Army National Guardsman, I was baffled by the number of acronyms that were used. Finally I turned to the colonel next to me and said, "You should have a translator here for civilians. I don't speak 'Acronym.' " "I guess I never thought about it," he said apologetically. "So what do you do for a living?" "Oh," I replied, "I work for a CPA."

— URSULA KLEIN

★ ★ ★ ★ ★ ★ ★ ★ ★ ★ ★ ★ ★ ★ ★ ★ ★

My squad leader decided to try to break the base record of 424 push-ups. With our physical-training instructor standing over him, he knocked out 100 quick ones before he settled into a steady rhythm. We were sure he'd break the record, but at 390 he paused at the top and began to shake his head from side to side before slowly continuing. After finishing his 402nd push-up, he paused again, shook his head, coughed, then collapsed. As we walked back to our barracks, our instructor cracked a rare smile. "You gotta give that guy credit," he said. "If he had just been able to shake that wasp away from his face instead of inhaling it, he'd have broken the record for sure."

— MSGT. PATRICK L. HATHAWAY

Two days before officers-training graduation, I bragged that my single demerit was the lowest in the company. The next day I saw with chagrin a slip on my bunk, and was thoroughly humbled when I read the list: 1 Demerit: Littering. Penny under bed 1 Demerit: Lincoln needs a shave and a haircut 1 Demerit: Trying to bribe an officer 1 Demerit: Bribe not enough.

— FREDERIC P. SEITZ

My daughter recently returned from Iraq on a civilian airplane. Before boarding, she and her squad went through the metal detectors. She'd forgotten she had her Swiss army knife in her pocket, and it was confiscated. Upset, she joined the other soldiers as they boarded the plane, carrying their M-16 rifles.

— MICHAEL DELUCA

★ ★ ★ ★ ★ ★ ★ ★ ★ ★ ★ ★ ★ ★ ★ ★ ★

Crew cut, flattop, buzz cut … . Whatever you call them, military haircuts are not always the height of fashion. And even the military recognizes that. While passing a U.S. armed services barbershop in Heidelberg, Germany, I saw these rates that were posted in the window: Haircuts: $7 Military Haircuts: $6

— ERIC GERENCSER

At the Oceana, Va., Naval Air Station, I was training a young ground-crew member on how to direct an F-14 into the fuel pit. I glanced over to check wing clearance and, when I looked back, discovered that he had taxied the aircraft too far forward for the fuel hose to reach. "You'll have to send him around again," I informed the trainee. "What?" he said, surprised. "They spend millions on these things and you can't put them in reverse?"

— JOHN G. RUTGERS

Flashlights used by my National Guard unit can withstand almost anything. And to prove it, they come with a lifetime warranty. Nevertheless, nothing is indestructible, which is why the warranty also cautions, "Void with shark bites, bear attacks and children under the age of five."

— CARMEN HILL

As a Marine captain stationed in Okinawa, Japan, I was accompanying the assistant commandant on his inspection of the troops. To break the silence, the general would ask some of the Marines standing at attention which outfit they were serving with. Ramrod straight, each would respond, "Marine Air Group 36, sir," or "Second Marine Division,

★ ★ ★ ★ ★ ★ ★ ★ ★ ★ ★ ★ ★ ★ ★ ★ ★

General." But near the end of the inspection, when the general asked a young private, "Which outfit are you in?" the Marine replied, "Dress blues, sir, with medals!"

— JOHN D. BRATTEN

Although fighting the enemy is considered normal, the Army frowns upon fighting among the troops. So much so that after one too many battles royal, my uncle was ordered to undergo a psychiatric evaluation in which he had to endure some odd questions. "If you saw a submarine in the Sahara, what would you do?" "Well, I'd throw snowballs at it," he answered. "Where'd you get the snowballs?" the doctor asked. "Same place you got the submarine."

— HANNAH ETCHISON

I was playing cards on my bunk by myself when I suddenly felt a presence looming over my shoulder. It was a young private. "Excuse me," the private finally said, as he tried to follow the game. "What are you playing?" "Solitaire," I replied. "Oh," he said, as he walked away. "I didn't know you could play that without a computer."

— ROBERT OWENS

Safety is job one in the Air Force. Overstating the obvious is job two, as I discovered when crawling into my military-issue sleeping bag. The label read:

"In case of an emergency, unzip and exit through the top."

— KEITH J. WALTERS

★ ★ ★ ★ ★ ★ ★ ★ ★ ★ ★ ★ ★ ★ ★ ★ ★

While my brother-in-law was in the Army, he had a desk job and his own office. At coffee breaks, he listened to officers complain about how they couldn't get their work done with all the interruptions. Once he got promoted, he knew what they were talking about. That's when they changed the nameplate on his door—to Corporal Meeting, from Private Meeting.

— JEANNE HAYNES

Don't Ask

Stationed on Guam, I was part of the SEAL team conducting a training mission to simulate terrorist activity. In the early hours of the morning, our duty officer called the area commander to report that the SEALs had cut a hole in the base perimeter fencing, broken into a building and taken hostages. Sleepily, the commander asked our duty officer if the hole in the fence was simulated. "Yes, sir" was his reply. "And were the break-in and hostages simulated?" After another affirmative answer, the commander asked, "Then why didn't you simulate this phone call?"

— RICHARD DESMOND

While on my desk assignment in the Army, I noticed that my coworker Rick never answered his phone. One day I asked him why. "If you had to pick up the telephone and say, 'Statistical section, Specialist Strasewski speaking,'" Rick replied indignantly, "you wouldn't want to answer it either!"

— KATHERINE FIDDLER

I arrived in Texas on a warm fall day, ready to begin my tour as an exchange student from the Canadian armed forces. When I met the commanding officer, he pointed out

★ ★ ★ ★ ★ ★ ★ ★ ★ ★ ★ ★ ★ ★ ★ ★ ★

how lucky I was to be in his state at this time of year. "Yes, sir," I agreed, "the weather here is much better than back in Ontario." "Weather?" said the colonel. "I'm talking about football season!"

— MICHAEL KYTE

One night my husband, Lee, a retired Army colonel, was watching a program on TV about paratroopers. As one D-Day jumper began to comment, my husband exclaimed, "That's Jack Norton! I served in both Korea and Vietnam with him." Then, after watching the man speak for a few moments, Lee quietly remarked, "You know you're getting old when you have more friends on the History Channel than in the news."

— SHERRY H. FAIR

The executive officer of the unit where I worked in the National Guard Armory went to a government office to take care of some business. The clerk there gave him two index cards with identical questions on them. The officer filled both out, but when he handed them in, he asked the clerk why she needed two cards with the same information. Stapling the cards together, she said, "That's in case we lose one."

— BILL JOHNSON

★ ★ ★ ★ ★ ★ ★ ★ ★ ★ ★ ★ ★ ★ ★ ★ ★ ★

When my husband was a civilian working overseas for the Air Force, he entered a golf tournament sponsored by the air base in Moron, Spain. He won the tournament, but he has always been reluctant to show off his award. The trophy reads, "First Prize Moron."

— FONTAINE CHASE

When my son joined the Marine Corps, his cousin was already an Army officer. The two were home on leave at the same time, and had a wonderful time exchanging stories. But after hearing one Marine joke too many, my son finally chastised his cousin with: "Man, haven't you learned what ARMY stands for?" "No, what?" "Ain't Ready for Marines Yet."

— ANNE HICKS

At the maritime museum where I work, we occasionally use midshipmen to do the "dirty work" of restoring a 100-year-old cruiser. One day the Navy sent a crew of 20 men, while the Marines sent a crew of three. Teasing one Navy midshipman, I said, "You mean it takes twenty Navy guys to do the work of only three Marines?" "Sir, no, sir," he snapped back. "The truth is, sir, it takes six or seven of us to supervise each one of those Marines!"

— BRIAN SMITH

Glenn, my husband, is stationed in Belgium, where his job includes proofreading English documents written by European officers. Once a German lieutenant colonel brought him a lengthy paper. "I should have my wife look it over," Glenn said. "She's an English major." "Oh," the colonel replied, "I didn't realize your wife was in the British army."

— ANNA MAGGARD

Getting By

While reading our headquarters' monthly training report, I noticed that it included a motto, "Committment to Excellence." I immediately notified the office that produces the report that commitment had but one "t" in the middle. On our next report, our motto had changed to "Committed to Excellence."

— WERNER WOLF

★ ★ ★ ★ ★ ★ ★ ★ ★ ★ ★ ★ ★ ★ ★ ★ ★ ★

During an exercise, I heard a radio transmission between a captain and a lieutenant who was a new platoon leader. After the lieutenant reported over an unsecured radio network that the unit was located at a certain map coordinate, the captain told his young charge that he should not give his location "in the clear." The lieutenant replied, "We're not in the clear. The platoon is located in the woods next to the farmer's barn."

— MAJ. RON MCCANDLESS

A friend recently went through Army Ranger training in Florida. During the second day of the brutal "swamp phase," as the soldiers were rowing an inflatable raft down a river, a fishing boat cruised by with two scantily clad sunbathers on deck. The harsh rigors of the training suddenly came into focus when my friend turned to his buddy and asked, "I wonder if they had any food in that cooler?"

— SAVOY WILSON

When my family lived on Okinawa, one of the biggest events of the year was the military's Fourth of July celebration, which culminated in a spectacular fireworks display. One year, as we joined the early evening crowd on the improvised midway, we watched with alarm as three tipsy airmen headed for the commanding officer. One of the men ambled up to the general and, without even a salute, cheerfully swatted his arm. "Say," the airman inquired, "what time do the fireworks start?" The general eyed him coolly for a moment then replied, "Any minute, son. Any minute."

— MEG FAVILLE

★ ★ ★ ★ ★ ★ ★ ★ ★ ★ ★ ★ ★ ★ ★ ★ ★ ★

A friend often told me about the problems he had getting his son to clean his room. The son would always agree to tidy up, but then wouldn't follow through. After high school the young man joined the Marine Corps. When he came home for leave after basic training, his father asked him what he had learned in the service. "Dad," hc said. "I learned what 'now' means."

— JAN KING

My son-in-law had just joined the Navy and had gone for a walk downtown to show off his brand-new uniform. After passing a few restaurants and bars, he decided to stop off for a refreshment. A waitress came over to him and said, "Draft, sir?" "Nope," he replied.

"Enlisted."

— BARBARA COOK

A quality-control clerk, I once was stationed at a Florida Navy base with a chief petty officer who had an attaché case identical to mine. The cases were stylish and durable, but it was nearly impossible to tell which side was the top. One day, after the chief spilled pens and papers on the floor of our office, he got fed up. He grabbed a can of spray paint and wrote "TOP" on the case. But he hadn't turned the case over before marking it, and I did all I could not to laugh at his mistake. "I can't believe I did that," he finally said with disgust. "I know," I said, chuckling. "You painted the bottom of your case." "It's worse than that," he said. "This isn't my case."

— BRUCE FRAZIER

★ ★

My husband, a Marine Corps drill instructor, walked into the barracks after boot-camp graduation and saw a new Marine and his family circling one of the large metal trash cans. When my husband asked his former charge what he was doing, the man replied, "Just showing my family the alarm clock."

— LISA M. JONES

At Travis Air Force Base in California, I was assigned to the electronic-component repair section of my shop. Because of the electrical hazards of the job, we were forbidden to wear watches and rings while performing our duties. One day our foreman walked through our area and admonished one of my coworkers for wearing a watch while repairing a part. "Oh, it's okay," the worker protested. "This watch says it's 'shock-resistant.'"

— SOURCE UNKNOWN

Thinking
FAST

★ So They Say

★ You Can't Win 'em All

★ ★ ★ ★ ★ ★ ★ ★ ★ ★ ★ ★ ★ ★ ★ ★ ★ ★

While stationed in Washington, D.C., I used Arlington National Cemetery as a shortcut on my way to give a briefing at Fort Myer. To my surprise, I encountered a road-block manned by the military police. An MP approached my car and asked in a stern voice, "Are you supposed to be here?" Unsure of what to say, I replied, "Not yet." He held back a smile and waved me on.

— DAVID T. LIPP

When I was stationed in Germany with the Air Force, we worked side by side with the Army but were governed by different regulations. One rule involved what we were allowed to do while on various watches. Those of us in the Air Force were allowed to read anything we wished, while Army members could read only manuals or, in some cases, nothing at all. One night during a long watch, one of my friends was quietly reading a comic book when an Army captain stormed over. "You know, the Army can't read here!" she said sternly. "That's okay," the airman replied calmly. "When I'm finished I'll let them look at the pictures."

— RHONDA ROLZ

During last summer's drought in Oklahoma, National Guard units were mobilized to assist by hauling in hay from other states. On one trip, I passed a convoy of National Guard trucks, each carrying 14 large hay bales. Chalked on the bumper of the lead truck was

"Operation Cow Chow."

— VIRGINIA BARLOW

★ ★ ★ ★ ★ ★ ★ ★ ★ ★ ★ ★ ★ ★ ★ ★ ★

Shortly after graduating from high school, my brother, Roger, joined the Air Force. We missed him terribly, and to make matters worse, he wasn't allowed to use the phone. After about two weeks my family was awakened in the middle of the night by the ringing telephone. Fearing something had happened to Roger, I hurriedly picked up the receiver and was relieved to hear his voice. "What happened?" I said. "I thought no one was allowed to call out?" "We're not," he answered. "But they left me guarding the phone!"

— KIMBER E. BUSH

During a recent joint exercise a Navy admiral repeatedly called a veteran Marine master sergeant "chief," the Navy's equivalent rank. On the last day of the operation, the admiral caught himself again calling the Marine "chief" and said, "I'm sorry, master sergeant, but if you were in the Navy, you would be a chief." "No, sir," the Marine replied. "If I were in the Navy, I'd be an admiral."

— CHRIS LAWSON

One of my first assignments as an Army lieutenant was to report to the contract-management detachment of the Boeing Company, maker of the Minuteman nuclear missile. As I rode the elevator to meet my commander, it stopped, and a Boeing employee entered. "Four, please," he said. I mistakenly pushed the button for the third floor. As I realized my error, the man from Boeing commented, "We're very happy to have you here, Lieutenant ... and not in a missile silo."

— BRYAN PIERNOT

★ ★ ★ ★ ★ ★ ★ ★ ★ ★ ★ ★ ★ ★ ★ ★ ★

As recruits at Lackland Air Force Base in San Antonio, we had a duty called "dorm guard." A rookie was required to stand a one-hour shift at the door of his dorm, allowing only authorized personnel to enter, and alerting the unit to the presence of an officer by calling everyone to attention. A colonel had been in the dorm for several minutes when we heard the guard call, "Atten-hut!" Everyone snapped to rigid attention awaiting the oncoming officer. In walked a lieutenant. Our drill instructor, realizing that the unwitting guard had called a colonel to attention for a subordinate officer, ran over to the guard and yelled, "You have a colonel standing at attention for a lieutenant! What are you going to do about this?" In his most commanding voice, the recruit shouted out, "Colonel, at ease!"

— KENNETH R. MCALISTER

When my son Jordan was graduating from Navy boot camp, parents were anxious to see their sons and daughters after what for most people had been the longest separation in their lives. When the ceremony began, the guest speaker noted that he'd had a conversation with a fellow officer regarding the topic to address. "What should I talk about?" he'd asked his colleague. "Considering the families haven't seen their recruits in nine weeks," the officer replied, "I'd say about two minutes."

— SUSAN RASH

During a review of radar basics, I asked some Coast Guard sailors, "What's the difference between a 2D radar and a 3D radar?" The genius in the front row answered, **"1D."**

— ROBERT KIPKE

★ ★ ★ ★ ★ ★ ★ ★ ★ ★ ★ ★ ★ ★ ★ ★ ★

Increasingly in the military, members of one branch are required to work with members of another, and sometimes this causes trouble. A friend, while working on a joint deployment, saw a veteran Army master sergeant become frustrated at a perceived lack of respect from a young Air Force airman. The master sergeant pointed to the six stripes arranged on his shoulder and asked his young counterpart, "Do you know what three up and three down mean?" "Sure," the young airman replied. "The end of an inning."

— RAY FARRELL

So They Say

One day I was all set to give a presentation at the Naval War College in Newport, R.I. When I learned that I was scheduled to be the final speaker, it was a point of pride for me. "In a relay race," I explained to a colleague, "the final runner is called the anchor. You always put your best runner in the anchor position." "But this is the Navy," my friend retorted. "In the Navy they throw the anchor overboard."

— TONY SCHULTZ

One coworker told me about a military funeral he attended. Everything went perfectly until one of the soldiers carrying the casket slipped and fell into the freshly dug grave. The crowd gasped and the officer in charge turned white. The young soldier, however, was a quick thinker. He pulled himself out and stated in a commanding voice, "Sir, the grave is fit for burial."

— FIRST LT. DAR PLACE

★ ★ ★ ★ ★ ★ ★ ★ ★ ★ ★ ★ ★ ★ ★ ★ ★

When my husband was a psychological operations company commander at Fort Bragg, a new first sergeant arrived who wanted the soldiers to clean up the area. At his initial formation, the sergeant bent down and picked up a piece of paper. "This is a signed four-day pass," he read, "to whoever brings this in to the first sergeant of A Company." Hoping to find another, the soldiers quickly picked up every scrap of paper, and the company area was the cleanest in the battalion.

— MELODY ALEGRE

With our aircraft carrier under way on an important exercise, the admiral called all of the pilots together to discuss safety. He sternly lectured the group, then glared at them and asked gruffly, "Any questions?" No one said a word, so he asked a second time. Still no takers. "No one is leaving," he demanded, "until I get a question." "So," came a weak voice from the back, "where you from?"

— JEFFRY L. EDGAR

The day before graduation from Army basic training, I stood on the edge of a blazing hot parade field watching a group of soldiers rake the freshly cut grass. Suddenly, a helicopter appeared and made a practice landing in anticipation of delivering a dignitary the following day. The sergeant in charge of the raking detail ran to the chopper and spoke to the pilot. He then jogged off the field, taking his group with him. The helicopter lifted off, made a few low passes over the field, then flew away. I asked the sergeant what maneuver the pilot had been practicing. He smiled and said, "Grass removal."

— ROBERT L. SELSER

★ ★ ★ ★ ★ ★ ★ ★ ★ ★ ★ ★ ★ ★ ★ ★ ★

The colonel who served as inspector general in our command paid particular attention to how personnel wore their uniforms. On one occasion he spotted a junior airman with a violation. "Airman," he bellowed, "what do you do when a shirt pocket is unbuttoned?" The startled airman replied, "Button it, sir!" The colonel looked him in the eye and said, "Well?" At that, the airman nervously reached over and buttoned the colonel's shirt pocket.

— G. DEARING, JR.

I was walking through the barracks of the Air Force unit I commanded in the Philippines when I noticed that a few of the airmen had posters of scantily clad young women on their lockers. I immediately told the sergeant in charge that only pictures of family members could be displayed. A few days later I went back through the barracks and saw that one of the posters remained, but that it now had an inscription. "To Joe," it read, "Love, Sis."

— ROBERT P. GATES

During survival training at Coast Guard boot camp, we were required to jump from a 30-foot-high platform into a swimming pool. One of my fellow recruits went to the edge of the platform but immediately backed off. The drill instructor quickly showed his disapproval. "What would you do if you had to abandon a burning, sinking ship?" he snapped. Eyeing the distance to the water, the recruit replied, "I'd wait until the ship sank a little lower before jumping."

— ZEKE CANDLER

★ ★ ★ ★ ★ ★ ★ ★ ★ ★ ★ ★ ★ ★ ★ ★ ★ ★

You Can't Win 'em All

After completing a celestial navigation training course in the Navy, I was eager to show off my new knowledge of the stars to my date for the evening. "That's Regulus," I said confidently, "and there's Polaris, the North Star." Impressed, she pointed to a bright light on the horizon. "And what is that?" she asked. "Oh, that's Venus," I replied. "Note the steady light typical of planets." Her awe quickly turned to amusement, however, when "Venus" slowly drew nearer, turned and began to lower its wheels for landing.

— KERRY ANDERSON CROOKS

I was a young Reserve first lieutenant on an assignment with some seasoned Marines. When it was time to return to base for chow, we discovered our bus wouldn't start. Not wanting the men to be late for dinner, our sergeant major suggested taking them back in the dump truck. So the Marines piled into the truck while the sergeant major took the wheel and I settled in beside him. As we were driving along, I said, "We shouldn't leave that bus here unattended, should we?" "No," he replied, "but I'm not concerned. We have something else to be worried about." "What's that?" I asked. "We're not supposed to be hauling people in a dump truck," he said. "But we have a bigger worry than that." "What?" I asked, getting nervous. "I don't have a license to drive a dump truck," he said. "But you know, that doesn't worry me at all." "Why not?" I replied. "Because," he said with a smirk, " you're in charge."

— LYNDA REARICK

★ ★ ★ ★ ★ ★ ★ ★ ★ ★ ★ ★ ★ ★ ★ ★ ★

When my husband visited our son, Michael, at boot camp, he found him marching smartly with his unit. Michael's father proudly approached the soldiers and began to snap photo after photo. Embarrassed and worried about getting into trouble, Michael looked straight ahead and didn't change his expression. Suddenly his drill sergeant barked, "Comito, give me 25 push-ups. And the next time your daddy wants your picture, you smile!"

— EDYTHE COMITO

When I was transferred to an Army unit in Germany, I immediately tried to put my high-school German to use. It was going well until one night on the subway. Sitting across from a nicely dressed couple, I initiated a conversation in German and asked for directions to a local shopping district. All this took about a minute. When I finally stopped talking, the woman looked at her husband and in a Southern drawl said, "Keep smiling, honey, and he'll go away."

— JAMES S. HOUK II

My brother, Shawn, was working the graveyard shift on an Air Force security detail in Germany when he fell asleep against the wheel of his vehicle. He was awakened only when the guard shack announced over his radio that his relief had arrived. "Get a good night's sleep?" my brother was asked by his sergeant back at the shack. "Oh, no, sir, I was wide awake," Shawn replied. "What makes you think I was sleeping?" "Airman," the sergeant said. "Look in the mirror." My brother looked in the mirror and grinned sheepishly when he saw the unmistakable Mercedes-Benz logo imprinted on his forehead.

— ROBERT F. FALCONER II

★ ★ ★ ★ ★ ★ ★ ★ ★ ★ ★ ★ ★ ★ ★ ★ ★ ★ ★

When a friend of mine was an Air Force base commander, he sent one of his formal, or "mess dress," uniforms to a tailor for alterations. After a few days the seamstress, who had a heavy German accent, called his office to say the uniform was finished. The secretary wrote down the message and handed it to an enlisted man for delivery. The airman entered the commander's office but was hesitant to say why he was there. The colonel asked what the young man wanted. Frustrated by his stammering, he ordered, "Out with it!" The enlisted man looked at him sheepishly and said, "Your mistress is ready."

— WYNNE YOUNG

During an important military exercise, another Air Force member and I were working in a radar van under a simulated attack. We were under strict orders not to open the door unless we received the secret code, which we had been given at the morning briefing. Later in the day, we heard knocking at the door. Remembering our orders, I yelled out "Fort" and waited for the correct response, "Knox." It never came. Several minutes later we heard more knocking, but again we didn't receive the proper response. Over the course of the afternoon, various others came to the door and knocked, but no one gave us the correct password. Proud of ourselves for not being tricked into opening up to the enemy, we later received a phone call from a furious superior officer who told us to open the door immediately. After we explained that we were simply following orders, he informed us that the code was not "Fort Knox," but four knocks.

— LYNDA C. LOVELL

★ ★ ★ ★ ★ ★ ★ ★ ★ ★ ★ ★ ★ ★ ★ ★ ★

I was standing at attention with a number of other recruits outside an airport in San Diego, eagerly awaiting the bus that would take us to Marine Corps boot camp. But our enthusiasm began to wane, and a creeping feeling of apprehension took its place. So it was no surprise when I heard a young man behind me say, "I think I've made a mistake." Not wishing to break my military bearing, I stared straight ahead and softly said out of the side of my mouth, "I know what you mean, but I'm trying to remain optimistic. I figure it's only 12 weeks, and it will all be worth it when we graduate and become Marines." "Thanks for clearing that up," came the whispered reply. "I thought this was the line for my rental-car shuttle bus."

— DAMIAN ROSSITTIS

 Are we there yet?

★ ★ ★ ★ ★ ★ ★ ★ ★ ★ ★ ★ ★ ★ ★ ★ ★ ★

Shortly after my cousin joined the Navy, my aunt repeatedly warned him about the dangers of getting a tattoo. To placate her, my cousin reluctantly agreed to call her should he ever contemplate getting one. The dreaded call finally came. My aunt thanked him for keeping his word, then surprisingly gave him her blessing without further questioning. My cousin was surprised at her attitude and pressed her for the reason she agreed so quickly. With a deep sigh of resignation, my aunt replied, "Because your younger sister came home with one the other day."

— B. FOLISI

Our six-week training camp at Fort Bragg, N.C., was capped by a traditional military graduation ceremony. With all of the families gathered in the stands, our commanding general watched the formation from his podium. After the Army Band played the national anthem, a three-cannon salute to the colors boomed across the parade grounds. The general was due to speak next, but his remarks were delayed—until the wailing of dozens of car alarms ended.

— DENNIS W. LAHMANN

As a professor at the Air Force Institute of Technology, I taught a series of popular courses on software engineering. The program was highly competitive and difficult to get into, but one prospective student made our decision whether to accept him quite simple. When asked to fax over his college transcript, the student told me, "Well, I would, but it's the only copy that I've got."

— JIM SKINNER

★ ★ ★ ★ ★ ★ ★ ★ ★ ★ ★ ★ ★ ★ ★ ★ ★ ★ ★

A friend had just completed Marine Corps recruit training at Parris Island, S.C., when his grandparents came to visit. Eager to show how proud they were of their young Marine, the couple went to a store where the grandfather bought a T-shirt emblazoned with the Marine Corps emblem. He immediately put it on before returning to the base, but soon noticed he was getting odd looks from passers-by. Later, when the man looked more closely at his new shirt, he realized why. Above the emblem was printed, "My boyfriend is a Marine."

— JOHN LICHTENWALNER

As a newly commissioned infantry lieutenant, I was eager to set an example for my platoon by cleaning my own M-16 rifle. While we were working on the weapons, one soldier complained about the unusual notched shape of the M-16's bolt and chamber, which makes it difficult to clean. "Lieutenant, they need to make something to clean this with," the soldier said. "They do," piped up a sergeant. "Really," I said with surprise, wondering why we had not ordered such a tool. "Yes, sir," replied the sergeant. "It's called a soldier."

— CHARLES ANDERSON

While in the Army, my son Gabe attended POSH (Prevention of Sexual Harassment) classes. During one session, the sergeant said to his men, "Before you tell a joke, ask yourselves, What would my mother think?" Gabe replied, "Sergeant, there's a problem with that." "What is it?" "If I listened to what my mother had to say, I wouldn't have joined the Army in the first place."

— ANGELA TRAYNOR

★ ★ ★ ★ ★ ★ ★ ★ ★ ★ ★ ★ ★ ★ ★ ★ ★ ★

My nephew, Chris, was assigned to drive in a truck convoy one night while serving in the Marine Corps. When he pulled away, he noticed the truck behind him was following much too closely. When he sped up, so did the other truck. When he slowed down, so did the other truck. He became concerned that the other driver would cause an accident. When he turned a corner and pulled up to the guard station, he noticed that the driver behind him had cut the turn too sharply and knocked down part of the gate. "He's been tailgating me since we left," Chris explained to the guard. "And look, now he's knocked down part of the gate." The guard eyed him coolly and said, "Corporal, you are towing the truck behind you."

— MARIE N. GOFORTH

The young training instructor at Lackland Air Force Base, fresh out of TI school, was doing everything by the book. Our group of 50 female basic trainees was gathered around as he showed us how to fold and hang our clothes military style. Using one of the women's lockers as an example, he referred to his TI school guide, fumbling with T-shirts and socks as he attempted to fold them into the prescribed shapes. Taking another long glance at the book, he reached into the locker and pulled out a set of lacy women's underwear. After a few awkward moments, he gave up. "Okay," he said, "just fold them like your mother taught you."

— DENISE L. FOX

★ ★ ★ ★ ★ ★ ★ ★ ★ ★ ★ ★ ★ ★ ★ ★ ★ ★

A sergeant in my Army bomb-clearing detail was asked to conduct a class for a group of visiting officers. Needing a prop to demonstrate, the sergeant retrieved a live bomb from the impact area. One class member, a second lieutenant, seemed nervous about a live bomb being used for the demo. He kept interrupting the class with, "Sergeant, I know you've done this before, but are you sure that you're doing it right?" After the fourth interruption, a voice called from the back of the room, "Lieutenant, I guarantee that in all your military career, you'll never meet anyone who's done this before and done it wrong!"

— DARRELL SMITH

While going through basic training in Texas, we were taught the Army's phonetic alphabet. Once when being quizzed by our drill sergeant, I had to give the representation for the letter "m." My mind went blank. I reasoned that since the letter "p" was represented by Papa, then "m" must be Mama. Looking forlornly at the sergeant, I bellowed, "Mama!" "Son," the sergeant responded, breaking into a grin, "even your mama can't help you now!"

— JOE LEE STOREY

At sea aboard the USS *Saipan*, I was passing by the ship's galley and overheard two sailors—a veteran and a new seaman—talking while they were on mess duty. "Hey, Bill," asked the younger, "what's the difference between a cook and a chef?" "Simple," answered his shipmate, "a chef doesn't have tattoos."

— K. I. SEPP

★ ★ ★ ★ ★ ★ ★ ★ ★ ★ ★ ★ ★ ★ ★ ★ ★

Tinker Air Force Base in Oklahoma was readying for an important inspection. Part of the sidewalk in front of the base commander's building was damaged, so a new section of concrete was poured to replace it. However, the new concrete did not match the darker color of the old sidewalk. Several remedies were suggested, but none could be completed in time for the inspection. "All right, men," an exasperated captain said, "let's smear some mud over the new section to match the colors." "Congratulations, sir," said the chief master sergeant. "Now you're thinking like an enlisted man!"

— STEVEN A. HOSELTON

When I came back to the United States after a tour of duty with the Marines in Vietnam, I stayed with my parents for a 30-day leave. Mom's rules were simple: I could come and go as I pleased, but I had to let her know when I returned home each night. After one long evening with friends, I crept into the house and didn't knock on Mom's door. Late the next morning when I came down for breakfast, she glared at me with icy silence. "Look, Mom," I said, "I'm sorry I didn't tell you I got home safely last night, but what did you do all the time I was in Vietnam?" "Well," she replied, "at least then I knew where you were!"

— BILL BRUCKNER

H^UH?

★ **Another Language?**

★ **Come Again?**

★ **Some Reassurance**

★ ★ ★ ★ ★ ★ ★ ★ ★ ★ ★ ★ ★ ★ ★ ★ ★ ★ ★

When you're stationed in Germany, you tend to have different priorities. A sign on our squadron's microwave read: "Do not use when coffeemaker is on. The circuit breaker will blow up and catch the beer on fire."

— DON HAMILTON

Stationed overseas with the Air Force, my wife and I collected miniature statues. Two of our favorites were replicas of the "Winged Victory" and "Venus de Milo." When we returned to the States and unpacked our boxes, our attention was drawn to the container holding our collection. The military movers, in an effort to protect themselves from liability, had written on the outside of the box: "Small statues; two already damaged—one missing head, another missing arms."

— LT. COL. LAYNE E. FLAKE

Before I could visit my daughter at her naval base in Japan, I was told I needed to supply her with some important information to give to security. The list included the following: passport number, height, weight, year of birth and anticipated hair color at time of arrival.

— DIXIE MCFARLAND

I drove my daughter to a weekend boot camp for teenagers sponsored by the Army. When we arrived, we didn't know whom to talk to. We asked a guy at the front desk, who nodded vaguely toward one of the officers standing behind him. Seeing my confusion, he added, "You can't miss him—he's wearing camouflage."

— K. L. CAMPBELL

★ ★ ★ ★ ★ ★ ★ ★ ★ ★ ★ ★ ★ ★ ★ ★ ★ ★ ★

My husband, daughter and son-in-law are active in the Civil Air Patrol, the auxiliary of the Air Force. Recently they all attended a state conference, where my daughter told me her father would be receiving an award. The evening of the banquet, my husband called home, and I asked how it was going. "Oh, pretty good," he said, and we chatted about it. I wondered why he didn't say anything about the award, but, fearing that he hadn't gotten it after all, I didn't mention it. When he returned home, he said very little except that everything had gone quite well. "So, did anything special happen?" I prodded, wondering if I should just come out and ask him about the award. Finally he produced a plaque from his bag. On it was inscribed: "Communicator of the Year."

— NANCY POLLOCK

Bumper sticker: "To err is human, to forgive divine. Neither is Marine Corps policy."

— TOM FRONCEK

Fort Monmouth in New Jersey was expecting a visit from a prominent two-star general. My husband, Bob, was in charge of decorating the lawn in front of the building where the festivities were going to be held. He had arranged to have an old, retired tank and some fake land mines placed near the entrance. Bob was standing there, overseeing the task, when an uninformed passerby paused, looked over the scene and remarked to him, "Gee, I guess they're really serious about not wanting us to walk on the grass."

— KIM LABARBIERA

★ ★ ★ ★ ★ ★ ★ ★ ★ ★ ★ ★ ★ ★ ★ ★ ★

Another Language?

My husband was telling me about a news item he heard on National Public Radio about how the U.S. military is enlisting honeybees to find land mines. The insects are trained to react to the scent of TNT, then are fitted with transmitters and sent out to search for underground explosives. "When they smell TNT," my husband explained, "the insects hover over the area and the military tracks them to the site to safely eliminate the land mine." "Gee," I remarked, "it gives a whole new meaning to the slogan 'Be all that you can be!' "

— ANITA RAYMOND

★ ★ ★ ★ ★ ★ ★ ★ ★ ★ ★ ★ ★ ★ ★ ★ ★ ★ ★

While standing watch in the Coast Guard station in Juneau, Alaska, I got a call from the Navy in the nearby city of Adak. They had lost contact with one of their planes, and they needed the Coast Guard to send an aircraft to go find it. I asked the man where the Navy aircraft had last been spotted so we would know where to search. "I can't tell you," the Navy man said. "That's classified."

— ALFRED MILES

My youngest brother, Tony, had just completed basic training and was home on leave prior to his first tour in Germany. Since I was an Army National Guard pilot and my other brother was my crew chief, we offered to take Tony to catch his transport overseas. When we landed at McGuire Air Force Base, several of Tony's fellow privates came out to greet him. Tony ran ahead, while my other brother and I followed with his gear. As Tony approached his buddies, he was bewildered by their dumbfounded stares. Finally, he realized his friends weren't seeing his two brothers giving him a lift; they were seeing a new private arrive in his own helicopter—with his captain and sergeant carrying his bags!

— GLEN H. WILLIAMS

Stationed in Okinawa, Japan, my son and his wife were expecting their first baby. I was elated when he called me at work with the wonderful news of my grandchild's birth. I took down all the statistics and turned to relate it all to my coworkers. "I'm a grandmother!" I declared. "It's a baby girl, and she weighs five pounds." "When was she born?" someone asked. Recalling the date my son told me, I stopped, looked at the calendar and said in amazement, "Tomorrow!"

— J. M. TURK

★ ★ ★ ★ ★ ★ ★ ★ ★ ★ ★ ★ ★ ★ ★ ★ ★ ★ ★

When I was in the Coast Guard at a small boat station in Hancock, Mich., the commanding officer announced that the admiral from the 9th Coast Guard District was coming to see us the next day to speak on gender equality. Then he added, "I would like your wives to make a dish for the potluck supper."

— TODD SHAFER

A quiet evening of guard duty at Camp Pendleton, Calif., turned hairy when my son and his buddy saw a pair of luminous eyes staring back at them. It slinked toward them ... a cougar. Retreating slowly, my son radioed the base. "We're being followed by a cougar," he said softly. "What do we do?" A voice responded, "Get the license plate number, and we'll send over some MPs."

— DENISE CHAFFIN

I had just been assigned to an Air Force fighter base in Arizona. I knew the culture would be different from the Ohio logistics base where I came from. One day I was playing golf, when a ball bounced just a few feet away from me. Instead of the customary "fore!" I heard someone yell, **"Incoming!"**

— ROBERT WIDO

Both my roommate and I are airborne engineer lieutenants at Fort Bragg, N.C. While we were looking for a new house to move into, we came upon a home that had a huge, open backyard. My roommate called me outside as I was inspecting the living room. "Hey, check this out," she yelled. "We've got our own drop zone back here!"

— BOB GORDON

★ ★ ★ ★ ★ ★ ★ ★ ★ ★ ★ ★ ★ ★ ★ ★ ★ ★

Seen on a Coast Guard bumper sticker: "Support Search and Rescue ... Get Lost!"

— CHRISTINA BURBANK

Come Again?

We were in the barracks when two guys threw down the gauntlet: 100 bucks to anyone who could do 150 push-ups. My friend disappeared into the latrine and returned minutes later, saying, "I'll take that bet." He got down on the floor and reached 50 before collapsing. "I don't get it," he said, gasping for air. "I just did 200 in the latrine."

— STEPHEN BEDICS

To bolster security at our Army post in Germany, we initiated Random Access Control Measures at our gates. This meant stopping and checking cars at various times of the day, resulting in terrible traffic. One senior officer came up with a solution: "We need more predictability in our randomness."

— JEFFREY CHURCH

Gen. George Armstrong Custer is buried on the grounds of the United States Military Academy at West Point. Since I was driving through the area, I decided to pay my respects. At the gate, the distracted young MP put down her book, checked my ID and asked the purpose of my visit. I explained that I was there to visit General Custer. As she picked up her book, she asked, "And is the general expecting you?"

— WILLIAM PARIS

★ ★ ★ ★ ★ ★ ★ ★ ★ ★ ★ ★ ★ ★ ★ ★ ★ ★

Our Army unit was overseas conducting maneuvers with the Marines. On shift one night, a Marine asked my sergeant where he was from. "I'm originally from Central America," said the sergeant. "Oh, yeah?" asked the Marine. "Kansas?"

— DAVID DENBEK

The subject of the meeting was whether or not to buy a new chandelier for the sergeants' mess hall. Some officers wanted to vote on it. But one holdout opted for prudence. "Before we spend money on a chandelier," he said, "shouldn't we find out if anyone can play the thing?"

— J. STEVENS

Overheard on the marine radio—a distress call to the Coast Guard from someone whose sailboat was taking on water: Coast Guard: "What is your position?" Distressed caller: "Vice president, State Street Bank!"

— A. KEENAN

Marine Corps pilots and aircraft maintenance technicians have a special bond. So I was unfazed when a flyboy described a vexing problem. "The radio," he said, "worked intermittently ... but only sometimes."

— JAMES BULMAN

File under Only in the Army.

A sign on the telephone in our barracks read
"If broken, please call maintenance."

— ANDREW DRUST

★ ★ ★ ★ ★ ★ ★ ★ ★ ★ ★ ★ ★ ★ ★ ★ ★ ★

While on leave, my Marine buddy and I met two nursing students from Southern California. After chatting them up awhile, the conversation turned to what we did in the service. When we told them we were in the infantry, the girls seemed very impressed, giving us big smiles as they told us how sweet that was. Since infantry and sweet are seldom used in the same sentence, I was a little confused. Until, that is, one of the girls said, "We admire any man who works with infants."

— TAEVEN THOMPSON

★ ★ ★ ★ ★ ★ ★ ★ ★ ★ ★ ★ ★ ★ ★ ★ ★

Imagine my surprise when I went to Tipler Army Medical Center for a heart bypass operation and discovered my surgeon's name was Dr. Eror. "What a name for a doctor," I said, not sure whether to laugh or cry. "Yeah," he agreed. "You can imagine the reaction I got when I was a major."

— GARY MEYERS

Life in the Navy is dangerous. Which is why a sign was posted on a pier at Guantanamo Bay, Cuba, reminding American sailors to "Drive Like You Work. Slow."

— DAVID HOLT

Some Reassurance

During the Cold War, I was an interpreter in the Air Force. We were testing a computer that purportedly could translate Russian into English, and vice versa. We began by uttering this English phrase, "The spirit is willing, but the flesh is weak." The Russian translation came out, "Vodka horosho, no myaca slabie." Or, in English, "The alcohol is good, but the meat is poor."

— SAM CONNOR

While in the Navy, my primary duty was to sight guns. Wanting to move up in the military, I went to law school and applied for the Judge Advocate General's Corps (JAG). My hopes of being a Navy lawyer were shot down, however, when I was rejected. It seems I suffered from poor vision.

— ALBERT MALONE

★ ★ ★ ★ ★ ★ ★ ★ ★ ★ ★ ★ ★ ★ ★ ★ ★

I was waiting for a flight to Texas along with four servicemen in desert camouflage uniforms. Over the top pocket of their uniform shirts was the branch of the military in which they served, followed by their last names. They were U.S. Navy, Ramirez, U.S. Army, Larkin and U.S. Army, O'Brien. The fourth man wasn't a soldier. Above his shirt pocket it read, "D.O.D. Civilian, Coward."

— WILLIAM COGGER

Our sergeant major was dimmer than a dying lightning bug. One day, I found a set of dog tags with his name on them in the shower. So, of course, I returned them. "Wow!" he said. "How'd you know they were mine?"

— JOSÉ RODRIGUEZ

Boarding a military transport plane, I noticed hydraulic fluid pouring from the tail section. "Excuse me," I said to a crew member. "Do you know the aircraft has a leak?" "Yep," he said as he continued on his way. "Aren't you concerned?" He shrugged. "Well," I asked, "how do you know when you're out of fluid?" "When it quits leaking," he answered.

— DAVID FORD

Fascinated by the military, my son went online to research everything there was to know about the armed forces, from training to equipment. Looking up bulletproof vests, he found one with an interesting warranty. It said: "Guaranteed or your money back."

— LORI SERVISS

★ ★ ★ ★ ★ ★ ★ ★ ★ ★ ★ ★ ★ ★ ★ ★ ★ ★

Everyone knows that physical fitness and safety are paramount in the military. Which may go a long way in explaining why a recent motivational campaign produced the following poster: "Safety—Now with fewer carbs!"

— LIN ALLEN

When I was stationed at March Air Force Base (now known as March Air Reserve Base) in California, the technicians who took identification card photos were apparently fed up with complaints about the quality of the IDs. This sign was posted where it could be seen by everyone coming in for a new card: "If you want a better picture, bring a better face!"

— ED MATTSON

HeY, MEDiC

★ **Stating the Obvious**

★ **Use What You Know**

★ ★ ★ ★ ★ ★ ★ ★ ★ ★ ★ ★ ★ ★ ★ ★ ★

The time came for annual immunizations at our overseas Air Force base. To get us all vaccinated as quickly as possible, they pressed the veterinary surgeon into helping out. I got my injection from the vet. "Wow," I said, "you did that so gently, I hardly felt it." "I have to be gentle," he said. "My patients can bite."

— ANTONY MWANGI

Newly minted as an ensign, I reported for duty at the naval medical center in San Diego, ready to follow all the rules. Expecting a no-nonsense environment, I was surprised to see a sign above the door of my new ward: "Welcome to Proctology. To expedite your visit, please back in."

— DIANE PENCE

My company was standing in line for shots and medical exams at the Naval Training Center Great Lakes. We each wore only an iodine number on our chests, and were surprised when a nurse suddenly walked in. Assessing the situation, she solved our problem when she yelled, "Close your eyes, fellows. I'm coming through."

— DANIEL RESPESS

I was new to the emergency medical branch at Fort Leonard Wood, Mo., where about ten platoon members and I were checking and stocking equipment. Suddenly a bell began to ring, and everyone dropped his equipment, grabbed his hat and headed for the exits. I did the same, scrambling to get out of the building. Concerned, I asked another soldier what was going on. "The ice-cream truck is here!" he replied.

— SUSAN HAL

★ ★ ★ ★ ★ ★ ★ ★ ★ ★ ★ ★ ★ ★ ★ ★ ★ ★

After joining the Navy, my husband underwent a physical. During the exam, it was discovered that, due to a bum shoulder, he couldn't fully extend his arms above his head. Perplexed, the doctor conferred with another physician. "Let him pass," said the second doctor. "I don't see any problems unless he has to surrender."

— BETTY LEE

When I worked as a medical intern in a hospital, one of my patients was an elderly man with a thick accent. It took a while before I understood that he had no health insurance. Since he was a World War II vet, I had him transported to a VA hospital, where he'd be eligible for benefits. The next day my patient was back, along with this note from the VA admitting nurse: "Right war, wrong side."

— M. MURRAY

A hospital corpsman and I were getting an elderly retired master chief petty officer out of his wheelchair, when I noticed the man had a tattoo on his knee. "What's that?" I asked, unable to make out the design. "It's a banjo," he said sheepishly. "I'm from Alabama."

— MARY K. PARKER

As a first-time patient at a naval dental clinic, I was looking around for the restrooms. I couldn't help but smile when I saw the sign pointing me in the right direction. It said **"Patients' heads located upstairs."**

— KEITH BROCATO

★ ★ ★ ★ ★ ★ ★ ★ ★ ★ ★ ★ ★ ★ ★ ★ ★ ★ ★

Stating the Obvious

My husband had been stationed in Europe and away from home for what seemed like years when I went for my annual gynecological checkup. My doctor asked the usual questions, including what I was using for birth control. I gave the only possible response I could: "The Atlantic Ocean."

— VICKI L. BAILEY

I was at an Air Force hospital as a second-year medical student. After assisting during a knee surgery, the nurse anesthetist and I were having trouble waking the patient. Our staff physician, however, knew what to do. "Marine," he shouted, "this is Colonel Smith." The patient then promptly sat straight up on the gurney and replied, "Sir!"

— 2ND LT. JOSHUA CAREY

My father-in-law, a retired Army officer, was recently in the hospital for surgery, and on the day of his operation, I went to wish him luck. I quickly found out he hadn't lost his military bearing—or his sense of humor. After I knocked, I heard him call out, "Friend or enema?"

— DEBORAH MARTIN

As a members of an Air Force Reserve medical unit, we worked with nurses just out of nursing school who were not used to military ranks. This notice appeared on our bulletin board: "There will be a meeting of all junior officers at 1300 hours today. If you are not sure if you are a junior officer, plan on attending."

— MARY SCHMIDT

During the time I was a first lieutenant at Seymour Johnson Air Force Base in North Carolina, the junior officers challenged the senior officers to see who would donate the most blood. After trying several times to locate a vein in my left arm, the technician applied a Band-Aid, then inserted a needle into my right arm, and after drawing blood, put a bandage on that arm as well. As I left the collection facility, I passed a colonel. Noting my two bandages, he looked at me and shook his head, saying, "I knew you young guys would find a way to cheat."

— JAMES H. DILDA

★ ★ ★ ★ ★ ★ ★ ★ ★ ★ ★ ★ ★ ★ ★ ★ ★

There was a long-standing practice at our hospital in Virginia that physicians with a rank of major or above did not have to rotate through nighttime emergency-room duty. A new commanding officer, however, issued an order that all physicians, regardless of rank, must take ER call. On his first night of emergency-room duty, our pathologist, a major, had to see a colonel's wife who was complaining of abdominal pain. "I'll try to evaluate you as best as I can," he said after introducing himself. "But I must inform you that you are the first living patient I've seen in fifteen years."

— JAMES R. RAYMOND, M.D.

When I entered the Army medical center on base 20 minutes prior to delivering my baby, I had a hard time convincing the staff that I was definitely in the last stages of labor. We had waited 10 minutes in the pre-admittance area when a nurse finally came in and said, "My name is Captain Smith, but you can call me Lisa." "I'm Chaplain Barclay," my husband responded, "but you can call me Kleet." "My name is Holly," I added in frustration, "but in a few minutes you can call me Mom!"

— HOLLY BARCLAY

While working as a Navy nurse in a military hospital's emergency room, I was required to introduce myself by my rank and full name. I usually refer to myself as Ensign Mike Payne, but one busy day I rushed into a patient's room and blurted, "Hi, I'm Ensign Payne." "Hi," the patient responded. "I'm in some pain, too."

— MIKE PAYNE

★ ★ ★ ★ ★ ★ ★ ★ ★ ★ ★ ★ ★ ★ ★ ★ ★

Use What You Know

While assigned to the Naval Medical Center in San Diego, I overheard this conversation between a pharmacy technician and a sergeant who needed a prescription filled for his son. Technician: "How old is your boy?" Sergeant: "Three months." Technician: "What's his weight?" Sergeant: "About two M-16s." Technician: "Loaded or unloaded?"

— MARCELO BUNDANG

As a physical therapist, I was working with a retired Army colonel. During part of his rehab, I had him walk back and forth while facing me the entire time. "Colonel," I joked, "you walk better backward than forward." "Yeah," he deadpanned. "My battalion retreated a lot."

— JENNIFER SEKULA

The scale at our clinic in Iraq was pitiful. Just to get it working properly required plenty of kicking and stomping. One day, as I was going through my weighing-in routine, a medic walked by. Watching as I pounded the scale with my feet, he wondered aloud, "Killing the messenger?"

— DAWN NEHLS

An odd thing happened when I contacted the Navy about my health care: They said their records listed me as "deceased." The petty officer I spoke to was very helpful and input my current information into the computer. But a window popped up and balked: "Are you sure you want to resurrect Joseph S. Clein?"

— JOSEPH S. CLEIN

★ ★ ★ ★ ★ ★ ★ ★ ★ ★ ★ ★ ★ ★ ★ ★ ★ ★

As an Army dentist, one day I treated a general on base. During his visit I had to make impressions of his teeth, and the puttylike substance I used smeared all over his lips and cheeks. After I was done I invited him over to the sink, gave him a moist towel and asked him to "clean up the mess I made" while I filled out the lab report. When I turned back around, my heart skipped a beat as I watched the general wipe up the counter around the sink.

— LT. COL. WILLIAM C. ELTON

During a visit to a military medical clinic, I was sent to the lab to have blood drawn. The technician there was friendly and mentioned that his mood improved every day because he was due to leave the service in two months. As he placed the tourniquet on my arm, he told me that taking the blood wouldn't hurt much. Then, noticing my Air Force T-shirt, he asked me what my husband did. When I replied that he was a recruiter, the technician smiled slyly and said, "This might hurt a little more than I thought."

— SHERRI VINIARD

While visiting a VA hospital with my son, I overheard a retired Army sergeant asking people which branch of the military they'd served in. Some said Army, a few Navy, others Air Force. "What were you in?" she asked a man who'd just entered the room. Confused, he mumbled, **"The bathroom."**

— SUSAN LOPSHIRE

★ ★ ★ ★ ★ ★ ★ ★ ★ ★ ★ ★ ★ ★ ★ ★ ★

Going through some of my grandfather's old books, I found a *Serviceman's Spiritual Handbook* from World War II. "I didn't know Pop Pop was in World War II," I said to my father. "Where was he stationed?" "He was in the Army at Cape Hatteras, assigned as a lookout to watch for German U-boats," my father replied. "So he was never in active combat abroad?" I queried. "That's right," my father answered. "The Army didn't think his eyesight was good enough."

— SARAH B. PAUL

Two weeks after having a vasectomy, I was discussing the procedure with a friend who was going to have one, too. "It was quick outpatient surgery," I assured him, "although I did experience some minor complications because of infection." He looked worried, so I tried to lighten the mood. "Hey, I only paid $15 for the operation after insurance—I guess you get what you pay for." "Oh, no," he exclaimed in alarm. "I'm having mine done at the naval hospital—and it's free!"

— STEVE M. WHALEN

The military is a stickler for rules, and when it comes to off-base medical treatment, the rules are that many procedures need to be preauthorized. So when we were expecting our first child, my husband and I did things by the book. After our son was born on September 22, the insurance statement showed that the obstetrician was not paid the full contracted amount. So I called our insurer's representative. "The problem is, your son was born early," she said, looking through my files. "And the Air Force hadn't authorized him to arrive for another two weeks."

— AMY AMSDEN

★ ★ ★ ★ ★ ★ ★ ★ ★ ★ ★ ★ ★ ★ ★ ★ ★

I didn't enlist in the Army—I was drafted. So I wasn't going to make life easy for anyone. During my physical, the doctor asked softly, "Can you read the letters on the wall?" "What letters?" I answered slyly. "Good," said the doctor. "You passed the hearing test."

— ROBERT DUPREY

RANK
★ and FiLE

★ **Pulling Rank**

★ **A Rose Is a Rose**

Reporting to Camp Lejeune, I was glad my husband had already explained to me that a "Commissioned Officers Mess (open)" is open to all officers, whereas a "Commissioned Officers Mess (closed)" is limited to officers residing on base. Therefore, I understood this message: "During the holidays the Commissioned Officers Mess (open) will be closed. The Commissioned Officers Mess (closed) will be open."

— PATRICIA W. MINER

My cousin, a senior airman in the Air Force, and my brother-in-law, a Marine sergeant, were comparing their experiences in the Saudi Arabian desert. They commiserated about the heat, sand and food. But when my Air Force cousin grumbled about the uncomfortable beds and the small tents, my Marine brother-in-law looked surprised. His astonishment grew as my cousin went on to complain about the unreliable air-conditioning and meager choice of cable channels. Finally the Marine spoke up: "Tents? You had tents!"

— A. K. MCNEILL

The theater group at our Navy base delayed the opening curtain until well after the 8 p.m. starting time because the commanding officer was still conspicuously absent from his reserved front-row seat. Since we were all aware of military protocol, everyone waited patiently. When a member of our drama club finally spotted the captain settling into his seat, we quickly dimmed the lights. That's when we heard the captain proclaim to his wife, "Great luck! We made it just in time."

— LEE R. FEATHERINGHAM

★ ★ ★ ★ ★ ★ ★ ★ ★ ★ ★ ★ ★ ★ ★ ★ ★ ★ ★

While visiting our daughter Susan, who was stationed at Fort Hood Army Base, we joined her at the officers club. Upon entering the building, Susan hung her cap in the hall, and I asked her if she wasn't afraid that someone might take it. "No, I'm not worried," she said, sighing. "No one wants to be a second lieutenant."

— DOROTHY THOMPSON

After being at sea in the Persian Gulf for 90 straight days, I went to the squadron command master chief to complain. "Chief, I joined the Navy to see the world," I said, "but for the past three months all I've seen is water." "Lieutenant," he replied, "three-quarters of the earth is covered with water, and the Navy has been showing you that. If you wanted to see the other quarter, you should have joined the Army."

— PAUL NEWMAN

I was scolding our pastor for his habit of starting church services five or ten minutes late. I mentioned that in my years with the Air Force, when the general scheduled us to take off at 0700 hours, he didn't mean 0705 or 0710. The pastor smiled at me and said, "My general outranks your general."

— BOB BALTZELL

While visiting my son on his Army base, I chatted with a colleague of his. "What rank are you?" I asked. "I'm relieved to say that I've just been promoted from captain to major." "Relieved? Why?" "Because," he replied, **"my last name is Hook."**

— BARBARA BLACKBURN

★ ★ ★ ★ ★ ★ ★ ★ ★ ★ ★ ★ ★ ★ ★ ★ ★

When we agreed to help our sergeant move to a new apartment, we didn't know the elevator wasn't working. So after hours of carrying heavy boxes and furniture up 11 floors, we were wiped out. And when the sergeant asked us to search for his favorite pot, no one moved. "I'll give a bottle of Scotch to whoever finds it," he shouted. Within minutes, a private found the pot. "Good," said the sarge. "Now look for the Scotch."

— WOO-KI SOHNN

Todd, my son, joined the Marines. When he went to take the placement and physical exams, he was in a room full of candidates for all the military services. Todd overheard someone near him say, "Aren't the Marines just a department of the Navy?" "Yes," came the response. "They're the men's department."

— EMILY MURPHY

When my husband was reassigned to Fort Knox, in Kentucky, he was told we couldn't live together off base. Instead, he'd have to stay in the barracks with the other grunts. My husband begged his sergeant to clear up the matter. But it was no use. "Son," said his sergeant, "if the Army wanted you to have a wife, we would have issued you one."

— DIANE RAY

★ ★ ★ ★ ★ ★ ★ ★ ★ ★ ★ ★ ★ ★ ★ ★ ★ ★

Pulling Rank

The enlisted guys may have won the annual softball game against the officers, but they lost the public relations war. Here's how I wrote it up for our naval base's Plan of the Day: "The officers powered their way to a second-place finish, while the noncoms managed to finish next to last."

— DAVID FRIEL

During a staff meeting at the Air Force base, the captain disagreed with everything being discussed. The commander, a general, grew annoyed, and let the younger officer know it. "Well, sir," said the captain, "I doubt you made general by agreeing with everything someone else recommended." "That's true," said the general, leaning in. "But that is how I made major."

— HAROLD R. LONGMIRE

My husband works in the fuels squadron at an Air Force base, and many of his coworkers complain about the superior attitude of the pilots. One day the fuel guys decided to put things in perspective for the proud pilots. They all came to work wearing shirts inscribed, "Without fuel, pilots are pedestrians."

— AMBER ANDERSON

Officer candidate school at Fort Sill, Oklahoma, was tough. During an inspection, a fellow soldier received 30 demerits for a single penny found within his area. Ten demerits were for "valuables insecure," ten because the penny wasn't shined, and ten because Abraham Lincoln needed a shave.

— JACK HOWELL

★ ★ ★ ★ ★ ★ ★ ★ ★ ★ ★ ★ ★ ★ ★ ★ ★ ★

My brother Ken was home on leave from his post in Hawaii, when he announced that he had just been promoted to lieutenant commander. We were all pleased with the news, but some of us less knowledgeable about military rankings asked Ken to explain what the promotion meant. After several failed attempts to get us to understand, he sighed and said, "Before, I was Hawkeye Pierce, and now I'm Frank Burns." Expressions of understanding immediately lit the room.

— JACQUELYN MILLER

Our patient in the hospital was a big, burly former officer. Just after surgery, and still half out of it, he became agitated and confused, tearing at his IVs and trying to escape his bed. The nurses gamely attempted to keep him calm, but were losing this battle. That's when my old Air Force training came in handy. "Colonel!" I commanded. "At ease." And with that, the colonel fell back to sleep.

— PATTY ANDREWS

My daughter, Emily, was telling a friend that her brother, Chris, was training to become a Navy submariner. The friend, who had just been assigned to a Navy destroyer, good-naturedly called Chris a Bubblehead. Later I related the story to Chris and asked if he'd heard the term. He said he had and added, "We also have a name for people who work on destroyers." "What is it?" I asked. "Targets."

— JO BARKER

★ ★ ★ ★ ★ ★ ★ ★ ★ ★ ★ ★ ★ ★ ★ ★ ★

 I've got attention deficit disorder, Sarge.

As a young Navy recruit, I discovered early on where I stood in the chain of command after stepping on a cockroach. "What have you just done?" demanded a petty officer who was walking by. "Just killed a cockroach, sir," I answered. "Next time salute it first. They have more time in the Navy than you do."

— TOM MAY

★ ★ ★ ★ ★ ★ ★ ★ ★ ★ ★ ★ ★ ★ ★ ★ ★

Credits

Laughter the Best Medicine

Cartoon Credits (alphabetically by artist) ©1997 Charles Barsotti from The Cartoon Bank™, Inc: p. 197 ©1997 Frank Cotham from The Cartoon Bank™, Inc: pp. 20, 44, 52, 64, 133, 145, 151, 165, 171, 174, 187, 189, 195; ©1997 Leo Cullum from The Cartoon Bank™, Inc: pp. 49, 79, 96, 117, 146, 162, 176, 182, 192; ©1997 Boris Drucker from The Cartoon Bank™, Inc: p. 103; ©1997 Joseph Farris from The Cartoon Bank™, Inc: pp. 59, 93, 167; Travis Foster ©2008 cover; ©1997 Mort Gerberg from The Cartoon Bank™, Inc: pp. 207, 213; ©1997 Ted Goff from The Cartoon Bank™, Inc: p. 30; ©1997 William Haefeli from The Cartoon Bank™, Inc: p. 39; ©1997 Glen Lelievre from The Cartoon Bank™, Inc: p. 153; ©1997 Arnie Levin from The Cartoon Bank™, Inc: p. 203; Robert Mankoff ©1984 from The New Yorker Magazine, Inc: p. 66; Robert Mankoff ©1988 from The New Yorker Magazine, Inc: p. 141; Robert Mankoff ©1995 from the New Yorker Magazine, Inc: p. 190; ©1997 Robert Mankoff from The Cartoon Bank™, Inc. pp.15, 26, 41, 47, 185; ©1997 Jerry Marcus from The Cartoon Bank™, Inc. pp. 85, 89, 99; ©1997 J.P. Rini from The Cartoon Bank™, Inc. pp. 73, 109, 112, 178, 201; ©1997 Bernard Schoenbaum from The Cartoon Bank™, Inc. p. 216; ©1997 Phil Somerville from The Cartoon Bank™, Inc: p. 9; ©1997 Peter Steiner from The Cartoon Bank™, Inc. p. 87, 131; ©1997 Mick Stevens from The Cartoon Bank™ ,Inc: pp. 82, 159; ©1997 P.C. Vey from The Cartoon Bank™, Inc: p.105; ©1997 Bob Zahn from The Cartoon Bank™, Inc: pp. 35, 69, 76, 125, 210; ©1997 Jack Ziegler from The Cartoon Bank™, Inc: pp. 13, 17, 26, 55, 127, 138, 148, 155

Quotable Quotes

©2008 Travis Foster - Cover

Humor in Uniform

Illustration Credits (alphabetically by artist) ©2008 Ian Baker pp. 562, 627; David Brown p. 465, 541; Patrick Byrnes p. 549; John Caldwell p. 455; Dave Carpenter pp. 449, 520, 532, 555, 619; Ken Catalino pp. 639; Joe CiDhiarro p. 574; Ralph Hagen pp. 529, 584; George McKeon cover; Dan Reynolds pp. 477, 515, 591; Steve Smeltzer pp. 443, 481, 504, 605; Thomas Bros. pp. 472, 494; Kim Warp pp. 491, 614